Sustainabilit

Sustainability Marketing
A Global Perspective

Frank-Martin Belz
and
Ken Peattie

A John Wiley and Sons, Ltd, Publication

Registered office

John Wiley & Sons Ltd, The Atrium, Southern Gate, Chichester, West Sussex, PO19 8SQ, United Kingdom

For details of our global editorial offices, for customer services and for information about how to apply for permission to reuse the copyright material in this book please see our website at www.wiley.com.

Library of Congress Cataloging-in-Publication Data

Belz, Frank-Martin.
   Sustainability marketing : a global perspective / Frank-Martin Belz and Ken Peattie.
      p. cm.
   Includes bibliographical references and index.
   ISBN 978-0-470-51922-6 (pbk.)
 1. Marketing 2. Sustainability. I. Peattie, Ken. II. Title.
   HF5415.B42887 2009
   658.8'02–dc22

                                       2009005655

A catalogue record for this book is available from the British Library.

Typeset in 9/13pt Kuenstler 480 BT-Roman by Thomson Digital, India

Printed in Great Britain by Bell & Bain, Glasgow

The authors would like to dedicate this book to their families, who they depend upon, particularly to Mirjam (Frank's wife) and to Eva (Ken's mother).

They would also like to dedicate it to all life on earth, from all the other people we share this planet with, down to the tiny microbes upon which all life depends.

Thank you.

Contents

Preface

The world has changed a great deal in the quarter century that preceded the publication of this book. In 1987 the Brundtland Report brought the concept of sustainable development to mainstream attention, and made it clear that our pre-existing approach to economic development, our systems of production and our patterns of consumption were environmentally and socially unsustainable. At the millennium, the setting of the Millennium Goals, and the report from the Millennium Ecosystem Assessment that followed, demonstrated the enormous challenge involved in tackling the scourge of global poverty, on a planet whose productive capacity was being eroded by damage to natural systems and resources. In 2005 *An Inconvenient Truth* pulled together the threads of the arguments concerning climate change, and the threat it posed to the future well-being of people all over the world, with clarity and Oscar-winning style. In 2006 the Stern Report put a price tag on the economic damage that climate change would cause, and the following year's Report of the Intergovernmental Panel on Climate Change put beyond doubt that climate change represents a clear and present danger to the future welfare of all societies. In 2008 the economic meltdown that accompanied the global 'credit crunch' also demonstrated that our existing way of living and of doing business was economically, as well as environmentally, unsustainable.

All this time, and through all these momentous changes, the way in which we teach marketing, and the books from which we teach it, have barely changed. They may have evolved to reflect the use of new technologies in marketing or to register that environmental and ethical concerns are one type of issue that may influence consumers' behaviour or companies' strategies, but they have never sought to rethink marketing in light of the new realities. Conventional marketing continues to exist within an economic hyperspace in which there are no physical limits on the availability of resources or on the number of holes into which waste can be poured. It also exists within the artificial bubble of the consumer society, in which the customer is king and no consideration is given to the consequences of consumption or the interests of the billions of people who cannot afford to join the consumer classes. Conventional marketing thought and practice have struggled to adapt to a world that we now realize could be destroyed (or at least impaired to the impoverishment of us all) by unconstrained consumption as we strive to satisfy an ever-longer list of wants for an ever-growing global consumer class.

This book attempts to change this situation, by providing a vision of marketing for the twenty-first century, starting right now, which will help it become environmentally, socially and economically sustainable. It does not claim to provide a one-step solution to the question of how any or all of our current systems of consumption and production can reach an absolutely sustainable state. Most markets, consumers and companies are not ready to complete that process yet. One of the metaphors frequently used to explain sustainable development is not as a destination, but as a journey towards a more ecologically oriented and socially equitable world. This book considers marketing's role in contributing to the journey of human society towards sustainability, by progressing beyond simply defending or reforming the status quo to begin to transform how we live, produce and consume.

The *vision of this book* is not one of an 'alternative' kind of marketing, because, in very simple terms, if more sustainable marketing continues to exist as an alternative in parallel to the conventional marketing mainstream, then we are all in trouble. The vision of this book is for *a new sustainability-oriented marketing mainstream*. This will combine the existing strengths of conventional marketing with the sustainability perspectives of ecological and ethical marketing, and insights from the field of relationship marketing, to create a new marketing paradigm based on forging sustainable, value-based relationships with consumers. That, in a nutshell, is sustainability marketing. The book takes a consumer marketing focus. This is not to downplay the importance of business-to-business or organizational marketing, but we will leave developing a more sustainable vision of those fields to others with greater expertise in them. The book also takes a managerial focus, with an emphasis on applied marketing decision-making, rather than a macromarketing focus on the overall impact of the field of marketing on society (although those issues are touched on). Hence the book is called *Sustainability Marketing – A Global Perspective* and it considers marketing management at corporate and product brand levels.

The subtitle promises a 'global' perspective, which deserves some explanation. The book uses illustrative cases, simple examples and research data from many different countries, but is still biased towards those countries in which the greatest progress in sustainability marketing practices or research has been made, and in which the authors have the greatest experience. Sustainability marketing efforts need to be considered from a global perspective, however, because in a spatial sense the environmental and social issues at the heart of the sustainability agenda are global in nature (e.g. limited nonrenewable resources, climate change, loss of biodiversity, population growth, poverty, and fair distribution of the costs and benefits of economic activity). Also, from an economic perspective, the supply chains that serve our wants and needs are global in nature. Conventional marketing books tend to focus on the needs of consumers in the industrialized economy and what the marketer there can do to accomplish a successful exchange with them or build a lasting relationship with them. A sustainability perspective frames this as part of a globalized system of production and consumption. Therefore behind the successful sale of an American computer to a European consumer will be a story encompassing component production and assembly in numerous (and often relatively prosperous) parts of Asia. The story is also likely to end in Asia, in one of its poorer communities, with the computer reduced to a mixture of reclaimable materials and polluting waste. As well as being global in space, this book also seeks to go beyond the 'here and now' perspective of conventional marketing books and their obsession with short-term thinking and the latest trends and fashions. It seeks to take both a long-term perspective by placing the emerging environmental, social, economic and marketing crisis in its historical context to understand how we came to be where we are today, and a future-oriented perspective that deals with issues like product longevity and the development of sustainable consumer solutions and relationships.

This book is the reflection of the efforts of the two authors who, between them, have more than 36 years of research experience in wrestling with the issue of how to integrate sustainability issues into marketing thought and practice. They were both among the vanguard of academics who developed sustainable marketing concepts as an 'alternative' marketing, and with this book they are now seeking to begin the process of making sustainability marketing the new mainstream. They also both have many years of experience of teaching sustainability marketing concepts in the classroom, and have had ample opportunity to develop ways of making some of the complex ideas involved accessible and interesting for students.

The target audiences for this book are threefold. First are students who want to understand how marketing and sustainability issues can and do come together. This will include marketing students who want to understand sustainability as a new marketing paradigm and a practical marketing challenge; business students studying courses in general management, strategic management, innovation, business ethics or corporate social responsibility who want to understand the marketing implications of sustainability; and sustainability or environmental management students who wish to learn about the field of marketing and how it deals with environmental and social challenges. Although we would expect the book to be most relevant to students studying at advanced bachelor's, master's or doctoral level, we would not want to discourage anyone at other levels from reading it. Secondly, those working in marketing research or business intelligence functions may find this book a useful tool to help them escape the traps that are set by a reliance on the conventional way of looking at the physical world, the business environment and how consumers respond to sustainability issues. Finally, marketers working in companies or business organizations could find this book a useful way of reconsidering their world from a sustainability perspective and of 'unlearning' some of the lessons of their business school education.

The book is organized in five sections and twelve chapters, and would be ideally suited to a course of twelve lectures (although to suit a ten-week course, the first two and last two chapters could be combined to support single lectures instead). The book encompasses both theoretical dimensions of sustainability marketing and a focus on practical sustainability marketing issues through the chapters on the new sustainability marketing mix (the 'four Cs'). Each chapter includes:

- Learning objectives.
- Sustainability marketing stories in the beginning of each chapter to introduce the chapters and to illustrate what might be considered good practice (or even 'best practice').
- Case studies and illustrative examples deliberately selected to focus on consumption sectors with the greatest sustainability impacts, including housing and home energy, food and drink, mobility and clothing. The cases also include a mixture of small and medium-sized companies (SMEs) and multinational companies (MNCs), demonstrating that sustainability applies to organizations

of all sizes, and a variety of sectors and countries, including Europe, the United States and Asia.

- Review questions.
- Discussion questions.

Sustainability marketing challenge cases are also included at the end of Chapters 2 to 10 in order to apply the concepts and discuss some of the decisions, difficulties, uncertainties and problems involved in making sustainability marketing management a reality. The book is accompanied by a website to support both lecturers and students: www.wileyeurope.com/college/belz.

Last but not least, we would like to thank the students at the Technische Universität München (TUM), Cardiff University and the University of St Gallen (HSG), where we have taught sustainability marketing management courses for a number of years. The students at advanced bachelor's, master's and doctoral levels provided us with invaluable insights and feedback to enhance the concept and the cases of sustainability marketing management. We are also grateful to Roxana Codita at the Technische Universität München, who drafted one of the chapters and did research on the case materials. Finally, we would like to thank our colleagues, especially Hanna-Leena Pesonen, who encouraged us to write this book.

It has been a pleasure to work with entire Wiley team, namely Nicole Burnett, Céline Durand and Georgia King. Thank you very much for your continuing support, encouragement and enthusiasm!

Frank-Martin Belz
Technische Universität München

Ken Peattie
Cardiff University

PART I

UNDERSTANDING SUSTAINABILITY AND MARKETING

CHAPTER 1

Marketing in the Twenty-First Century

After Studying this Chapter You Should be Able to:

1. Understand why the legacies of the twentieth century have created challenges for society and the discipline of marketing for the twenty-first century.
2. Explain the basic concept and key principles of sustainable development.
3. Analyse why 'modern mainstream marketing' as it has evolved is being challenged by emerging concerns about sustainability.

LOOKING AHEAD: PREVIEWING THE CONCEPTS

This chapter explores the historical context of sustainability marketing through a short history of both the world and of marketing. The evolution of society and economic activity, particularly during the twentieth century, has created social and environmental consequences that threaten the planet's environmental systems and the future well-being and prosperity of society. Sustainable development is an alternative approach to human progress that seeks to balance economic prosperity with social justice and the protection of environmental quality. The chapter charts the evolution of marketing and how it seeks to take account of social and environmental issues.

SUSTAINABILITY MARKETING STORY: OF PIRATES AND GIANTS

'We don't consider ourselves sea bandits,' declared the Somali pirates' spokesman, Sugule Ali, in an interview with the *New York Times*. 'We consider sea bandits those who illegally fish in our seas and dump waste in our seas and carry weapons in our seas.' The interview was given by satellite phone from the bridge of the *Faina*, a Ukrainian cargo ship that was hijacked about 300 km off the coast of Somalia on 25 September 2008. Piracy in Somalia has become a highly organized and lucrative business based on ransoms. In 2008 alone, Somali pirates hijacked more than 30 ships from sailing yachts to oil tankers, and in many cases they were paid million-dollar ransoms to release the ships and their crew.

Since the collapse of the Somali central government and the beginning of a civil war in the early 1990s, piracy there has posed a constant threat to international shipping. With no patrols along its shorelines, Somalia's waters, which are rich in tuna, were soon plundered by commercial fishing fleets from around the world. Somali fishermen then began arming themselves and confronting illegal fishing boats with demands for a 'tax' for the use of Somalia's waters. 'From there, they got greedy,' said Mohamed Osman Aden, a Somali diplomat in Kenya. 'They started attacking everyone.' By the early 2000s, many of the former fishermen had traded in their nets for machine guns and were hijacking any vessel they could catch: sailboats, oil tankers and even UN-chartered ships delivering humanitarian assistance.

Millions of Somalis depend on food aid. Somalia is one of the poorest countries of the world, with an estimated annual per capita GDP of $600 (€ 433). In 2008 over 70% of the population lived on a daily income below $2 (€ 1.44). Frequent pirate attacks have been threatening the delivery of humanitarian assistance. 'Pirates may have a romantic image on the silver screen these days,' says World Food Programme executive director Josette Sheeran, 'but the picture might not be quite so pretty from the point of view of someone stuck in a camp for internally displaced people in Somalia, dependent on food assistance for survival.' It is easy to feel pity for the plight of Somali refugees, but should we also sympathise with the pirates who were once fishermen?

During 2008 the illegal actions of the Somali pirates in seizing international vessels caused global outrage, sparked massive media interest and posed a challenge for many governments whose economies rely on the shipping routes through the Suez Canal and the Gulf of Aden. Behind it lies another story, one about international vessels seizing and destroying natural resources, often illegally, usually without much media or government interest, and all done in the name of satisfying consumer demand. It does not excuse the actions of the pirates, but the depletion of the natural resources that their communities once depended on provides at least a partial explanation.[1]

Illegal, unreported and unregulated fishing is a key contributor to the overfishing of marine resources and the depletion of global fish stocks. According to the Food and Agriculture Organization (FAO), 52% of the fish population is already fully exploited, 17% is overexploited and

7% depleted. Since the 1970s depleted and overexploited fish populations have been rising dramatically. Total world fisheries production has steadily increased from 19 million tons in 1950 to over 100 million tons in 1989 and 142 million tons in 2005. The production figures are in line with research studies that provide evidence that humanity is gradually emptying the oceans: 90% of all large predatory fish have already been removed from the global ocean and marine communities. While whales and sharks are commonly acknowledged to be endangered species, some commercial fish like bluefin tuna and cod are also on the WWF's list of endangered species.

The consumer goods giant Unilever with annual sales of over € 40 billion employs 200 000 people and operates in about 100 countries. Until 2006 Unilever was also one of the largest fish processors worldwide (the frozen fish business unit was sold to an investment company that year). Faced with the crisis of overfishing and depleting fish stocks, Unilever cooperated with WWF to found the Marine Stewardship Council (MSC) in 1997. MSC is a global, nonprofit organization that promotes sustainable fishing practices by certifying fisheries and using an eco label to give consumers a choice. The blue MSC label signals to consumers that the wild-caught fish comes from marine sources that are managed in a responsible and sustainable manner. The MSC programme became mainstream when Wal-Mart made a switch to sustainable fish. In 2006 the retail giant announced that within three years it would source only MSC-certified fresh and frozen seafood. That commitment was a clear signal to suppliers and consumers alike, which has led to a tremendous growth in the supply and demand for sustainable fish: 35 fisheries were MSC certified in 2008, up from 14 in 2005, and more than 100 fisheries were under assessment. In addition, 1700 MSC-certified seafood products were available in 2008, compared to 300 in 2005. The retail value of seafood products bearing the blue MSC label was close to $1 billion (€ 721 million) in the fiscal year 2007/08.[2]

A Very Short History of the World

The world we know is made up of two types of system. There are the natural environmental systems on which all life on Earth depends and which have evolved over the 4.5 billion-year history of the planet. These include systems that underpin the formation of rocks and soils, distribute water and govern our weather, and the ecosystems that integrate the resources and species that coexist on the planet in ways that sustain life. There are also systems created by humans, one of the planet's more recently evolved species that has existed for around 200 000 years. The past 10 000 years have witnessed the emergence of new man-made systems such as agriculture, politics, economics, education, culture and technology.

As humankind has evolved, so its relationship with the planet has changed. As hunter-gatherers, humans as a species initially formed an integral part of many ecosystems and depended directly on them for the provision of food, water, shelter and medicines. The evolution of agriculture between 8500 and 7000 BC allowed humans to shape their environment by harnessing other species and deliberately alter and direct ecosystems in order to meet our needs. The food surpluses provided by agriculture allowed for the development of permanent settlements and more specialized skills and roles among people. As civilization emerged with innovations such as cities and writing, humankind began to search for, accumulate and communicate knowledge about our world and how it worked. During the eighteenth century, the scientific knowledge of the Enlightenment, when combined with the emerging technologies of the Industrial Revolution, allowed humans to begin to alter and control their environment to an unprecedented extent. As individuals, during the last two centuries our direct dependence on, and experience of, the natural environment has declined compared to that of our ancestors. Collectively, however, we have developed the power to transform that environment in ways our ancestors could never have imagined. Where the rhythms and limits of natural systems and seasons once dictated human behaviour and how society was organized, now science and technology are able to change those rhythms and limits, either purposefully or unintentionally.

The mix of forces that has determined the evolution of social systems around the world, and determined the relationship between humankind and the planet, has changed over time. For many centuries politics and technology have been important drivers of change, particularly when combined in warfare. In recent centuries economics has also been important, particularly when combined with evolving technologies through business and commerce. Ideas and beliefs relating to religion, democracy, ethics and personal responsibility have also all been important, along with those individuals who have articulated and championed them.

During the twentieth century a new driver of change emerged that has in many ways integrated, subsumed, harnessed or in some cases replaced those that came before it. That new driver of change is called *marketing*. Viewing marketing as a force that can shape the world might seem like nothing more than self-aggrandisement on the part of marketers. However, in the liberal consumer democracies that make up the majority of the world's richest societies, we are familiar with the idea that the products we consume are marketed to us. Less obviously, marketing processes also determine the political leaders we are invited to choose between and the policies that they seek to pursue. Marketing increasingly helps to determine where we invest our savings, where we go to learn, which countries we visit on vacation, which charitable causes we support, what information we are exposed to through the media, and whether or not we take proper care of our own health or support a range of social initiatives.

The Twentieth Century – The Century that Transformed the World

The scale and scope of change on planet Earth that occurred during the twentieth century in many fields eclipsed the changes of the previous thousand years. The human population was estimated to have passed the one billion mark during the 1830s, and it took another hundred years to double to reach two billion. During the twentieth century it tripled, to exceed six billion by 2000.[3] This population growth was driven partly by improvements in medical science that raised average global life expectancy and partly by the 'green revolution' in agriculture that expanded global food production. The twentieth century was also the era of world wars, of flight, of space exploration, of mass tourism, of computerized information technology, of cheap and plentiful oil and of the 'great car economy'. It was the era that saw the end of colonial empires and the growth of a more globalized popular culture and the concept of the 'global village'. Yet perhaps the greatest change was the unprecedented expansion in our material wealth. The twentieth century witnessed the *democratization of consumption* and the rise of the mass market, and it saw marketing emerging as a force that could both shape and change the world.

The paradigm or mindset that dominated during the twentieth century was based on several key ideas. One was that economic growth was a prerequisite to improving the quality of life for humankind and was necessary to generate the wealth through which challenges like poverty or the need for environmental protection could be addressed. A second was a belief that the physical problems linked to the use of resources and the generation of waste and pollution caused by a rapidly expanding global population and economy could be solved through the application of science and technology (sometimes referred to as the 'Promethean view'[4]). By the end of the century humankind had developed the ability to manipulate genes, to harness nuclear power for constructive or destructive purposes and to embark on engineering projects from the nano to the interplanetary scale. In her book *Science as Salvation*,[5] Mary Midgeley suggested that faith in science to solve our problems had largely replaced the faith in divine intervention that had been widespread in western society in previous centuries. A third key idea was a belief that markets were not only the most effective way to allocate scarce resources, but also the most effective way to deal with the provision of many social services and benefits that had previously been provided through the state, and to tackle many of the social (and some of the environmental) consequences created by economic and population growth. The collapse of the communist economics of eastern Europe, the failures of many state-owned enterprises and the perceived failure of many government service providers to meet the needs of their 'customers' led to a much greater emphasis on the role of private enterprise and markets to meet society's needs. As more and more of our society became governed by markets, particularly during the last decades of the century, so more aspects of it became influenced by marketing.

There was considerable evidence to judge as a success the approach to managing humankind's development that was founded on the pursuit of economic growth, particularly through the application of technology and markets. Simply during the last 30 years of the century, life expectancy in many developing countries rose by up to 20%, infant mortality halved, food-production rates managed to rise ahead of population increases, and incomes and literacy rates improved. On the basis that, at its end, more people than ever before were living a relatively comfortable, safe and free life, the twentieth-century project could be judged a clear success. In spite of this, critics of existing political and business approaches highlighted the fact that many social problems remained stubbornly intractable, some had worsened, and new social and environmental challenges were emerging.

Challenges for the Twenty-First Century

In 2000, the beginning of a new century, and indeed a new millennium, provided an opportunity for reflection about the state of the world and the future prospects for humankind. The United Nations' projects to establish the Millennium Development Goals[6] and conduct a Millennium Ecosytem Assessment[7] were symptomatic of that moment of reappraisal. The rapid population growth, technological changes and unprecedented economic growth of the twentieth century all combined to pose a number of challenges for the new century, including the following:

- *Population*. In 2000, the United Nations estimated that the world's population had recently passed the 6 billion mark and was growing at an annual rate of 1.14% (or about 75 million people).[8] On its growth trajectory at the time of writing, global population is expected to reach nearly 9 billion by the year 2050. Over 95% of the population growth that occurred in the five years after 2000 was in Asia, Africa and Latin America.
- *Poverty*. The unprecedented scale of economic growth during the twentieth century might logically be assumed to have had a major impact in terms of reducing poverty. However, with almost 3 billion people living on less than \$2 (€ 1.44) per day, and up to 30 000 child deaths daily being directly attributable to poverty,[9] it appears to be a challenge that has endured. Over a billion people entered the new millennium unable to read or to sign their own name.[10] As former UN Secretary General Kofi Anan said in a speech for the International Day for the Eradication of Poverty in 2000, 'Almost half the world's population lives on less than two dollars a day, yet even this statistic fails to capture the humiliation, powerlessness and brutal hardship that is the daily lot of the world's poor.'
- *Health*. Health remains one of the primary determinants of quality of life, and although improvements in health technologies and public health practices raised life expectancies in most countries during the twentieth century, a number of health issues continued to threaten or impair the quality of lives worldwide. Curable diseases still accounting for large numbers of deaths include tuberculosis (an estimated 3.5 million deaths in 2000) and malaria (an estimated 1 million deaths).[11] In comparatively rich nations, emerging health challenges tend to be linked more to lifestyle than disease, particularly concerns about rises in both obesity rates and mental health disorders.
- *Urbanization*. Population migration into, and growth within, cities was a key trend during the twentieth century, and by 2000 almost half of the world's population were urban dwellers. There is an increasing number of so-called megacities containing more than 10 million inhabitants, including Tokyo, New York, Mexico City, Buenos Aires, Mumbai, São Paulo and Karachi. Based on trends in births and migration, the United Nations predicts that 2 billion people will be living in slums by 2030,[12] with profound implications for future challenges linked to health and poverty.
- *Peak oil*. The fossil fuels, and particularly oil, that underpinned the economic growth of the twentieth century are known to be finite resources. There is considerable controversy over when existing fossil fuel resources will be depleted to a point that 'peak oil' output is reached, leading to subsequent reductions in supply and rises in price. Known reserves are likely to expand through new discoveries and technologies to exploit 'unconventional' and currently uneconomic resources. However, growing demand for oil from large and rapidly industrializing economies such as China and India will also rapidly absorb new supplies. During 2008 global crude oil prices breached the \$100 (€ 72) per barrel

level for the first time, before then both hitting a new peak ($147 = €106), and dropping to almost a five-year low (below $37 = €26.70) in the space of less than six months. Such price volatility has already raised concerns about the long-term viability of existing 'suburban' patterns of living that have become widespread in North America and Europe. Urban development in which our places of work, residence and consumption are geographically distant and rely on widespread private car ownership and use to connect them became the norm in the latter part of the twentieth century. Now there are concerns about whether more remote communities in many parts of the United States can remain viable in an era where communities have become far less self-sufficient, once oil prices return to mid-2008 levels.

- *Ecosystem damage.* In 2005 the results were published of the United Nations' Millennium Ecosystem Assessment,[13] a four-year research project to assess the health of the natural environment, the impact of human development on natural systems and their ability to support life and provide 'ecosystem services'. These services including providing food, water, fuel and materials such as wood and fibres for shelter, clothing and other products. Ecosystems also provide benefits by regulating climate and temperature, preventing flooding and diseases and managing water quality and wastes. They also contribute to our well-being through recreational, health and spiritual benefits. The results of the project showed that 60% of world ecosystem services have been degraded and species extinctions are running at between 100 and 1000 times the 'natural' background rate. For example, during the last 20 years of the twentieth century, about 35% of mangroves were lost, removing the protection they provide for coastlines from damage by hurricanes. The overall conclusions of the assessment were that unparalleled economic growth during the second half of the century had 'resulted in a substantial and largely irreversible loss in the diversity of life on Earth' and that 'gains in human well-being and economic development . . . have been achieved at growing costs in the form of the degradation of many ecosystem services . . . and the exacerbation of poverty for some groups of people. These problems, unless addressed, will substantially diminish the benefits that future generations obtain from ecosystems.'[14]

- *Food.* Despite progress in agricultural productivity, at the millennium around 800 million people in developing counties were still chronically undernourished.[15] The expansion of agricultural production during the previous century largely relied on the use of artificial fertilizers based on oil. Increasing oil prices, competition for agricultural land for uses such as biofuels, extreme weather and growing demand from countries such as China and India all combined to push up global food prices. By the beginning of 2008 global food reserves had reached their lowest level for 25 years.

- *Water.* More than 1 billion people in developing countries lack adequate access to water, and 2.6 billion lack basic sanitation. In sub-Saharan Africa the costs associated with water and sanitation deficits equate to around 5% of GDP (which exceeds the totals provided in aid flows and debt relief during 2003).[16]

- *Climate change.* One consequence of the economic growth of the twentieth century and the burning of fossil fuels to provide much of the energy that drove our economies was the release of carbon dioxide (CO_2) into the atmosphere. There is a clear scientific consensus that the role of CO_2 as a 'greenhouse gas' that traps the incoming energy from the sun (combined with other greenhouse gases such as methane released by both natural processes and human activity) is raising average global temperatures in ways that will increasingly disrupt global climatic systems resulting in potentially disastrous changes in climate.[17] Climate change has become an issue that has woven together many of the other challenges facing humankind as either a cause or an effect. Changes in our climate will have a profound impact on the distribution and availability of water supplies and on the viability of food-production systems, and are likely to exacerbate the loss of species who cannot adapt and to further damage fragile ecosystems. Many of the most severe impacts of climate change will be experienced by those in poorer countries, and this is likely to increase their vulnerability to health problems. Health may also be affected in the richer countries in the northern hemisphere as warming temperatures lead to changes in the pattern and prevalence of disease.

Climate change, and the risks it poses to the future quality of life for much of the world's population and to future economic growth, is an issue that has recently galvanized politicians, businesses, consumers and citizens to confront the fact that if humankind retains the twentieth-century approaches to politics, economic development, business, consumption and lifestyles during the early stages of the twenty-first century, the consequences are likely to be disastrous. In 2006 a report by Sir Nicholas Stern on the economics of climate change[18] examined the challenge not simply as a looming environmental and humanitarian crisis, but in economic terms. His conclusion was that we need to invest 1% of global GDP *per annum* to avoid experiencing the most severe effects of climate change that could forcibly shrink the global economy by up to 20%.[19] The Stern Report portrayed climate change as likely to provoke the greatest and widest-ranging market failure ever seen unless we act to both prevent it from worsening, and to adapt to those changes that cannot be prevented.

Some of the responses to climate change also illustrate the limitations of an over-reliance on new technologies or market mechanisms to provide solutions to such challenges. Faced with mounting evidence about the potentially disastrous effects of climate change, there has been a rush to develop alternative technologies that allow for existing lifestyles and patterns of consumption and development to remain relatively unchanged while changing the technologies of products and production to reduce their impact on the climate. A key example is the move towards biofuel-driven cars with the expectation that since plants absorb carbon as they grow, this will offset the carbon released when the fuel is burnt, creating a carbon-neutral fuel. This idea led to the enthusiastic promotion of corn-based ethanol, particularly in the United States, where the Renewable Fuel Standard law required the country's refineries to blend 9 billion gallons of biofuels into the national fuel supply during 2008. The rush to biofuels has been partly responsible for the rise in food prices, which led to riots on the streets of cities in Mexico and other poorer countries. The environmental benefits of biofuels have also been questioned through studies showing that the oil used to grow and process the corn and therefore 'embedded' in the ethanol makes it a contributor rather than a solution to climate change.[20] It also takes around 1700 litres of water to create one litre of ethanol. The biofuel story demonstrates that meeting the challenges of the twenty-first century will not be achieved through the development of individual technologies or particular types of market that address specific problems. Instead, we need an approach to our thinking that integrates the economic viability of particular technologies and systems of production and consumption with a consideration of their social significance and environmental impact in a far more holistic way.

Sustainable Development

In 1987 the United Nations' World Commission on Environment and Development (often referred to as the Brundtland Commission as it was chaired by Norwegian Prime Minister Dr Gro Harlem Brundtland) published the influential report *Our Common Future*.[21] This report provided the enduringly memorable encapsulation of sustainable development as 'meeting the needs of the present without compromising the ability of future generations to meet their needs'. The report recognized the interdependencies between the natural environment, human social welfare and economic activity, and the need to establish and maintain a dynamic balance between these three elements. The key principles of sustainability are either explicitly expressed in the Brundtland definition or implied by it:

- *Needs*. The Commission's focus on 'needs' shows both a concern for social justice and an anthropocentric, rather than biocentric, viewpoint. Anthropocentrism, or human-centredness, frames the maintenance of a healthy and sustainable environment as necessary for human well-being. It places humans and their needs above the interests of other living creatures on Earth. In contrast, biocentrism is commonly defined as the belief that all forms of life are equally valuable and that human beings should not be pre-eminent. Anthropocentrism has been identified by some environmentalists as a root cause of the ecological crisis, human overpopulation, and the extinction of many nonhuman species.[22]
- *Equity*. The Commission called for development with a fairer distribution of the costs and benefits of economic development among different countries, regions, races and age groups and between the sexes. The economic growth of the twentieth century failed to close the gap between the richest and poorest nations. According to United Nations Development Programme figures, by the turn of the century the richest 20% of the global population within the industrialized nations were consuming 86% of global resources, while the poorest 20% of the global population shared a mere 14% of the planet's resources. Over 80% of people live in countries where income differentials are widening rather than reducing.[23]
- *Intergenerationality*. The Commission takes a long-term perspective by seeking a balance between present needs and those of future generations. This principle of futurity ensures that the needs of existing people are balanced against our ability to meet the needs of future generations of citizens, consumers, investors and workers.
- *Global environmentalism*. The final principle recognizes that the environment is a holistic, dynamic and vulnerable physical system with a finite ability to provide our production and consumption systems with resources, and to absorb waste and pollution without impairing the quality of the environment and the services that it provides. Over half of the global poor rely directly on 'eco-system services' for their survival, and the majority of their consumption and production activity exists outside the framework of the monetary economy and is therefore largely 'invisible' from the perspective of conventional economic development.

Unlike much of the ecological concern voiced during the 1970s, sustainable development is not based on a 'zero growth' agenda, but on ensuring that economic growth will not ultimately become self-defeating because its consequences lead to environmental or social crises. As such, sustainable development provided a concept that businesses, politicians and pressure groups could all endorse, and an ideological space within which constructive dialogue could take place. The broad definition and basic principles of sustainability provided by the Brundtland Report allowed for a myriad of different interpretations of 'sustainable development' to emerge. By 1992 around 70 different definitions of sustainable development had been noted[24] and over the following decade the proliferation of definitions and the frequent hijacking of the term continued.[25] The many different suggested approaches to sustainable development were often roughly split between 'hard' sustainability (which focused on the preservation of environmental quality by protecting the environment from economic activity) and 'soft' sustainability (which focused on ensuring that economic development could be maintained by keeping it within environmental and social limits).

In the 1990s the Brundtland Report gained widespread political and business support for the principle that the scale and nature of the human economy should not exceed what the planet can physically sustain. It also begged the question of what the limits of the planet might be, and how and when human activity might go beyond what the planet can sustain. This question has been at least partly answered by the science of 'eco-footprinting', which seeks to calculate the level of resources we consume (as individuals, organizations, cities, regions and nations, or as humanity as a whole) and compares this with the resources nature can provide and sustain in terms of land, water, energy and other resources. The first global eco-footprint for humanity was published by WWF in 1998. This showed that around the time of the Brundtland Report's publication in 1987, humankind began to exceed the physical capacity of the planet to support our numbers, activities and lifestyles indefinitely.[26] To use a financial analogy, at this point we stopped living off the 'income' provided by natural systems and began instead to use up 'natural capital' and therefore to reduce the productive capacity of natural systems. By the turn of the twenty-first century humankind's eco-footprint was exceeding the Earth's sustainable productive biocapacity by some 20% (see Figure 1.1). Despite the widespread agreement about the need to change the nature of economic development, the existing dominant social paradigm and the trajectory of social, economic and technological development have proved remarkably resistant to significant change.

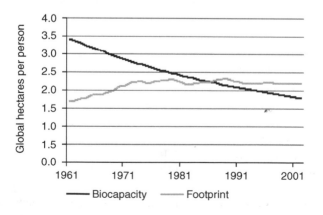

Figure 1.1 Ecological footprint vs global biocapacity

Source: Global Footprint Network, www.footprintnetwork.org (26 December 2008).

Sustainable Development – Towards Transformation

The debate about what might represent sustainable development, and how it might be achieved, has continued for more than 20 years. Hopwood *et al.* suggested that simply dividing up sustainability approaches into hard and soft disguised the many variations that existed among them in terms of emphasis and intensity.[27] They created a 'map' of sustainability approaches according to the extent to which they offered alternatives to our existing patterns of development, government and business that were more environmentally oriented or sought to deliver greater social equality (or both). They suggested that whatever the balance between social and environmental issues, the different approaches to sustainability all belonged in one of three groups:

- *Status quo oriented.* The first group consists of relatively 'soft' approaches primarily oriented towards maintaining our current lifestyle and ensuring that it is not disrupted by environmental catastrophes or social crises. The efforts of democratically elected governments or organizations such as the World Bank or Organization for Economic Cooperation and Development (OECD) are geared towards preserving patterns of economic activity and not changing them. The state-funded 'bailouts' of car companies announced during the credit crunch of 2008 were also used by some governments to promote the adoption of cleaner car technologies. However, the agenda was more a desire to retain an economically viable car industry than to promote a more sustainable personal mobility agenda. Seeking to make positive changes while largely preserving the status quo is also typical of environmentally concerned businesses, as represented by the World Business Council for Sustainable Development and the 'green' or 'ethical' consumers to whom such businesses often market.
- *Reform oriented.* The second group involves reforming existing approaches to development and systems of consumption and production. It encompasses the work of mainstream environmentalist groups such as the International Union for Conservation of Nature, and organizations promoting alternative development policies such as the Real World Coalition.
- *Transformation oriented.* The final group consists of approaches that seek to transform societies and economies into something more profoundly sustainable. They take the far more radical approaches to social and economic development put forward by the Club of Rome's *Limits to Growth* work,[28] Schumacher's *Small is Beautiful*[29] or *Natural Capitalism* from Hawken, Lovins and Lovins.[30] Such approaches seek to create a society that is socially equitable, ecologically oriented and ultimately (meaning intergenerationally) sustainable.

The challenges set out in the Millennium Development Goals, and reported in the Millennium Ecosystem Assessment, demonstrate that seeking to maintain the status quo in relation to patterns of development, production and consumption is no longer defensible. We inhabit a planet that must accommodate 75 million new citizens every year, that suffers enduring problems linked to poverty and inequality, and that faces growing concerns about the future impact of climate change and the likelihood of related crises in food, water, health and ecology. Addressing these challenges requires action to achieve substantive reforms and ultimately to achieve a fundamental transformation within many spheres of human activity. One of the metaphors frequently used to explain sustainable development is not as a destination, but as a journey towards a more ecologically oriented and socially equitable world. This book considers marketing's role in contributing to the journey of human society towards sustainability, by moving beyond defending or reforming the status quo to begin to transform how we live, produce and consume.

The Evolution of Marketing Thought

Marketing can be considered in many ways: as a commercial activity, as a management function or department, as a business process, as a philosophy or as a discipline. As a word, 'marketing' can be traced back at least 400 years and until the twentieth century it had a very literal meaning relating to activities that brought buyers and sellers together, usually in the context of a physical marketplace. Such marketing activities are as old as commerce itself.

Early in the twentieth century the idea emerged that marketing could be an academic discipline and a subject for study. In 1905 the University of Pennsylvania established one of the first explicit marketing course concerning the marketing of products. By 1920 a number of institutions were offering courses covering subjects such as marketing, advertising, salesmanship and marketing research, and the first books explicitly dealing with marketing practice had been published. The early days of the marketing discipline brought together experience from sales and advertising, insights derived from the developing field of psychology, and the increasingly sophisticated and analytical use of market research data. This early marketing sought to increase and to shape demand, and to develop new mass markets for the products created by new mass production systems. The emphasis of the early days of marketing can be summarized as 'how to sell more stuff to people'.

The emergence of mass production allowed supply to outstrip demand in many markets, forcing companies to seek new ways to become more competitive. The emergence of mass markets also created an increasing distance between consumers and producers. In a matter of decades, relatively localized systems of production and supply were replaced by mass production and marketing operations serving national or international mass markets. Producers no longer interacted so directly with their consumers, and lacked the direct knowledge of consumers and their preferences that pre-industrial producers possessed. From the 1950s onwards we see the emergence of what we could term 'modern marketing', as both a business philosophy and a management discipline. The emphasis of marketing moved beyond selling more products to customers towards understanding customers and how to meet their needs and wants.

By the end of the 1970s, the evolution of the core components of modern mainstream marketing thinking was largely complete. Although they would be refined and supplemented by new ideas that reflected changes in technology and the growth in international trade, the core elements we still use to teach and understand marketing were largely in place. The following core components are the foundations of marketing theory and practice:[31]

- *The marketing philosophy,* founded on the idea that meeting the needs and wants of the customer is the principle around which a business should be organized and from which success in the market and profitability will flow.

- *The marketing environment*, the principle that marketing should be an outwardly focused function within a business, helping it to understand and respond to the environment within which it exists.
- *Marketing research*, to ensure that the marketing decisions, particularly concerning customers and their wants, are based on insights derived from research.
- *Market segmentation and targeting*, to ensure that significant differences among customer groups and types revealed by marketing research are accounted for in the strategies and market offerings of companies.
- *The marketing mix*, a set of variables that marketers can control and adjust in order to meet customer needs more effectively than the competition, and to meet the differing needs of particular market segments. The mix was originally defined as the 'four Ps': product, price, place and promotion. The original four Ps mix model has received much criticism,[32] but it has also simply endured due to a combination of its simplicity, memorability and relatively universal applicability.
- *Competitive advantage*, the principle that through an understanding of consumers and their marketing environment a business can provide something unique that generates competitive advantage.
- *The marketing planning and management process*, the principle that marketing success is delivered through a systematic approach to marketing activities and decisions.

Beyond 'Modern' Marketing

The evolution of marketing thinking did not end once the ideas of modern mainstream marketing were in place. The social, technical and cultural environment that shapes marketing thought and practice has continued to evolve. Dramatic changes involving the globalization of markets, the rise of electronic commerce and renewed concerns about the environment created new pressures on marketing to respond and evolve. At the end of the 1970s and early 1980s, the field of macromarketing emerged to integrate many of the debates about the impacts of marketing activity and the relationships between markets, regulation and social welfare that had surfaced periodically since the beginning of the twentieth century. Macromarketing sought to consider more systematically the inter-relationship between marketing systems and society, with a particular emphasis on the (often unintended) consequences of marketing activities on environmental quality and societal welfare.[33]

Discussions about the evolution of marketing thought also shifted to consider what 'postmodern' marketing might look like. Stephen Brown, a leading thinker within the postmodern marketing movement, critiqued both mainstream marketing thinking and many of the alternatives proposed to it with wit and insight.[34] He noticed an emerging literature composed of what he termed 'marketing panaceas', alternatives to mainstream thought and practice that were proposed as solutions to marketing's supposed ills. A review of these panaceas by Badot *et al.*[35] uncovered 70 different forms of 'new' marketing that had been proposed between 1985 and 2005 and that could be applied across different forms of market (unlike, say, arts marketing, bank marketing or political marketing).

An analysis of this parade of panaceas shows that they vary in several ways. Some concern the scope and focus of marketing efforts both geographically and within the market, such as niche marketing, micromarketing, one-to-one marketing and geo-marketing. Other ideas include new ways of defining and targeting market segments through ideas such as tribal marketing, family marketing, community marketing or ethnic marketing. Some approaches aim to help smaller companies or those with limited resources to compete within markets, including entrepreneurial marketing and guerrilla marketing. Other approaches sought to reorientate marketing in terms of one particular aspect of the marketing process, such as:

- *Time*, through time-based marketing, real-time marketing and slow marketing.
- *Information systems*, through database marketing and knowledge marketing.
- *Style of communication with customers*, through stealth marketing, street marketing, network marketing, viral marketing and grass-roots marketing.
- *Style of appeal*, through trend marketing, nostalgia marketing, emotion marketing and cause-related marketing.
- *Consumer experiences*, through experiential marketing and sensory marketing.

There are a number of common themes running through these panaceas. Many of them use a particular metaphor to recast marketing thought and practice, such as guerrilla marketing, tribal marketing, viral marketing or turbo marketing. Many of them seek to balance the rather rational analytical perspectives of conventional 'Kotlerian' marketing through a greater emphasis on emotion and the subjective experiences and perceptions of consumers. What many of them also have in common is that as a 'new' form of marketing, they represent nothing that is significantly different to the established marketing mainstream. Mostly they represent a focusing of marketing efforts around particular segments, communications approaches or company capabilities.

Nevertheless, there are two groups among the panaceas that propose an approach to marketing that does not just refocus, adjust or enhance existing marketing thinking and practice, but seeks to challenge these and provide a substantially different perspective.

The first group is based on a shift of focus in marketing away from the commercial transaction with customers and towards the relationship that is formed and maintained with them. Relationship marketing, total relationship marketing, co-marketing, loyalty marketing, solution marketing and symbiotic marketing are within that group of alternative marketing approaches.

The other group consists of those marketing approaches that seek to address the lack of fit between marketing as it is currently practised and the ecological and social realities of the wider marketing environment. This group includes marketing approaches such as macromarketing, societal marketing, green marketing, environmental marketing and eco-marketing.

The Marketing of the Future

The debates about postmodern marketing, marketing panaceas and the various forms of 'new' marketing share a common theme: that the marketing of the future will have to be different to the marketing of the past. In a world that is coming to understand the social and environmental consequences of the unsustainable economic growth of the twentieth century, it is clear that we need alternative approaches to production and consumption for the future. Changing our production and consumption systems cannot be achieved without changing marketing mindsets and practices, and forever abandoning the assumption that the issue at the root of marketing activity is 'how to sell more stuff to people'.

In his book *In Search of a New Logic of Marketing*, leading marketing scholar Christian Grönroos opens with a chapter entitled 'Marketing – A Discipline in Crisis'.[36] The crisis he describes is one in which marketing is an area of business thought and practice that has failed to evolve, and where a marketing executive who travelled in time from 50 years ago would be quite comfortable in the same role in a contemporary marketing department (albeit with a little catching up to do about digital media). The picture Grönroos paints is one of an increasingly costly function whose strategic role and credibility within business are eroding because it has been unable to break out of its existing ways of thinking to evolve:

> The productivity of marketing cannot be improved within the existing frameworks and structures. As long as marketing's major responsibility is customer acquisition and promise-making, the costs of marketing will continue to grow, and its effectiveness will continue to go down ... The development of brand management and adopting a branding terminology in marketing is only more of the same, in some situations making conventional marketing more effective perhaps, but offering no innovative new avenues for customer management. Marketing is a discipline is in crisis. And marketing as a business practice responsible for customer management is losing credibility.

The irony in Grönroos's diagnosis is that the crisis that marketing faces comes from a failure to apply the marketing philosophy thoroughly enough to the discipline itself. The emphasis on marketing has been on the management of the marketing mix and the traditional four Ps, which are inherently producer-oriented. They focus on the company's products and how it prices, distributes and promotes them. Such thinking tends to focus marketing thinking inward and onto the variables that the marketer can control. Customers become something that need to be acquired through the promise of value and benefits. As Grönroos phrases it, 'Mainstream marketing continues to be orientated towards doing something *to* customers, instead of seeing customers as people *with whom* something is done.'[37] He proposes an alternative vision of marketing that is centred around a process of managing relationships with customers rather than facilitating exchanges with them. In doing this, it shifts the focus away from the marketing of products to customers, and instead emphasizes the need to deliver value to customers.

The need for an alternative vision of marketing is often portrayed rather simplistically as a clash between 'old' marketing (i.e. mainstream Kotlerian marketing) and a 'new' alternative approach to marketing that seeks to replace it.[38] The reality is more subtle and complex. The mainstream concept of marketing as it was encapsulated by the first edition of Kotler's *A Framework for Marketing Management* in 1967[39] may no longer be as well suited to the world within which it exists, but rather than simply allowing itself to be replaced, it continues to adapt and evolve. It was perhaps significant that the first European edition of *Principles of Marketing* by Kotler *et al.*[40] to be published in the twenty-first century opened with a chapter entitled 'Marketing in a Changing World: Satisfying Human Needs', which emphasized the central issues of marketing as demand management, the management of relationships and of connectivity. Similarly, the second chapter concerned marketing and society with a focus on social responsibility and marketing ethics, transforming sustainability issues in mainstream marketing from afterthought to context.

Towards Sustainability Marketing

In view of the sustainability challenges facing society, a logical question confronting the marketing discipline is: 'What would a sustainability-oriented vision of marketing look like?' This is the question that this book seeks to answer. In short, the answer comes in the form of a pseudo-mnemonic. Sustainability marketing is marketing that endures forEVER, in that it delivers solutions to our needs that are:

- *Ecologically oriented*, taking account of the ecological limits of the planet and seeking to satisfy our needs without compromising the health of ecosystems and their ability to continue delivering ecosystem services.
- *Viable*, from technical feasibility and economic competitiveness perspectives.
- *Ethical*, in promoting greater social justice and equity, or at the very least in terms of avoiding making any existing patterns of injustice worse.
- *Relationship-based*, which move away from viewing marketing in terms of economic exchanges, towards viewing it as the management of relationships between businesses and their customers and other key stakeholders.

In other words, sustainability marketing represents an evolution of marketing that blends the mainstream economic and technical perspectives with the emerging concepts of relationship marketing and the social, ethical, environmental and intergenerational perspectives of the sustainable development agenda. This evolution is shown in summary in Figure 1.2. It is not exactly a 'new' marketing, but it is an 'improved' marketing in drawing insights and strengths from these different perspectives. It is about marketing that is intended to endure.

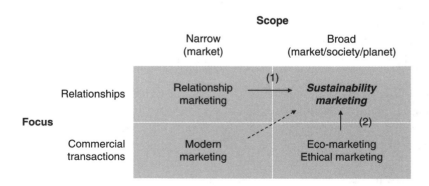

Figure 1.2 Towards sustainability marketing

The marketing of the future will be shaped by many forces, and this chapter has encapsulated only a few of them. The perceived crisis in the marketing discipline, the growing importance of relationship management and the rise of new technologies of production and communications will all play a part. Growing concerns about the environmental and social impacts of economic growth, and particularly concerns about the impacts of climate change, are also bound to push businesses and marketers to search for more sustainable ways of maintaining relationships with customers and delivering value to them. These issues are explored in more detail in Chapters 2 and 3. Ultimately, if humankind is to avoid environmental and social disaster caused by the unsustainable patterns of business, growth and lifestyle that emerged during the twentieth century, marketing has a very important role to play as a pathway to delivering transformation for sustainable development in the twenty-first century.

List of Key Terms

Brundtland Report
Climate change
Ecological footprinting or eco-footprinting
Economic growth
Ecosystems
Equity
Global environmentalism
Intergenerational perspective
Marketing 'panaceas'
Modern marketing
Need
Peak oil
Population
Postmodern marketing
Poverty
Sustainable development
Transformation
Urbanization

REVIEW QUESTIONS

1. Why did the scale and nature of economic growth during the twentieth century create problems?
2. What is the Brundtland Report's basic definition of sustainable development and what are the key principles within it?
3. What are the three groups of sustainability approaches identified by Hopwood *et al.* and what are the differences between them?

4. What are the core components of the modern mainstream marketing discipline?
5. On what basis does Christian Grönroos criticize mainstream marketing?

DISCUSSION QUESTIONS

1. Do you think that the former fishermen of Somalia have the right to confront illegal fishing boats and demand a tax for the use of Somalia's waters?
2. Would it be fair to characterize the consumers of today as 'pirates' seizing resources at the expense of the citizens of tomorrow and their quality of life?
3. Why has the principle of sustainable development proved easy for many different groups to endorse, but difficult for them to define or put into practice?
4. Would embracing sustainability principles represent an evolutionary reform of the marketing discipline, or a revolutionary transformation?

Endnotes

1. Gettleman, J. (2008a) 'Somali pirates capture tanks and global notice', *New York Times*, http://www.nytimes.com/2008/09/27/world/africa/27pirates.html, accessed 26 December 2008; Gettleman, J. (2008b) 'Somalia pirates tell their side: They want only money', *New York Times*, 1 October 2008, http://www.nytimes.com/2008/10/01/world/africa/01pirates.html, accessed 26 December 2008; Khan, S.A. (2007) 'Tackling piracy in Somali waters: Rising attacks impede delivery of humanitarian assistance', *UN Chronicle Online Edition*, http://www.un.org/Pubs/chronicle/2007/webArticles/073107_somalia.htm, accessed 26 December 2008; www.msc.org (accessed 26 December 2008); www.unilever.com (accessed 26 December 2008).
2. FAO (2006) *The State of World Fisheries and Aquaculture 2006*, Rome: Food and Agriculture Organization of the United Nations.
3. UN (2005a) *World Population Prospects: The 2004 Revision*, New York: United Nations.
4. Dryzek, J. (1997) *The Politics of the Earth*, Oxford: Oxford University Press.
5. Midgley, M. (1994) *Science as Salvation: A Modern Myth and its Meaning*, London: Routledge.
6. UN (2005b) *The Millennium Development Goals Report 2005*, New York: UN.
7. World Resource Institute (2005) *Ecosystems and Human Well-being: Synthesis Report (Millennium Ecosystem Assessment)*, Washington, DC: Island Press.
8. UN (2005a) *op. cit.*
9. UNICEF (2000) *Progress of Nations Report*, Paris: United Nations Children's Fund.
10. UNICEF (1999) *The State of the World's Children*, Paris: United Nations Children's Fund.
11. WHO (2000) *World Health Report 2000*, Geneva: World Health Organization.
12. UNFPA (2007) *State of the World's Population 2007*, New York: United Nations Population Fund.
13. World Resource Institute (2005) *op. cit.*
14. *Ibid.*, p.1.
15. World Resource Institute (2001) *Pilot Analysis of Global Ecosystems: Food, Feed and Fiber Section*, Washington, DC: World Resource Institute.
16. United Nations Development Programme (2006) *Human Development Report 2006*, New York: UN.

17. IPCC (2008) *Climate Change 2007 – Impacts, Adaptation and Vulnerability: Working Group II Contribution to the Fourth Assessment Report of the IPCC*, Cambridge: Cambridge University Press.

18. Stern, N. (2006) *The Stern Review Report: The Economics of Climate Change*, London: HM Treasury.

19. To reflect the worsening situation, Stern revised that number in 2008 from 1% up to 2% of global GDP per annum.

20. Crutzen, P.J., Mosier A.R., Smith, K.A. & Winiwarter, W. (2007), 'N$_2$O release from agro-biofuel production negates global warming reduction by replacing fossil fuels', *Atmospheric Chemistry and Physics Discussions*, 7: 11191–205.

21. WCED (1987) *Our Common Future (The Brundtland Report)*, World Commission on Environment and Development, Oxford: Oxford University Press.

22. See Foreman, D. (1993) *Confessions of an Eco-Warrior*, New York: Crown Publishing Group; and Manes, C. (1993) *Green Rage: Radical Environmentalism and the Unmaking of Civilization*, Boston, MA: Little Brown.

23. United Nations Development Programme (2006) *op. cit.*

24. Kirkby, J., O'Keefe, P. & Timberlake, L. (1995) *The Earthscan Reader in Sustainable Development*, London: Earthscan.

25. Welford, R. (1997) *Hijacking Environmentalism: Corporate Responses to Sustainable Development*, London: Earthscan.

26. WWF (1998) *Our Living Planet*, Geneva: WWF.

27. Hopwood, B., Mellor, M. & O'Brien, G. (2005) 'Sustainable development. Mapping different approaches', *Sustainable Development*, 13: 38–52.

28. Meadows, D.H., Meadows, D.L., Randers, J. & Behrens, W.W. (1972) *The Limits to Growth*, New York: Universe Books.

29. Schumacher, E.F. (1973) *Small Is Beautiful: Economics as if People Mattered*, London: Frederick Muller.

30. Hawken, P., Lovins, A. & Lovins, H. (1999) *Natural Capitalism: Creating the Next Industrial Revolution*, Boston, MA: Little, Brown.

31. This approach is also sometimes referred to as 'Kotlerian' marketing, recognizing the dominance of Professor Philip Kotler's core teaching textbooks in business schools since the late 1960s (although, depending on your perspective, this gives him either too much credit or too much blame for shaping orthodox thought within an entire discipline).

32. See Constantinides, E. (2006) 'The marketing mix revisited: towards the 21st century marketing', *Journal of Marketing Management*, 22(3/4): 407–438; and Grönroos, C. (1994) 'From marketing mix to relationship marketing: Towards a paradigm shift in marketing', *Management Decision*, 32(2): 1–19.

33. See Fisk, G. (1981) 'An invitation to participate in affairs of the Journal of Macromarketing,' *Journal of Macromarketing*, 1(1): 3; and Hunt, S. (1981) 'Macromarketing as a multidimensional concept', *Journal of Macromarketing*, 1(1): 7–8.

34. Brown, S. (1995) *Postmodern Marketing*, London: Routledge.

35. Badot, O., Bucci, A. & Cova, B. (2007) 'Beyond marketing panaceas: In praise of societing', in Saren, M., Maclaran, P., Goulding, C., Elliott, R., Shankar, A. & Caterall, M. (eds) *Critical Marketing*, London: Butterworth-Heinemann, pp. 85–95.

36. Grönroos, C. (2007) *In Search of a New Logic for Marketing*, Chichester: John Wiley & Sons Ltd.

37. *Ibid.*, p. 17.

38. The 'Old Marketing vs New Marketing' debate is caricatured amusingly by marketing commentator Kathy Sierra and presented on her 'Creating Passionate Users' marketing blog, http://headrush.typepad.com/creating_passionate_users/ (accessed 26 December 2008).

39. Kotler, P. (1967) *A Framework for Marketing Management*, Upper Saddle River, NJ: Prentice Hall.

40. Kotler, P., Armstrong, G., Saunders, J. & Wong, V. (2001) *Principles of Marketing: Third European Edition*, London: Financial Times/Prentice Hall.

CHAPTER 2

Framing Sustainability Marketing

After Studying this Chapter You Should be Able to:

1. Understand the key elements of sustainability marketing.
2. Relate sustainability marketing to corporate social responsibility.

LOOKING AHEAD: PREVIEWING THE CONCEPTS

In this chapter we will briefly describe the evolution of the marketing perspective with particular regard to social and environmental issues. Then we will introduce you to the main elements of sustainability marketing: socio-ecological problems; consumer behaviour; sustainability marketing mission and objectives; sustainability marketing strategies; the sustainability marketing mix; and sustainability marketing transformations. Toyota is a company that has embraced the concept of sustainability marketing. In the chapter-opening marketing story we will have a look at Toyota's sustainability mission and the worldwide launch of the Toyota Prius.

SUSTAINABILITY MARKETING STORY: TOYOTA PRIUS – THE WAY FORWARD

Hollywood star Cameron Diaz drives a Toyota Prius. So do Leonardo DiCaprio, Harrison Ford, Tom Hanks, Jack Nicholson, Gwyneth Paltrow, Susan Sarandon, Robin Williams and many others. The Toyota Prius is a hybrid car combining the power of a petrol engine with the efficiency of an electric battery. The electric motor starts the car and operates at low speed. At higher speed the Prius automatically switches to the petrol engine. Under normal driving conditions, the hybrid runs at 4.3 litres per 100 kilometres and emits 104 grams CO_2 per kilometre – less than most petrol and diesel cars of the same category. The Prius looks stylish and comfortably seats five. It combines environmental performance with power, convenience and safety.

The hybrid synergy drive system is a key step for Toyota towards cleaner and greener cars. Simultaneously, Toyota is exploring other options such as compressed natural gas engines and fuel cells to reduce exhaust emissions. The ultimate aim is a car that does not generate any emissions and is totally recyclable ('zero emissions, zero waste'). In order to reach this aim Toyota conducts extensive life cycle assessments (LCA); sets quantitative targets for design for the environment (DFE); reduces waste and energy consumption in manufacturing; and reuses and recycles cars and car parts at the end of their lifetime.

Toyota launched the first mass-produced hybrid vehicle in Japan in 1997 and began selling it in North America, Europe and elsewhere in 2000. When the Prius was introduced to North America, it flew out of the dealers' showrooms. The initial sales success can be attributed to Toyota's clever pre-marketing. Two years before the introduction in North America, Toyota began educating consumers about the Prius by establishing a website to disseminate information and send out e-brochures. Ads running before the actual introduction used the tag line: 'A car that sometimes runs on gas power and sometimes on electric power, from a company that always runs on brain power.' These ads helped to position Toyota as a leading environmental company and, more subtly, stressed the technological aspect of the hybrid car. After its introduction, the ads appealed more to the emotions. One of the print ads shows the Prius easily passing a large truck, the head line reading 'Eat my voltage', referring to the high performance and power of the hybrid system. Another print ad shows the Prius at a stoplight with the tag line saying 'When it sees red, it charges', a reference to the way the car recharges during the deceleration/braking phase. Again, the appeal is based on the car's technology.

Technology pioneers are an important target group for the Prius. These 'techies' are early adopters, who are interested in the latest innovation and must be the first 'on the block' to own this technology and embrace it. The environmentally concerned are another important customer group. They know about the environmental impact of motoring and would like to do something about it. To reach this target group, Toyota sent out green seed cards shaped like its logo to prospective buyers at Earth Day, wrapped some Priuses in green and gave away cars at Earth Day events. A third major customer group are the value conscious, who look for the ideal combination of high fuel economy and low maintenance cost in the long run at an affordable price.

The rise of petrol prices had a positive effect on product sales. Between 2003 and 2005, the world-wide annual sales of Toyota hybrid cars quintupled from approximately 50 000 to 250 000 units, including the Toyota Prius and two sport utility vehicles introduced in spring 2005. Should petrol prices again reach the high levels experienced during 2008, fuel efficiency as a buying criterion will favour hybrid cars. Toyota believes that although diesel and petrol engines will remain the dominant technology in the world for the next decade or more, hybrid and fuel cell technologies will progressively take their place beside them in the mainstream. Hydrogen fuel cells may have the potential to provide practical, reliable and affordable zero-emission propulsion, but commercialization of this technology is still years away. That is not the case with hybrid cars. They are relatively environmentally benign and commercially viable. For Toyota, hybrid cars represent a key stepping stone on the way towards sustainable mobility in the twenty-first century and it is determined to lead the way.[1]

Evolution of Marketing

Leading companies such as Toyota are market-oriented and strongly customer-focused. This has not always been the case. The role of marketing in organizations has evolved over time. For the purpose of a simple classification, we may say that during the first half of the twentieth century companies were mainly production-oriented. Manufacturers responded to unsatisfied demand by focusing on mass production to increase output, expand supply and lower cost. One of the most famous examples from the mass production era was the Model T Ford. As mass production capabilities improved, distribution and sales became more important. However, manufacturers were still primarily production-oriented.

This changed during the second half of the twentieth century. The expansion of mass production led to overcapacity in many markets as supply overtook demand. The challenge of increasingly saturated and competitive markets led to the birth of an explicit marketing and customer orientation: the production-centred 'make and sell' philosophy was superseded by a customer-centred 'sense and respond' philosophy.[2] Consumers' needs and wants became the centre of attention and the starting point of innovation and production. Consumer-driven companies set up marketing departments and appointed marketing directors. The basic assumption was that knowing the needs and wants of your target markets, and satisfying them better than your competitors do, allows organizational goals to be achieved as well. Thus, marketing and customer orientations are the means to the end of ensuring that an organization can survive and thrive by generating growth and profit.

The satisfaction of (immediate) consumer wants is not always in the best interest of society and, in the case of products such as cigarettes or high-fat foods, not even necessarily in the best interests of the consumer. Since the 1960s there has been an on-going debate about the impact of marketing on the physical environment and on health, employment, education and welfare. Macromarketing is the discipline that has emerged to deal with these issues. Literally, macromarketing means marketing in general or on an aggregated level, which implies marketing from the perspective of whole systems and groups of institutions, such as channels, conglomerates, industries and associations, rather than from the perspective of individual 'players'. Macromarketing also refers to the social context of micromarketing, its role in the national economy and its application to noneconomic goods and goals.[3] Generally, macromarketing asks how marketing should be carried out to meet the goals of society and to optimize social benefits and is complementary to micromarketing, which focuses on the marketing activities of individual companies or business units within them.

The evolution of the marketing perspective is depicted in Figure 2.1. The production orientation is internally focused and mainly concentrates on organizational goals. The consumer orientation emphasizes people's needs and wants. The societal orientation considers ecological and social goals as well.

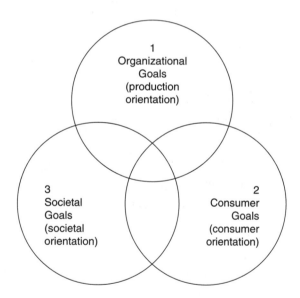

Figure 2.1 Evolution of the marketing perspective
Source: Bartels, R. and Jenkins, R.L. (1977) 'Macromarketing', *Journal of Marketing*, 44(4): 17–20. Reprinted with permission.

Emergence of Sustainability Marketing

Since the 1970s several marketing concepts have emerged that deal with ecological and social issues in some way or other, including societal marketing, social marketing, ecological marketing, green marketing, environmental marketing, sustainable marketing and sustainability marketing.

Societal Marketing

Societal marketing suggests that the intersection of the three perspectives of organizational goals, consumer goals and societal goals leads to long-term marketing opportunities and success.[4] It questions the implicit assumption of marketing (and more broadly of neoclassical economics) that the collective satisfaction of individual customer needs and wants is always in the best long-term interests of consumer welfare and society. The societal marketing concept differentiates between immediate consumer satisfaction and long-run consumer benefits. According to these two dimensions, products can be classified in four categories (Figure 2.2). Deficient products neither fulfil immediate customer satisfaction nor work in the long-run interest of consumers and society (e.g. unsafe cars). Pleasing products give a high level of immediate satisfaction, but they may hurt long-run consumer welfare (e.g. sports cars). Salutary products have low appeal, but they may benefit consumers and society in the long run (e.g. electric cars or car sharing). Desirable products give both immediate customer satisfaction and serve long-term consumer and societal interests (e.g. hybrid cars).

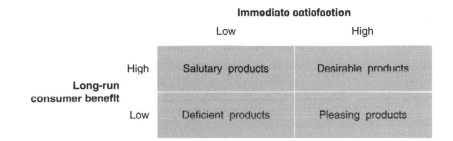

	Immediate satisfaction	
	Low	High
High	Salutary products	Desirable products
Low	Deficient products	Pleasing products

(Long-run consumer benefit)

Figure 2.2 Societal classification of products
Source: Kotler, P. (1972) 'What consumerism means for marketers', *Harvard Business Review*, 50(3). 48–57.

Based on the societal product classification, companies can develop four basic strategic norms: (1) elimination of deficient products; (2) incorporation of pleasing qualities into salutary products; (3) incorporation of salutary qualities into pleasing products; and (4) investment in the development and marketing of desirable products, which meet both consumer and societal goals.

One of the unsolved problems with the concept of societal marketing is who defines what is, and what is not, in the interests of consumers and society?[5] Another problem lies in pleasing products, which serve immediate customer wants and are highly profitable, but are not necessarily beneficial for consumers and society in the long run. Wants and needs are typically treated as synonymous within the marketing literature, but there is often a difference between what we want and what is good for us. Consider fast food, which may cause obesity and other health problems if consumed regularly, as demonstrated by Morgan Spurlock in his documentary *Supersize Me*; or think of sport utility vehicles, which consume a disproportionate amount of fuel and generate excessive emissions.

Social Marketing

Social marketing refers to the application of marketing principles, concepts and tools to problems of social change.[6] Social marketing programmes are designed to influence individuals' behaviour to improve their well-being or that of society. Social marketing is concerned with macromarketing issues, but it generally takes a micromarketing perspective; that is, social marketing programmes are usually planned and implemented by individual organizations focusing on a specific issue.

Social marketing campaigns involve more than just advertising in print media, radio or television. They may include a broad range of tools such as sponsorship or online marketing. Public health campaigns aim at reducing smoking, alcoholism, drug abuse, overeating and unsafe sex. Environmental campaigns promote wilderness protection, conservation, clean air and energy efficiency. Still others address issues such as family planning, human rights, corruption and gender as well as racial equality. Social marketing campaigns are usually planned and implemented by governmental or nongovernmental organizations, although business organizations may be involved in social marketing campaigns as partners.

Ecological Marketing

Ecological marketing was developed during the 1970s, drawing attention to both the negative and positive impacts of marketing on the natural environment.[7] In relation to ecology, it dealt mainly with the depletion of energy and nonenergy natural resources and the pollution created as a by-product of production and consumption. The roots of the concept lay in the environmental concerns expressed in renowned books such as *Silent Spring* by Rachel Carson and *Limits of Growth* by the Club of Rome.[8]

Generally, ecological marketing deals with marketing activities that cause environmental problems and that provide remedies for environmental problems.[9] It looks at the marketing mix from an ecological point of view. In terms of product policy, ecological marketing raises questions regarding the use of critical substances and energy consumption, as well as the amount and type of packaging used. In distribution, the recycling of products and packaging are key issues. Promotion's role is ambiguous, since on the negative side it stimulates demand but on the positive side it may benefit environmentally superior products. Pricing is concerned with externalities and the total cost of products.[10]

Some scholars in the 1970s, namely Fisk, Henion and Kinnear, raised profound questions concerning the interdependency of marketing and ecology. Their ground-breaking concept of ecological marketing moved marketing thought and practice beyond an abstract economic and social worldview to embrace the physical realities of a tangible world. In practice, however, the ecological marketing debate was limited to the most damaging industries such as oil, chemicals and cars, and very few companies changed their marketing behaviour. The majority of companies continued to see environmental problems as a constraint and a cost factor, and as concerning regulatory compliance rather than markets or marketing. To reduce pollution and meet legal requirements, 'end-of-pipe' solutions were implemented in production processes and products (e.g. catalytic converters in cars).

Although ecological marketing emerged as a reaction to the worst examples of environmental damage, some pioneering companies at the time proactively embraced environmental and social values as central to their business. The Body Shop was opened by Anita Roddick in 1976 and ice-cream company Ben & Jerry's was founded by Ben Cohen and Jerry Greenfield in 1978. Their founders were value driven and entrepreneurial rather than driven by customer needs and market pressures. Consumers began to take an interest during the 1980s following a series of critical incidents, including the Bhopal gas tragedy in 1984, the nuclear reactor accident at Chernobyl in 1986, the chemicals leak at the Sandoz factory in 1986 and the *Exxon Valdez* oil spill in 1989. Media coverage of these and other disasters stoked public concern about the environment so that it entered the mainstream as a political and business issue.

Green Marketing and Environmental Marketing

During the late 1980s the environmentally conscious and active 'green consumer' emerged in western Europe and North America, armed with a range of bestselling green consumer guides. In markets as diverse as batteries, beverages, cars, cleaning products, detergents and food, the environment became a competitive factor. *Green marketing* or *environmental marketing* concepts were developed, focusing on the target group of green consumers who would be willing to pay premium prices for more environmentally friendly products.[11] New instruments such as life cycle assessment (LCA) allowed ecological considerations to be introduced into marketing decisions. According to the Society of Environmental Toxicology and Chemistry (SETAC):

> Life Cycle Assessment is a process to evaluate the environmental burdens associated with a product, process, or activity by identifying and quantifying energy and materials used and wastes released to the environment; to assess the impact of those energy and materials used and releases to the environment; and to identify and evaluate opportunities to affect environmental improvements. The assessment includes the entire life cycle of the product, process or activity, encompassing, extracting and processing raw materials, manufacturing, transportation and distribution; use, re-use, maintenance; recycling, and final disposal.[12]

Based on LCA, environmentally improved packaging materials and products were developed and promoted by pioneering and leading companies, as documented in a number of green marketing success stories.[13]

In contrast to ecological marketing in the 1970s, green marketing was not merely concerned with the depletion of nonrenewable resources and critical substances. Green marketing also included environmental issues like the loss of species, the destruction of ecosystems and habitats, and poverty in developing countries. From the viewpoint of marketing practice, the second phase during the late 1980s and early 1990s was much more significant than the first during the 1970s for a number of reasons. Firstly, environmental problems were not only issues of public controversy and political regulation, but became a competitive factor in the market. Secondly, the focus was not only on production processes but also on packaging and products. Thirdly, there was a broadening beyond the original 'front line' of industries with the most direct impact on the natural environment, such as oil, mining, chemistry and cars, to consider a wide variety of consumer goods industries and even service markets such as tourism or financial services.

Despite the 'win–win' logic and rhetoric, it became obvious during the second half of the 1990s that it can be difficult to generate and sustain competitive advantage from superior environmental performance.[14] There was something of a backlash against green marketing.[15] Green products often proved vulnerable to competitive tactics such as discounting, or attacks on the level of technical performance offered or the credibility of their environmental claims. Competing on the basis of environmental quality can be very difficult, since what constitutes the 'greenest' product in any market is open to debate. It is easier to demonstrate which is the fastest or the cheapest car on the market than to define the greenest. The glass industry claimed glass as a greener packaging material than plastic because of its naturalness and recyclability, while the plastics industry claimed the upper hand on the basis of weight and associated energy and cost savings in distribution. Diesel engines use less fuel and emit less CO_2 than conventional engines, but emit NO_x particles that are hazardous to human health. Overall, environmental problems and dimensions were shown to be complex, controversial and not easily solved simply by particular product substitutions.

Another problem for green marketing was that the green consumer, who is willing to buy greener products at premium prices, frequently proved to be something of a myth. Consumer studies regularly reported that there was a gap between reported environmental consciousness and actual environmental behaviour, and that an enduring cynicism towards corporate greening efforts among consumers tended to undermine their willingness to buy green products. Therefore in practice, the opportunities for green marketing proved to be far less than had been predicted in the early 1990s. The concept of green marketing assumes that producers are market driven, but overestimates consumer demand for green products. In contrast, the concept of ecological marketing argues that environmental issues should not depend on consumer demand, but overestimates the willingness of producers to develop environmentally superior production and products.[16] As long as the institutional setting and the price signals remain unchanged, neither ecological marketing nor green marketing will be adopted by the majority of companies in the mainstream.

Sustainable Marketing

Sustainable marketing accepts the limitations of a market orientation and acknowledges the necessity of regulatory alterations to the market mechanism.[17] Instead of avoiding regulations, sustainable marketing fosters corporate and collective commitment to necessary alterations of institutional settings and price signals in favour of sustainable development. From this perspective, sustainable marketing is a macromarketing concept.[18] It embraces the idea of sustainable development, which requires a change in the behaviour of virtually everyone, including both producers and consumers. In addition to the macromarketing perspective, sustainable marketing emphasizes the triple bottom line of ecological, social and economic issues; unlike green marketing, which tends to focus on environmental problems and the reduction of the environmental burden.[19]

For this book, we have chosen to use the term 'sustainability marketing' rather than sustainable marketing. The distinction between the two, although subtle, is important. The adjective 'sustainable' can be used to mean durable or long-lasting. Therefore 'sustainable marketing', can be interpreted as a kind of marketing, which builds long-lasting customer relationships effectively – without any particular reference to sustainable development or consideration of sustainability issues. Sustainability marketing more explicitly relates to the sustainable development agenda. In the next section we will describe the managerial approach of sustainability marketing and its main elements.

Elements of Sustainability Marketing

Marketing management usually adopts a micro orientation to consider marketing from the perspective of the individual manager within the organization. Marketing management refers to planning, organizing, implementing and controlling marketing resources and programmes to satisfy consumers' wants and needs, in order to achieve organizational objectives. For it to be successful, the entire organization should support a market and customer orientation.[20] Corresponding with that definition, *sustainability marketing management* refers to planning, organizing, implementing and controlling marketing resources and programmes to satisfy consumers' wants and needs, while considering social and environmental criteria and meeting corporate objectives. In more general terms, *sustainability marketing* may be defined as building and maintaining sustainable relationships with customers, the social environment and the natural environment.[21] A common characteristic of sustainability marketing and relationship marketing is the long-term orientation. Both concepts are long-term and relationship-oriented, as opposed to transaction marketing, which is rather short term and sales-oriented.

The managerial approach of sustainability marketing comprises six key elements:

- socio-ecological problems
- consumer behaviour
- sustainability marketing values and objectives
- sustainability marketing strategies
- sustainability marketing mix
- sustainability marketing transformations[22]

The first two elements are part of an analysis of the corporation's external environment. They help marketers to identify key socio-ecological issues in the marketplace and develop new marketing opportunities. The third and fourth elements are strategic marketing decisions at a corporate level. They are part of the planning phase and set the ground for the sustainability marketing mix at a product level. The sixth element of sustainability marketing is the active participation of companies in public and political processes to change institutions in favour of sustainability.

Here it becomes clear that sustainability marketing is a micro/macro concept. Conventional marketing thinking provides a highly abstracted view of the relationship between individual companies and their target markets, in which the time frame is relatively short; key socio-environmental impacts are assumed away as 'externalities'; and the marketing environment is considered an important influence on companies and consumers, but companies and consumers are assumed to have no power to shape that environment. Sustainability marketing provides a more realistic view of markets in which the key players have some power to influence their environment; in which companies and consumers take some responsibility for the social and environmental impacts of production and consumption; and in which the impact of today's decisions on future generations of consumers, citizens, investors and managers is considered. The six key elements of sustainability marketing depicted in Figure 2.3 represent the outline and structure of this book.

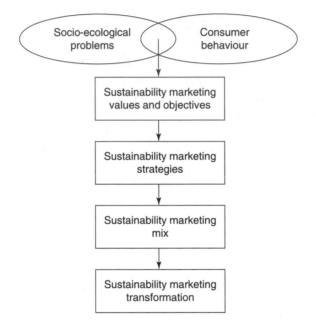

Figure 2.3 Framing sustainability marketing

The point of departure in sustainability marketing is an understanding of social and environmental problems in general (macro level) and an analysis of the social and ecological impact of corporate products in particular (micro level). The relevance and importance of social and ecological issues vary by business, by size, by sector and by geographic region. In contemporary society, socio-ecological issues are not purely about scientific fact, they are also socially constructed. Mass media and pressure groups play a significant role in determining which issues attract high or low attention from the general public. For example, there are many ecologically important species that are at risk of extinction, but it tends to be the large and 'attractive' species such as elephants, tigers and polar bears that dominate media coverage and public concern on the issue.

The analysis of consumer behaviour includes the purchase, use and post-use of products. In the context of sustainability, all three stages of consumer behaviour are important: many significant contributions that consumers can make towards environmental and social quality come in product use, maintenance and disposal, or in delaying a purchase or avoiding it altogether.[23] Sustainable consumption considers ecological and social criteria in the purchase, use and post-use of products. The intersection of socio-ecological problems and consumer wants sets the context for sustainability marketing and can create significant new market opportunities for innovative companies.

The sustainability marketing mission presents the company's values and vision, its markets, customers, products and services in the light of the sustainability challenge. The sustainability marketing mission may be an implicit element of corporate values or explicitly articulated within written documents such as corporate mission and value statements. Corporate sustainability statements and codes of practice are nevertheless of little use if they are not integrated into the processes of setting goals and developing and implementing strategies. Sometimes ecological, social and economic objectives are complementary. However, in many cases there are trade-offs to be made between them, and between the short and the long term. Finding the right, responsible balance between ecological, social and economic goals is both a demanding challenge and a continuous process and it will be an increasing feature of marketing in the twenty-first century.

At the strategic level of sustainability marketing there are a number of issues to consider for marketing managers: innovation, segmentation, targeting, positioning and timing. Sustainability innovations are a fundamental part of successful sustainability marketing (e.g. passively heated houses, solar cells, organic food, fair trade products, hybrid cars and car sharing). If these kinds of sustainability innovations are developed, which are the main target groups? What roles do social and environmental aspects play in positioning? What is the unique sustainable selling proposition (USSP)? When is the right moment to enter the market with sustainability innovations?

To implement sustainability marketing strategies, a comprehensive marketing mix has to be developed. The classic concept classifying marketing activities is the 'four Ps' of product, price, place and promotion.[24] However, the classic mix takes the seller's viewpoint, not the buyer's. In the age of customer relationships and sustainable development, we think that the 'four Cs' are better suited to classify the sustainability marketing mix. The fours Cs – customer solutions, customer cost, communication and convenience[25] – take the point of view of the customer. *Customer solutions* go beyond selling physical products and present solutions to customers' problems. They imply knowing customers and their needs well and offering products and services that satisfy customer needs and that consider social as well as environmental aspects. *Customer Cost* does not only include the financial price a buyer has to pay for a product or a service, it also considers the psychological, social and environmental costs of obtaining, using and disposing of a product. *Communication* goes beyond promotion, which is a form of persuasion and a one-way communication from seller to buyer. Communication is a process of interactive dialogue within which it is essential to build trust and credibility. *Convenience* means that customers want to use products and services that meet their needs and that are easy and convenient to access and use.

Sustainability marketing transformations are about the active participation of companies in public and political processes to change institutions in favour of sustainability (macromarketing).[26] Within the present institutional framework, the successful marketing of sustainable products is possible, but limited. The institutional design fails to set positive incentives for sustainable behaviour, both for producers and consumers. On the contrary, it allows – and often even encourages – unsustainable behaviour. That is why changes in institutions are necessary to expand the intersection between socio-ecological problems and consumption, and to set up conditions for the successful marketing of sustainable products beyond market niches. Sustainability pioneers and leaders can harness enlightened self-interest to change public and political institutions and thus enhance sustainable development.[27] The more societal and political institutions favour sustainable consumption, the easier it is for companies to market sustainable solutions successfully. Sustainability marketing is therefore linked to corporate social responsibility, a concept that has gained widespread acceptance in politics and practice since the turn of the twenty-first century.

Corporate Social Responsibility (CSR)

Unlike sustainability marketing, *corporate social responsibility (CSR)* is not new. For a long time businesses have shown varying degrees of responsibility to society, and political concerns about the social and environmental impact of economic activity can be traced back literally thousands of years. Modern ideas about CSR began emerging with the corporate philanthropists of the nineteenth century,[28] but systematic reasoning about the issue started in the USA only about half a century ago.[29] Two key questions in the debate on CSR are: Besides economic responsibilities, do corporations have social responsibilities? If so, what is the nature of these responsibilities?[30] The answers to that second question have been many and varied, leading to many different principles and conceptions of CSR. A good definition is suggested in the Green Paper 'Promoting a European Framework for Corporate Social Responsibility' by the European Commission:

> CSR is a concept whereby companies integrate social and environmental concerns in their business operations and in their interaction with stakeholders on a voluntary basis.[31]

Let us have a closer look at this definition. First, it is important to notice that the European Commission defines the nature of social responsibilities broadly, considering both social and ecological aspects. In contrast, the World Business Council for Sustainable Development makes a distinct differentiation between corporate social responsibility, corporate environmental responsibility and corporate financial responsibility, forming the triple bottom line of *corporate responsibility* (see Figure 2.4).

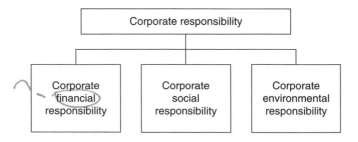

Figure 2.4 Corporate responsibility

Source: World Business Council for Sustainable Development (1999) *Corporate Social Responsibility*, Geneva: Switzerland, p. 3.

From this perspective, the term corporate social responsibility is strictly limited to social issues such as employee rights, human rights and community involvement. Theoretically, this distinction makes sense. In everyday business talk, however, the concept of CSR becomes blurred. Often CSR includes both social and environmental responsibilities, as suggested by the European Commission.

Another differentiation is made between the internal and external dimensions of CSR.[32] The internal dimension refers to employee rights, health and safety at work, the management of natural resources and the environmental impacts of production. The external dimension of CSR refers to local communities, business partners, suppliers, consumers, human rights and global environmental concerns. Companies have varying degrees of influence over CSR issues.[33] With regard to core operations, companies have a high degree of control. Companies, especially large multinationals, also exert direct influence on business partners along the supply chain. On governments, local communities, media and the general public, corporations have only an indirect influence.

A second feature of the European Commission's CSR definition is that social and environmental concerns are integrated into all business operations. From this point of view, CSR is not seen as a purely philanthropic activity, nor as an optional 'add-on' to core business activities, but as the way in which businesses are managed.[34] Social and environmental responsibilities are part of purchasing, operations, sales, marketing and so on. In this sense, CSR is viewed as a comprehensive set of policies, practices and programmes that are integrated into business operations, supply chains and decision-making processes throughout the company.[35] Systematic approaches to integrating environmental responsibilities into business operations and decision-making processes include environmental management systems such as EMAS and ISO 14000. These approaches go beyond legal requirements and businesses usually adopt them on a voluntary basis.

Another element of CSR is the interaction with stakeholders. The main starting point of stakeholder theory is that corporations are not simply managed in the interests of their owners and shareholders, but that there is a whole range of groups such as customers, employees, suppliers, government, local communities and environmental organizations that have a legitimate interest in the corporation as well (see Figure 2.5). Since the 1990s the involvement and expectations of stakeholders have increased significantly, with direct and indirect impacts on companies and their economic performance.

Many companies have responded to the heightened attention being paid to CSR by publishing reports that showcase their social and environmental good deeds. For example, 64% of the 250 largest multinational corporations published CSR reports in 2005, either within their annual reports or separately. As one critic sarcastically says:

> It would be a challenge to find a recent annual report of any big international company that justifies the firm's existence merely in terms of profit, rather than 'service to the community'. Such reports often talk proudly of efforts to improve society and safeguard the environment – by restricting emissions of greenhouse gases from the staff kitchen, say, or recycling office stationery – before turning hesitantly to less important matters, such as profits.[36]

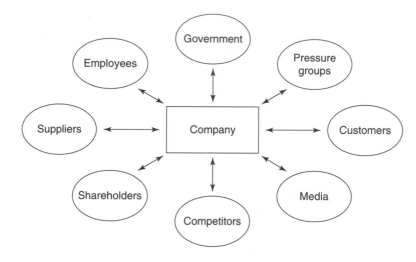

Figure 2.5 Stakeholder model

Source: Freeman, R.E. (1984) *Strategic Management: A Stakeholder Approach*, Boston: Pitman Publishing.

These remarks indicate that many CSR activities and reports are relatively cosmetic, with an emphasis on their public relations value. They are neither strategic nor operational in terms of being integrated into core business activities, as suggested by the European Commission. Porter and Krämer argue that the prevailing approaches to CSR are so disconnected from business as to obscure many of the greatest opportunities for companies to benefit society.[37] They suggest that corporations should use the same kinds of framework as those that guide their core business choices. If they do so, they would discover that CSR can be much more than an obligation, a cost or a constraint; it can in fact be an opportunity for innovation and competitive advantage.

Steps towards a systematic and strategic CSR approach include identifying, prioritizing and addressing the social and environmental issues that matter the most, or the ones on which the company can make the biggest impact. From a strategic point of view social and environmental issues fall into three categories: general social and environmental issues; value chain social and environmental impacts; and social and environmental dimensions of competitive context.[38] The first category describes generic social and environmental issues that may be important for society, but are neither significantly affected by company operations nor do they influence the long-term competitiveness. The second category characterizes social and environmental issues that are significantly affected by corporate activities in the ordinary course of business. Here the entire value chain or the whole product life cycle from cradle to grave has to be taken into account. The third and last category describes social and environmental issues that significantly affect the underlying drivers of competition. The classification of social and environmental issues varies by sector, by business and by geographic region. Water may be a general issue for financial services, a negative value chain impact for agriculture and a competitive factor for beverages. The AIDS pandemic in Africa may be a general issue for a British retailer, a value chain impact for a pharmaceutical company and a competitive context issue for a South African mining company that depends on local labour for its operations.[39] The identification and prioritization of social and environmental issues set the ground for an affirmative and coherent corporate social agenda that tries to achieve social and corporate objectives simultaneously. Such an agenda must be responsive to stakeholders and their expectations, but it moves beyond good corporate citizenship and mitigating harmful value chain impacts.

Strategic CSR transforms value chain activities to benefit society and to reinforce competitive strategy (see Figure 2.6). Take Whole Foods Market, which offers organic, natural and healthy food products to its customers. This North American retailer integrates social and environmental concerns into its entire business operations by purchasing organic food products from local farmers; screening out foods containing unhealthy ingredients; converting vehicles to run on biofuels; composting spoiled produce and biodegradable waste; and purchasing renewable wind energy credits equal to 100% of its electricity use in all of its stores and facilities.[40] This kind of strategic approach to CSR adds social and environmental dimensions to a company's value proposition. When this is the case, CSR is closely associated with sustainability marketing as defined previously and described further in this book.

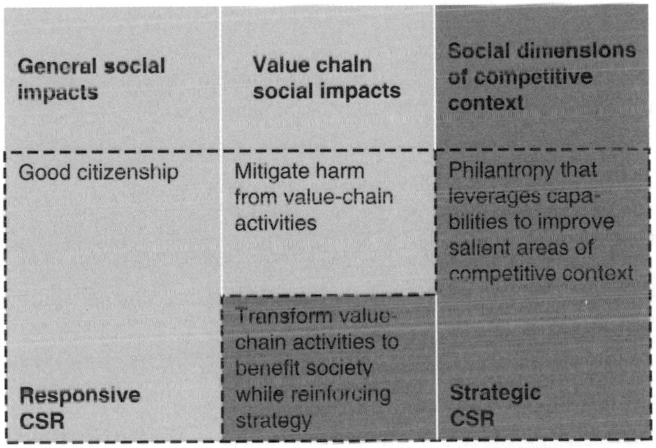

General social impacts	Value chain social impacts	Social dimensions of competitive context
Good citizenship	Mitigate harm from value-chain activities	Philanthropy that leverages capabilities to improve salient areas of competitive context
	Transform value-chain activities to benefit society while reinforcing strategy	
Responsive CSR		**Strategic CSR**

Figure 2.6 Responsive and strategic approaches to CSR
Source: Porter, M.E. and Krämer, M.R. (2006) 'Strategy and society', *Harvard Business Review*, 84(12): 89.

However, there are differences between CSR and sustainability marketing: the former focuses on the corporate level and stakeholders, whereas the latter emphasizes the product level and customers as the 'forgotten stakeholder'. In subsequent chapters each element of the sustainability marketing concept is presented in more detail, including theoretical foundations, empirical insights and illustrative case examples from companies all over the world.

Marketing has evolved over time. Saturated and competitive markets led to companies substituting the production-centred 'make and sell' philosophy with a customer-centred 'sense and respond' philosophy. However, the satisfaction of consumer wants and needs is not always in the best interests of society. Since the 1970s different marketing concepts such as societal marketing, social marketing, ecological marketing, green marketing and environmental marketing have been developed to deal with social and environmental issues. The managerial approach to sustainability marketing explicitly refers to the concept of sustainable development. The framework of sustainability marketing consists of six key elements: socio-ecological problems; consumer behaviour; sustainability marketing mission and objectives; sustainability marketing strategies; the sustainability marketing mix; and sustainability marketing transformations. Sustainability marketing is complementary to corporate social responsibility (CSR), a concept that integrates social and environmental concerns into business operations on a voluntary basis.

List of Key Terms

Corporate responsibility
Corporate social responsibility
Ecological marketing
Environmental marketing
Green marketing
Social marketing
Societal marketing
Sustainable marketing
Sustainability marketing

REVIEW QUESTIONS

1. Define societal marketing and social marketing. What are the similarities and differences between the two concepts?
2. Define ecological marketing and green marketing. What are the similarities and differences between the two marketing concepts?
3. During the second half of the 1990s it became obvious that it is difficult to generate and sustain competitive advantage on the basis of superior environmental quality. What are the main reasons for the so-called backlash against green marketing?
4. What are the main elements of sustainability marketing? Why is the concept called 'sustainability marketing' instead of 'sustainable marketing'?
5. Define corporate social responsibility (CSR). What is the link between CSR and sustainability marketing?

DISCUSSION QUESTIONS

1. The Toyota Prius was the first mass-produced hybrid vehicle. Do you think that a hybrid car using less petrol and emitting less CO_2 than other cars in the same category is a contribution to the aim of intragenerational equity?

2. One of the unsolved problems of societal marketing is who defines what is, and what is not, in the interest of long-run consumer benefit. In your opinion, who should define the long-run benefits of products and services?

3. The green and environmental marketing concepts of the 1990s assume that companies are market driven, aiming at the target group of green consumers. What are the limitations of such a concept from a) the marketing point of view and b) the ecological point of view?

4. Corporate social responsibility (CSR) is defined as 'a concept whereby companies integrate social and environmental concerns in their business operations and in their interaction with stakeholders on a voluntary basis'. Is CSR really adopted 'on a voluntary basis'? In which situations and to which degree are companies free to decide whether to adopt a CSR approach or not? Give specific examples of companies that were required to take on social responsibilities.

5. In your experience, which kind of companies adopt sustainability marketing management? Give specific examples and discuss to which extent they implement sustainability marketing.

Endnotes

1. Toyota Motor Corporation (2006) *Sustainability Report 2006. Towards a New Future for People, Society and the Planet*; Toyota Motor Europe (2006) *Toyota European Sustainability Report 2006*; www.toyota.com/prius (accessed 21 August 2007).
2. Kotler, P. & Armstrong, G. (2004) *The Principles of Marketing*, 10th edn, Upper Saddle River, NJ: Prentice Hall, pp. 12–13.
3. Bartels, R. & Jenkins, R.L. (1977) 'Macromarketing', *Journal of Marketing*, 44(4): 17–20.
4. Kotler, P. (1972) 'What consumerism means for marketers', *Harvard Business Review*, 50(3): 48–57.
5. Crane, A. & Desmond, J. (2002) 'Societal marketing and morality', *European Journal of Marketing*, 36(5/6): 548–69.
6. Kotler, P. & Zaltman, G. (1971) 'Social marketing: An approach to planned social change', *Journal of Marketing*, 35(3): 3–12; www.social-marketing.org (accessed 21 August 2007).
7. Fisk, G. (1974) *Marketing and the Ecological Crisis*, New York: Harper & Row; Henion, K.E. II (1976) *Ecological Marketing*, Columbus, OH: Grid; Henion, K.E. II and Kinnear, T.C. (1976) *Ecological Marketing*, Chicago, IL: American Marketing Association. For an overview of the evolution from ecological marketing to environmental marketing, see Peattie, K. (2001) 'Towards sustainability: The third age of green marketing', *The Marketing Review*, 2: 129–46.
8. Carson, R.L. (1962) *Silent Spring*, New York: Houghton Mifflin; Meadows, D.H., Meadows, D.I., Randers, J. & Behrens, W.W. III (1972) *The Limits to Growth*, New York: Universe Books.
9. Henion, K.E. II & Kinnear, T.C. (1976) *Ecological Marketing*, Chicago, IL: American Marketing Association.
10. Fisk, G. (1974) *Marketing and the Ecological Crisis*, New York: Harper & Row, pp. 84–126; Henion, K.E. II (1976) *Ecological Marketing*, Columbus, OH: Grid, pp. 77–240; Henion, K.E. II & Kinnear, T.C. (1976) *Ecological Marketing*, Chicago, IL: American Marketing Association, pp. 1–2.
11. Charter, M. (1992) *Greener Marketing: A Responsible Approach to Business*, Sheffield: Greenleaf Publishing; Coddington, W. (1993) *Environmental Marketing. Positive Strategies for Reaching the Green Consumer*, New York: McGraw-Hill; Meffert, H. & Kirchgeorg, M. (1993) *Marktorientiertes*

Umweltmanagement, Stuttgart: Schaeffer-Poeschel; Ottman, J.A. (1993) *Green Marketing. Challenges and Opportunities for the New Marketing Age*, Lincolnwood, IL: NTC Business Books; Peattie, K. (1992) *Green Marketing*, London: Pitman Publishing; Peattie, K. (1995) *Environmental Marketing Management. Meeting the Green Challenge*, London: Pitman Publishing.

12. Society of Environmental Toxicology and Chemistry, www.setac.org (accessed 3 January 2009). See Chapter 3 for a further description of LCA.

13. Charter, M. (1992) *Greener Marketing: A Responsible Approach to Business*, Sheffield: Greenleaf Publishing; Meffert, H. & Kirchgeorg, M. (1993) *Marktorientiertes Umweltmanagement*, Stuttgart: Schaeffer-Poeschel; Ottman, J.A. (1993) *Green Marketing: Challenges and Opportunities for the New Marketing Age*, Lincolnwood, IL: NTC Business Books; Peattie, K. (1992) *Green Marketing*, London: Pitman Publishing.

14. Peattie, K. (2001) 'Towards sustainability: The third age of green marketing', *The Marketing Review*, 2: 129–46.

15. Crane, A. (2000) *Marketing, Morality and the Natural Environment*, London: Routledge.

16. Van Dam, Y.K. & Apeldoorn, P.A.C. (1995) 'Sustainable marketing', *Journal of Macromarketing*, 15(3): 45–56.

17. The term was first coined by Sheth, J.N. and Parvatiyar, A. (1995) 'Ecological Imperatives and the Role of Marketing', in M.J. Polonsky & A.T. Mintu-Wimsatt (eds) *Environmental Marketing. Strategies, Practice, Theory, and Research*, New York: Hawarth Press, pp. 3–20. The authors' fundamental proposition is that sustainable development can be achieved only by active corporate marketing and government intervention.

18. Van Dam, Y.K. & Apeldoorn, P.A.C. (1995) 'Sustainable marketing', *Journal of Macromarketing*, 15(3): 45–56.

19. Charter, M., Peattie, K. Ottman, J. & Polonsky, M.J.(2002) *Marketing and Sustainability*, Cardiff: Centre for Business Relationships, Accountability, Sustainability and Society (BRASS).

20. Lazer, W. & Culley, J.D. (1982) *Marketing Management. Foundations and Practices*, Boston MA: Houghton Mifflin.

21. Belz, F.M. (2006) 'Marketing in the 21st century', *Business Strategy and the Environment*, 15(3): 139–44.

22. *Ibid.*

23. Peattie, K. (1999) 'Rethinking Marketing', in M. Charter & M.J. Polonsky (eds) *Greener Marketing. A Global Perspective on Greening Marketing Practice*, Sheffield: Greenleaf Publishing, pp. 57–70.

24. The classification of the four Ps was first suggested by Mc Carthy, E.J. (1960) *Basic Marketing: A Managerial Approach*, Homewood, IL: Irwin.

25. Lauterborn, R. (1990) 'New marketing litany: 4 Ps passé; C-words take over', *Advertising Age*, 1 October 1990, p. 26; Kotler, P. & Armstrong, G. (2004) *The Principles of Marketing*, 10th edn, Upper Saddle River, NJ: Prentice Hall, p. 58.

26. Belz, F.-M. (2001) *Integratives Öko-Marketing: Erfolgreiche Vermarktung von ökologischen Produkten und Leistungen*, Wiesbaden: Gabler.

27. Bendell, J. & Kearins, K. (2005) 'The political bottom line: The emerging dimension to corporate responsibility for sustainable development', *Business Strategy and the Environment*, 14(6): 372–83.

28. World Business Council for Sustainable Development (1999) *Corporate Social Responsibility*, Geneva: World Business Council for Sustainable Development.

29. Carrol, A.B. (1999) 'Corporate social responsibility: Evolution of a definitional construct', *Business and Society*, 38(3): 268–95.

30. Crane, A. & Matten, D. (2004) *Business Ethics*, Oxford: Oxford University Press, pp. 41–7.

31. Commission of the European Communities (2002) *Corporate Social Responsibility: A Business Contribution to Sustainable Development*, COM (2002) 347 final, Brussels: Commission of the European Communities, p. 5.

32. World Business Council for Sustainable Development (1999) *Corporate Social Responsibility*, Geneva: World Business Council for Sustainable Development, p. 3., pp. 9–16.

33. World Business Council for Sustainable Development (2002) *Corporate Social Responsibility: The WBCSD's Journey*, Geneva: World Business Council for Sustainable Development, p. 4.

34. Commission of the European Communities (2002) *Corporate Social Responsibility: A Business Contribution to Sustainable Development*, COM (2002) 347 final, Brussels: Commission of the European Communities, p. 5.
35. Business for Social Responsibility, www.bsr.org (accessed 21 August 2007).
36. Crook, C. (2005) 'A survey of corporate social responsibility', *The Economist*, 22 January, pp. 3–18.
37. Porter, M.E. & Krämer, M.R. (2006) 'Strategy and society', *Harvard Business Review*, 84(12): 78–92.
38. *Ibid.*
39. *Ibid.*
40. Whole Foods Market, www.wholefoodsmarket.com (accessed 3 January 2009).

PART II

DEVELOPING SUSTAINABILITY MARKETING OPPORTUNITIES

3

Socio-ecological Problems

After Studying this Chapter You Should be Able to:

1. Understand the main socio-ecological problems on a macro level.
2. Identify the main socio-ecological impact of products on a micro level.
3. Understand the use of life cycle assessment (LCA) as a tool to understand the social and ecological issues related to a given product.

LOOKING AHEAD: PREVIEWING THE CONCEPTS

In the last chapter, you learnt about the core concepts of sustainability marketing. In this chapter, we will first look at key ecological and social problems at a global level (macro level). Then we take a look at the socio-ecological impact of products (micro level). Here the whole life cycle from cradle to grave has to be taken into account. Life cycle assessment (LCA) is an instrument used to analyse the impact of products on the natural and social environments. Neglecting the impact of products on the social and ecological environments is risky for business and brands, whereas understanding the impact of products opens up new perspectives and market opportunities.

SUSTAINABILITY MARKETING STORY:
STARBUCKS – FILLING SOULS AND BELLIES

Starbucks is the largest coffee house chain in the world. It started back in 1983, when Howard Schultz had the idea of bringing a European-style coffee house to North America. He believed that people needed to slow down – to 'smell the coffee' and enjoy life a little more. Starbucks does not sell just coffee, it sells the 'Starbucks experience'. The company treats customers to poetry on its wallpaper and tabletops, jaunty apron-clad barista behind the espresso machine, and an interior ambience that is both cosy and slick, marked by earth tones, brushed steel and retro music. As one Starbucks' executive puts it: 'We're not in the business of filling bellies, we're in the business of filling souls.'

Since the coffee crisis, Starbucks has been in the business of filling bellies as well. Between 1994 and 2004 the price of coffee beans plummeted, which had a devastating impact on farmers worldwide. Coffee provides a livelihood for more than 20 million farmers and their families living within the 'bean belt', tropical and subtropical countries such as Brazil, Colombia, Costa Rica, Ethiopia, Guatemala, India, Indonesia and Vietnam. Over two thirds are smallholders cultivating less than five hectares. Before the sharp fall in the coffee price, the income farmers used to get from coffee was enough to sustain them. They were able to eat and feed themselves and their children, buy clothes, take their children to school, go to health centres when they were sick and get involved in some community-based activities. After the coffee crisis this had all become a distant dream. The money the small farmers received from the middlemen was insufficient to cover production costs and provide a decent living. Low earnings caused multiple effects. The peasants stopped investing in their farms. In many cases children were withdrawn from school and the daily diet worsened. The small farmers were also unable to afford clothes, shoes, basic medical attention and repayment of credit.

A large portion of Starbucks' coffee is grown on small family farms, often located in remote, hilly areas where the fruit is harvested by hand. Coffee beans are the seeds inside the small red fruit of the coffee tree, which is larger than a typical shrub but smaller than most trees. One plant usually produces enough fruit every season for one pound (453 grams) of roasted coffee beans. In traditional poly-culture systems the small coffee trees are surrounded by larger leguminous trees, which provide shade. On coffee plantations, shade trees are often stripped away and replaced with tight rows of coffee trees that are directly exposed to the bright sun. Such monocultures, which are characterized by high inputs in terms of fertilizers and pesticides, deliver high crop yields, but the quality is often lower than coffee grown in a more natural, shaded setting.

Starbucks' approach to sustainable coffee purchasing is customer and quality driven. The willingness of Starbucks customers to pay high prices for coffee is largely based on the company's promise to deliver exceptional quality. That is why it buys only the finest arabica coffee that meets its rigorous standards for high quality. Starbucks recognizes that high-quality arabica coffee is more expensive to produce than lower-grade arabica or robusta coffee. Thus, it pays premium prices for higher-quality arabica beans, sold as speciality coffee, to help farmers make profits and support their families. Furthermore, Starbucks adopted CAFE, an integrated approach that strives to improve the lives of farmers and increase the amount of high-quality coffee that is grown, processed and traded in a sustainable matter. CAFE stands for Coffee And Farmer Equity, which emphasizes the importance of farmer equity in relation to Starbucks coffee. The approach defines a set of sustainability criteria, developed by Starbucks in cooperation with farmers, suppliers and independent nongovernmental organizations such as Conservation International and the Rainforest Alliance. The guidelines contain 28 indicators covering five areas: product quality, economic accountability (transparency), social responsibility, environmental leadership in coffee growing and environmental leadership in coffee processing. Farmers and suppliers that demonstrate the use of best practice according to the CAFE guidelines, and obtain independent verification of their performance, may become preferred and strategic Starbucks partners. To build trust and credibility, Starbucks retained Scientific Certification Systems (SCS) for the development, training and auditing of CAFE practices. SCS is a third-party evaluation and certification firm. To collaborate with farmers and provide them with the technical support and training needed to ensure the sustainable production of high-quality coffee, Starbucks opened up a farmer support centre in Costa Rica.

In addition to setting up CAFE guidelines, Starbucks buys some coffee that has been grown or sold in ways that help to preserve the natural environment and promote economic stability; that is, conservation coffee (shade grown), certified organic coffee and Fair Trade certified coffee. Starbucks environmental commitment also goes beyond the growing of coffee. It covers the whole product life cycle from bean to barista. To measure and monitor progress, Starbucks has set up key environmental key metrics, which are reported against on a regular basis.[1]

Many other companies face social and environmental problems that affect their business, short-term success and long-term survival. Consumers are becoming increasingly interested in the world behind the product. They want to know how and where and by whom the product has been produced. Thus, marketers have to understand the main socio-ecological problems in general and the impact of products in particular.

Socio-ecological Problems on a Macro Level

You may well have seen one of the photos of Earth taken from space in the middle of the twentieth century (Figure 3.1). The photos show a blue and green ball, small and seemingly fragile in the vastness of space. This vision had a great impact on the thinking of humankind. It made people aware that there are limits to natural resources and to the ability of the biosphere to absorb the effects of human activities.[2] The Earth is the only planet in the solar system known to harbour life. About 70% of its

Figure 3.1 Earth from outer space

surface is covered by water, which is essential to life. The rest is land, mostly in the form of continents that rise above the oceans.

The overall impact of human activities on the planet and the natural environment is the result of three factors: population, consumption per person (affluence) and technology. This can be expressed through the *IPAT formula*:[3]

$$\text{Impact} = \text{Population} \times \text{Affluence} \times \text{Technology}$$

Population

Population is the total number of people living on Earth. The world population grew from 2.5 billion in 1950 to 6.5 billion in 2005 (+160%). The vast majority of the world population lives in Asia, especially in China and India. In the year 2005 around 3.9 billion people lived in Asia, 730 million in Europe, 560 million in Latin America and 330 million in Northern America. By 2050 the world population is projected to grow to approximately 9 billion (Figure 3.2).

The population in the more developed regions of 1.2 billion is estimated to remain fairly constant between 2005 and 2050. During this period most of the population growth is expected to take place in less developed regions. Here the population is projected to increase from 5.2 billion to 7.8 billion (+50%). The population of the least developed countries is expected to more than double between 2005 and 2050, rising from approximately 760 million to 1.7 billion (+123%). The high fertility levels

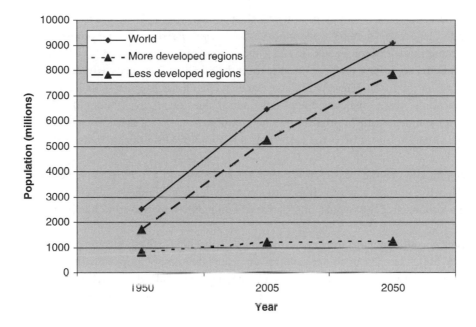

Figure 3.2 World population 1950–2050

prevailing there are mainly responsible for the increase, despite high mortality rates due to poverty, hunger, malnutrition and epidemic diseases such as HIV/AIDS, malaria and tuberculosis.[4]

Affluence

Affluence relates to the amount that each person consumes. Based on the consumption per capita three classes can be distinguished on a global scale: the poor, the middle and the affluent (see Table 3.1).[5]

The world's poor include all households with less than $700 a year per family member; that is, they live on less than $2 (€ 1.44) a day. The poor live in huts and shanties. They do not travel far and mostly

Table 3.1 World Consumption Classes

Category of Consumption	Poor	Middle	Affluent
Annual income	Less than $700	Between $700 and $7500	Above $7500
Housing	Huts, shanties	Moderate buildings	Climate-controlled buildings
Diet	Insufficient grain, unsafe water	Grain, clean water	Meat, packaged food, soft drinks
Transport	Walking	Bicycles, buses	Private cars, airplanes
Materials	Local bio-mass	Durables	Throwaways

Source: Based on Durning, A. (1992) *How much is enough? The Consumer Society and the Future of the Earth*, New York: W.W. Norton Company, p. 27.

go on foot. They eat grains, root crops and beans. Seldom do they have access to clean, healthy water. According to the United Nations' *Millennium Development Report*, extreme poverty remains a daily reality for more than 1 billion people on the globe, who subsist on less than $1 (€0.72) a day.[6] More than 800 million people have too little to eat to meet their daily energy needs. Children from the poorest of the poor suffer the most. They are malnourished and less likely to go to school and receive a proper primary education, which might give them choice and enable them to live a better life. When it comes to extreme poverty, hunger, child mortality and epidemic diseases, sub-Saharan Africa is the worst affected, whereas the situation in southern and eastern Asia has improved significantly since 1990.

The world's middle income class earn between $700 (€503) and $7500 (€5414) per family member per year. They live in moderate buildings with electricity for lights, radios and refrigerators. They eat a diet based on grains and clean water, and they travel on public transportation like buses and railways.

By definition, the affluent consumer class includes all households whose income per family member is more than $7500. They live in climate-controlled, heated buildings, equipped with refrigerators, washing machines, dishwashers and many other electricity-powered gadgets. They eat meat and processed, packaged food, and enjoy soft drinks and other beverages from disposable containers. The dominant modes of transportation in the affluent consumer class are automobiles, and increasingly airplanes. They typically use televisions, telephones and the Internet. These kinds of products have a considerable impact on the natural environment. However, equally important are the ideas and consumption culture that mass media transmits. Television offers news and entertainment, but also exposure to consumer products and lifestyles, which are shown in advertisements and during programmes.

The members of the affluent consumer class enjoy a kind of material lifestyle that has never been experienced before in the history of humankind. The 'democratization of consumption' started in North America and expanded to western Europe and Japan in the past half century. Since the 1990s the consumer culture has been spreading across the world. According to the latest estimates 1.7 billion people belong to the so-called *global consumer class*, which is about a quarter of the world population. Although most consumption spending still occurs in more developed regions, the number of consumers is increasing in less developed regions. Almost half the global consumer class now lives in less developed countries (Table 3.2).[7]

In east Asia there are approximately 240 million Chinese and 120 million Indians belonging to the affluent consumer class. In sum, this is more than the affluent consumer class in all of western Europe (349 million), not to mention the United States and Canada (270 million). Whereas 80% of the population in industrializing countries belongs to the global consumer glass, it is less than 20% in developing countries, indicating a large potential for future consumption demand. If the same levels of consumption that several hundred million of the most affluent people enjoy today were replicated across the world tomorrow, the impact on water supply, air quality, climate, biodiversity and human health would be severe. Thus, the ecological question is also a social question of resource equity in a world with limited resources.[8] As resource scarcity increases due to world population growth and the rise of the affluent consumer class, achieving an equitable distribution of natural capital, goods and services becomes more

Table 3.2   Affluent Consumer Class in Developed and Less Developed World Regions

Region	Number of People Belonging to the Affluent Consumer Class (Million)	Affluent Consumer Class as Share of Regional Population (%)	Affluent Consumer Class as Share of Global Consumer Class (%)
United States and Canada	271.4	85	16
Western Europe	348.9	89	20
East Asia and Pacific	494.0	27	29
Latin America and the Caribbean	167.8	32	10
Eastern Europe and Central Asia	173.2	36	10
South Asia	140.7	10	8
Australia and New Zealand	19.8	84	1
Middle East and North Africa	78.0	25	4
Sub-Saharan Africa	34.2	5	2
More developed regions	912	80	53
Less developed regions	816	17	47
World	1,728	28	100

Source. Bently, M. (2003) *Sustainable Consumption: Ethics, National Indices and International Relations*, PhD dissertation, Paris: American Graduate School of International Relations and Diplomacy.

difficult and makes conflicts over oil, natural gas, water and arable land more likely. An increase in resource and energy efficiency is a contribution to intragenerational and intergenerational equity as well as a contribution to a policy of security and peace. New technologies might help to make the best use of natural resources.

Technology

Technology has two different meanings: In a narrow sense, technology refers to tools and machines that may be used to help solve problems. In a broad sense, technology is the current state of our knowledge of how to combine resources to produce desired products, to solve problems, to fulfil needs or to satisfy wants. Technology, in this sense, includes skills, processes, technical methods, tools and raw materials. In modern societies technology is pervasive; it seems to be everywhere. Often technology is quite complex. Most modern tools are difficult to understand: they require intensive training to manufacture and use (e.g. computers). For their manufacture and proper use, many modern tools also depend on other modern tools. Cars, for example, have a huge supporting industrial complex for their manufacture and maintenance. To use them requires infrastructure such as roads, streets, highways, fuel and service stations.

On the one hand, technology has many positive, intended effects. Cars help people to move around and transport goods. On the other hand, technology frequently has unintended, negative consequences (e.g. car accidents and air emissions). The negative effects of technology on the natural environment are both obvious and subtle. The more obvious effects include the depletion of nonrenewable resources such as oil and the added pollution of air, water and land. The more subtle effects include debates over long-term impacts (e.g. global warming).

The technology part of the IPAT formula can be broken down into two separate elements: the amount of resources used to produce a unit of consumption (input side), and the amount of waste or emissions generated by a unit of consumption (output side). Most technologies were designed first for economic or ergonomic effect, without the natural environment in mind. In the future it is safe to assume that ecology will become an important criterion in the design of new technologies (e.g. fuel-cell cars and low-energy houses). In principle, it is possible – and necessary – to boost the resource productivity and energy efficiency of technologies. If we go on with business as usual, world energy consumption is projected to double by 2050, which would have a devastating effect on the natural environment. According to leading scientists, the stabilization of the global climate requires a halving of the world energy consumption as compared to 1990. If we could quadruple our resource productivity and energy efficiency (known as *Factor 4*), it would help us to reduce worldwide energy consumption and stabilize the global climate while maintaining our lifestyles (see Figure 3.3).[9] Some people think that even more radical changes are needed to prevent an environmental crisis. They ask for a revolution of resource productivity and efficiency by *Factor 10*.[10]

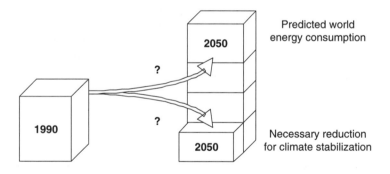

Figure 3.3   Factor 4 – Doubling wealth and halving environmental impact

Some technologies are designed specifically with the environment in mind, for example recycling facilities, solar cells and wind power generators. However, these kinds of technologies are not completely free of environmental impact either. Some types of solar cells contain hazardous materials and wind power generators need land as well as infrastructure such as roads.

The best-known standpoints often emphasize only one of the three PAT factors as the dominant cause of the rising human impact on the natural environment: inexorable population growth, excessive consumption or polluting technology. An essential point of the IPAT formula is that all three factors are important and intertwined. None can be safely ignored or postponed. There are no easy, single-faceted solutions to the ecological challenges of the twenty-first century. Population control, the equitable distribution of opportunity, the ingredients of prosperity and the redirection of technology must all be accomplished if there is to be a future worth having.

What is the connection between the IPAT formula and marketing? What role does marketing play when it comes to population, affluence and technology? Marketing has relatively little direct effect on population – although marketers involved in the manufacture of condoms and contraceptive pills or the operation of dating agencies might see things differently. However, marketing does have an influence on both the level of affluence and the technology that creates it.[11] In this respect marketing plays an ambivalent role. On the one hand, it promotes a consumer society and materialistic lifestyles, which impose problems on the social and natural environments. On the other hand, marketing helps develop and diffuse sustainability innovations to make the revolution of resource productivity and energy efficiency come true. Furthermore, sustainability marketing can facilitate new lifestyles that are less materialistic and more sustainable. In this respect, marketing is not just a problem but can also be a part of the solution.

Environmental Impact

Environmental *impact* is the outcome of the three factors in the IPAT equation. The natural environment is the source of renewable and nonrenewable resources (input side). It is also the sink for disposals and emissions in the air, water and soil (output side). Both functions of the natural environment are jeopardized due to a growing world population, increasing levels of consumption and polluting technologies.

Sources

Natural resources are commonly divided between renewable and nonrenewable resources. *Renewable resources* include air, water supplies, food crops, fish stocks and timber. A renewable resource has a way of regenerating itself. If managed properly and used at the rate of regeneration, renewable resources provide steady yields virtually for ever. However, if used at a greater rate than that at which it can regenerate, a renewable resource may become nonrenewable. In the example of groundwater, the removal of water from pore spaces within soil and rocks may cause permanent compaction that cannot be reversed. Natural resources such as coal, oil and gas take million of years to form. Since fossil fuels do not reform at the rate at which we use them up, they are considered *nonrenewable resources*. In this sense, mined resources such as stone, metals, uranium and various other minerals are also nonrenewable resources.[12]

Water is a natural, renewable resource. It is essential to life: all known forms of life depend on fresh water. Although more than 70% of the Earth's surface is covered with water, only 3% of that water is fresh, and over two thirds of this is frozen in glaciers and polar ice caps. Some regions of the world have large amounts of fresh water, others hardly have any. In 2005 one third of the world's population lived in water-stressed countries; by 2025 this is expected to rise to two thirds. Water shortages will be more prevalent among poorer countries where resources are limited and population growth is rapid. Around 70% of the water worldwide is used for agriculture. The rest is used for industrial, household, recreational and environmental activities. Overpumping of groundwater is causing water tables to decline in key agricultural regions in Asia, North Africa and the United States. As a result of the excessive use of fertilizers and pesticides, heavy metals discarded by industry and petrochemicals leaking out of storage tanks and long-distance pipelines, the quality of groundwater is also deteriorating.[13]

Food crops are also renewable resources. Globally, about a quarter of the planet's land area is used for cropland and pasture, which is roughly 3.3 billion hectares. While the world population more than doubled in the last half century, global food production more than kept up. The increase in food production was possible due to the conversion of forests and natural grassland to cropland, as well as the use of commercial fertilizers and pesticides. In 2005 much of the world's best cropland was already taken. Increasingly, farmers have to turn to marginal land. A key constraint for agriculture is fresh water, which is scarce in some regions of the world. As a result of monocultures and excessive use of fertilizers, soil degradation is becoming a problem that is reducing agricultural productivity. In addition, many pesticides lose their effectiveness as the pests acquire resistance.

Fossil fuels such as coal, oil and natural gas have been the main energy sources since the Industrial Revolution. Modern life would be impossible without the use of fossil fuels, especially oil, on which we depend for 90% of transportation, and for pharmaceuticals, chemicals, food and many other things.[14] Fossil fuels are nonrenewable, limited resources. Depending on the current stocks and the exploitation rate, the availability of nonrenewable resources varies significantly. The larger the world population and the higher the demand and the exploitation rate, the shorter will be the availability of nonrenewable resources. Experts estimate that current reserves of oil will only last about 40 years. Natural gas is a suitable replacement for oil, but it is not infinite either. There is still plenty of coal, but it causes high pollution levels. All three fossil fuels have a high carbon content, which goes back to the photosynthesis of plants millions of years ago. If fossil fuels are burnt, they release the carbon into the atmosphere in the form of carbon dioxide.

Biological diversity or biodiversity is the diversity of life on Earth. It may be defined as the totality of the genes, species and ecosystems of a region. The biodiversity found on Earth today is the result of 4 billion years of evolution. It is hard to say how many species there are. Estimates of the present global species vary from 2 million to 100 million, with a best estimate of somewhere near 10 million. Most biologists agree that humans are responsible for the sixth great wave of mass extinction. We were not here for any of the other previous mass extinctions, but this time our sheer preponderance leaves less room for other species. The conversion of forests and natural grasslands leads to habitat loss and eventually to the extinction of other species. Some argue that species have a high economic value. Others argue that each species has a value in itself and should be saved. It is a matter of fact that we depend on many species to keep us alive, to purify water, to fix nitrogen, to recycle nutrients and waste and to pollinate crops.[15]

Sinks

The surface of the Earth is surrounded by a layer of gases called the atmosphere. The atmosphere includes a balance of gases that trap heat from the sun, resulting in a moderate climate suitable for water to exist in liquid form. Since 1750 the global atmospheric concentrations of carbon dioxide, methane and nitrous oxide have increased significantly. The global increases of carbon dioxide are primarily due to fossil fuel use and land-use changes, while those of methane and nitrous oxide can be traced back to agriculture.

There is mounting scientific evidence that the build-up of carbon dioxide and other gases in the atmosphere leads to global warming. According to the Intergovernmental Panel on Climate Change (IPCC), a consortium of several hundred independent scientists around the world, the average global temperature has risen approximately 0.75°C since the late nineteenth century. It is very likely that most of the warming observed over the last 50 years is attributable to human activities. All of the warmest years have occurred since 1990. Based on climate models, IPPC predicts an increase of average temperatures between 1.1 and 6.4°C by 2100.[16] Nobody can say exactly how fast it may happen, what will happen and who will be most affected. Global warming could take the Earth into uncharted territory, with possible consequences including rises in sea levels; increases in extreme weather events such as floods, droughts, heat waves and hurricanes; changes in agricultural yields; glacier retreats; or contribution to biological extinctions.[17] That is why climate change is probably the biggest global environmental challenge.

Pollution is the release of contaminants to the air, water and soil. Arguably, the main source of air pollutants worldwide is motor vehicle emissions. The World Health Organization (WHO) reports that 3 million people worldwide are killed annually by outdoor air pollution from vehicle and industrial emissions. Water pollutants consist of a wide range of organic and inorganic chemicals such as heavy metals, petrochemicals, chloroform and bacteria. Each year over 2 million people die from diarrhoeal diseases associated with poor water quality. Among the most significant soil contaminants are heavy metals, herbicides and pesticides. Often soil contamination is associated with water pollution due to the involvement of runoff and groundwater. It occurs when chemicals are released by spills, when underground storage tanks leak or when farming land is overfertilized. Eventually, the chemical pollutants in the soil and water climb the food chain from plants and animals to humans, a finding that received widespread publicity following Rachel Carson's *Silent Spring*.[18]

Despite increased scientific attention to environmental problems, many of the potentially serious threats are far from being completely understood. When you are studying living organisms and complex ecosystems, scientific uncertainty is the norm rather than an exception. Generally, the response of the natural environment to human activities is long-term, nonlinear and sometimes irreversible. Global warming or the extinction of species, for instance, cannot be undone at any cost. To be on the safe side, it is useful to follow the precautionary principle and take action based on scientific evidence that supports probable – although not certain – future outcomes. Waiting too long to take action on an ecological issue to guarantee certainty might allow irreversible consequences to set in.[19]

Socio-ecological Impact of Products on a Micro Level

Neo, the hero of the science fiction movie *The Matrix*, is in on a secret: the reality that forms the lives of millions of human beings is not in fact real. The world that seems real to most people is in fact a computer-generated simulation, but hardly anybody notices this. While humans seem to walk around in ordinary life, their minds are radically deceived.[20] So are the minds of business students: in ordinary marketing classes they learn about the benefits of products and how to sell them, but they do not see the reality behind those products. Most marketing students are unfamiliar with the biophysical dimensions of products. What kind of impacts do products have on the natural and social environments? To which extent do products contribute to environmental and social problems on a macro level? Such questions are rarely asked or answered in conventional marketing classes.

To assess the impact of products on the natural and social environments, it is necessary to take the whole physical *product life cycle* into account; that is, extraction of raw materials, transportation, manufacturing, distribution, use and disposal. The product life cycle from cradle to grave depicted in Figure 3.4 should not be confused with the product life cycle model commonly used in marketing. The former views the product life cycle in socio-ecological terms, whereas the latter charts the life of a product in economic terms. The conventional product life cycle model proposes that products follow a life cycle of birth, growth, maturity and death, in which sales and profits rise and finally fall.[21]

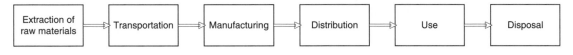

Figure 3.4 Product life cycle from cradle to grave

The stages of this life cycle vary by industries and product categories. The simplified life cycle of an automobile 'from well to wheel', for example, includes resource extraction, material manufacturing, automobile manufacturing, automobile use/maintenance and automobile disposal. The food chain 'from farm to fork' mainly consists of agriculture, food processing, food distribution, food consumption, recycling and disposal.

The product life cycle in Figure 3.4 is a simplified model. In reality, the life cycle consists of entire networks instead of a single product chain. Industrialized agriculture, for example, depends on a number of actors, such as agrochemical industry (fertilizers, pesticides), seed industry, fodder industry, energy and water suppliers, machine and automobile industries. Food-processing companies are supplied by agriculture, packaging companies, food ingredient producers and others. Moreover, many product life cycles stretch across nations and markets. An automobile, for instance, consists of thousands of different parts and raw materials such as iron, steel and plastics, which come from all over the world.

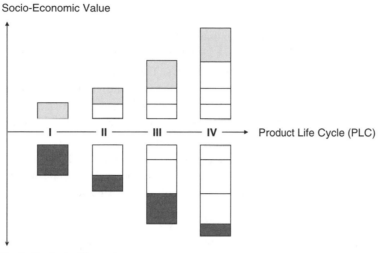

Figure 3.5 Value and impact of products

Products create both value and impact along the whole life cycle from cradle to grave (Figure 3.5).

The manufacturing of products generates jobs, incomes for workers, and revenue and profits for companies. The use of products satisfies customers' needs and wants. This kind of social and economic value is in contrast to the social and environmental impact induced by products. Product value and impact are two sides of the same coin. They do not necessarily balance in each phase of the product life cycle, however.

Take a cotton T-shirt, which is nice to wear and relatively cheap for consumers, but which comes with high costs for the natural environment and workers.[22] Cotton is the world's best-selling fibre. However, many pesticides commonly used on cotton are 'extremely hazardous', according to the World Health Organization's classification. Many cotton farmers all over the world get sick and some die as a result of pesticide exposure. In addition, the chemicals and pesticides used on cotton have a high impact on the natural environmental, animals and wildlife. Shipping the cotton from farm to factory requires energy, typically fossil fuels. At the end of processing, T-shirts are usually dyed and treated with fabric finishes. Chemical dyes often contain heavy metals like copper and zinc, which are toxic and can pollute water through factory runoff. China is the world's top producer of T-shirts, supplying about 65% of the total. Garment factory workers in China earn low wages and work long hours. Does the socio-economic value match the socio-ecological impact in the initial life cycle phases of a cotton T-shirt?

The thorough environmental and social assessment of products is the point of departure for credible sustainability marketing.[23] In general terms, there are qualitative and quantitative methods of life cycle assessment.[24]

Socio-ecological Impact Matrix

The *socio-ecological impact matrix* is a qualitative instrument.[25] It is a heuristic for analysing and visualizing the social and environmental 'hot spots' of a product. It takes a life cycle perspective and considers all relevant social and environmental aspects. The horizontal axis of the matrix depicts the major phases of the product life cycle from cradle to grave. The vertical axis presents the relevant environmental and social dimensions. The phases and dimensions on the two axes may vary from one product category to another. The fields in the matrix indicate the impact of the corresponding product life cycle phase on the natural or social environment. The assessment in the fields is based on ABC analysis: black fields symbolize a high impact on the natural and social environments, grey fields represent medium impact and white ones low impact. The assessment is based on several sources such as scientific and social studies, socio-ecological indicators, statements by experts and written documents.

Let us take a closer look at the impact of automobiles and coffee, two different kinds of consumer goods that you are probably familiar with from everyday life. Which are the main socio-ecological problems of these products along the whole life cycle from cradle to grave? As pointed out before, the life cycle of automobiles encompasses the following phases: resource extraction/material manufacturing, automobile manufacturing, automobile use/maintenance and automobile disposal. The following categories are relevant from a socio-ecological perspective: resource and energy consumption, air, noise, waste, water, land use, health and accidents.

The impact matrix of automobiles depicted in Figure 3.6 shows at a glance that the usage stage is of the utmost importance from a socio-ecological perspective. The driving phase is responsible for approximately 80% of the energy consumption and air emissions throughout the vehicle life cycle.[26] Worldwide motor vehicle emissions are arguably the main source of air pollutants (CO_2, NO_x, SO_x). Noise emissions are another problem, especially in highly populated countries and cities. Cars require a large amount of infrastructure (roads, highways, fuel stations, maintenance companies, private and public parking), which accounts for land use. Traffic influences human health directly and indirectly. Worldwide there are millions of car accidents annually, often resulting in injuries and death. Additionally, vehicle air emissions affect the respiratory tract. Some of the vehicle emissions are suspected of causing cancer. In addition to the usage phase, the first phase of the vehicle life cycle is also relevant. Key problems at this stage are the extraction of nonrenewable resources, water consumption and wastes. About two thirds of passenger cars consist of steel and iron, which have high 'ecological rucksacks'. In the last phase of disposal the wide variety of plastics involved is problematic, since they are difficult to recycle.[27]

Let us also have a look at the impact of coffee, which was the subject of the chapter-opening marketing story on Starbucks. Coffee is the second most valuable commodity in the world. It is estimated that coffee generates around \$80 (€57.6) billion per year worldwide. The main life cycle phases of roasted coffee encompass cultivation, primary processing, roasting/packaging, distribution and consumption/disposal. The socio-ecological dimensions include energy, air, water, soil, waste, ecosystems, health and equity. The impact matrix as depicted in Figure 3.7 shows that the major impact of coffee

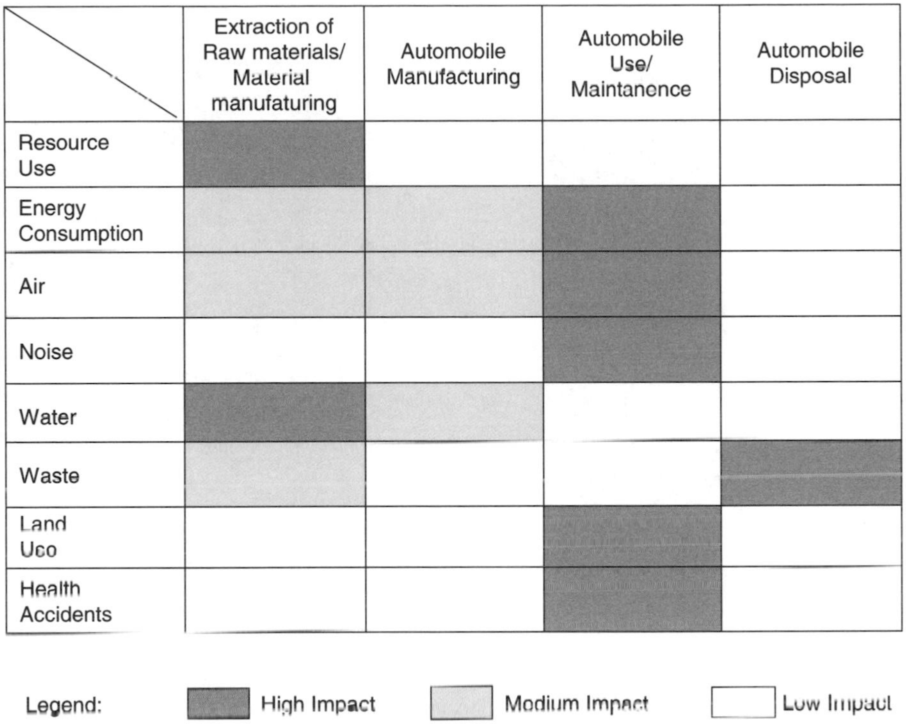

	Extraction of Raw materials/ Material manufaturing	Automobile Manufacturing	Automobile Use/ Maintanence	Automobile Disposal
Resource Use	High Impact	Low Impact	Low Impact	Low Impact
Energy Consumption	Medium Impact	Medium Impact	High Impact	Low Impact
Air	Medium Impact	Medium Impact	High Impact	Low Impact
Noise	Low Impact	Low Impact	High Impact	Low Impact
Water	High Impact	Medium Impact	Low Impact	Low Impact
Waste	Medium Impact	Low Impact	Low Impact	High Impact
Land Use	Low Impact	Low Impact	High Impact	Low Impact
Health Accidents	Low Impact	Low Impact	High Impact	Low Impact

Legend: ▓ High Impact   ░ Medium Impact   ☐ Low Impact

Figure 3.6 Impact matrix of automobiles

Source: Belz, F.-M. (2001) *Integratives Öko-Marketing: Erfolgreiche Vermarktung von ökologischen Produkten und Leistungen*, Wiesbaden: Gabler, p. 175.

on the natural and social environments is related to the first and last stages of the product, that is, cultivation and primary processing as well as consumption and disposal.[28]

Coffee is produced in a continuum of cultivation systems differing in degree of intensification, from traditional polyculture systems to industrial monoculture production. The former uses few if any agrochemicals, has a low plant density of 1000–3000 per hectare and yields 200–300 kg per hectare of coffee; whereas the latter usually involves high use of agrochemicals, has more than 5000 plants per hectare and provides yields above 1300 kg per hectare.[29] Unshaded monocultures deliver high yields, but they are dependent on high external inputs in terms of irrigation, fertilizers, pesticides and machinery, which require a lot of energy. Furthermore, the intensive use of industrial fertilizers often leads to the problem of eutrophication of groundwater and surface water. The biodiversity on site is very low due to the monocultural farming practices and the high use of pesticides and herbicides. Once the coffee berries are picked, there are two methods for obtaining green coffee beans. The 'dry' method simply involves sun-drying or heat-drying the berries, while the 'wet' method uses water to remove the pulp from the beans.[30] The wet method offers better quality control but consumes up to 60–70 litres of water per kilogram of coffee and generates large volumes of effluent.

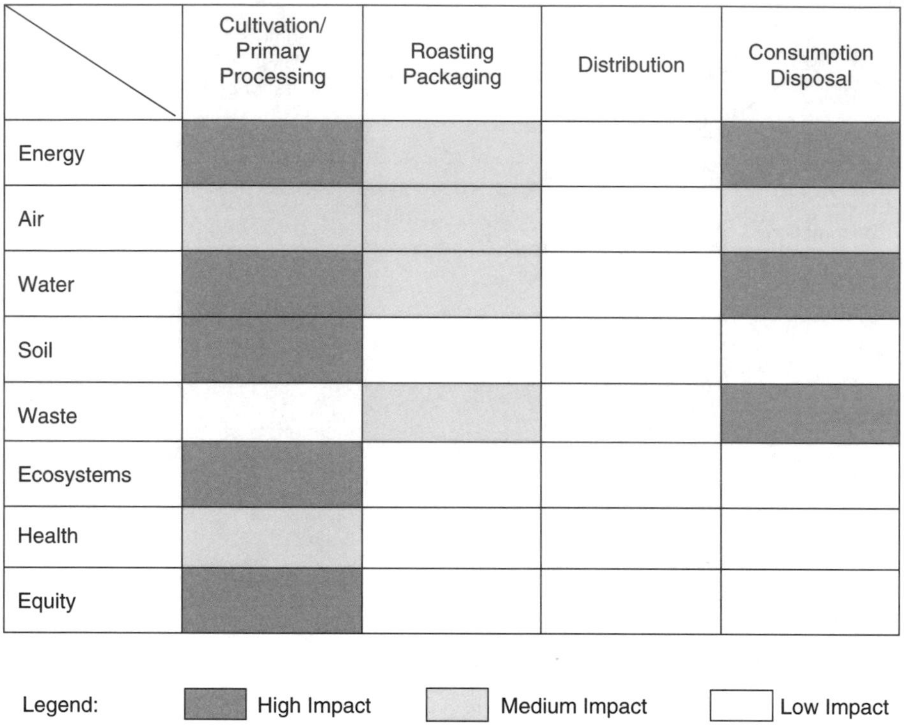

	Cultivation/ Primary Processing	Roasting Packaging	Distribution	Consumption Disposal
Energy	High Impact	Medium Impact	Low Impact	High Impact
Air	Medium Impact	Medium Impact	Low Impact	Medium Impact
Water	High Impact	Medium Impact	Low Impact	High Impact
Soil	High Impact	Low Impact	Low Impact	Low Impact
Waste	Low Impact	Medium Impact	Low Impact	High Impact
Ecosystems	High Impact	Low Impact	Low Impact	Low Impact
Health	Medium Impact	Low Impact	Low Impact	Low Impact
Equity	High Impact	Low Impact	Low Impact	Low Impact

Legend: ■ High Impact   ▢ Medium Impact   ☐ Low Impact

Figure 3.7 Impact matrix of coffee

Source: Adapted from Belz, F.-M. (1995) *Ökologie und Wettbewerbsfähigkeit in der Lebensmittelbranche*, Bern: Paul Haupt, p.37.

Social problems also play an important role in the first two stages of the coffee life cycle, as highlighted in the chapter-opening story. The sharp decline in world coffee prices between 1994 and 2004 contributed to the misery of millions of coffee farmers and their families in South America, Africa and Asia, raising questions of intragenerational equity. Aside from cultivation, the purchasing, preparation and disposal of coffee are very significant from an ecological point of view. The brewing and heating of coffee in millions of households and offices result in high levels of energy consumption as well as waste in terms of coffee grounds and packaging. In comparison to that, the roasting of coffee is relatively unimportant. Even more astonishing is that the transportation of coffee from the 'bean belt' to North America or western Europe contributes only slightly to overall energy demand and global warming potential.

As illustrated by the examples of automobiles and coffee, the impact matrix provides an idea of the major problems of a product along its whole life cycle from cradle to grave. The black and grey fields in the matrix visualize the socio-ecological 'hot spots'. On the one hand, the key problems represent risks. If they become significant in the market, consumer behaviour may change and affect the position of existing products. On the other hand, the socio-ecological hot spots open up new market opportunities. The impact matrix is therefore a starting point for sustainability innovations and a useful tool for new sustainable product and service developments.[31] Having said that, we have to remember that the impact matrix only gives an overview of relevant environmental and social problems. Often a more thorough analysis of these problems is necessary to provide quantitative data and detailed results.

Life Cycle Assessment

Life cycle assessment (LCA) is a quantitative instrument that measures and assesses the impact of products on the natural environment and human health. The Society of Environmental Toxicology and Chemistry (SETAC) developed a conceptual framework and guidelines for LCA in the early 1990s.[32] Since 1997 the process of conducting LCA studies has been standardized by the International Organization for Standardization (ISO). The latest standards of ISO 14040 and ISO 14044 released in 2006 provide an overview of the framework, requirements and guidelines of LCA.[33]

The process of LCA consists of four interrelated phases: (1) definition of the goal and scope; (2) life cycle inventory analysis; (3) life cycle impact assessment (LCIA); and (4) life cycle interpretation (Figure 3.8).

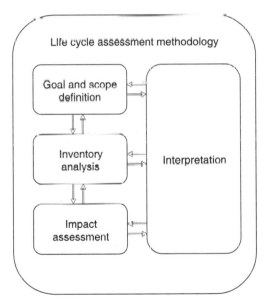

Figure 3.8 Life cycle assessment methodology

Source: ISO 14040 (2006). Permission to reproduce extracts from BS EN ISO 14040:2006 is granted by BSI. www.bsigroup.com/shop.

In the first phase, the objectives and scope of the study are defined. The objective of an LCA might be the comparison of two alternative packages (e.g. glass versus plastic bottles). The scope refers to the functional unit of analysis, the system boundaries and the geographic extent of coverage. The idea of a functional unit is central to LCA, which is used to compare alternative ways of providing a certain functionality or utility to the consumer. Take the functional unit of one litre of milk, which might be packed in a glass bottle or in a board container. System boundaries dictate how far to follow the life cycle and which stages to include in the analysis. Practical considerations and the objectives of the study influence these decisions.

In the second phase a life cycle inventory (LCI) is taken of the material and energy flows related to the functional unit of analysis. Here the inputs and outputs of processes are measured in physical terms (e.g. energy use in kilowatt hours, water consumption in litres, and solid waste in square metres). As you can imagine, even simple consumer goods like coffee, detergents or clothes require numerous processes corresponding with different kinds of material and energy flows. Professional software tools like SimaPro can display the processes in greater detail and use data specifically gathered for the LCA study in combination with more generic data from external sources. The Swiss ecoinvent database, for instance, contains international industrial life cycle inventory data on energy supply, resource extraction, material supply, chemicals, metals, agriculture, waste management services and transport services.[34]

In the third phase a life cycle impact assessment (LCIA) is carried out, involving at least three steps: selection and definition of impact categories; assignment of inventory input and output data to the selected impact categories; and aggregation of inventory input and output data within the category. In LCIA according to ISO 14040 the following impact categories are considered: use of resources (fossil resources, regenerative resources, mineral resources and water); land use; global warming; ozone depletion; photochemical oxidant formation (smog); acidification; eutrophication; and human toxicity.

In the fourth and last phase of an LCA study, the data from the inventory analysis and impact assessment are interpreted and practical conclusions are drawn.

LCA is conducted by environmental engineers, environmental scientists and consultants worldwide, and has become a valuable source of insights into the impact of products and providing relevant information for decision-making processes. There are many possible areas of application for LCA: it provides important information for research and development, marketing, strategic planning and public policymaking. It also forms the basis for eco-labelling schemes, which are an effective tool for communicating 'green' claims to the consumer.[35]

To illustrate the application of LCA, let us have a look at a study conducted by the Fraunhofer Institute and commissioned by Kraft Jacobs Suchard (KJS), one of the largest coffee roasters in the world.[36] The subject of the study was roasted ground coffee in vacuum packaging. The goal was to quantify the environmental energy and material flows induced by the consumption of a defined amount of coffee. The functional unit was 1000 kg of roasted coffee purchased and prepared by the consumer, the equivalent of 21 430 litres of prepared coffee. The study considered the following stages of the life cycle: cultivation, primary processing, roasting, packing, distribution of the coffee, its purchase and preparation by the consumer, and the waste treatment of the coffee grounds, the packaging and the filter bags.

The LCA study carried out an impact assessment considering the following categories: energy, mineral resources, water and waste as well as the potential for eutrophication, acidification and global warming.

The use of land resources and the effect on human beings were not considered. The main results are depicted in Figure 3.9, showing the relative contribution of all life cycle stages on the selected impact categories. Overall, the first stage of cultivation and the last stages of consumption and disposal are of high importance from an ecological point of view. The transportation, roasting process and packaging materials seem to be less important.

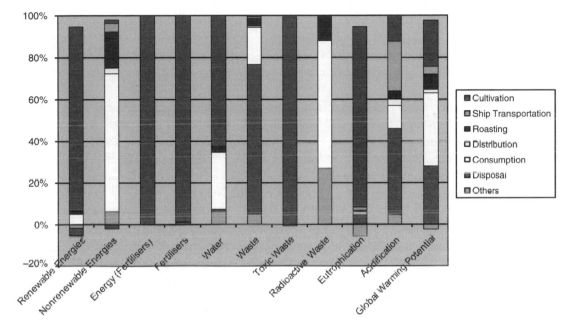

Figure 3.9 Main results of the LCA of coffee

Source: Diers, A., Langowski, H.-C., Pannkoke, K. & Hop, R. (1999) *Produkt-Ökobilanz vakuumverpackter Röstkaffee*, Landsberg: Ecomed, p. 85.

LCA is a relatively new approach with some serious limitations.[37] One of the problems is the definition of scope. If basic assumptions regarding the functional unit of analysis, system boundaries and geographic scope vary, the LCA of different products or packaging materials are hardly comparable. Another problem is the perishability of information: new materials and rapidly changing technologies associated with production, distribution and waste recovery can cause LCA interpretation to become obsolete overnight.[38] Furthermore, the selection of impact categories is limited to environmental dimensions and human health. Other social dimensions (such as equity or cultural diversity), which are difficult to quantify, are not considered at all. The socio-ecological impact matrix and LCA therefore work in a complementary way. The matrix gives an overview of the main ecological and social impacts of a given product and is a good starting point for a detailed, in-depth LCA. The impact matrix is also helpful for presenting and discussing the complex results of an LCA to both internal and external groups.

The Role of Media

Many environmental and social problems are not experienced directly by people. Global warming, scarcity of water in some distant regions of the world, pollutants in the soil, child labour and unacceptable working conditions in developing countries are problems to which many people cannot relate in everyday life. Thus, there is reason to believe that mass media plays a decisive role in putting environmental and social issues on the public agenda.[39] Impacts on the natural environment and human health are discovered by science and transmitted by news media. Since public attention is a scarce commodity, environmental and social issues compete with other issues for a share of it. According to the *issue attention cycle*, public attention rarely remains focused on an issue for long. Usually an issue is taken up by the media and discussed for a period until public attention moves on.[40]

Nonetheless, the environment has stayed quite high on the public agenda since the 1970s. One reason for the continuing high level of public attention is that an endless variety of new environmental problems has emerged, ranging from local toxic contamination to global threats such as climate change, and that these have blended together to create a sense of continual deterioration.[41] Another reason might be that environmental organizations have succeeded in presenting environmental problems in dramatic and persuasive terms.[42] Environmental activists like Greenpeace, for example, deliver symbolic pictures for the news media. The dispute over the planned sinking of the oil facility *Brent Spar* in 1995 created a sense of drama. The encounter between Greenpeace and the oil giant Shell was perceived by the general public as similar to the fight of David against Goliath and therefore that of good against evil – regardless of the scientific evidence and factual arguments involved. However, continual bombardment with environmental messages can eventually also lead to the saturation and de-dramatization of this kind of problem.[43] While the oil spill from the *Exxon Valdez* in Alaska in 1989 received widespread media and public attention, a similar accident on the Spanish coast in 2002 was still considered newsworthy, but hardly received the same kind of media and public attention.

News media influence the perception of environmental and social issues in two ways. First, the media choose which kind of topics appear on the public agenda (first-order framing). Many people presume that the media take notice of problems in some kind of objective way according to their relevance to society. This is not necessarily the case. Some issues are too complex to explain, others are difficult to put into pictures. Take pandas and microbes. The panda is on the verge of extinction. It is a seemingly cute and charming mammal that gains a lot of public attention. Thus, a significant share of conservation effort goes into creatures like this. In contrast, little things like soil microbes, on which the world depends, are among the least-known species of all. Microbes may appear in special features on the Discovery Channel, but they are not present in the mass media for the simple reasons that they are too small and are not newsworthy.

In addition to selecting topics according to newsworthiness and 'media friendliness', the media also decide in which way environmental and social issues are presented (second-order framing).[44] In the 1980s and 1990s the media often exaggerated environmental and social problems. In addition, they put sustainability pioneers in a very positive light. Eventually this kind of framing loses its newsworthiness. New and competing kinds of framing, such as denying or downplaying socio-ecological problems, reporting on 'black sheep' and presenting sustainability pioneers in a negative light, then become newsworthy and have gained more attention in the mass media since the beginning of the twenty-first century.[45] As a consequence, many consumers are becoming sceptical regarding products' ecological and social claims.

List of Key Terms

Affluence
Environmental impact
Factor 4
Factor 10
IPAT formula
Life cycle assessment (LCA)
Nonrenewable resources
Population
Product life cycle from cradle to grave
Renewable resources
Socio-ecological impact matrix
Technology

REVIEW QUESTIONS

1. What does the IPAT formula say? What is the link between the IPAT formula and marketing?
2. Explain the phenomenon of global warming as one of the main global environmental problems and its possible consequences for nature and human beings.
3. Describe the concept and the stages of the product life cycle from cradle to grave. Compare it to the conventional product life cycle commonly used in marketing.
4. Define life cycle assessment (LCA) and describe the process of conducting an LCA study.
5. What role do the media play in 'constructing' social and environmental problems?

DISCUSSION QUESTIONS

1. Why is the ecological question also a social question of resource equity in a world with limited resources? Discuss.
2. Describe the entire product life cycle of a textbook.
3. Develop a socio-ecological impact matrix for a cotton T-shirt. Which stages of the product life cycle and which categories should you consider? What are the main social and environmental problems associated with cotton T-shirts?

4. What conclusions can we draw from qualitative and quantitative life cycle assessments of coffee? What implications could these have for the sustainability marketing management of coffee companies such as Starbucks?
5. Describe the issue attention cycle of environmental problems associated with consumer goods packaging in your country.

SUSTAINABILITY MARKETING CHALLENGE: VESTAS – NO. 1 IN MODERN ENERGY

The growth in the world population and increasing affluence in developing countries, especially China and India, will lead to a growing demand for energy, despite technological developments and energy-efficiency improvements. The International Energy Agency expects the world's energy consumption to rise by 45% between 2006 and 2030. As a supplement to nonrenewable forms of energy such as oil and gas, renewable energy will play a vital role in the coming years in securing energy supplies and curtailing rising emissions of greenhouse gases.

Vestas is a pioneer in the wind power industry. The Danish company sold and installed its first wind turbine in 1979. Since then Vestas has developed into the world's leading supplier of world power solutions, having installed more than 35 000 wind turbines in 63 countries and employing 15 000 people. Its core business includes the development, manufacturing, sales, marketing and maintenance of wind power systems that use wind energy to produce electricity. In 2007 Vestas achieved revenue of €4.8 billion and an operating profit of €440 million. In that year wind power with a capacity of approximately 20 000 megawatts (MW) was installed worldwide. With a delivery of 4500 MW, Vestas had a global market share of 23%. Its main customers come from Germany, the United States, Denmark, Spain, India, Italy, the Netherlands and China.

To accommodate the fast-growing demand for wind energy and optimize logistics in the principal markets, Vestas opened a number of factories in recent years, including in 2007/08 in Tinanjin (China), Windsor, Colorado (USA) and Daimiel, Castilla-La Mancha (Spain). All production facilities around the world are certified according to the ISO 14001 environmental management standard and the OHSAS 18001 occupational health and safety standard. Thus, Vestas sets high international standards for environment and safety, which go further than local legislation in a number of countries. To make production as environmentally sound as possible, Vestas purchases electricity from renewable resources. In 2007, electricity from renewable sources accounted for 66% of its total electricity consumption.

Vestas does not simply sell and install wind turbines. Instead, it offers potential customers solutions to the problem of generating electricity from renewable sources without any CO_2 emissions. To ensure the commercial viability of such an investment, the careful scoping of the wind power project to ensure an appropriate match to the environment and stable operations are vital. Vestas assists its customers with:

- Scoping the wind power project
- Choosing wind turbine type
- Installing the wind farm
- Commissioning and monitoring the wind farm
- Servicing and maintaining the wind turbine throughout its lifetime.

We can see that Vestas follows a sustainability marketing approach, which aims at maintaining long-lasting relationships with both its customers and the natural environment. It has a wide portfolio of wind turbines that are suited to specific conditions and requirements. The various wind turbines mainly differ in size and power. The latest generation of wind turbines is called V90-3.0 MW. The blades of this product type have a width of 90 metres and generate an output of 3 MW at a wind speed of 15 metres per second.

Since 1999, Vestas has conducted comprehensive life cycle assessments (LCA) for three different types of wind turbines to document and improve its environmental performance. Manufacturing of raw materials for the wind turbines and production of the wind turbines both have a negative impact on the environment. The major impacts in the first two stages of the life cycle derive from ore processing and metal extraction. Environmental impacts during the usage stage comprise the visual impression of wind turbines in the countryside, sound from operating wind turbines and the impact on animals and plants. On the other hand, the energy production from the wind turbines has a positive impact on the environment. In a good location a V90-3.0 MW wind turbine will produce approximately 284 000 MWh over the expected lifetime of 20 years. That corresponds to approximately 129 000 tonnes of CO_2 reductions compared with electricity generated by a modern coal-fired power station. It also means that this type of wind turbine generates 35 times as much energy during the expected lifetime as that required for production, transport, installation, operation and dismantling. At the end of the life cycle more than 80% of the wind turbine can be recycled, primarily through the collection and remelting of metals.

Since 2005 Vestas has claimed to be 'No. 1 in modern energy'. This new corporate mission rejects the perception of wind energy as 'a romantic flirtation' with alternative energy forms, and instead states that wind is a competitive energy source on a par with oil and gas. Vestas bases its strategy on making wind energy the preferred supplement to conventional energy sources. The global market leader states that wind power is a clean, stable and unlimited resource.[46]

Questions for Discussion

1. What does the energy mix in your region look like? What is the role played by electricity from renewable sources, especially wind power?
2. What is the energy outlook for your region in 2030? Discuss the assumptions of the different scenarios for predicted energy consumption.

3. What do energy utilities in your region do to promote renewable energies?
4. What are the advantages and disadvantages of wind power as compared to a) oil; b) nuclear power; and c) solar power? Discuss on the basis of available life cycle assessments (LCA).
5. Do you think wind power is the 'preferred supplement to conventional energy sources', as proclaimed by Vestas?

Endnotes

1. Kotler, P. & Armstrong, G. (2004) *The Principles of Marketing*, 10th edn, Upper Saddle River, NJ: Prentice Hall, pp. 48–50 and 277–8; Starbucks Corporation (2006) *Beyond the Cup. Corporate Social Responsibility/Fiscal 2005 Annual Report*, Seattle, WA: Starbucks Corporation; Starbucks Corporation (2007) *My Starbucks. Corporate Social Responsibility/Fiscal 2006 Annual Report*, Seattle, WA: Starbucks Corporation; Schultz, H. & Yang, D.J. (1997) *Pour Your Heart Into It. How STARBUCKS Built a Company One Cup at a Time*, London: Hyperion; The Fairtrade Foundation (2002) *Spilling The Beans on the Coffee Trade*, London: The Fair Trade Foundation.
2. World Commission on Environment and Development (1987) *Our Common Future*, Oxford: World Commission on Environment and Development.
3. Ehrlich, P.R. & Ehrlich, A.H. (1990) *The Population Explosion*, New York: Simon and Schuster, pp. 58–9; Ehrlich, P.R., Ehrlich, A.H. & Holdren, J.R. (1977) *Ecoscience. Population, Resources, Environment*, 3rd edn, pp. 720–34; Ehrlich, P.R. & Holdren, J.P. (1971) 'Impact of population growth', *Science*, 171 (March): 1212–16; Holdren, J.R. & Ehrlich, P.R. (1974) 'Human population and the global environment', *American Scientist*, May–June: 288–91.
4. UN (2005) *World Population Prospects: The 2004 Revision*, New York: United Nations, p. 1.
5. See the seminal work by Durning, A. (1992) *How Much Is Enough? The Consumer Society and the Future of the Earth*, New York: WW Norton, pp. 26–36.
6. UN (2005) *The Millennium Development Goal Report 2005*, New York: United Nations.
7. Gardner, G., Assadourian, E. & Sarin, R. (2004) 'The State of Consumption Today', in E. Assadourian *et al.* (eds), *State of the World 2004*, New York: WW Norton, pp. 3–21.
8. Wuppertal Institut für Energie Klima Umwelt (2005) *Fair Future. Begrenzte Ressourcen und Globale Gerechtigkeit*, Munich: C.H. Beck; www.redefiningprogress.org (accessed 23 August 2007).
9. Von Weizsäcker, E., Lovins, A.M. & Lovins, L.H. (1998) *Factor Four: Doubling Wealth, Halving Resource Use*, London: Earthscan.
10. Weaver, P. & Schmidt-Bleek, F. (2000) *Factor 10. Manifesto for a Sustainable Planet*, Sheffield: Greenleaf Publishing.
11. Peattie, K. (1995) *Environmental Marketing Management. Meeting the Green Challenge*, London: Pitman Publishing, p. 49.
12. Meadows, D., Randers, J. & Meadows, D. (2004) *Limits of Growth. The 30-Year-Update*, White River Junction, VT: Chelsea Publishing.
13. Gardner, G., Assadourian, E. & Sarin, R. (2004) 'The State of Consumption Today', in E. Assadourian *et al.* (eds), *State of the World 2004* New York: WW Norton, pp. 3–21.
14. Rifkin, J. (2003) *The Hydrogen Economy*, New York: Jeremy P. Tarcher/Penguin.
15. Wilson, E.O. (2001) *The Diversity of Life*, London: Penguin.
16. Intergovernmental Panel on Climate Change (2007) *Climate Change 2007: The Physical Science Basis*, Fourth Assessment Report of the Intergovernmental Panel on Climate Change, Working Group 1, Geneva.
17. Intergovernmental Panel on Climate Change (2007) *Climate Change 2007: Climate Change Impacts, Adaption and Vulnerability*, Fourth Assessment Report of the Intergovernmental Panel on Climate Change, Working Group 2, Geneva.
18. Carson, R.L. (1962) *Silent Spring*, New York: Houghton Mifflin.

19. Holdren, J.R. & Ehrlich, P.R. (1974) 'Human population and the global environment', *American Scientist*, May–June: 288–91.
20. Vasilou, I. (2006) 'Reality, What Matters, and the Matrix', http://whatisthematrix.warnerbros.com/rl_cmp/new_phil_iakovos.html (accessed 23 August 2007).
21. Peattie, K. (1995) *Environmental Marketing Management. Meeting the Green Challenge*, London: Pitman, pp. 186–7.
22. Rivoli, P. (2005) *The Travels of a T-Shirt in the Global Economy: An Economist Examines the Markets, Power and Politics of World Trade*, Chichester: John Wiley & Sons Ltd; Pennybacker, M. (2004) 'Behind the Scenes: Cotton T-Shirts', in E. Assadourian *et al.* (eds), *State of the World 2004*, New York: WW Norton, pp. 162–3.
23. Rex, E. (2005) 'Premises for Linking Life Cycle Considerations with Marketing', thesis for the degree of Licentiate of Engineering, Göteburg: Chalmers University of Technology.
24. Fuller, D.A. (1999) *Sustainable Marketing. Managerial-Ecological Issues*, Thousand Oaks, CA: Sage Publications, pp. 56–72.
25. Belz, F.-M. & Hugenschmidt, H. (1995) 'Ecology and competitiveness in Swiss industries', *Business Strategy and the Environment*, 4(4): 229–36.
26. Toyota Motor Europe (2006) *Toyota European Sustainability Report 2006*, Brussels: Toyota.
27. Keoleian, G.A. (1998) 'Is environmental improvement in automotive component design highly constrained? An instrumental panel study', *Journal of Industrial Ecology*, 2(2): 103–18
28. The most comprehensive qualitative life cycle assessments of coffee are provided by Belz, F.-M. (1995) *Ökologie und Wettbewerbsfähigkeit in der Lebensmittelbranche*, Bern: Paul Haupt; Diers, A., Langowski, H.-C., Pannkoke, K. & Hop, R. (1999) *Produkt-Ökobilanz verkuumverpackter Röstkaffee*, Landsberg: Ecomed publishers; Salome, R. (2003) 'Life cycle assessment applied to coffee production: Investigating environmental impacts to aid decision making for improvements at company level', *Food, Agriculture and Environment*, 1(2): 295–300.
29. Pelupessy, W. (2003) 'Environmental Issues in the Production of Beverages: Global Coffee Chain', in B. Mattson & U. Sonnesson (eds), *Environmentally-Friendly Food Processing*, Cambridge: Woodhead Publishing.
30. *Ibid*.
31. See Chapter 6 for further information on sustainability innovations and sustainability innovation processes involving consumers.
32. SETAC (1991) *A Technical Framework for Life Cycle Assessment*, Washington, DC: Society of Environmental Toxicology and Chemistry; SETAC (1993) *A Conceptual Framework for Life Cycle Impact Assessment*, Penasacola, FL: Society of Environmental Toxicology and Chemistry; SETAC (1993) *Guidelines for Life Cycle Assessment: 'A Code of Practice'*, Penasacola, FL: Society of Environmental Toxicology and Chemistry.
33. ISO 14040 and ISO 14044.
34. www.ecoinvent.ch (accessed 24 August 2007).
35. Rex, E. (2005) 'Premises for Linking Life Cycle Considerations with Marketing', thesis for the degree of Licentiate of Engineering, Göteburg: Chalmers University of Technology
36. Diers, A., Langowski, H.-C., Pannkoke, K. & Hop, R. (1999) *Produkt-Ökobilanz verkuumverpackter Röstkaffee*, Landsberg: Ecomed Publishers.
37. Fuller, D.A. (1999) *Sustainable Marketing. Managerial-Ecological Issues*, Thousand Oaks, CA: Sage, pp. 65–8.
38. *Ibid*.
39. Anderson, A. (1997) *Media, Culture and the Environment*, London: UCL Press; Thøgersen, J. (2006) 'Media attention and the market for green consumer products', *Business Strategy and the Environment*, 15(3): 145–56.
40. Downs, A. (1972) 'Up and down with ecology – the "issue-attention cycle"', *The Public Interest*, 28: 38–50.
41. Dunlap, R.E. (2002) 'An enduring concern', *Public Perspective*, 13 (September/October): 10–14.
42. Anderson, A. (1997) *Media, Culture and the Environment*, London: UCL Press.
43. Hilgartner, S. & Bosk, C.L. (1988) 'The rise and fall of social problems: A public arenas model', *American Journal of Sociology*, 94(1): 53–78.

44. Weaver, D., McCombs, M. & Shaw, D.L. (2004) 'Agenda-setting Research: Issues, Attributes, and Influences', in L.L. Kaid (ed.), *Handbook of Communication Research*, Mahwah, NJ: Laurence Erlbaum, pp. 257–83.
45. Thøgersen, J. (2006) 'Media attention and the market for green consumer products', *Business Strategy and the Environment*, 15(3): 145–56.
46. International Energy Agency (2008) *World Energy Outlook (WEO) 2008*, Paris: International Energy Agency; www.vestas.com (accessed 3 January 2008); Vestas (2008): *Vestas annual report 2007*, Randers, Denmark: Vestas.

CHAPTER 4

Sustainable Consumer Behaviour

After Studying this Chapter You Should be Able to:

1. Understand the whole consumption process from a sustainability perspective.
2. Appreciate the range of potential influences on the behaviour of a consumer and how these might influence consumers to be more or less sustainable in their consumption behaviour.
3. Explain why there are significant differences in the way that different types of consumers respond to the sustainability agenda, and why understanding those differences is helpful for sustainability marketers.

LOOKING AHEAD: PREVIEWING THE CONCEPTS

In this chapter we explore the process of consumption, and the behaviour of consumers in relation to the sustainability agenda and the social and environmental challenges outlined in Chapter 3. This requires an understanding of consumption as a holistic process that goes beyond the economic activity of purchasing, and also of how the purchasing context influences consumer behaviour. Although sustainability is relevant to all forms of consumption, those consumption sectors with the greatest sustainability impacts are highlighted as a future focus for sustainability marketing efforts. Three schools of thought that have contributed to our understanding of sustainable consumption behaviour are explored, reflecting rational, psychological and sociological explanations of behaviour. The chapter ends by looking at the evolving concept of sustainable consumer behaviour and ways to promote it, including effective market segmentation and expectations management.

SUSTAINABILITY MARKETING STORY: COASTING TOWARDS SUSTAINABILITY WITH SHIMANO

If there is a 'public enemy number one' in the sustainable consumption debate, the private motor car has got to be the leading contender. If we are serious about making a transformation towards a more sustainable society, one of the main things that will need to change will be the 'great car economy'. Dependence on cars to make relatively short journeys will need to stop being a social norm. However, people are not going to get out of their cars unless they are offered a convenient and appealing alternative. In some cases public transport services, car-sharing services or even walking can offer a solution. For other relatively short journeys, the obvious way to achieve more sustainable transport is not a new technology but a relatively old one, the bicycle, which is still the main mode of transport in China. As a means of transport it offers the added health benefits of exercise, which will be important in societies like the USA where obesity rates have soared in recent decades.

A key sustainability marketing question therefore is: How can we get more people on their bikes? This is less easy than it sounds. The existing market for bikes is composed of several segments. The largest consists of cycling enthusiasts. These are people who own a lot of lycra, read cycling magazines and are enthralled by the techno-speak of modern bikes. For these people their bikes are central to their leisure activities. Another key segment is those with an actively 'green' lifestyle, for whom a bike is a means of transport and a part of the way they live.

The challenge for bike manufacturers is to expand into the mass market of consumers who are active neither as bike enthusiasts nor as environmental enthusiasts (since members of both of those groups are likely already to own a bike). Japanese cycle component manufacturer Shimano decided to tackle this challenge through some market research in partnership with Californian design firm IDEO. The market research conducted by IDEO among American consumers came up with two key insights. First, the average consumer and would-be casual bike rider was intimidated by bike stores, by the technical complexity of most sports bikes and by the zealous enthusiasm of lycra-clad salespeople. Secondly, most of them had fond memories of cycling as a child that were tied up with a sense of freedom and simplicity.

This consumer research led to collaboration with manufacturers to produce a new bike 'platform' to appeal to the 161 million Americans who could potentially ride a bike, but currently didn't.

The result was the 'Coasting' bike concept, a simple, comfortable, affordable, low-maintenance and easy-to-use bike stripped of complex controls. Instead of many-speed gear systems to allow it to traverse mountains, it uses a simple (but hidden) automatic three-speed gear system designed for casual riding, including a micro-chip control that shifts gears as the bike speeds up or slows down. Its coaster brake is based on the old-fashioned technology of pedalling backwards. The concept was based around the user's needs, with nothing to learn or master: it was a bike you could simply jump on and ride, just like when you were a child.

The Shimano Coasting concept made its debut in 2007 with bikes from three of the top manufacturers, Giant, Raleigh and Trek, and another seven introduced models during 2008. The concept went on to win the Gold Award in the International Design Excellence Award (IDEA) competition presented by the Industrial Designers Society of America (IDSA) and sponsored by *BusinessWeek*. The success of the design in appealing to consumers was not related to marketing it explicitly on the benefits of cycling for the environment or for health. It tapped into nostalgia for the childhood freedom that a bike once brought and created a sustainability-oriented consumer outcome, by providing a solution that was based around enjoyment and simplicity.[1]

Sustainability and Consumption

In developing the Coasting bike, Shimano was doing more than simply trying to sell more product, it was seeking to shape the lifestyles and behaviours of consumers in ways that would both expand the market for its products, and achieve the sustainability goal of getting people out of their cars and onto a bike. The behaviour of consumers, in terms of what products they buy, how they use them and what they do with them afterwards, shapes almost every aspect of our planet to an extent that only the forces of nature can rival. Buying and consuming an individual product, like a cup of coffee on the way to work or class, might seem such a trivial action that, although it refreshes us, it leaves no lasting impression or memory. However, that action will combine with those of other consumers to contribute to the economic success of the coffee retailer, the overall growth in the economy and the volume of waste with which local government must deal. It will influence the demand for, and the price of, coffee beans and milk, and in doing so will influence the lives and prosperity of thousands of farmers throughout the world, and shape their investment and planting decisions for next year. It will have knock-on impacts in terms of the demand for pesticides, fertilizer, packaging materials and energy. The economic impact of that coffee will contribute to the future share price of the retailers and the levels of income and investment they will enjoy. At a national level, it will contribute to national prosperity and in doing so will influence future policies on taxation and interest rates.

We tend to think of consumption as an economic phenomenon that addresses our individual wants and drives the economy through our collective behaviour, but it is also a social and cultural process through which we all express our identity and establish our place within society. It is also a physical process tht literally consumes resources. What we eat, how we heat our homes and how we travel to work or for pleasure may seem like nobody's businesses except our own. However, the collective consequences of those consumption decisions, and the ways in which our needs are met, are a principal driver behind climate change that will have consequences for people, countries and species across the globe. In some cases the connection is even more vivid, as in the African rhino being pushed towards extinction because its horn is prized for dagger handles in the Middle East or for traditional medicines in Asia, or the Tibetan antelope facing a similar fate because of the demand in the fashion houses of New York, Paris and London for the *shahtoosh* shawls made from its fine, soft wool. In conventional marketing the emphasis is on the benefits of consumption to the individual consumer. In sustainability marketing this is balanced by concern for the collective social and environmental costs.

The Consumption Process

The focus in conventional marketing has always been strongly on the actual purchase of products and services. This is logical, since this is generally the point at which a contract is established (explicitly or implicitly) between the buyer and seller, money changes hands, and ownership of products transfers to the consumer. From a legal and economic perspective, the purchase is all important. From a social and environmental context, however, the impacts of a product will relate to other stages of the total consumption process that precedes and follows the purchase. As the negative social and environmental consequences of the consumer society, and the systems of production and consumption within it, have become increasingly pronounced, they have gradually begun to influence consumer attitudes and behaviour within each stage of the total consumption process (see Figure 4.1).

Figure 4.1 Total consumption process

Recognition of a Want or Need

Humans have a number of intrinsic and fundamental needs for food and drink, clothing, security and shelter and to reproduce and nurture their children. Beyond this they also have a number of more social and emotional needs for acceptance and status, for amusement and for love and self-fulfilment. Somewhat confusingly, most people also display a mixture of a need to establish their individual identity along with a need for belonging and social conformity, with the balance between these two conflicting needs varying considerably between cultures. These relatively broad and enduring forms of need are translated into more specific individual wants, which within a consumer society are usually expressed as a demand for a particular product or service. Mainstream marketing thinking has tended to consider only one consumer want or need at a time, but in practice humans have a complex set of wants and needs that can interact and even conflict. Therefore we might want to own a car to provide safe and convenient transportation for our family, yet also desire to raise that family within a car-free environment. Part of progressing towards a more sustainable and equitable economy will also require a greater understanding of what constitutes a 'want' as compared to a 'need'[2] (see pp. 105–7).

Information Search

Although it is possible to leap straight from the recognition of a want to making a purchase (e.g. through an impulse buy at a supermarket checkout), many purchases involve the passive or active accumulation and then processing of relevant information. The key sources of information are personal sources, such as family and friends; commercial sources from advertising, on-pack information or in-store displays; public sources from the mass media, pressure groups or from consumer organizations or guides; and experiential information from handling or using a product.[3]

Consumers are increasingly exposed to information about sustainability issues such as climate change or global poverty via all these sources, and particularly news reports, documentaries or interest group campaigns. The connections between particular products and sustainability issues are also being communicated to consumers through product advertising and labelling, and through consumer guides or product comparison websites. One problem for marketers is the risk that in our information-rich society consumers are becoming overloaded with information and may become unwilling or unable to process the range of technical, economic, social and environmental issues and information linked to individual purchases.[4] This leads to consumers relying on particular brands or trusting to the social responsibility of particular retailers in order to avoid having to process increasing volumes of purchase information. The B&Q home improvements chain, for example, has produced a series of consumer-friendly, magazine-style sustainability publications emphasizing that the company has eliminated tropical hardwoods and volatile organic compounds and adopted responsible supply-chain policies across the board, encouraging consumers to trust in the retailer's broad CSR credentials rather than worry about the issues individually.[5]

Evaluation of Alternatives

Conventional marketing tends to assume that before a purchase is made different products and brands are evaluated and a choice made between them. There may also be a choice to be made between different ways of accessing a product or service (e.g. a choice between retailers). From a sustainability perspective, a broader set of alternative ways to meet consumer wants and needs may be considered. Ways of meeting needs that do not involve a purchase (such as borrowing an item from friends or family) or that involve the purchase of a service rather than a product (possibly by renting the product) may be considered as alternatives. Not purchasing may be a valid alternative where a consumer decides not to satisfy a particular want because of the social or environmental consequences of doing so.

Purchase

The actual purchase has always been the focal point of mainstream marketing's view of consumption, and whether or not consumers can be persuaded to change their purchasing behaviour to discriminate in favour of more sustainable products and services is a key element of the sustainability marketing agenda. Measuring purchases is also a central measure of success in commercial marketing, and repeat purchase levels are often used as a proxy measure for consumer satisfaction. This emphasis on purchase, however, may lead to aspects of consumers' behaviour being overlooked when their social and environmental concerns are expressed by boycotting a product or finding an alternative way to meet their needs. The process of purchasing products will have its own sustainability impacts, particularly in an era in which retailing has become dominated by large out-of-town retailers. In the UK in 2006 the average Briton made 219 shopping trips, of which 91 involved them driving by car an average distance of 9 km.[6]

Use

For many durable products, particularly energy-using appliances, the use phase will generate more environmental impacts than either the production or disposal phases. Whether or not mechanical items such as cars or boilers are properly maintained; whether electrical equipment is switched off or left on standby; the speed at which cars are driven; and whether or not attempts are made to repair broken products will all influence the ultimate sustainability impacts linked to use. The duration of use also has an impact on the resource efficiency of a product. In many markets the working life of products has shortened as rates of technical innovation and product replacement rates have increased[7] or as fashion has become an increasing influence on purchase, use and disposal decisions. This is reflected in the concept of *disposable fashion*, in which retailers produce clothes that are highly fashionable, but at low cost and low quality levels, to be worn only for a single season (or a single occasion) and then thrown away.[8] The markets for an increasing number of products that were once considered to be durables, such as home furnishing or entertainment technologies, have become more fashion-oriented so that products reach the end of their use long before the end of their useful life.

Post-Use

Mainstream marketing rarely considered the post-use behaviour of consumers beyond the opportunity for a repeat purchase that the end of an existing product's life or use might present. Sustainability concerns about overburdened landfills have made the post-use phase of the consumption process increasingly important. Extended producer responsibility regulations in markets such as cars and electronics have given some companies a legal obligation to take back and deal with post-use products.[9] There are a variety of possible types of consumer behaviour in the post-use phase:[10] disposing of the product, either to landfill or into systems that will reuse, recycle or remanufacture it; selling, trading or giving it to others (either directly or through alternative channels such as charity retailers); or renting or loaning it to other consumers temporarily; putting it into storage; or converting it to another use.

Understanding Sustainable Consumer Behaviour

Consumer behaviour is at the very heart of marketing. Consumers' purchasing behaviour will determine the success or failure of new products and services that are marketed on the basis of their sustainability performance. Because of the role of consumers in determining sustainability impacts during the use and disposal phases of the consumption process, their overall behaviour will also strongly influence the sustainability performance of all goods and services. For sustainability marketers, success is based on understanding consumer behaviour throughout the consumption process so that they can develop a marketing strategy and mix that will meet consumers' needs more effectively (and more sustainably) than their competitors.

The marketing process is founded on the use of market research to identify a company's current and potential customers, and to understand their nature, motivations and behaviour. This can allow the potential available market to be assessed and segmented into consumer groups that share certain key characteristics, which enables suitable market offerings to be developed and targeted at specific and distinctive market segments.

The field of consumer behaviour seeks to understand, explain and predict the behaviour of consumers, mostly by developing models of consumer preference and behaviour. Many of these models have been used and adapted to try to explain how and why consumers do or do not incorporate sustainability issues into their purchasing behaviour.[11] Some of this research has been applied to environmental concerns in researching the 'green' consumer, and some to social issues such as Fair Trade in researching the 'ethical' consumer.[12] Such research efforts have demonstrated that there are considerable difficulties involved in trying to model sustainable consumer behaviour, reflecting the degree to which individuals vary and the diversity in the types of purchases they make and the consumption behaviours in which they engage.

Most research into sustainability and consumers has focused on the purchase phase of the consumption process, and on trying to identify potential purchasers of more sustainable products and services. This makes sense from a conventional marketing perspective, but from a sustainability perspective it does not provide a full picture, since for some key products such as homes, cars and domestic appliances, much of the sustainability impact accrues after the purchase phase during use or post-use. There have been some studies that have focused on post-use behaviour, for example by seeking to identify the type of people who are 'recyclers',[13] and a 2006 study by McDonald and Oates sought to understand consumer behaviour across a range of 40 different types of sustainability-oriented consumption activities.[14] However, to develop a more holistic understanding of consumer behaviour for sustainability, a more balanced understanding through all phases of the consumption process will be required.

Sustainable Consumption in Context

One of the most consistent findings in the research into sustainability and consumer behaviour has been inconsistency. There is a widely acknowledged lack of consistency between the majority of consumers' expressed concerns about sustainability issues and their willingness to reflect those concerns in their consumption choices and behaviours (usually referred to as the attitude–behaviour or intention–behaviour gap).[15] There also tends to be inconsistency within the behaviour of individual consumers, with few consumers incorporating sustainability concerns into all types of consumption activities, or across all types of goods and services. The sustainable consumption agenda contains a wide spectrum of individual issues, and consumers will vary in the selection of issues that they will connect with and respond to most within their consumption behaviour. Some may favour socially oriented ethical consumption issues such as Fair Trade, while others will favour environmental issues such as organic produce or carbon reduction. Some consumers may have a broad spread of socio-ecological issues to which they respond, while others may feel passionately about a very specific issue such as animal cruelty.

Similarly, there is a common finding within sustainable consumer research that even a highly concerned consumer will often have an 'indulgence' that is immune to the influence of their sustainability concerns. McDonald and Oates identified a specific type of consumer whom they labelled *Exceptors*, consumers who were strongly sustainability oriented across a range of behaviours, but who had one area (such as foreign flight-based travel) that remained as an exception, which would effectively negate the sustainability benefits of their other behaviours.[16] This was also confirmed by a major study from the British Market Research Bureau showing that a market segment of adult Britons with the strongest environmental attitudes and behaviours, accounting for only 1.3% of the population, were also the group who flew the most often (19% of them taking three or more return flights by air in the previous 12 months, compared with 12% of the overall British adult population).[17]

Although the conventional approach to sustainability marketing has been to attempt to understand different types of consumer according to their sustainability concerns, an alternative approach is to try to understand the different type of sustainable consumption contexts. This was explored using the 'purchase perception matrix'[18] shown in Figure 4.2, which sought to explain the inconsistencies within consumer behaviour at the purchase stage (and also the success and failure of different past sustainability marketing strategies) by differentiating between types of sustainability purchase on two dimensions:

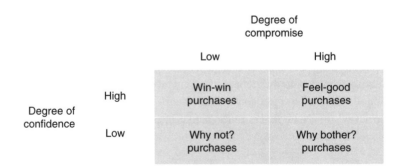

Figure 4.2 Sustainable purchase perception matrix

Source: Peattie, K. (1999) 'Trappings versus substance in the greening of marketing planning', *Journal of Strategic Marketing*, 7: 131–48.

1. *Degree of compromise.* This can take a variety of forms, such as having to pay more or travel further in order to purchase a more sustainable product. It could also mean that purchasing a more sustainable equivalent might involve a sacrifice in the performance of the product or in convenience during use.

2. *Degree of confidence.* This is how sure the consumer is that the product addresses a genuine sustainability issue, that the product or service offered is superior in its sustainability performance, that the company behind it can be trusted and that there will be a worthwhile benefit from a purchase.

The implications of the matrix are useful for marketers in two ways. Firstly, instead of taking a product-oriented view of quality and sustainability performance, it takes a consumer-oriented view of what compromises are required from the consumer and whether the product or service inspires confidence among consumers (these issues are explored further in Chapters 7–10). Secondly, the matrix provides marketers with a simple two-pronged strategy through which to pursue the successful marketing of sustainable products and services: reduce the compromises that are asked of consumers, and build their confidence in the worth and benefits of making sustainable consumption choices.

There are a number of other characteristics of different types of purchase or other consumption behaviours that can influence whether or not consumers will be willing and able to reflect social and ecological concerns in their behaviour, including:

- *Value*: purchases vary from the level of a postage stamp or a newspaper to that of a house or a car, and the level of effort put into gathering and considering information relevant to the purchase is likely to vary accordingly. Similarly, in terms of post-use a consumer will be more likely simply to dispose of a low-value product after use, whereas they may seek to resell a high-value product to reclaim some of the residual value.
- *Frequency*: purchases also vary in frequency from habitual daily purchases to once-in-a-lifetime purchases, and again the decision-making process will not be the same throughout. Purchases that are frequent and low-value will tend to become a 'habitual' rather than a considered behaviour. Similarly, a product-use activity such as switching a television to standby mode may be done so often that consumers do not consider its energy-use implications in the same way as they would when undertaking an infrequent activity like choosing to buy a new television.
- *Visibility*: purchases vary in the degree to which they are socially visible to other people. Therefore a consumer might buy Fair Trade coffee because it may be explicitly offered to guests or visible in their kitchen, but may not buy Fair Trade versions of other products such as sugar or dried fruit because it will be less visible. Similarly, putting out waste for kerbside collection for recycling may appeal to consumers because it is a relatively visible and socially responsible post-use behaviour.
- *Complexity*: purchasing a computer is considerably more complex than purchasing a bottle of milk or a newspaper, so a consumer is more likely to seek out and analyse information about it and to use the advice of others to help them to cope with complexity. Sustainability issues can tend to increase the complexity of purchases where they are adding a dimension to the purchase on which products will vary. Vegetables could be seen as extremely simple products to purchase, but once a consumer tries to weigh up the relative sustainability benefits of local versus organic versus Fair Trade, it becomes far more complex. Similarly, complex products like computers create more post-use options than simple products. An old computer could be resold, donated to charity, disassembled for use as parts or upgraded to allow second use by another family member.

- *For self or for others*: a person may happily content themselves with a used product or a no-frills, resource-efficient version for their own use, but would not consider that as a gift for others. Alternatively, a personally 'disinterested' consumer might make an overtly sustainable purchase as a gift for a loved one with a strong interest in sustainability issues. In terms of use and post-use, when buying products for others the original purchaser loses control over what happens to the product.
- *Necessity or indulgence*: consumers may be more willing to consider social and environmental issues in relation to purchases that are everyday necessities rather than luxuries. One of the challenges for marketing Fair Trade chocolate, compared to the more established Fair Trade coffee, is that chocolate is seen by many consumers as an indulgence that they already feel slightly guilty about, therefore they will not want to spoil the sense of indulgence by considering Fair Trade issues.[19] A product that is a necessity will tend to be used frequently and in a relatively resource-efficient way that gets a high degree of value from the resources that went into the product or service. Luxurious indulgences may be used infrequently and may also be more likely to be sold on or disposed of before the end of their useful life.

For sustainability marketers it is important to understand that consumers will respond differently in their consumption behaviour in relation to goods and services that vary across these dimensions. A person who may habitually seek out sustainable choices in their everyday consumption behaviours may not do so when making a complex, high-value and infrequent choice such as buying a house. The purchase phase of the consumption process can also be shaped by a number of situational factors, including time pressure, whether the consumer is shopping alone or is accompanied, and by the immediate purchase environment, which in the case of fast-moving consumer goods (FMCG) includes the retail environment and overall retail experience of the consumer. Retailers can use lighting, music or even scents to create an environment that is conducive to people spending time and money within their stores. Behaviour in the post-use phase can also be influenced by a variety of structural factors, such as the availability of recycling services, the availability of channels for resale or whether charitable organizations exist to provide opportunities for reuse.

Key Consumption Contexts

It is clear that consumer behaviour, even among those consumers most concerned about sustainability issues, is not consistent across all types of purchase and all consumption contexts. From a sustainability perspective, we also know that all types of consumption are not equally important in terms of their sustainability impacts.

Seeking to change the behaviour of consumers across every sector of consumption is potentially counterproductive, as consumers are likely to be overwhelmed with sustainability-oriented offerings and information. Greater progress may come from focusing on consumption behaviours linked to those products with the most significant impacts. For the environmental impacts of individuals' consumption in industrialized economies, the majority relate to a small number of product categories. The

European Environmental Impact of Products (EIPRO) Project[20] provides a rigorous analysis of research into the environmental impacts of products consumed by households. The project's input–output-based methodology assesses 255 domestic product types against a wide range of environmental impacts. It concludes that 70–80% of total impacts relate to food and drink consumption; housing (including domestic energy use); and transport (including commuting, leisure and holiday travel). This creates a front-line agenda for sustainability marketing efforts; which is not to say that sustainability marketing is not important or does not offer opportunities across all market sectors. Ideally, all aspects of our consumption behaviours and production systems will become oriented towards sustainability, but initially significant progress would be achieved through:

1. *Sustainable food and drink consumption choices*: consumption levels that are more conducive to health; a reduced consumption of meat products due to their contribution to climate change; choosing organically produced and locally sourced, seasonal produce; and greater composting of biodegradable food waste.
2. *Sustainable housing consumption choices*: including more emphasis on purchasing homes constructed using sustainable materials and choosing and creating homes with high levels of insulation and energy efficiency. This also involves energy usage within the home based on sustainable energy sources, and the avoidance of energy waste while living within the home (e.g. through energy-efficient refrigerators and energy-saving bulbs).
3. *Sustainable travel behaviour*: which may mean reducing the amount of travel undertaken (e.g. through home-working or teleconferencing services) or finding alternative transport means for journeys such as cycling for leisure rather than driving. In terms of tourism consumption behaviours, it means seeking tourism offerings that try to protect the global and local environment and also the cultures within tourism destinations. It could be argued that there is no such thing as sustainable tourism, and that the socially and environmentally concerned tourist should simply stay at home. From a sustainability perspective things are not so simple, given the proportion of the economy of many poorer countries devoted to tourism. Simply to stop tourism completely would create a social and economic disaster in these countries and contribute to the liquidation of important natural environmental resources (such as forests), which support tourism as a result. Therefore responsible tourism companies are offering consumption choices such as carbon-offset programmes and encouraging consumers to respect the cultures and environments of destinations during their trips.

These consumption areas represent the core agenda for sustainability marketing in the future, and therefore they form the focus of many of the examples throughout this book. It will also be important for sustainability marketing efforts to help consumers understand the connections between their behaviour as consumers of these key products, and the resulting social and environmental consequences. This will make the sustainability issues more personally relevant and hopefully allow consumers to feel confident that they can do something (i.e. alter their consumption behaviour) to respond. In this way consumers can become proactive partners in developing sustainability solutions, not simply feel themselves to be a cause of sustainability problems.

Consumer Behaviour for Sustainability

For their sustainability marketing efforts to succeed, companies need to do one (or more) of three things. They may be able to identify a particular segment of the market who are enthusiastic about sustainability issues, and market a sustainable product or service to that segment on that basis. This is the strategy successfully adopted by many of the pioneering sustainable companies and brands, but it suffers from the disadvantage that it tends only to address a small niche within the market. To make a real contribution to progress towards sustainability, it is important for more sustainable products to penetrate the mass market. A second approach is to try to persuade consumers within the bulk of the mass market to change their behaviour and accept a more sustainable option (or to make their use or post-use consumption behaviour more sustainable). A third approach is to market more sustainable products and services to consumers, but not explicitly or principally as sustainability-oriented. This is the strategy that Shimano adopted with its Coasting bike, although to succeed this strategy requires a product to excel in other ways than in terms of sustainability.

Whichever approach a sustainability marketer adopts, understanding consumers and their motivations, and why they may, or may not, accept a particular product or facet of sustainable consumption, requires a very clear understanding of consumers, their motivations and the barriers they may face to making more sustainable consumption choices. The research evidence on these issues is summarized comprehensively by Tim Jackson in *Motivating Sustainable Consumption* (which is recommended reading for anyone wanting to understand the full complexities of sustainability and consumer behaviour).[21] In general terms there are three theoretical approaches to understanding, explaining and predicting consumer behaviour from a sustainability perspective – that is, why consumers sometimes will make sustainable consumption choices and sometimes won't, even though they say they will – rational, psychological and sociological explanations. Each of these schools of thought is potentially helpful in understanding the behaviour of consumers, but none has the power to explain the full complexity of that behaviour on its own.

Rational Explanations

Some of the earliest research into consumer behaviour and sustainability relied on rational explanations. This perspective emphasizes the economics of sustainable consumption, and how consumers weigh up the functional benefits and relative affordability of a product or service. Behavioural models based around economic rationality tend to assume a high degree of self-interest on the part of the consumer. Unfortunately, this often works against promoting more sustainable consumption because, since all social and environmental costs are not typically reflected in the prices that consumers pay, our existing unsustainable consumption is effectively subsidized and made more attractive.[22] However, it can be used as the basis on which government can reduce consumption and the environmental impacts of certain products such as fuel or flights through the use of taxation. A broader approach to rational consumer choice is the concept of *perceived costs and benefits*, which includes non-economic 'costs' such as time, inconvenience, social unacceptability or psychological 'wear and tear'. The basic assumption is that consumers will choose the alternative with the highest perceived net benefit, as in the formula below:

| Perceived Benefits – Perceived Costs = Perceived Net Benefit |

Take the example of organic versus conventional food. If the perceived net benefit of organic food outweighs the perceived net benefit of conventional food (from the consumer's viewpoint), he or she will choose the former. In the case of this product category perceived benefits may include taste, appearance and a good environmental conscience. Perceived costs involve price, search costs, transport costs and time to prepare the food product. In studies of 'green' consumer behaviour, the balance of perceived costs and benefits is one of the most consistently significant factors.[23] The major implication for sustainability marketers is the need to increase the perceived net benefits of sustainable solutions as compared to conventional offerings. This is accomplished by increasing the benefits and/or reducing the costs of sustainable products and services as perceived by consumers (see Chapters 7–10).

Rational explanations have also emphasized the role of knowledge in moving consumers towards sustainable choices. This assumes that increasing knowledge about environmental or social issues, and increasing levels of education, will lead to a reasoned response that more sustainable consumption is in our collective best interests. This would then lead consumers to buy more sustainable goods and services (although paradoxically, increasing knowledge may make consumers aware of the absolute sustainability shortcomings of existing market offerings and the production systems behind them). This is, however, a slightly dangerous assumption for marketers to rely on, since consumers will vary considerably in the connections they make between different sustainability issues and particular products and services.

The emphasis on the role of economics, knowledge and education within the rationalist school of thought means that it has tended to rely on demographic factors (such as age, sex,[24] socio-economic grouping or level of education[25]) when attempting to identify consumers likely to engage in sustainable consumption for rational reasons, either economic or social. As a strategy this has been largely unsuccessful, and attempts to identify green market segments, using demographic bases, have produced largely inconsistent and often conflicting results.[26]

Psychological Explanations

As a complement to rational explanations for consumer behaviour, there has been research into the psychology of sustainable consumption and more emotional or irrational explanations of our behaviour. Much of this focuses on *consumers' attitudes and beliefs* about sustainability issues. Three important sets of attitudes that influence consumers' willingness to engage with sustainability issues are perceived personal relevance, social responsibility and trust. Perceived personal relevance concerns the extent to which consumers see a connection between their lives and consumption behaviour and a particular issue. For sustainability issues there is a challenge in trying to inform and educate consumers about environmental issues because of the potentially demotivating mismatch between the *problem frame* (global environmental challenges) and the *personal frame* of 'my life, home, work and family'.[27] Social responsibility concerns the sense of shared responsibility for particular social and environmental issues and a willingness to take part in collective responses to them. For example, one international survey of consumers found that only 10% trust what companies say about climate change, 25% trust corporate claims about energy-efficient products and services, and 70% want third-party verification of climate change claims.[28]

Another important set of attitudes and beliefs connected to personal relevance concerns *perceived consumer effectiveness (PCE) and self-efficacy.* The belief that the actions of an individual consumer can have a meaningful impact on a social or environmental issue determines PCE. Across a range of sustainable consumer behaviour studies, this is one of the factors that most consistently features as a statistically significant influence[29] (the other being perceived costs and benefits). The implication is that we are most likely to engage in behaviours that we believe will make a difference (and it is therefore closely linked to generating the confidence needed among consumers implied by the purchase perception matrix model). PCE was originally developed to explore purchases, but it can also be adapted and applied to other aspects of consumption behaviour[30] such as recycling.[31] Related to PCE is the concept of self-efficacy, the belief that one is able to engage in a particular behaviour effectively.[32]

Also important to the psychology of sustainable consumption are the values that we hold as individuals and the things that we believe are important, which will tend to influence our behaviours in relation to products and consumption. Research into the influence of values[33] suggests that several value shifts will need to occur within society to allow progress towards a more sustainable society and economy, including:

From	To
Egocentric (me first)	Altruistic (others first)
Conservative	Open to change
Indulgent	Frugal
Materialist	Post-materialist
Technocentric (technology rules)	Ecocentric (nature knows best)
Anthropocentric (human centred)	Biocentric (all species matter)

Researchers seeking to understand the psychological dimensions of consumer behaviour have relied on psychographics as an alternative to demographics as a means of categorizing consumers. Psychographics seeks to describe consumers in terms of psychological factors that reflect, and often combine, values, behaviours and lifestyles.

Sociological Explanations

Another set of theories suggest that our behaviour as consumers is not simply a reflection of the rational dimensions of the costs and benefits of a particular consumption activity and what we know about it, nor is it fully explained by how we perceive the consumption activity as an individual. It is also explained by how we think our consumption activities will be perceived by others, and how that might reflect and influence our place in society. We tend to refer to those industrialized countries within which most of the world's marketing activity and consumption take place as the 'consumer society'. This is a slightly problematic term, because a defining feature of any society is the collective production, consumption and exchange of goods and services. In a consumer society the act of consumption moves beyond the process of meeting basic individual wants and needs to become the primary mechanism through which relationships within society are structured. In a consumer society, the process of consumption becomes the accepted route to individual happiness, expression, meaning and status and to national wealth and success. The consumer society has also become a force for global change in itself, as a globalized media has promoted images of homogenized consumer lifestyles and values that are eroding the cultural diversity of societies throughout the world.

The consumer society represents the backdrop to the consumption behaviours with which the marketing discipline deals. To be a member of the consumer society, an individual needs to have sufficient discretionary spending power to be able to make consumption choices that go beyond the meeting of basic subsistence needs, and to make decisions that reflect their sense of identity and aspirations to be a 'consumer'. There are somewhere in excess of 1.7 billion people on the planet that could fit this description, and this figure is increasing rapidly with the emergence of large middle classes in populous nations such as China and India. The half of the global population existing on less than $2 (€1.44) per day is therefore excluded from the consumer society.

Within conventional marketing, if a person cannot afford a particular product they are not considered as part of the potential target market and therefore their needs and interests are not considered, even though the marketing of a product and its consumption by others may affect them. The conventional view of the marketing environment is in terms of the influence that social, economic and technological trends have on the players within a particular market. The impact that the behaviour of the players within a market has on society and the economy more broadly is rarely considered within marketing (although it is the focus of the more specialized academic field of macromarketing, as described in Chapter 2).

One reason conventional marketing struggles to dealing with sustainability is that its frame of reference is the consumer society, and the behaviour of the minority of the world's population who exist within it. Within a consumer society many social norms, which are a powerful influence on behaviour, are based around consumption. Notions of consumer sovereignty, consumer rights and overconsumption are all accepted as normal. Harnessing social norms will be important for pro-sustainability behaviours such as engaging in recycling, which is influenced by the behaviour of peers and neighbours. Consumers' willingness to change their behaviour for the common good is influenced by their belief in whether or not others will do likewise.[34] How 'normal' sustainable consumption activities are perceived to be also has a significant influence on whether or not consumers are willing to engage in them.

In the context of the consumer society, many purchases become important beyond the functional benefits they provide, in that they contribute to the construction of an identity for the consumer. Food and clothing may be basic human needs, but consuming a vegetarian diet or dressing in the latest fashion says a great deal about who we are (or how we would like to be perceived by ourselves and others). Therefore among the products we buy, many will have important symbolic meanings. As noted in Jackson's review:

> The insight that consumer goods attain symbolic properties clearly has some resonance with popular psychology about our relationship with material possessions. A child's favourite teddy bear, a woman's wedding dress, a stamp collector's prized first day cover, the souped-up, low-sprung sports car of the 'boy racer': all these examples suggest that there is much more at stake in the possession of material artefacts than simple functional value.[35]

Both mainstream marketers and those trying to promote more sustainable consumption have sometimes been guilty of an overly rational and functional approach to how and why products are consumed. Consumers may be reluctant to give up a particular product, not for what it is but for what it represents.

Conventional marketing theory and research tend to focus on the consumer as an individual, and many purchase decisions are a reflection of individual wants, needs, tastes and desires. Although there is an increasing trend in many countries towards people living individually, the majority still live as part of a family or household in which there is a shared element in consumption decisions and behaviours. This has implications in terms of the nature of their consumption and its social and environmental impacts. A person living on their own will consume on average around three times as many products and generate more than twice the amount of packaging waste as a member of a household comprised of three people.[36]

The nature of the community within which people live will also shape their behaviour with respect to sustainability issues. Aspirations will be influenced by the lifestyles of neighbours. Transport decisions will be shaped by the availability of public transport within their community. Recycling and waste-disposal behaviours will be influenced by local waste-handling provision. Purchases will be shaped by the nature of retail provision within the local community.

Another important influence on consumption behaviour is the notion of lifestyle. Again, the conventional approach to marketing tends to deal with particular needs and purchases individually, but in practice many individual purchases and behaviours combine to create a particular lifestyle for an individual or family. Progress towards more sustainable consumption is therefore not simply a question of what products and services are purchased, it is about the adoption of a lifestyle in which sustainability is reflected in all aspects of consumers' behaviour. The most advanced form of sustainable consumption behaviour is among those identified as *voluntary simplifiers*, whose lifestyle is based around five key values:

- *Material simplicity:* involves consuming fewer products and services, and tending to seek out products that are resource efficient, durable and with a reduced ecological impact.
- *Human scale:* following Schumacher's principle of 'small is beautiful' in tending towards working and living environments that are smaller, simpler and less centralized. This includes moving away from consuming mass-produced anonymous goods and from being part of an impersonal and industrialized work experience.
- *Self-determination:* through a reduced reliance on large commercial businesses, or even large public-sector organizations, to meet one's needs, or even to influence what those needs might be.
- *Ecological awareness:* in terms of conservation of resources and reduction of waste in order to protect the environment.
- *Personal growth:* emphasizing the creation of satisfaction through experiences and the development of personal abilities instead of through commercially provided consumption experiences.

Voluntary simplification as a consumer behaviour or lifestyle has been typically associated with the creation of 'alternative consumption communities', typified by Findhorn in Scotland or the Centre for Alternative Technology in Wales. However, in recent years many of the key traits of voluntary simplification have been exhibited in a less extreme, but more widespread way, through the phenomenon of *downshifting*. Downshifting involves a change of lifestyle and consumption patterns that exchange a relatively highly paid/highly pressurized career and a relatively high-spend/consumption intensive lifestyle, for an occupation that is lower paid/lower stress but more rewarding, and shifting to a lower level of material consumption but a higher level of quality of life and personal satisfaction.[37]

These three theoretical perspectives capture most of the key ideas explaining consumption behaviour in relation to sustainability. They are not however exhaustive, and even when combined cannot easily explain the behaviour of all consumers, across all types of consumption at all times. Tim Jackson's review of research into motivating sustainable consumer behaviour[38] identifies a number of important external influences, including:

- The institutional context in which consumer choice is framed (e.g. trading standards and regulations governing product marketing).
- Business practices and their influence on employees as consumers.
- The initiation and facilitation of community-based social change and resulting behaviours (particularly through social marketing approaches).
- The government's own environmental and social performance.
- The social and cultural context in which priorities are set and cultural values determined.

Figure 4.3 seeks to demonstrate how all the different types of influence on consumer behaviour, including the efforts of marketers, extend across all the stages of the consumption process. This model also provides examples of how sustainability concerns can prompt new and different responses among consumers throughout the consumption process.

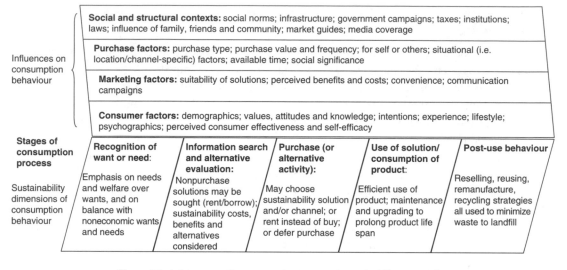

Figure 4.3 Influences on the consumption process: A sustainability perspective

Harnessing Consumer Behaviour for Sustainability

The practical question for the sustainability marketer is how to use insights into the behaviour of consumers to encourage them to engage in more sustainable behaviours. The early work in the field followed the conventional marketing approach of seeking to identify and respond to particular aspects of consumers, in order to influence their purchasing preferences in favour of particular products and brands. In other words, it was about trying to harness the concerns of consumers that led them to boycott certain products or companies (often using the guidance of publications such as the original *Green Consumer Guide*[39] and its many international variants), to motivate them to purchase more sustainable products and services (through a 'buycott'[40]). This emphasis on different and 'better' purchasing of certain products is only one part of the challenge of harnessing consumer behaviour for sustainability. To make progress towards sustainability, there are three areas in which theory and practice in relation to consumer behaviour need to progress:

1. Sustainable consumption behaviour needs to evolve from pro-sustainability purchases of certain goods and services to encompass the full consumption process across a wide range of goods and services, particularly those with the greatest impacts (homes, food, travel and tourism).
2. Sustainable consumption behaviour needs to extend from the segment of the market with the greatest sustainability concerns to encompass the mass market.
3. To change from a situation in which unsustainable lifestyles and consumption are a social norm, to one in which sustainable consumption behaviour and lifestyles are the social norm, commercial marketers (and social marketers working in the public sector) will need to be effective in changing behaviour. This requires an understanding not just of what might motivate consumers to change

their behaviour to become more sustainable, but also of what economic, practical, psychological and social barriers consumers might face.

The assumption inherited from conventional marketing is that sustainable consumption (i.e. when considered as the purchase of goods and services differentiated on the basis of better sustainability performance, and likely to have a premium price) is something mainly engaged in by relatively well-off consumers with high levels of discretionary spending power. However, consider for a moment which consumer's lifestyle is the more sustainable: the relatively poor consumer with absolutely no interest in social or environmental issues who only consumes what they can afford; or the relatively wealthy consumer who buys Fair Trade coffee and organic food, drives a Smartcar, goes on eco-tourism holidays, holds ethical investments and tries to recycle as much as they can. Both common sense and ecological footprint analysis[41] tell us that it is the former.

Sustainable Market Segmentations

Understanding how to motivate consumers to engage in more sustainable consumption behaviours relies on an understanding of the differences between people in how they perceive and respond to the sustainability agenda. Despite the complexities and inconsistencies revealed by research, there have been numerous attempts to group consumers into meaningful and measurable market segments according to their attitudes, behaviours and other characteristics.[42] Segmenting a market allows marketers to cope better with the diversity of consumers and their behaviour, to focus efforts towards serving those segments with the greatest potential for success, and to vary their market offerings to suit the needs of different segments. Some of the earliest were very simple segmentations based on a combination of interest in sustainability and willingness and ability to pay a premium for more sustainable products (for example Roper Research's separation of the US population into four groups ranging from 'True-Blue Greens', who would happily purchase more sustainable products, to 'Basic Browns', who wouldn't).[43]

A more sophisticated segmentation developed by the British Market Research Bureau for the UK Government's Department of the Environment and Rural Affairs (Defra) considered a wider range of motivators and barriers to sustainable consumption behaviour that divided the UK population into seven distinct segments.[44] The emphasis was on environmental dimensions, but the insights it provides are useful in relation to ethical consumption as well. The segmentation was as follows:

1. *Greens*: who are driven by a belief that sustainability issues are critical. They are well educated about these issues, feel involved with and connected to the issues and arguments, and do not view people who respond to them in their lifestyles or consumption as strange or eccentric.
2. *Consumers with a Conscience*: who want to be 'seen to be green'. They are motivated by environmental and social concerns and seek to avoid feeling guilty about environmental damage. They are focused on consumption and making positive choices.
3. *Wastage Focused*: who dislike waste of any kind and seek to avoid it. They have good knowledge of wastage and local pollution, but lack awareness of other issues and behaviours. Interestingly, this group see themselves as ethically distinct from the greens.

4. *Currently Constrained*: who would like to be more sustainable, but who don't think there is much they can do in their current circumstances. They have a focus on balance, pragmatism and realism.

5. *Basic Contributors*: who are sceptical about the need for behaviour change. They tend to think about their behaviour relative to that of others and are driven by a desire to conform with social norms. They have relatively little knowledge of, or interest in, environmental issues and behaviours.

6. *Long-Term Restricted*: who have a number of serious life priorities to address before they can begin consciously to consider their environmental impacts. Their everyday behaviours often have relatively low impacts, but for reasons other than environmental or social concerns.

7. *Disinterested*: who display no interest or motivation to change their current behaviours to make their lifestyle more sustainable. They may be aware of climate change and other environmental or social issues, but this has not affected their current decision-making processes or behaviours.

This research also demonstrated that segments varied in the factors that might motivate them to adopt more sustainable consumption behaviours, and which barriers might prevent them. Such insights will be helpful to both marketers of sustainability-oriented products and services and governments seeking to promote sustainability as a social goal.

This segmentation allowed a 'mapping' of a range of potential sustainability-oriented consumer behaviours that particular segments would likely be willing and able to adopt (see Figure 4.4). Some behaviour could be applied to all segments, while other behaviours would be more acceptable to, or suited to, some segments more than others. Seeking to market to the 'Disinterested' segment is likely to be a waste of time and effort, as they are only likely to respond to regulations or fiscal measures in the short term, or education efforts to move them into a different segment in the longer term. This helps to guide the strategy options for policymakers seeking to promote sustainable citizenship, but can equally well guide marketers in the development of commercial strategies and sustainable market offerings. As the Shimano Coasting bike story illustrated, even for consumers who are not particularly interested in sustainability issues, it is still possible to motivate them to move towards more sustainable consumption behaviours if their needs, interests and nature are properly researched and understood.

Longhurst[45] suggested that commercial marketers seeking to encourage behaviour change among consumers needed to consider three levels of change. The first level consists of simple behaviour changes in product use or disposal such as engaging in recycling, reusing carrier bags or switching off lights, which often need little more than communications efforts aimed at raising awareness and reminding consumers (but which are only 'symbolic' in the context of the main environmental impacts of an individual's consumption activities). The second level involves encouraging product-purchase behaviour change, to motivate consumers to buy free-range eggs, or Fair Trade brands or use public transport, for instance. Longhurst warns that such changes are susceptible to decay as old product or brand preferences re-emerge should problems emerge with the new choice, or if the marketing of more

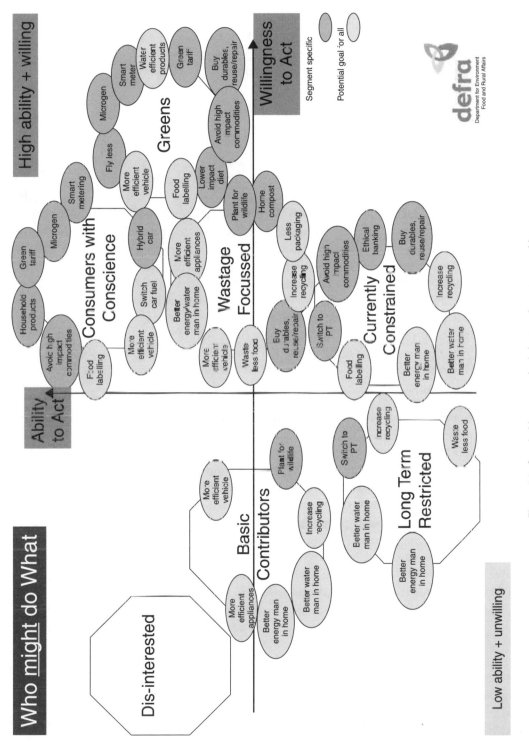

Who might do What

High ability + willing

Ability to Act

Dis-interested

Basic Contributors

Consumers with Conscience

Greens

Wastage Focussed

Long Term Restricted

Currently Constrained

Willingness to Act

Low ability + unwilling

Segment specific

Potential goal for all

defra
Department for Environment
Food and Rural Affairs

Figure 4.4 Sustainable consumption behaviour change opportunities

Source: Barr, A., Gilg, A. & Shaw, G. (2006) *Promoting Sustainable Lifestyles. A Social Marketing Approach*, Final Summary Report to Defra, London.

sustainable alternatives becomes less obvious. The third level is fundamental lifestyle change, a level that it will be difficult for marketers in either the public or commercial sector to achieve without considerable help from other economic and social pressures, although it might be something that could be 'marketed' as part of a more fulfilling, 'downshifted' lifestyle.[46]

Expectations Management

The satisfaction we derive from consumption is not a simple matter of the quality of the product or service and the price that we paid for it. It is also a function of our prior expectations regarding the consumption experience. This is something that service marketers in particular have realized: that consumer satisfaction can be improved either by raising the quality of service, or by managing the expectations of a customer down to realistic levels. Expectations play an important part in the opportunities to move towards a more sustainable economy. During the latter part of the twentieth century, within the rapidly globalizing and increasingly liberal economy, investors became used to historically atypical high levels of return from financial investments. Consumers became used to declining prices in real terms for food products, electronic products and air travel. Decades of double-digit investment returns and cheap food, televisions and travel have created expectations among investors and consumers that are simply not sustainable. However, it can be difficult for either marketers or elected representatives to break the habit of a lifetime to promise either consumers or voters less rather than more. This partly explains the desire to limit the debate about sustainable consumption to 'win–win' scenarios in which there is no sacrifice for consumers and yet still potentially competitive advantage for businesses.

Sustainable consumer behaviour is a complex and evolving subject, and simple answers rarely provide substantive progress towards creating a more sustainable society. As well as considerable variations in behaviour among different consumer types, individuals often vary in how they behave across a range of consumption contexts, which makes it important for sustainability marketers to understand both the consumer and the consumption context. Conventional marketing approaches have tended to consider consumers and their wants and needs individually, and have focused largely on the purchase phase of the consumption process. From a sustainability perspective, consumption needs to be understood more holistically as a total process, as part of a broader consumer lifestyle and as a process that is strongly influenced by the social context in which it takes place. Individual changes in purchasing behaviour can contribute to progress towards sustainability, but progress also depends on support from deeper changes occurring within consumer lifestyles and throughout society.

List of Key Terms

Attitudes
Consumer behaviour
Consumer ethics
Consumer society

Consumption process
Downshifting
Economic rationality
Expectations
Ethical consumption
Green consumption
Lifestyles
Perceived consumer effectiveness
Perceived net benefit
Purchase
Segmentation
Social context of consumption
Social norms
Values
Voluntary simplicity

REVIEW QUESTIONS

1. Why have marketers conventionally focused on the purchase phase of the consumption process?
2. What characteristics of a particular purchase may influence the consumer's willingness to behave in a way that takes account of social or environmental concerns?
3. According to the findings of the EIPRO Project, which areas of consumption account for 75–80% of our environmental impacts as consumers?
4. Which three schools of academic thinking provide partial explanations for sustainable consumer behaviour?
5. What are the five key values of voluntary simplifiers?

DISCUSSION QUESTIONS

1. Should consumers be expected to take responsibility for the social and environmental impacts of their consumption behaviours, or should that be the responsibility of companies and governments?
2. Why might it be challenging for a consumer with deep concerns about social and environmental issues to live a more sustainable lifestyle within the consumer society?
3. How can barriers to changing lifestyles and promoting more sustainable consumption be overcome, and how can marketers and marketing contribute to this process without damaging their own commercial interests?

SUSTAINABILITY MARKETING CHALLENGE: A SUSTAINABLE CIGARETTE?

Can any company develop a more sustainable product to offer to its consumers? It is an interesting question, particularly when applied to an industry such as tobacco. As the former editor of the *Journal of Business Ethics*, Patrick Murphy, was fond of remarking, the cigarette is a unique product from an ethical perspective because it is the only one that, if used as directed, will kill the consumer (provided nothing else kills them first). It is an industry that kills three million people annually worldwide and, through its use of pesticides, monoculture cropping and the use of unsustainable wood as a fuel for tobacco curing in many poorer countries, is also responsible for significant environmental damage. Over 80% of tobacco is grown in developing countries and it is linked with the destruction of ancient woodland, soil depletion and pollution from fertilizers and the 16 pesticide applications recommended during its growing season. Economically in the UK alone tobacco use costs the National Health Service around $3 (€ 2.16) billion, and employers forfeit an estimated $10 (€ 7.2) billion in absenteeism, lost productivity and fire damage.[47] If ever there was a candidate for a complete consumer boycott of a product on the basis of social and environmental impacts, tobacco would rate second only to cars. However, just as many of us are metaphorically addicted to our cars, smokers are literally addicted to consuming cigarettes. This makes rational consumer choice barely relevant to consumer decision-making, since many smokers profess a desire not to smoke, but are unable to break the habit.

The irony is that in terms of technology to reduce the health damage cigarettes cause, tobacco companies have developed a range of alternatives, including improved filters or special curing processes that when combined with microwaving virtually eliminate nitrosamines (a key class of carcinogens). Most of these technologies have not been implemented in the industry, and part of the explanation may lie in a leaked memo written by British American Tobacco's chief executive in 1986, which said: 'In attempting to develop a "safe" cigarette you are, by implication, in danger of being interpreted as accepting that the current product is "unsafe". This is not a position I think we should take.'

For campaigns aimed at helping consumers to change their behaviour and become nonconsumers of cigarettes, success has come from a variety of factors. One is to recognize the role that smoking often plays in the lifestyles and identities of smokers, particularly those in disadvantaged communities. Satisfying the craving to smoke creates a sense of well-being that can act as a moment of self-indulgence and reward in an otherwise bleak day, and communal cigarette breaks can create social bonds and a feeling of belonging that are important to smokers. Another is to offer people an alternative to smoking, even if only to the physical addiction to the nicotine through patches or gum. Weaning smokers off cigarettes partly requires an understanding of why they smoke, to allow the development of alternative, and more sustainable, ways of meeting their needs. Weaning tobacco companies and tobacco farmers off the product to find an alternative way of generating wealth may be an even greater challenge.[48]

Questions for Discussion

1. What issues do you think influence the behaviour of cigarette consumers during each stage of the total consumption process?
2. Given what this story says about cigarettes and their impact on consumption and production, why might consumers concerned about sustainability issues continue to smoke (over and above physical addiction)?
3. Would the only really socially responsible strategy for tobacco companies be to diversify out of cigarettes as quickly as practicable?

Endnotes

1. See www.coasting.com (accessed 26 December 2008).
2. Jackson, T., Jager, W. & Stagl, S. (2004) 'Beyond Insatiability: Needs Theory, Consumption and Sustainability', *Sustainable Technologies Programme Working Paper* (2004/2), Guildford: Centre for Environmental Strategy, University of Surrey.
3. Kotler, P. & Armstrong, G. (2004) *Principles of Marketing*, 10th edn, Upper Saddle River, NJ: Prentice Hall.
4. Geyer-Allely, E. (2001) *Towards Sustainable Household Consumption: Trends and Policies in OECD Countries*, Paris: OECD.
5. Green, K., Morton, B. & New, S. (1998) 'Green purchasing and supply policies: Do they improve companies' environmental performance?' *Supply Chain Management*, 3(2): 89–95.
6. Department for Transport (2007) *National Travel Survey*, London: TSO.
7. Cooper, T. (2005) 'Slower consumption: Reflections on product life spans and the "throwaway society', *Journal of Industrial Ecology*, 9(1–2): 51–67.
8. Fletcher, H. (2008) 'Disposable fashion: For sale, hardly worn, two million tonnes of clothes', *The Times*, 15 December available at: http://women.timesonline.co.uk/tol/life_and_style/women/fashion/article5332366.ece (accessed 26 December 2008).
9. Toffel, M.W. (2003) 'The growing strategic importance of end-of-life product management', *California Management Review*, 45(3): 102–29.
10. Jacoby, J., Berning, C.K. & Dietvorst, T.F. (1977) 'What about disposition?', *Journal of Marketing*, 41(3): 22–8.
11. Jackson, T. (2004) *Motivating Sustainable Consumption: A Review of Evidence on Consumer Behaviour and Behavioural Change*, Guildford: Centre for Environmental Strategy, University of Surrey.
12. *Ibid.*
13. Barr, S. (2002) *Household Waste in Social Perspective: Values, Attitudes, Situation and Behaviour*, Aldershot: Ashgate.
14. McDonald, S. & Oates, C.J. (2006) 'Sustainability: Consumer perceptions and marketing strategies', *Business Strategy and the Environment*, 15(2): 157–70.
15. Vermeir, I. & Verbeke, W. (2006) 'Sustainable food consumption: Exploring the consumer attitude–behavioral intention gap', *Journal of Agricultural and Environmental Ethics*, 19(2): 169–94.

16. McDonald, S. & Oates, C.J. (2006) 'Sustainability: Consumer perceptions and marketing strategies', *Business Strategy and the Environment*, 15(2): 157–70.
17. BMRB (2007) *Can Fly Will Fly*, London: British Market Research Bureau.
18. Peattie, K. (1999) 'Trappings versus substance in the greening of marketing planning', *Journal of Strategic Marketing*, 7: 131–48.
19. Golding, K. (2008) 'Fair trade's dual aspect: The communications challenge of fair trade marketing', *Journal of Macromarketing*, December.
20. Tukker, A., Huppes, G., Guinée, J. *et al.* (2005) *Environmental Impact of Products (EIPRO): Analysis of the Life Cycle Environmental Impacts Related to the Total Final Consumption of the EU25*, Brussels: IPTS/ESTO, European Commission Joint Research Centre.
21. Jackson, T. (2004) *Motivating Sustainable Consumption: A Review of Evidence on Consumer Behaviour and Behavioural Change*, Guildford: Centre for Environmental Strategy, University of Surrey.
22. Pretty, J. (2001) 'Some Benefits and Drawbacks of Local Food Systems', briefing note for Thames Valley University/Sustain AgriFood Network Inaugural Seminar and Meeting, 2 November.
23. Straughan, R.D. & Roberts, J.A. (1999) 'Environmental segmentation alternatives: A look at green consumer behaviour in the new millennium', *Journal of Consumer Marketing*, 16(6): 558–75.
24. Roberts, J. (1993) 'Sex differences in socially responsible consumers' behaviour', *Psychological Reports*, 73: 139–48.
25. Olli, E., Grendstad, D. & Wollebark, D. (2001) 'Correlates of environmental behaviors: Bringing back social context', *Environment and Behavior*, 33: 181–208.
26. See Wagner, S.A. (1997) *Understanding Green Consumer Behaviour*, London: Routledge; Kilbourne, W.E. & Beckmann, S.C. (1998) 'Review and critical assessment of research on marketing and the environment', *Journal of Marketing Management*, 14(6): 513–32; and Straughan, R.D. & Roberts, J.A. (1999) 'Environmental segmentation alternatives: A look at green consumer behaviour in the new millennium', *Journal of Consumer Marketing*, 16(6): 558–75.
27. Rose, C., Dade, P. & Scott, J. (2007) Research into Motivating Prospectors, Settlers and Pioneers to Change Behaviours that Affect Climate Emissions, Campaignstrategy.org.
28. AccountAbility & Consumers International (2007) *What Assures Consumers on Climate Change?* London: AccountAbility and Consumers International.
29. Straughan, R.D. & Roberts, J.A. (1999) 'Environmental segmentation alternatives: A look at green consumer behaviour in the new millennium', *Journal of Consumer Marketing*, 16(6): 558–75.
30. McDonald, S. & Oates, C.J. (2006) 'Sustainability: Consumer perceptions and marketing strategies', *Business Strategy and the Environment*, 15(2): 157–70.
31. Oates, C.J. & McDonald, S. (2002) 'What can marketing do for recycling?', *Proceedings of the Academy of Marketing Conference*, Nottingham: Academy of Marketing.
32. Sparks P. & Shepherd R. (1992) 'Self-identity and the theory of planned behavior: The role of identification with "green consumerism"', *Social Psychology Quarterly*, 55: 388–99.
33. For a review see Gilg, A., Barr, S. & Ford, N. (2005) 'Green consumption of sustainable lifestyles? Identifying the sustainable consumer', *Futures*, 37: 481–504.
34. Thøgersen, J. (2005) 'How may consumer policy empower consumers for sustainable lifestyles?', *Journal of Consumer Policy*, 28: 143–78.
35. *Ibid.*
36. Biffa (2003) *Future Perfect*, High Wycombe: Biffa Waste Services.
37. Peattie, K. & Peattie, S. (2009) 'Social marketing: A pathway to consumption reduction?', *Journal of Business Research* 62:260–268.
38. Jackson, T. (2004) *Motivating Sustainable Consumption: A Review of Evidence on Consumer Behaviour and Behavioural Change*, Guildford: Centre for Environmental Strategy, University of Surrey.
39. Elkington, J. & Hailes, J. (1988) *The Green Consumer Guide*, London: Victor Gollancz.
40. Friedman, M. (1996) 'A positive approach to organized consumer action: The "buycott" as an alternative to the boycott', *Journal of Consumer Policy*, 19: 439–51.
41. WWF Cymru (2002) *The Footprint of Wales*, Report to the Welsh Assembly Government, Cardiff: WWF Cymru.
42. See Straughan, R.D. & Roberts, J.A. (1999) 'Environmental segmentation alternatives: A look at green consumer behaviour in the new millennium', *Journal of Consumer Marketing*, 16(6): 558–75.

43. SC Johnson/Roper Starch (1993) *The Environment:Public Attitudes and Individual Behavior*, Racine, WI: Roper Starch.
44. Defra (2007) *Survey of Public Attitudes and Behaviours toward the Environment*, London: Department of the Environment and Rural Affairs.
45. Longhurst, M. (2006) 'Mediating for sustainable consumption', *Consumer Policy Review*, 16(4): 131–8.
46. Peattie, K. & Peattie, S. (2009) 'Social marketing: A pathway to consumption reduction?', *Journal of Business Research* 62: 260–268; and Naish, J. (2008) *Enough*, London: Hodder.
47. NICE (2007) *Workplace Smoking*, London: National Institute for Health and Clinical Excellence. Available at: http://www.nice.org.uk/phi005 (accessed 22 December 2008).
48. For further details see Denker, K. (2001) 'Smoke clearing', *Green Futures*, April, available at http://www.forumforthefuture.org/greenfutures/articles/60717 (accessed 22 December 2008).

PART III

DEVELOPING SUSTAINABILITY MARKETING STANDARDS AND STRATEGIES

CHAPTER 5

Sustainability Marketing Values and Objectives

After Studying this Chapter You Should be Able to:

1. Understand and reflect on the basic assumptions and values of sustainability marketing (in contrast to conventional marketing).
2. Explain the different kinds of objectives pursued in sustainability marketing.

LOOKING AHEAD: PREVIEWING THE CONCEPTS

Values are the normative foundation of sustainability marketing. In the first part of this chapter, we discuss the basic assumptions and values of sustainability marketing in contrast to those of conventional marketing. We discover and reflect on the underlying beliefs and myths of marketing theory and practice regarding markets, consumers, needs and nature. In the second part of the chapter, we present economic, ecological and social objectives for sustainability marketing. You will see that meeting the triple bottom line is not an easy proposition for prospective sustainability marketers.

SUSTAINABILITY MARKETING STORY: HIPP BABY FOOD

Hipp offers baby foods of the highest quality in harmony with nature. In fact, the company represents the largest processor of organic raw materials worldwide, supplied by around 6000 farmers.
Founded in 1932, the family-owned and family-run business has been one of the pioneers of organic
farming. Since the 1980s the whole production process has been converted to organic quality. Hipp
baby foods are distributed by conventional food retail chains, chemists and pharmacies and offered
in most European countries, with total revenues of €400 million in 2007. The headquarters are
located in Pfaffenhofen, Germany. Altogether, the company employs around 1000 people.

Prof. Dr Claus Hipp is the company's managing director. He has a strong faith and is a practising
Christian. Thus, Christian and human values have always played a vital role in his decision making. Since 1999, Hipp has had an 'Ethics Declaration'. This is a voluntary agreement, signed by the
family owners, which commits Hipp to discuss and reflect on ethical questions regarding corporate decisions in a transparent and systematic way. Furthermore, it binds the company to an ethics
charter, which has continuously developed. The Hipp ethics management programme defines the
company's procedures, its organizational structure and the communication of its ethical values
and rules. A key element of the ethics management programme is the ethics commission, consisting of five company members (director, ethics programme manager, human resource manager and
two representatives from Marketing/Sales as well as Operations). They come together twice a year
to discuss and decide on challenging ethical motions suggested by employees. The ethics committee analyses the motions and consults with experts. Finally, the committee makes a decision
to accept or reject the motions. In every case, detailed answers are given to whoever filed them.
Accepted motions become part of the Hipp ethics charter, which is binding for all employees. The
ethics charter is a set of written guidelines for appropriate corporate behaviour covering five key
areas: behaviour in the market, behaviour towards employees, behaviour of employees, behaviour
towards the state and society and behaviour in nature. The first Article, 'Behaviour in the market',
and the fifth Article, 'Behaviour in nature', are of special interest for us, since they are at the centre
of sustainability marketing.

Generally, Hipp recognizes the social market system and competition as institutions that guarantee
the dignity of humanity and contribute to wealth. Hipp explicitly aims to be oriented to the long
term, even if that involves short-term losses. It invests in the future of the company to stay
competitive, to guarantee its survival and to optimize profits in the long run (Article 1.1). Delivering
the highest quality is a vital part of all activities and a permanent challenge laid down for all
employees. Quality encompasses the whole company, its processes and products, which are valued
by customers (Article 1.2). The main purchasers of the company's products are large food retail
chains. Hipp is against any kind of unfair practices (e.g. listing fees, paid to the retailer to guarantee
shelf space), which are commonplace in the food industry due to the high level of competition
and the increasing purchasing power of large food retail chains. Instead, Hipp is interested in
long-term relationships with its customers and suppliers based on trust (Articles 1.3 and 1.4).

The behaviour towards competitors is shaped by mutual respect. Hipp believes that competition enhances innovations, which in turn increase customer satisfaction (Articles 1.5 and 1.6).

The fifth Article of the Hipp ethics charter particularly deals with the natural environment. It is noteworthy that this Article says 'Behaviour *in* nature', not 'Behaviour *towards* nature'. The latter would imply that the natural environment is perceived as something out there; nature would be detached from the company. The former acknowledges that the company is part of the natural environment; it is nature which underpins the economy, not the other way round. Thus, environmental protection plays a key role at Hipp. It defines it as a company that wants to satisfy the needs of the present generation without comprising the needs of future generations. All employees are integrated into environmental management systems striving for continuous environmental improvement (Articles 5.1 and 5.2). Often environmental activities lead to competitive advantages enhancing the corporate image, contributing to product differentiation or reducing costs. However, there are instances in which environmental activities may lead to competitive disadvantages endangering the long-term survival of the company. In these cases Hipp feels obliged to take part in the public and political discourse to develop the existing market system further in favour of the natural environment and sustainable development (Article 5.3).[1]

Sustainability Marketing: Basic Assumptions and Values

The example of Hipp shows that values matter in business and marketing. Sustainability values set the foundation of credible and responsible sustainability marketing management, but extending the concept of marketing values to include sustainability and embracing ethics can be challenging for marketers. Usually, marketers avoid talking about ethical values or dealing with moral questions of right and wrong. Seldom do they reflect on the basic assumptions underlying the concept of marketing. Instead, they have a strong preference for viewing marketing as amoral. Andrew Crane states that *amoralization* is a significant feature of marketing theory and practice to the extent that implicit values, moralities and aims are hidden so that they become ideological.[2] Regardless of what marketers say, conventionally they have a strong set of (implicit) values based on the principles of the sanctity of markets, consumer sovereignty and meeting consumer needs as justification for all they do.

In this chapter we present and challenge the basic assumptions and beliefs of marketing in the light of sustainable development.[3] As opposed to the amoral view in conventional mainstream marketing, we propose a values driven approach to sustainability marketing.

The Sanctity of Markets?

Marketing is a child of economic theory, which places its faith in the invisible hand and the functioning of markets. Since the publication of *The Wealth of Nations* by Adam Smith in 1776, markets have been seen as crucial to the generation and distribution of wealth. Economic theory blossomed in the Victorian era of imperial expansion in which vast new continents were being opened up and explored. Then it seemed reasonable to assume that the world and its resources had no practical limits, and that the only costs that needed to be attached to their exploitation were the costs of extraction. However, as all continents are explored and as the world population has grown tremendously, it has become clear that there are indeed limits that are not considered by markets.

In practice, the vast majority of the biosphere is not covered by price (air, water, common land, habitat, species, ozone layer etc.).[4] The environmental and social costs of production, product use and disposal are largely excluded from the price consumers pay. These costs are treated as 'externalities' to be met by society. If all environmental and social costs associated with production and consumption were covered by the price paid, it would be a major step forward on the way to sustainable development. However, even if markets could work with perfect efficiency, they suffer from some fundamental flaws:

- Markets have great difficulty valuing environmental resources. How do you value biodiversity? What is the price for the extinction of a particular species? Which monetary value do the aesthetics of a beautiful landscape have?
- Markets do not consider thresholds. Up to a certain point ecosystems are resilient to stress factors. However, if the critical thresholds are breached, the ecosystem or population may fall below its sustainable level before the price of the remaining stock becomes high enough to encourage preservation.
- Markets do not take irreversible processes into account. Ecosystem failures are often difficult to correct. Once the rainforest has been cleared, the land becomes incapable of supporting rainforest growth, whatever price or value is placed on it.
- Markets cannot predict the future demand for species and other resources. The Pacific yew, which reached the brink of extinction after the forestry industry burned it in massive numbers because it obstructed the harvesting of economically valuable species, went on to prove invaluable in the fight against cancer as the source of the drug Taxol.

Considering these fundamental flaws, blind faith in free markets is misplaced. Nevertheless, we have to acknowledge that the market system is a powerful institution influencing the behaviour of billions of people. There is hardly any alternative in sight to the functioning of markets. That is why the institutional framework of markets has to be changed so that environmental and social costs are included in the prices of products and services. The so-called *internalization of external costs* would be a major step towards a sustainable future. We think that the development of sustainable institutional frameworks is not just a task of the public, policy and politics, but also a challenge for business. We will return to this idea in Chapter 11, when we discuss sustainability marketing transformations.

The Sovereignty of Consumers?

Central to marketing is the customer or the consumer: who they are, what they buy and how much they are willing to pay. This is entirely right, but the current vision of consumers is mistakenly myopic and clings with blind obedience to the notion that 'The customer is king'. Consumer sovereignty and choice are sacred articles of faith within marketing, to the extent that they are equated with other fundamental societal values like democracy and freedom. However, freedom to consume needs to be balanced against the rights of nonconsumers, and against freedom from the consequences of others' consumption. Dedicated smokers view smoking as their right, but often without equal consideration of the nonconsumer's right to breathe unpolluted air. People in industrialized countries will claim a consumption driven lifestyle as their right, but often without equal consideration to the right of the poorest of the poor to consume as well. Ultimately, consumers are not sovereigns, with a God-given right to rule the fate of others, whom the marketer must obey.

A more enlightened and contemporary view sees consumers as a constituency with members who vary in their needs and priorities, and with rights and responsibilities that must be balanced against the rights and responsibilities of others. 'Dethroning' consumers to become a constituency demands that marketers no longer devolve responsibility for their decisions and actions by portraying themselves as the passive servants of the customer. Otherwise there is the danger that the concept of consumer sovereignty is being used by companies as a shield and as an excuse to avoid internalizing costs and providing more sustainable products.

The conventional faith placed in consumer choice to guide marketing strategies and activities also assumes that the consumer is faced with a free choice and complete information. In reality, however, both assumptions are flawed: neither a full freedom of choice nor complete information is actually given. Choices are carefully constructed and restricted by others. Large retail chains choose the products and brands that are put on the shelves of the supermarket, automobile companies determine which kinds of cars and engine systems are developed and offered, scientists and politicians decide which kinds of technologies are researched, and so on. Furthermore, information provided about many products is incomplete and often misleading. Given the lack of general literacy regarding environmental and social issues within the population, it is extremely optimistic to expect consumers to be able to make the decisions that will lead us towards sustainable development. Thus, companies and other industry stakeholders have a role to play in providing balanced information on the environmental and social consequences of products and services.

The Satisfaction of Needs?

Core concepts of marketing are needs and wants.[5] Basically, needs are the internal forces that drive or guide our actions. There is a great variety of needs such as subsistence, protection, affection, understanding, participation, leisure, creation, identity and freedom.[6] The satisfaction of needs yields positive feelings, whereas the dissatisfaction of needs will yield negative feelings (see Table 5.1).

The needs described above become wants once they are directed to a specific objects that might satisfy the need. An American needs food but may want a hamburger, French fries and a soft drink. A person in Mauritius needs food but may want rice, lentils, beans and a mango drink.[7] Americans build skyscrapers to satisfy the needs for protection and participation. Inuit people build igloos to satisfy those needs. Whereas human needs do not change much, wants vary over time and across cultures. The latter are

Table 5.1 Satisfaction and Dissatisfaction of Needs

Basic Need	Satisfaction of Needs (Positive Feelings)	Dissatisfaction of Needs (Negative Feelings)
Subsistence	Satiated, replete	Hungry
Protection	Safe	In danger, anxious
Affection	Love/being loved	Hate/indifference
Understanding	Intellectual well-being, smart, clever	Intellectual frustration, dumb, stupid
Participation	Belonging, related, involved	Lonesome, isolated, forsaken
Leisure	Playful, relaxed	Bored, weary, stressed
Creation	Creative, inspired	Uninspired
Identity	Self-assured, confident, positive self-image	Uncertain, insecure, negative self-image
Freedom	Free, independent	Entangled, chained, bounded, captured, tied

Source: Max-Neef, M. (1992) 'Development and Needs', in P. Ekins & M. Max-Neef (eds), *Real-Life Economics: Understanding Wealth Creation*, Routledge: London and New York.

shaped by society and the natural surroundings. Whereas needs are finite and few, wants are numerous in variety.[8]

Basic assumptions of conventional marketing are that wants are insatiable and that satisfaction will flow from consumption of material and immaterial goods. Growth in consumer demand is seen as a prerequisite for an improvement in the quality of our lives. Increasing consumption is regarded as synonymous with a better standard of living.[9] This assumption underlying modern consumer societies is both right and wrong at the same time. Empirical research in a number of countries shows that up to a certain point there is indeed a positive correlation between income per capita and life satisfaction. In other words, the more people earn and the more they can spend on food, housing, education, leisure and so on, the happier they are. However, once a certain level of income has been reached, life satisfaction does not increase any more. Even if people earn and consume more, they are not happier with their life (see Figure 5.1). This kind of evidence leads us to the conclusion that at least some of our consumption may not be contributing positively to the satisfaction of any of our needs. Obviously, some needs like affection, understanding and participation cannot simply be satisfied by the consumption of material and immaterial goods. They are instead satisfied by human relationships, which may suffer if we are preoccupied with making money to spend on goods. Thus, the environmental imperative to consume less may be good for the environment as well as ourselves. There is the possibility of living better by consuming less.[10]

The difficulty is to determine which part of consumption makes us happy and which does not. All too often there is a conflict between short-term and long-term satisfaction.[11] The consumption of fast food may satisfy our immediate appetite, but may not be good for our health. After all, people are complex, individual, inconsistent, and possessed of many and often conflicting wants. In many cases explicit wants conflict with our inherent needs as human beings for a healthy diet, an active lifestyle or a manageable level of stress. Sustainability marketing is about respecting consumers and perceiving

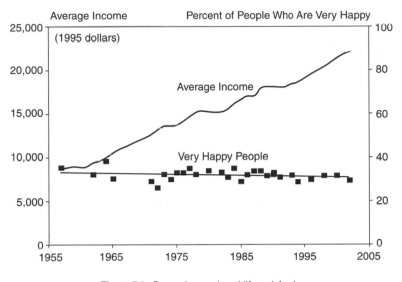

Figure 5.1 Economic growth and life satisfaction

Source: Myers, D.G. (2000) *American Paradox: Spiritual Hunger in an Age of Plenty*, New Haven, CT: Yale University Press.

them as human beings with different, sometimes conflicting needs and wants instead of reducing them to 'units of consumption'. Sustainability marketing tries not just to satisfy wants and meet needs, but also to generate opportunities and happiness and to achieve lasting satisfaction.

When we talk about needs and wants, we usually have consumer societies in mind. The poorest of the poor, who live on less than $2 (€1.44) per day, are widely neglected by conventional marketing. According to the United Nations they represent more than one third of the world population (circa 2.8 billion people).[12] The main reason for discrimination against the so-called base of the pyramid is that they do not have sufficient purchasing power. However, sustainable development is about meeting the needs of the present, which includes the poor as well as the rich. Thus, one aspect of sustainability marketing is to generate opportunities for the poorest of the poor, and include them within markets through new and innovative products, business models and pricing models.[13] Embracing the world's poor in the view of sustainability marketing may help them to consume more and lead a decent life satisfying their basic needs. However, introducing them to the consumer society will also worsen environmental problems (at least without 'Factor 10'-style improvements in resource efficiency; see Chapter 3). That leads us to the next basic assumption of conventional marketing, the peripheral nature of nature.

The Peripheral Nature of Nature?

In the conventional marketing paradigm, the macro environment is made up of the technological, social, political, legal and economic environments that influence the actors within a market, their strategies and behaviours. Standard textbooks on marketing dedicate whole chapters to these, but the physical environment is generally ignored or widely neglected. At best, environmental problems are fitted into the conventional model as a social concern or a driver of legislation in the political environment.[14]

The nature of the natural environment is treated as peripheral. This viewpoint overlooks the fact that technological, social, political, legal and economic environments ultimately depend on the natural environment. It is nature that underpins them all.

In the paradigm of sustainability marketing the natural environment is the point of departure. Ecology is highly relevant and integrated into each chapter of this book. Additionally, a whole chapter is mostly dedicated to ecological problems on the macro and micro levels; (see Chapter 3). We think that it is crucial for marketing students to learn at least the basics about the physical environment that surrounds us and about the environmental impacts of products and services. Instruments such as life cycle analysis (LCA) enables you, the future decision-makers in marketing, to analyse and reduce the negative impacts of products and services on the natural environment. The main focus of attention is on the reduction of the negative impacts of products and services on the natural environment to avoid the instability of ecological systems. The underlying assumption is that ecological systems are fragile and vulnerable. They have to be preserved and kept in balance. Winn and Kirchgeorg characterize this viewpoint as the 'inside-out' perspective: the primary perspective is to look from the firm (=inside) to the external environment (=outside).[15]

The prevailing inside-out perspective of sustainability marketing is to some extent myopic. It hardly pays any attention to the reverse effects; that is, the impact of the external environment on firms, characterized as the 'outside-in' perspective. Unpredictable ecological discontinuities can have a disastrous impact on the stability of social and economic systems. Think of the Hurricane Katrina when it hit New Orleans (USA) in the summer of 2005. If extreme weather events and natural disasters such as droughts, heatwaves, storms, floods and fires increase in number and severity, the outside-in perspective will become increasingly important. From this point of view, the natural environment is not as romantic and harmonious as it seems at first glance. Nature is instead perceived as wild, merciless and potentially dangerous to the life and health of human beings. On the one hand the outside-in view sensitizes companies to the possibility of ecological discontinuities and the development of catastrophic scenarios. On the other it creates new markets, products and services that help us to prepare for and respond to unpredictable ecological discontinuities. Consider the Netherlands, one of the most densely populated and low-lying countries of the world, which is endangered by flooding due to global warming and the rise of the oceans. To keep up with that challenge, creative planners and architects from the Dutch construction company Dura Vermeer developed 'floating houses', which rest on land but are built to rise with the water level.[16] We can see that it is useful to complement the prevailing inside-out perspective of sustainability marketing with the outside-in perspective. The two are different and yet complementary perspectives on the natural environment (see Figure 5.2).

Sustainability Marketing Values

The underlying values of sustainability marketing should reflect the visions, missions, philosophies or principles of the companies in the vanguard. Such statements express the core values of companies and, like a deeply rooted DNA code, differentiate one company from another.

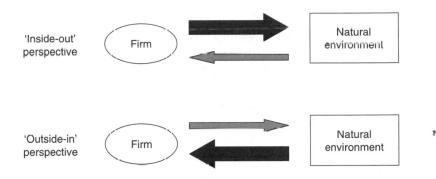

Figure 5.2 Two complementary views of the natural environment

Take SC Johnson, which operates in nearly 70 countries offering household products for cleaning and hygiene. You probably recognize some of the brands it makes, including Mr Muscle, Glade, Oust, Duck, Pledge and Shout. In 1976 the family company first formulated its basic principles. At the turn of the twenty-first century it restated, clarified and reaffirmed its commitment to upholding them. The corporate philosophy states the company's beliefs in relation to the five groups of people to whom it is responsible and whose trust it has to earn: employees, consumers and users, general public, neighbours and hosts, and world community.

SC JOHNSON – A FAMILY COMPANY

'This We Believe' – A Statement of Business Philosophy

Employees: We believe that the fundamental vitality and strength of our worldwide company lies in our people.

Consumers and Users: We believe in earning the enduring goodwill of consumers and users of our products and services.

General Public: We believe in being a responsible leader within the free market economy.

Neighbours and Hosts: We believe in contributing to the wellbeing of the countries and communities where we conduct business.

World Community: We believe in improving international understanding.

The company says that it has to earn the 'enduring goodwill' of consumers and users, which is oriented towards a long-term relationship. SC Johnson commits itself to 'develop and market products which are environmentally sound and which do not endanger the health and safety of consumers and users'. It applies environmental thinking at every phase of the product life cycle, starting with product design and continuing through manufacturing, use and disposal. It packages and labels products in such a way that consumers and users can make informed value judgements. In addition, it disseminates information to consumers and users that promotes full understanding of the correct use of its products and services (e.g. cautionary statements and/or symbols). Furthermore, SC Johnson provides the general public with information about its activities so that they have a better understanding of the worldwide company regarding economic, ecological and social aspects. Profits of each local company are shared with those who have contributed to it, by rewarding employees, giving a share to the local community, developing better products for the benefit of consumers, and providing the owners with a reasonable return on their investment.

Note that shareholders are not one of the five major groups to whom SC Johnson feels responsible. This is because as a family company it is not – and does not want to be – a public company listed on the stock market. SC Johnson explicitly says in its corporate philosophy: 'Our way of safeguarding these beliefs is to remain a privately held company. Our way of reinforcing them is to make profits through growth and development, profits which allow us to do more for all the people we depend.' Although SC Johnson does not explicitly refer to sustainable development, it embraces the different facets of the concept and integrates them into its daily business. The corporate philosophy is the normative foundation of the sustainability marketing approach that this family company pursues.

Both Hipp and SC Johnson are family-owned and family-run businesses, which express their beliefs, values and norms in written statements and pursue an active approach towards sustainability marketing. That does not imply that public companies listed on the stock market cannot do that too. It might be more difficult, because public companies have to consider the interests of shareholders as well, but it is without any doubt possible, as shown by the examples of Electrolux and Toyota.

The founder of Electrolux, Axel Wenner-Gren, pioneered the development of modern vacuum cleaners and refrigerators in the first half of the twentieth century. One of the key success factors was a deep commitment to engaging with consumers in the home in order to understand their needs and wants. More than 80 years later, Electrolux is a global leader in household appliances such as refrigerators, dishwashers, washing machines, vacuum cleaners and cookers. Some of the main brands of the multinational company include Electrolux, AEG-Electrolux and Frigidaire. More than ever the company devotes a lot of time, knowledge and thought to devising products that are not simply innovative and functional, but are also aesthetically beautiful, and easy and enjoyable to use. This commitment to the customer is communicated by the tagline 'Thinking of you' (Figure 5.3). All Electrolux products and services share the same philosophy: to make an extra effort to find out what people really need and want. However, 'Thinking of you' goes beyond meeting and exceeding customers' needs. The motto also underpins the company's attitude to its environmental and social responsibility: it communicates Electrolux's

Figure 5.3 Electrolux: Thinking of you
Source: Electrolux. www.electrolux.com.

commitment to make appliances safe for use, for the environment and for future generations. Thus, it is a good example of value-driven sustainability marketing and branding. The tagline communicates that the company really cares. If the thoughtfully designed Electrolux products live up to their promises, they create positive experiences and the familiar brand will become a 'friend' that consumers trust.

Japanese company Toyota is a global leader in the automobile business and is listed on the major stock markets around the world. The 'Toyota Way' is characterized by respect for the natural environment, for other people and for the communities around the company. The other key values, the gene code of the company, are teamwork, challenge, Genchi Genbutsu (going to the source to make the right decisions) and Kaizen (continuous improvement). To help put the Toyota Way into practice, the company established guiding principles and formulated its commitment to sustainable development.

TOYOTA'S COMMITMENT TO SUSTAINABLE DEVELOPMENT

We, Toyota Motor Corporation and our subsidiaries, take initiative to contribute to harmonious and sustainable development of society and the earth, based on our Guiding Principles.

We comply with local, national and international laws and regulations as well as the spirit thereof and we conduct our business operations with honesty and integrity.

In order to contribute to sustainable development, we believe that management interacting with its stakeholders as described below is of considerable importance, and we will endeavour to build and maintain sound relationships with our stakeholders through open and fair communication.

Customers: Based on our philosophy of 'Customer First', we develop and provide innovative, safe and outstanding high quality products and services that meet a wide variety of customers' demand to enrich the lives of people around the world . . .

Employees: We respect our employees and believe that the success of our business is led by each individual's creativity and good teamwork . . .

Business Partners: We respect our business partners such as suppliers and dealers and work with them through long-term relationships to realize mutual growth based on mutual trust . . .

Shareholders: We strive to enhance corporate value while achieving a stable and long-term growth for the benefit of our shareholders.

Global Society/Local Communities: We aim for growth that is in harmony with the environment throughout all areas of business activities. We strive to develop, establish and promote technologies enabling the environment and economy to coexist harmoniously and to build close and cooperative relationships with a wide spectrum of individuals and organizations involved in environmental preservation . . . We constantly search for safer, cleaner and superior technology to develop products that satisfy the evolving needs of society for sustainable mobility . . .

The five key stakeholders for Toyota are customers, employees, business partners in the supply chain, shareholders and the global society/local communities, including the natural environment. Toyota seeks to respect and build and maintain sound relationships with each one of them. Customers, their needs and wants come first. To reconcile the evolving needs of society for mobility with the requirements of the natural environment, Toyota explores simultaneously a broad variety of solutions for developing cleaner, greener vehicles (e.g. alternative energies like compressed natural gas, diesel clean advanced technology, hybrid systems, electric vehicles and fuel cells). Toyota's vision of sustainable mobility can be summed up in two words: 'zeronize' and 'maximize'. The first refers to the aim of reducing the harmful effects of automobiles on people and nature to zero. In other words: zero emissions, zero congestions and zero accidents. The second represents Toyota's goal of providing ever-greater comfort, fun and excitement in its vehicles.[17]

If we take a look at these companies and their corporate principles, we can see four common traits, despite the differences regarding legal status, history, nationality, products and industries. First, the companies seek to treat the group of people they depend on with respect and trust. Their goal is to build and maintain long-term relationships with key groups. Secondly, long-term thinking is more important to them than short-term thinking. Thirdly, quality and innovation are part of their culture and a factor behind their success. Finally, they feel responsible for the natural and social environments around them and integrate them into their daily business activities, including marketing. Thus, environmental and social criteria are an integral part of the products and services they offer.

The corporate values are the normative foundation of the sustainability marketing approach the companies pursue. We will see that incorporated values help sustainability marketers make decisions on strategic and operational levels. The incorporated values are also reflected in corporate brands, which have become increasingly important for a number of reasons:[18]

- Whereas product brands mainly aim at consumers, corporate brands appeal to a number of stakeholders, including actual and potential employees, shareholders and nongovernmental organizations. Often, large organizations are under scrutiny. Corporate responsibility is demanded by different stakeholders. Corporate brands, which embody environmental and social excellence, help companies to take a stance.
- Corporate brands also enhance identity and generate a sense of common purpose, especially in large organizations like Toyota, Electrolux and SC Johnson with thousands of employees all over the world.
- Due to globalization and internationalization, the attribute 'Made by' becomes more important than the attribute 'Made in'. Most Electrolux products are not made in Sweden, but in the rest of the world. Similarly, Toyota has factories all over the world, manufacturing or assembling vehicles for local markets.
- Last, but not least, corporate brands can support product brands in a positive way. The different kinds of branded household products for hygiene, which are sold by SC Johnson, profit from the positive image of the family company. If corporate brands and product brands are one and the same (e.g. Hipp), the positive effects are even more obvious.

Corporate Leaders

Written corporate statements do not mean much if corporate leaders do not live up to the core values. Owners and managers have to live by them, and be seen to live by them. They have to communicate the core corporate values continually to their employees. Empirical studies show that owners and managers are among the main drivers for an active sustainability marketing approach.[19] Consumers play a significant role in this context too, but to begin and continue such an endeavour it is crucial for leaders to hold strong beliefs. This leads to the questions: Why do companies pursue a sustainability marketing approach? What are the motives for leaders to do so? Generally, we can distinguish ethical-moral and economic-strategic motives. Accordingly, there are four different types of sustainability marketers, as shown in Figure 5.4:

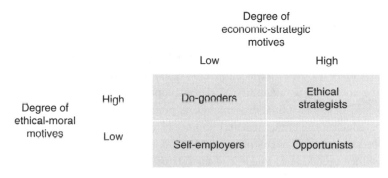

Figure 5.4 Four different types of sustainability marketers

- *Self-employers* want neither to change the world nor to get rich. They do not have a distinct ethical or economic motive. They just want to survive in the market and make a decent living. There are many small family businesses, lifestyle businesses or those operating in highly traditional or arts and creative markets, where the business reflects the lifestyle and the personal priorities of the owners.
- *Do-Gooders* care deeply about ecological and social responsibilities. Their mission is to use business to make the world a better place. They put principles before profits. A well-known example of this type of corporate leader was Anita Roddick, who founded The Body Shop in 1976. She built up the business according to her ethical values. She sold relatively natural cosmetics in simple and recyclable packaging, aiming to do the minimum harm to the natural environment. All the cosmetic products were formulated without animal testing. The natural ingredients were often sourced from developing countries and for some product lines a percentage of the profits was donated to environmental and social groups.
- *Opportunists* mainly believe in making money regardless of the means. As opposed to do-gooders, they put profits before principles. As long as it is within the legal requirements (and sometimes not even that), economic rationalists take their chances and offer any kind of product to any kind of market. If consumers demand environmental attributes and they could be delivered at a greater profit, opportunists would supply them; otherwise they would not. Take the German market for organic food products. As it grows and an increasing share of consumers buy organic, even the

'hard discounters' offer these kinds of products. They jump onto the bandwagon of environmental concern. It is safe to assume that the hard discounters primarily do so for economic and strategic reasons.

- *Ethical strategists* have mixed motives. They try to balance principles and profits by meeting the triple bottom line of sustainability marketing: ecological, social, and economic objectives. Claus Hipp is an example of such a corporate leader. He is a religious person and lives according to Christian values. He truly believes in the preservation of nature and in serving the community. It is not a simple marketing gimmick. In his case these positions are maintained regardless of immediate consumer wants. Environmental product attributes are, for the most part, nonnegotiable. By thinking in terms of years and decades, Hipp seeks to generate long-term profits and responsibly balances them with ecological and social goals.

Anita Roddick was a vocal advocate of putting passion before profits. She had high ethical values and personal morals when she founded and run her business. She also gave morality a meaning in the process of sustainability marketing. So do Claus Hipp (Hipp), Seth Goldmann (Honest Tea), David and Mike Hartkop (Solar Roast Coffee), Aaron Lamstein (WorldWise) and many other leaders of value-led companies pursuing an active sustainability marketing approach. However, often the personal moralities of those involved in the sustainability marketing process are understated and pragmatic. Many leaders argue that reducing the environmental and social impact of products is just a good thing to do. 'Rational' business arguments of customer satisfaction, revenues, costs and profits are used to promote the sustainability agenda both inside and outside the company. The rhetoric of 'win–win–win' solutions prevails, meaning that what is good for the natural and social environments is also good for customers and long-term profits. 'Emotive' discourses over moral conscience, social responsibility or ecological duty are, on the whole, avoided. This phenomenon is called amoralization as opposed to moralization.[20] Whereas the former means removing moral meaning from sustainability marketing, the latter implies that moral meaning is attached to it.

Sustainability Marketing Objectives

Well-intended corporate sustainability statements expressing concern for social and environmental issues are of little worth if they are undermined by the pursuit of short-term economic objectives. That is why sustainability issues have to be incorporated in the goal-setting process. In general, objectives should be specific, measurable, time-related, challenging and yet attainable. Sustainability marketing objectives state where the company intends to be at some specific time in the future. What is to be achieved? When are the results to be accomplished? Typically, marketing objectives relate to products and services. The baby food company Hipp, for example, may have the following marketing objective: Increase the market share of Hipp baby food products from 60% to 65% in the German food market by the end of next year. Conventionally, marketing performance is measured in terms of sales, profits and market share. However, if they focus on financial and growth-oriented objectives, marketing managers are not likely to engage in sustainability issues. That is why the economic objectives of marketing have to be complemented by ecological and social objectives. They may guide and motivate sustainability marketers, especially if remuneration is coupled to them; that is, if they reach specific social and/or ecological goals, marketers receive a bonus at the end of a specific period.

Economic Objectives in Sustainability Marketing

Economic objectives are predominant in conventional marketing and are still relevant for sustainability marketing. Classical marketing objectives are revenues, market shares, profits and profitability. They are related to market transactions and are relatively easy to track. For established companies an important economic sustainability objective may be to increase the revenues and shares of sustainable products and services as compared to conventional ones. One of Toyota's goals is to raise the public awareness of the benefits of Toyota's full hybrid systems and increase the global sales of hybrid cars to one million by 2010.[21]

As the focus shifts from single transactions to long-term relations, customer satisfaction and customer value become relevant marketing objectives as well. Customer satisfaction measures how products or services supplied by the company meet customer expectations. The higher the satisfaction of a customer, the greater is the likelihood that they will stay loyal to the company and repurchase its products in the future. Customer lifetime value represents the monetary worth of a customer throughout its economic life. Purchases and repurchases of products and services are taken into account and discounted to calculate the net present value. In reality, it is difficult to make accurate calculations of customer lifetime value due to the complexity and uncertainty surrounding customer relationships.

Whereas conventional marketing objectives such as revenues focus on the results of actual consumer behaviour, psychographic marketing objectives address the mental process of consumer behaviour. It is safe to assume that positive attitudes and perceptions of a product or brand influence the propensity of consumers to buy it. Psychographic marketing objectives include recognition rate, attitude, preferences and intentions to buy a product or brand. Electrolux, for example, may formulate the following objectives: We want to raise the unaided recognition rate of the Electrolux brand from 20% to 30% in China by the end of next year. Furthermore, we want to enhance the positive image of the Electrolux brand regarding quality, design and environment in our Chinese target groups. Unlike actual consumer behaviour, psychographic variables cannot be observed directly. That is why they are difficult and costly to measure.

Ecological Objectives in Sustainability Marketing

Economic objectives mostly concern the cumulative results of customer purchases in terms of contribution to revenues, market share or profits. Ecological objectives will reflect the need to manage the ecological impacts of the consumption and production of a product or service through all phases of the physical product life cycle. For some sectors, the impacts of products and services during their usage phase (e.g. the fuel consumption of a car, the water consumption of a washing machine) and at the end of their useful life in disposal can equal or exceed those of the production phase. To make sustainability marketers aware of the environmental impact of products and services along the entire life cycle and to make them consider it in decision-making, ecological indicators and objectives are crucial. The information can be drawn from life cycle assessments (LCA) or documents related to product design and development. Ecological objectives in sustainability marketing include:

- Materials use (e.g. use of nonrenewable and renewable energies, use of toxic materials)
- Water use (e.g. volumes used during production and/or product use)
- Emissions (e.g. greenhouse gases, toxic, ozone-depleting emissions)
- Effluents (e.g. effect on water quality of production and/or use)
- Waste (e.g. no ability to reclaim, toxic materials/compounds).[22]

The combined fuel consumption of the Toyota Prius, for example, is 4.3 litres of petrol per 100 kilometres, corresponding to 104 grams of CO_2. Ecological objectives would be to reduce the combined fuel consumption of the Toyota Prius to less than 4 litres of petrol and 100 grams of CO_2 per 100 kilometres by 2010. The actual fuel consumption and emissions of cars depend on personal driving habits. To encourage fuel-efficient driving Toyota designed the gear shift indicator, which indicates to the driver the optimized points at which to shift gears taking drivability and exhaust emissions into account.

The disposal of products and packaging materials at the end of their use is becoming an increasingly important environmental challenge. Establishing effective recycling and reuse schemes to close the loop can contribute to increased resource efficiency. The recycling quota can be calculated as follows:

$$\text{Recycling quota} = \frac{\text{Products and their packaging materials reclaimed within the reporting period}}{\text{Products sold within the reporting period}} \times 100$$

The higher the recycling quota, the better able the company is to collect and convert used products, components or materials into useful materials for new production processes. This indicator gives insight into potential sources of competitive advantage (differentiation or costs), particularly in sectors facing formal requirements to recycle products and their packaging materials.[23]

To make informed decisions consumers need adequate information on the environmental and social impacts of products and services along the entire life cycle. Thus, providing appropriate information and labelling with respect to products and services is essential for sustainability marketing. A possible objective is to increase the awareness of customers of a particular environmental brand and/or label by a certain percentage in a given period of time.

Social Objectives in Sustainability Marketing

Besides external environmental impacts, health and safety are vital issues in sustainability marketing. Customers expect products and services to perform well and not to pose a risk to their health and safety and that of others. General goals in sustainability marketing are to improve the safety of products during use and to reduce the potential negative impact on health.[24]

An increasing number of customers also consider the 'world behind the product'; that is, where and under what conditions it was produced. Thus, the physical protection and well-being of people at work are important indicators of sustainability marketing. This applies to employees as well as to workers within supply chains. Industries such as footwear or apparel, which depend on developing countries for production capacity, are faced with social challenges. In the mid 1990s Nike, for example, was confronted with accusations linking its products to sweatshop labour. The bad publicity endangered the image and sales of its products. Since then the company has sought to change and to take responsibility for conditions within its supply chains. The Nike Code of Conduct seeks partners that manufacture Nike-branded products that will respect the rights of their employees, provide them with safe and healthy work, and pay at least the minimum wage, or the prevailing industry wage, whichever is higher. Helping to improve contractors' factory conditions and enhance workers' rights is one of Nike's most important corporate responsibility efforts. For the financial year 2011 it set the following targets:

- Implementation of human resource management programmes in all focus contract factories.
- Implementation of freedom of association educational programmes in all focus contract factories.
- Conduct of a survey on satisfaction and empowerment of workers in focus contract factories.
- Zero excess overtime in focus contract factories.[25]

Companies can have both positive and negative impacts on the communities in which they operate. Generally they will aim to increase the positive social impacts and decrease the negative impacts. Many companies contribute to the well-being of communities by means of donations and involvements in social, cultural and educational projects that enhance the quality of life. However, most of these companies follow a rather reactive approach to CSR (see Chapter 2).[26] Often, the donations and involvements are detached from the core business of the company. In contrast, Nike pursues a strategic approach to CSR that is closely linked to the core business, adding value to the corporate and product brands. Nike believes that sport is a catalyst for positive change in young people and the communities in which they live. Thus, its community investments focus on a programme called 'Let Me Play', which gives excluded youth around the world the chance to play because access to sport can enhance their lives. Nike provides products, resurfaces playing fields, supports community-based programmes and helps young people to create their own communities. In 2005/06 Nike invested $100 (€72) million worldwide in 'Let me play' community-based sports initiatives. Until 2011 it will invest an additional $315 (€227) million on the programme. By doing good for society the company enhances its corporate image and strengthens its brand.

Economic, ecological and social objectives can have positive, negative or mutual interdependencies. Many marketers in practice still think that the three different kinds of objectives cannot be reconciled. As opposed to the prevailing view in marketing practice, the literature of sustainability marketing points out the positive relations between environmental, social and economic marketing goals. To underline this point of view, many case examples and anecdotal evidence are given in this chapter. However, this kind of 'win–win–win' rhetoric is at best naïve and at worst counterproductive.

A mistake made by some marketers is that they respond to sustainability concerns by simply 'bolting on' some social and environmental objectives into their existing goal set. Making substantive progress towards sustainability will require social and ecological objectives to reflect corporate sustainability values and develop marketing objectives in ways that balance and integrate the three aspects and balance long-term and short-term priorities. Meeting the triple bottom line of ecological, social and economic objectives is not an easy proposition. The interdependencies between the environmental, social and economic objectives of sustainability marketing are complex, difficult to measure and ever-changing.

Usually, it takes patience and perseverance to be successful in the long run. Think of Hipp, who was considered an outsider when he switched to organic baby food. Or take Toyota, when it launched the Prius in 1997. At that time gas-guzzling sport utility vehicles were the name of the game. Energy-efficient cars or alternatively powered vehicles were not top priorities for most automobile companies. And although motorists voiced their concern about the natural environment, many purchased cars with yet more power. Developing hybrid energy systems or electric cars requires time and investment. Changing consumer perceptions may take even more time and money. So finding the right balance between ecological, social and economic objectives is a very demanding challenge for sustainability marketers. It is a continuous process that will never end. Thinking long term without forgetting about short-term objectives is vital in the sustainability marketing decision-making process.

List of Key Terms

Amoralization
Base of the pyramid
Consumer sovereignty
Corporate philosophy
Corporate values
Do-Gooder
Ecological objectives
Economic objectives
Ethical strategist
External costs
Moralization
Needs
Opportunist
Self-employer
Social objectives
Wants

REVIEW QUESTIONS

1. What is the difference between needs and wants? Which factors influence wants?
2. Explain the 'inside-out' perspective of the natural environment as opposed to the 'outside-in' perspective.
3. Describe the four types of sustainability marketers with respect to ethical-moral and economic-strategic motives.
4. What does the term 'amoralization' mean?
5. List five social and ecological objectives in sustainability marketing.

DISCUSSION QUESTIONS

1. Voluntary simplicity is a lifestyle that individuals choose for a number of reasons to minimize the 'more-is-better' pursuit of wealth and consumption. What are the positive and negative consequences of such a lifestyle for individuals and society?
2. Do companies like Hipp, SC Johnson, Electrolux, Toyota and Nike live up to their core corporate values? Search websites that are critical towards these companies and discuss the gap between rhetoric and reality.
3. As compared to many other automobile companies, Toyota's contribution to sustainable development is no doubt far-reaching, but it faces some criticisms too. Discuss Toyota's basic assumptions regarding markets, consumer sovereignty, needs and wants.
4. What are the advantages and disadvantages of formulating specific and measurable objectives in sustainability marketing?
5. One of the most pressing issues sustainability marketers face is how to balance economic, ecological and social objectives. Give examples of negative interdependencies between the different kinds of objectives. Discuss how they could possibly be solved.

SUSTAINABILITY MARKETING CHALLENGE: BP – BEYOND PETROLEUM?

In February 2008 Tony Hayward, CEO of BP, hinted that he might be considering a sale of the company's alternative energy business. He made clear that everything, including renewable fuels, must pay their way at a time when BP is under pressure to restore its financial standing. 'The year 2007 was one of change for BP. In terms of financial performance it was one which most of us will be glad to leave behind, we are judged by investors in relation to our peers. In that regard our financial performance was not good enough,' Hayward said candidly. In 2007 BP's annual profits fell by 22% to $17.3 (€12.5) billion – at a time of record oil prices.

Selling off all or part of the renewables business would reverse a major part of the company's strategy under the former CEO Sir John Browne, who saw renewable energy as core to BP's operations and image. Browne had been recognized as a successful corporate leader. He transformed BP from a sleepy second-tier European oil company into one of the largest oil majors of the world by acquiring Amoco and Arco. The deal to buy Amoco for $56 (€40) billion in 1998 was the largest industrial merger ever. 'This guy is a visionary,' said Oppenheimer analyst Fadel Gheist. Whether the issue was consolidation, opportunities in Russia or global warming, 'Browne saw it coming before the competition.' In 1997 Browne was the first major oil CEO to acknowledge a link between emissions and global warming. Consequently, he emphasized environmental responsibility and started changing BP from the 'inside out'. The new BP mission statement says:

> Our products and services contribute to a better quality of life. They provide the freedom to move, to heat, to see. We believe this freedom is inseparable from the responsibility to produce and consume energy in ways that respect both human rights and the natural environment. Maintaining this balance is our life blood.

The 18 groups including health, environment and safety, people and capability, external relationships and performance help BP managers and employees to put the mission statement into guides for practical action. Thereby BP claims 'environmental leadership', taking a lead in developing solutions that will help address the world's energy paradox. Under Browne's leadership, BP worked to reduce emissions in the exploration and production of oil, began to market cleaner fuels like natural gas, and made significant investments in renewable energy sources such as hydrogen, wind and solar. In fact, BP is one of the largest producers and users of solar panels worldwide. To express the new values and strategies of the company BP replaced the 'green shield' logo with the symbol of Helios, the Greek sun god. The logo has a sunflower pattern with green and yellow colours. Since 2000, BP has spent several hundred million dollars on repositioning the corporate brand and communicating the tagline 'Beyond Petroleum' in its advertising. In 2005, the company set up the business unit BP Alternative Energies to bundle its sustainability marketing efforts. In 2007, BP also announced that it would spend $8 (€5.8) billion over ten years to research alternative methods of fuel, including natural gas, hydrogen, solar and wind.[27]

Questions for Discussion

1. How does BP's financial performance compare to that of its peers? Research the latest annual reports of Shell, Exxon and BP and analyse the most important financial figures.
2. What is meant by the 'world energy paradox'? What are viable options to solve this paradox?
3. What do you think of the corporate leadership of former BP CEO Sir John Browne?
4. Does the new logo of BP and its tagline express the environmental shift of the company?
5. From your point of view, is the environmental shift of the oil major credible? Is it reality or rhetoric?

Endnotes

1. Hipp (2006) *Hipp Ethik-Charta*, 3rd edn, Pfaffenhoffen: Hipp; Hipp (2007) *Hipp Ethik-Management*, 3rd edn, Pfaffenhoffen: Hipp; www.hipp.de (accessed 3 January 2009).
2. Crane, A. (2000) *Marketing, Morality and the Natural Environment*, London: Routledge, , pp. 121–71.
3. For the following discussion of basic marketing assumptions and beliefs about the sanctity of marketing, the sovereignty of consumers and the satisfaction of needs, see Peattie, K. (1999) 'Rethinking Marketing', in Charter, M. & Polonsky, M.J. (eds), *Greener Marketing. A Global Perspective on Greening Marketing Practice*, Sheffield: Greenleaf Publishing, pp. 57–70; and Peattie, K. (2007) 'Sustainable Marketing: Marketing Re-thought, Re-mixed and Re-tooled', in Saran, M., Maclaran, P., Elliott, R. *et al.* (eds), *Critical Marketing: Defining the Field*, London: Butterworth-Heinemann, pp. 193–210.
4. Gray, R. (1990) 'The accountant's task as a friend to the earth', *Accountancy*, 102(1192): 65–9.
5. Kotler, P. & Armstrong, G. (2004) *Principles of Marketing*, 10th edn, Upper Saddle River, NJ: Prentice Hall, p. 6.
6. Max-Neef, M. (1991) *Human-Scale Development: Conception, Application and Further Reflection*, London: Apex Press; Max-Neef, M. (1992) 'Development and Needs', in Ekins, P. & Max-Neef, M. (eds), *Real-Life Economics: Understanding Wealth Creation*, London: Routledge.
7. Kotler, P. & Armstrong, G. (2004) *Principles of Marketing*, 10th edn, Upper Saddle River, NJ: Prentice Hall, p. 6.
8. Jackson, T., Jager, W. & Stagl, S. (2005) *Beyond Insatiability: Needs Theory, Consumption and Sustainability*, Working Paper Series Number 2004/2, Guildford: Centre for Environmental Strategy, University of Surrey, p. 13.
9. *Ibid.*, p. 5.
10. *Ibid.*, p. 20.
11. Kotler, P. (1972) 'What consumerism means for marketers', *Harvard Business Review*, 50(3): 48–57.
12. UN (2005) *The Millennium Development Goal Report 2005*, New York: United Nations.
13. Winn, M.I. & Kirchgeorg, M. (2006) 'Sustainability marketing for the poorest of the poor', *Business Strategy and the Environment*, 15(3): 171–84.
14. For the following discussion on the peripheral nature of nature, see Winn, M.I. & Kirchgeorg, M. (2005) 'The Siesta Is Over: A Rude Awakening from Sustainability Myopia', in Sharma, S. & Starik, M. (eds), *Corporate Environmental Strategy and Competitive Advantage*, Cheltenham: Edward Elgar Publishing, pp. 232–58.
15. Winn, M.I. & Kirchgeorg, M. (2006) 'Sustainability marketing for the poorest of the poor', *Business Strategy and the Environment*, 15(3): 171–84.
16. www.duravermeer.nl (accessed 3 January 2009). Water flooding is not just a Dutch problem. In 2007 there were catastrophic floods across the world, including Vietnam, India, Bangladesh, Mexico, Australia and Great Britain.
17. Toyota (2005) *European Environmental and Social Report 2005. Towards Sustainability*, Brussels: Toyota Motor Europe, pp. 4–7; Toyota (no date) *Aim: Zero Emissions*, Brussels: Toyota Motor Europe.
18. Hermann, S. (2005) *Corporate Sustainability Branding*, Wiesbaden: Gabler pp. 40–42.
19. Belz, F.-M. & Schmidt-Riediger, B. (2009) Marketing Strategies in the Age of Sustainable Development: Evidence from the Food Industry. *Business Strategy and the Environment* (forthcoming).
20. Crane, A. (2000) *Marketing, Morality and the Natural Environment*, London: Routledge, pp. 121–71.
21. Toyota (2008) *Sustainability Report 2008: Towards a New Future for People, Society and the Planet*, available at http://www.toyota.co.jp/en/csr/report/08/index.htm (accessed 4 January 2009).
22. Global Reporting Initiative (2009) *Indicator Protocols Sets: Environment*, Version 3.0, p. 33, available at www.globalreporting.org (accessed 3 January 2009).
23. *Ibid.*, p. 34.
24. Global Reporting Initiative (2009) *Indicator Protocols Sets: Product Responsibility*, Version 3.0, p. 3, available at www.globalreporting.org (accessed 3 January 2009).
25. Nike (2007) *Innovate for a Better World, Nike FY05-06 Corporate Responsibility Report*, Beaverton, OR: Nike. To ensure transparency Nike lists all contracted factories with names and addresses at the end of corporate responsibility report.

26. Porter, M.E. & Krämer, M.R. (2006) 'Strategy and society', *Harvard Business Review*, 84(12): 78–92.

27. BP (2009) *Our Values*, www.bp.com (accessed 3 January 2009); Bergin, T. (2008) 'BP sees no gain from green energy', *International Herald Tribune*, 27 February, http://www.iht.com/bin/printfriendly.php?id=10472441 (accessed 3 January 2009); Doh, J. & Holt, E. (2004) 'Lord John Browne and BP's Global Shift, In-Depth Integrative Case 1', in Hodgetts, R.M., Luthans, F. & Doh, J.P. (eds), *International Management: Culture, Strategy and Behavior*, 6th edn, Columbus, OH: McGraw-Hill/Irwin, pp. 516–20; Macalister, T. (2008) 'BP goes back to petroleum. The shift to renewables has been ditched for a carbon intensive future', *The Guardian*, 21 February, htpp://www.guardian.co.uk/business/2008/feb/21/bp.oik/print (accessed 3 January 2009); Schwartz, N.D. (2004) 'Inside the Head of BP. He doesn't like meat. He thinks green. What is John Browne doing running the world's largest oil company?', *CNNMoney.com*, 26 July, http://money.cnn.com/magazines/fortune/fortune_archive/2004/07/26/377141/index.htm (accessed 3 January 2009).

Sustainability Marketing Strategies

After Studying this Chapter You Should be Able to:

1. Understand the role that the marketing environment plays in influencing the development of sustainability marketing strategies.
2. Discuss the opportunities and threats that sustainability issues and concerns within society are creating for marketers and understand some of the key elements that might be involved in creating a marketing strategy to respond to them.
3. Appreciate sustainability strategy from the perspective of different stakeholders.

LOOKING AHEAD: PREVIEWING THE CONCEPTS

The strategies that marketers adopt are not simply a response to the values and the objectives of the company, the wants and behaviour of customers, and the extent to which both are oriented towards sustainability. In this chapter we consider the marketing environment and the actors and forces within it, which also shape the strategy of a company, sometimes creating barriers to the pursuit of sustainability and sometimes providing encouragement and pathways towards it. Meeting the sustainability challenges of the twenty-first century and transforming our systems in production and consumption will require many innovations in products, technologies and marketing strategies. Sustainability marketing strategies focus on the *When?* *Where?* and *How?* questions necessary to introduce innovations to the market successfully.

SUSTAINABILITY MARKETING STORY: MARKS & SPENCER'S 'PLAN A'

Marks & Spencer (M&S) is one of the UK's longest established and most successful retailers. It has always seen itself as a values-led organization. In January 2007 the company launched a £200 (€210) million, five-year sustainability plan 'Plan A'. This represented one of the most ambitious sustainability strategies to be developed by a leading company and sought to position M&S ahead of rivals like ASDA, which had recently pledged to stop landfill waste, and Tesco, which had promised to halve its carbon footprint. The 100-point Plan A sought to address the key sustainability challenges that the business faced, grouped under five headings:

- Climate change: with the aim of making the business carbon-neutral by 2012.
- Waste: with the aim of eliminating waste to landfill from its operations by 2012.
- Sustainable sourcing: particularly to extend M&S's use of organic and free-range produce.
- Ethical trading standards: to use the power of M&S as an own-brand retailer to improve the livelihoods of its suppliers and supplier communities worldwide.
- Helping customers and employees to live a healthier lifestyle.

In unveiling the plan, M&S Chief Executive Stuart Rose commented:

Every business and individual needs to do their bit to tackle the enormous challenges of climate change and waste. While M&S will continue to sell great quality, stylish and innovative products, our customers, employees and shareholders now expect us to take bold steps and do business differently and responsibly. We believe a responsible business can be a profitable business. We are calling this 'Plan A' because there is no 'Plan B' ... This is a deliberately ambitious and, in some areas, difficult plan. We don't have all the answers but we are determined to work with our suppliers, partners and Government to make this happen. Doing anything less is not an option.

Turning the 100 sustainability pledges in the original Plan A into a strategy for the marketing of the business and its products has led to a variety of innovations and required the company to forge new types of strategic relationships. This has included the opening of three pilot 'eco-stores' in different parts of the UK in which around 80 new environmentally oriented systems and technologies are trialled in each. The packaging for its pizza range, for example, was redesigned to use 62% less material, sales of organic food products increased 48% in the first year and new Fair Trade and organic cotton, organic linen and recycled polyester products were introduced in homeware. For some pledges the company sought to work with consumers to change their behaviour, for example contributing to a shift in the percentage of clothing washes done at 30°C from 23% to 31% or introducing charges on carrier bags to encourage reuse. There was also considerable work done on the operational side of the company, including a 'carbon footprint' audit of its food business and a campaign to reduce energy-related CO_2 emissions in its stores and offices that yielded a reduction of 55 000 tonnes over 12 months.

Partnerships were an integral part of the strategy, and the company sought to work with its supply chain to help suppliers reduce their sustainability impacts, for example through a programme of assisting supplying farmers to introduce small-scale renewable energy resources. In the case of Pledge 44, M&S had promised to help customers to reduce their waste clothing by 'making sure that, within five years, you need throw none of our clothing away as waste after you've finished with it. We will start by researching alternatives into clothing disposal, including donation, composting and recycling.' Although the obvious solution was to develop an in-house clothes reclamation and recycling scheme, this posed a significant reverse logistical challenge for a retail operation geared towards providing rather than reacquiring products. Instead the company met this pledge through a partnership with Oxfam, one of the UK's best-known charities. As well as being dedicated to tackling poverty and promoting development globally, Oxfam possessed a national retail network of over 750 high-street shops that represented the most extensive retail network involved in recycling secondhand goods, particularly clothes.

Market research into the nation's wardrobes from YouGov showed that an estimated 2.4 billion items (representing almost half of people's clothes) had sat in a wardrobe without being worn once in the past year. Consumers in the 25-34 age group had the most expensive unworn clothes collection, worth an average of £228 (€239). These unworn clothes were providing no value to consumers, yet represented a store of value that could be converted into clothes that Oxfam could sell to fund its work tackling poverty and that other consumers could purchase and benefit from. Even clothes unsuitable for resale could be reused in other ways through Oxfam's own textile-sorting operation, Wastesaver, based in Huddersfield

Although the two organizations had never worked together before, they shared an interest in tackling key sustainability issues including waste and poverty, and there was considerable overlap in the demographics and attitudes of their core customer groups. The resulting 'M&S and Oxfam Clothes Exchange' scheme offered M&S customers a special Clothes Exchange voucher if they made a donation to Oxfam containing at least one piece of M&S labelled clothing or accessory. The voucher was valid for one month (to motivate consumers to act) and incentivized consumers through a £5 (€5.25) discount at M&S if customers spent more than £35 (€36.70) on clothing, beauty or home-wear products. The deal provided a tangible reward for consumers rather than simply appealing to their ethical instincts by asking for surplus M&S clothes to be donated to Oxfam.

The communications campaign generated considerable public interest and follow-up research showed that it reached an audience of approximately 45 million people and generated public relations benefits valued at £4.5 (€4.7) million. The commercial success of the scheme was such that in just the first seven weeks Oxfam had issued over 140 000 vouchers in exchange for an average of 4.85 items per donation. Donations to Oxfam increased by 40% and an estimated 341 tonnes of clothing that might otherwise have ended up in landfill were reused or recycled. By the end of the first six months of the scheme, the forecast additional income for Oxfam would represent around £1.5 (€1.57) million (on an annual basis) to invest in its campaigns to tackle poverty and promote development.

The success of the Clothes Exchange scheme shows all the hallmarks of successful sustainability strategy formulation. It was underpinned by clear values and specific targets. It was based on sound research, had a strong customer orientation and involved an innovative strategic relationship with a partner which, although a very different type of organization, had the right synergies in terms of culture, values and core customer base. It also achieved a balanced 'win–win' result for the different parties. It offered consumers a simple and rewarding way to recycle clothes, provided economic benefits for both M&S and Oxfam, and delivered sustainability benefits linked to the environment and to promoting sustainable development in poorer countries.

Marketing Strategy and Sustainability

The marketing strategy of a company reflects its overall corporate strategy and objectives, its vision, mission and values. It will be shaped by the nature of the company's market and its wider marketing environment. It will also reflect the relationships that evolve between the company and the key actors within that environment. A company's marketing strategy in practice will typically be a mixture of carefully planned and deliberate steps, and more informal patterns of decisions and actions that emerge as managers react to events and improvise. Normative sustainability marketing determines the broad *What?* and *Why?* questions in establishing a more sustainable approach to marketing (see Chapter 5). Strategic sustainability marketing focuses more on answering the *How?*, *Where?* and *When?* questions necessary to translate sustainability marketing values into a commercially viable marketing strategy.

Three ideas underpin business thinking about strategy, and each is a metaphor from beyond business. The first equates business to warfare, as a confrontation between a company and its competitors in the quest to dominate a market. When marketers talk of objectives, targeting and territory, or of guerrilla marketing or defending a position in the market, it reflects the roots of business strategy thinking in military science.[1] The second metaphor likens companies to machines and focuses on issues of structure, efficiency and control systems. The final metaphor has ecological roots and compares a business to an organism whose success depends on being well suited to its environment and able to adapt to environmental change.[2] This follows Darwin's principle of *survival of the fittest* that, although often mistakenly interpreted as survival of the strongest, originally meant survival of those best suited to their environment. The companies most able to respond and adapt to a changing economic, social and physical environment in the twenty-first century will be the best placed to survive and thrive.

The concept of survival is fundamental to business and marketing strategy. Strategic marketing processes help companies to look outward into their environment, and forward in time to identify potential threats to their survival or opportunities to exploit. Strategic marketing and sustainability therefore share a future orientation and an external focus, and both seek to prevent (or at least manage) disruptive environmental and social change. Although there has been a tendency for people to think about 'green' or sustainability marketing as an oxymoron,[3] from the strategic perspective of ensuring that a business can survive, thrive and endure, sustainability and marketing are highly compatible concepts.

Understanding the Marketing Environment

Being well suited to your environment is fundamental to the ecological metaphor of marketing strategy and to a sustainability perspective on marketing. The marketing environment is the world in which marketers, their customers and competitors all exist and interact. Its complexity is usually simplified by subdividing it into levels or issues.

A distinction is usually drawn between a company's micro environment (also referred to as the task or proximate environment) and its macro environment. The micro environment includes a company's market and those *actors* it interacts with directly and relatively regularly. The macro environment consists of broader and less direct influences on the business such as regulation and technology. Market research informs companies about their customers, while broader marketing research provides information about the wider market and macro environment, to identify trends, opportunities and threats. As sustainability issues have become more strategically important, so companies have used marketing research to understand their strategic implications. Independent marketing research organizations such as MORI in the UK and Roper in the USA have regularly published research on different aspects of the sustainability agenda, and companies seeking to develop sustainability-oriented strategies or products will also conduct or commission their own studies.

Micro environment

The key actors within the *micro environment* include the following.

Customers

Customers play the leading role in shaping a company's strategic response to the sustainability agenda. Customers can include individuals, households, retailers, other businesses, government bodies, public service providers or some other type of organization (although this book focuses on marketing to the final consumer). How a customer responds to a company, its values and market offering depends on their nature, their perceptions, the behaviour of the company and a range of other influences within the marketing environment. Although many companies may initially adopt sustainability strategies proactively to reflect corporate values or market opportunities, others will embrace sustainability more reactively in response to direct pressure from customers.

Competitors

The strategies adopted by companies may follow the lead of a particular competitor, best exemplified by the idea of a 'Me too' strategy. This was the case with the marketing of 'rod and line caught' sustainable tuna under the Starkist brand or the introduction of phosphate-free washing detergents.

Suppliers

A company's strategy and the quality of its products depends on its ability to purchase the necessary goods and services from suppliers. The concept of the ecological product life cycle means that the sustainability performance of a product will depend on the 'embedded' social and environmental impacts inherited through the supply chain. The social pressure that companies such as Nike and Gap experienced over the use of child and sweatshop labour was a reaction to the behaviour of their suppliers rather than of the companies behind the brands. Marketers also directly purchase from suppliers of services such as advertising, public relations, design and marketing research.

Intermediaries

Most manufactured products reach customers through intermediaries such as retailers, wholesalers or distributors. They facilitate marketing exchange and build marketing relationships by aggregating products for customers and often by aggregating customer information to improve marketing decision making. They may also assist customers through the provision of information and advice, financing and delivery services. In some markets moves towards sustainability are resulting from intermediaries taking a lead by 'choice editing' or deselecting unsustainable products on behalf of consumers.[4] Wyevale Garden Centres in the UK, for example, took a lead in destocking patio heaters from its product assortment, a move that was followed by B&Q, the company that has traditionally positioned itself as the leader in sustainability performance within the British do-it-yourself market. ASDA, part of the Wal-Mart Group, announced in 2006 that it would cease to sell endangered North Sea cod products.

Communities

Wherever businesses are located, they will interact with the local communities in ways that can create benefits (such as jobs and wealth) or costs (such as pollution or congestion). In an era of increasingly globalized business, local communities might seem virtually irrelevant to marketing strategy. However, for small businesses the majority of their customers and employees may be drawn from their local community, and this makes relations between the business and the community significant.[5] For more international companies, their relationships with local communities will have an impact on their corporate reputation and perceptions of whether or not they operate in an ethical, responsible and sustainable way. The concept of communities can even be relevant for those engaged in e-commerce through the response of *virtual communities of interest* who share a connection based on interests rather than geography.

Government

The challenge for government at all levels is to promote the economic and social benefits of business in the short term, while minimizing the negative social and environmental impacts. In the longer term the challenge will be to create a policy framework that brings about a sustainable and harmonious balance between the economy, society and the environment. Governments can influence corporate marketing strategies through command-and-control-style regulation, financial measures including taxation and incentives, the promotion of industry self-regulation and the provision of the infrastructure on which business activity depends. Governments also represent a key customer group for many companies, and the purchasing power and requirements of government organizations can act as an incentive for companies to embrace good sustainability practices.

Investors

For publicly owned companies, investors supply the financial resources needed for operation and expansion. In return, investors expect companies to deliver value for shareholders through earnings (dividends paid on an 'earnings per share' basis), and through a return on investment from share price increases. Both are determined by the profit generated by the business, but while dividends reflect the current levels of profit generated by a business, the share price represents future expectations of profit. There is a common misconception that the pursuit of short-term profit maximization to benefit shareholders is responsible for the unsustainability of business. Although profit is attractive to shareholders, to managers growth is even more attractive because it typically provides greater prestige, rewards for managers and security from acquisition. To move towards more sustainable businesses, investor expectations will need to be adjusted to accept a return on their investment that is sustainable (and certainly below the double-digit returns experienced during much of the 1990s). What constitutes a sustainable return on investment is a difficult and complex question that goes far beyond the scope of this book. What is clear, however, is that the field of marketing will not be able to make substantive progress towards sustainability without a similar evolution in thinking and practice in other disciplines, including finance and accounting.

Financial Institutions

Investors include both individuals and financial institutions such as banks, insurance companies and pension funds. These financial institutions can play a significant role in encouraging businesses towards sustainability by acting on behalf of their customers and through the financial services that they offer to companies. Many businesses require loan finance or insurance for their operations, and the social and environmental risks associated with a business will partially determine its risk profile and therefore the likely terms of the loans or insurance provided.

Media Organizations

The media plays a crucial role in shaping the opinion of customers, investors, politicians and the general public in relation to both the sustainability agenda and perceptions about particular products, companies and technologies. Media coverage of social and environmental issues influences which have the highest priority among consumers, voters and investors and which industries come under the greatest pressure to change. Businesses will also use the media for their own purposes of marketing and corporate communications, and business advertising will create a revenue stream for many media organizations that they may be unwilling to jeopardize.

Interest Groups

Other actors can be influenced by the campaigns of interest groups linked to social and environmental causes. Such groups vary from the global to the local, and can focus on a single issue such as Fair Trade or encompass a range of socio-environmental issues. Some have existed for hundreds of years, while others exist only temporarily to campaign against a development, project or technology at a specific time and place. The relationship between interest groups and businesses varies from confrontation (such as that between Shell and Greenpeace over the *Brent Spar* oil platform) to dialogue and partnership. Partnership approaches became more common from the 1990s onwards and evolved into the concept of cause-related marketing, in which interest groups and businesses cooperate to develop a mutually beneficial promotional campaign.

General Public

Beyond the relatively direct stakeholders with an interest in the business, including customers, investors and interest groups, are the wider general public and their opinions, attitudes and beliefs. Public opinion can be important to marketers, because a product that is well liked by its consumers (such as cigarettes) may come under threat from disapproval by the general public or from regulation.

Macro Environment

The *macro environment* includes the wider strategic influences that can affect a company and the other actors within its market. Through most of the twentieth century the view of the marketing environment was curiously abstracted from the physical world. The macro environment was usually divided into manageable thematic chunks, with PEST (Political, Economic, Social, Technical) analysis being a simple but enduring approach.[6] Although the physical environment underpinned all companies' markets, it was rarely explicitly included in models of the marketing environment. If it was considered, it was as a 'social' issue reflecting consumers' environmental concern, or as a 'political' issue reflecting environmental regulations. The physical environment was primarily considered in relation to distribution and the geographic distances between producers and consumers, or in markets such as clothing, food or cars as an influence on consumer lifestyles and needs through climate or topography. Little attention was given to how marketing activity might be influenced by the physical environment if its ability to provide resources or absorb pollution and waste was exceeded.

Other models for categorizing the macroenvironment include the SCEPTICAL framework (Social, Cultural, Economic, Physical, Technical, Infrastructure, Communications, Administrative, Legal), which provides a more detailed way of analysing the forces within the macro environment and understanding how sustainability concerns may affect a particular business.[7]

Social

Although social values and priorities vary among societies around the world, there are many commonly shared values that can influence the perceived acceptability of a marketing strategy and the company behind it. With respect to the pursuit of sustainability a number of key social values are expressed in the UN's Millennium Declaration, including freedom and democracy, equality and shared responsibility. There are also broader social attitudes and values that create the framework within which sustainability strategies will need to operate,[8] including institutional trust and attitudes towards capitalism, globalization, technology, social change and sustainable development itself. An important set of values relates to social norms, or in other words what is socially accepted as 'normal'. The mainstreaming of sustainability concerns into consumption behaviour, management practices or investment practices depends on this becoming viewed as 'normal' as opposed to in some way 'alternative'.

Cultural

Culture refers primarily to how society expresses itself collectively, particularly through shared knowledge, learning, communication and the arts. Sustainability issues are increasingly reflected in the cultural landscape in ways that influence public and political opinion and consumer response. Coverage of social and environmental crises in the news media, the popularity of television wildlife documentaries, the adoption of social and environmental campaigns by bands like U2 and Coldplay or celebrities can all increase social awareness and concern about sustainability. In the case of climate change, a successful fictional movie (*The Day After Tomorrow*) and an Oscar-winning factual movie (Al Gore's *An Inconvenient Truth*) combined to raise public awareness more rapidly than decades of scientific reporting.

Economic

The economic climate profoundly influences the short-term viability of firms and their marketing strategies, and also the long-term prospects for the transition to a more sustainable economy. Unsustainable levels of economic growth created the sustainability crisis, yet ironically it is when economic growth is threatened that politicians and companies often shy away from pursuing sustainability strategies. The perceived higher costs of more sustainable technologies, the costs involved in making any form of significant change, and the renewed priority given to stimulating rather than transforming growth all combine to deter strategy makers from pursuing sustainability strategies in recessionary times. The full implications of the global 'credit crunch' in 2008/09 may take many years to unfold. The impact of reduced wealth for, and demand from, American consumers is likely to slow economic growth globally. This will reduce pressure on natural resources and systems and may create some opportunities for new sustainability marketing strategies and practices to emerge, provided that the necessary political will and corporate courage exist.

Physical

The physical environment is not a strategic constant, but represents a dynamic and potentially disruptive influence on marketing strategy. Climate change has the potential to have a direct impact on businesses whose production facilities, transport infrastructure or customers are located in low-lying coastal regions.[9] Tourism and agriculture are two of the largest global industries, and both would be threatened by disruption to current patterns of temperature and climate. For other industries, climate change concern may create strategic opportunities as society seeks to prevent it, or adapt to it. A 2008 McKinsey business survey found that 60% of respondents regarded climate change as strategically important, and a majority considered it important to product development, investment planning and brand management; 61% of managers expected efforts to tackle climate change to boost profits.[10]

Technical and Scientific

The scientific community provides the data on sustainability challenges that will inform governments and, through the media, the wider population. Science also plays a vital role in meeting the challenges of the twenty-first century and generating new technologies that will form the basis of smart materials, renewable energies, sustainable products and services (e.g. electric cars, fuel-cell cars, combined mobility, energy-generating houses and bioplastics).

International

The international climate can have a significant influence on marketing strategy. Tensions between countries can reduce the opportunities for the export of products and threaten the supply of key resources. International cooperation is also important in tackling many of the sustainability challenges outlined in Chapter 1.

Communications and Infrastructure

The established transport infrastructure within a market will partly determine the economics and environmental impacts of product-distribution strategies. The communications infrastructure, particularly in relation to integrated communications technologies and the Internet, will determine the opportunities to develop e-commerce strategies. This can create new opportunities for less resource-intensive forms of marketing such as the digital distribution of music.

Administrative and Institutional

Educational institutions and religious institutions are among those that exert a considerable influence on social and cultural attitudes and help to determine the social capital within a society. Administrative organizations can also influence sustainability strategies for companies. This is the case with the International Organization for Standardization (ISO), which administers business standards including the ISO 14001 series for environmental management systems (EMS) and which has developed a new standard, ISO 2600, for CSR.[11] Similarly, Social Accountability International has developed the SA8000 global social accountability standard for decent working conditions, which covers issues including child labour, forced labour, the rights to collective bargaining, basic pay, health and safety issues and working hours.[12]

Legal and Political

Since the publication of the Brundtland report, sustainability issues including poverty, climate change and waste have enjoyed an increased political profile leading to regulations that affect many businesses. Some of the most significant changes have come from the introduction of 'extended producer responsibility' regulations such as the European Directives on end-of-life vehicles or waste electrical equipment. These have profoundly changed the economics, structures and design priorities within automotive and electrical equipment markets by making producers responsible for reclaiming and largely reusing or recycling old products from consumers.

Effective marketing strategies match the demands of consumers and the marketing environment to the resources, strengths and weaknesses of the company in pursuit of its objectives in line with its values. This requires marketing strategists to understand the resources, strengths and weaknesses, and also the culture and competencies of the internal company environment. A sustainability marketing strategy also needs to be reinforced through management of the company's financial, human and physical resources. Implementing a company's sustainability marketing ambitions therefore requires a response from the entire company to ensure that the processes of acquiring materials, manufacturing products (or delivering services), managing human resources, distributing finished products and facilities management are made as sustainable as is practicable. This makes it important for the company also to audit its internal environment and the management of its other functions and all of its resources.

Management information systems play an important role in providing information for strategic marketing decisions as well as for management control. For sustainability marketing strategies, social audits and environmental management systems have become important to support strategy making and to provide information about social and environmental performance. Such systems can also become strategically important by helping a company to achieve sustainability-oriented standards certification (such as the ISO 14000 series or SA 8000) to satisfy customer requirements. To complement such management systems there are now also environmental knowledge management systems emerging to help managers understand the environmental impacts, linked to the full range of products, production processes and facilities that a manufacturing business will have.[13]

Sustainability Marketing Strategy

A good understanding of the marketing environment and the actors within it allows a company to tackle some of the key questions involved in marketing strategy development. Two of the most fundamental questions are 'Which markets should we compete in?' and 'Within each of our markets, how shall we compete?'. The answers will reflect the company's values and objectives, its marketing resources and organization, and the information it has about customer needs, competitor capabilities and the opportunities and threats created by the evolution of the wider marketing environment.

Market Choice

Decisions about what set of markets to compete in, and whether or not to enter a particular sustainability-oriented market or market segment, will be influenced by many factors. They will include the perceived attractiveness of the market, as defined by factors such as market size, maturity and growth rate, profitability, intensity of competition and potential market entry costs and barriers to entry (and a sustainability perspective also adds the sustainability of the market to that list of criteria). They will also be influenced by the potential strength of the company's competitive position within a market in terms of actual or potential market share, the life cycle stage of its products and technologies, and the company's ability to generate competitive advantage and occupy and defend a position within the market. It will also be influenced by the company's experience and competence, and the extent to which entering the market would be an extension of the company's existing product/market strategy, or whether it represents a new departure.

Marketing strategy is often discussed in terms of managing a dynamic portfolio of product/market businesses that will include a mixture of new and emerging, and established or even declining, product/market businesses (as set out in the well-known 'Boston Box' growth–share matrix model[14]). The logic behind such a portfolio is that the revenues generated by the mature 'cash cow' businesses can be used to fund new and emerging products and technologies as the basis for future businesses. By the same logic, relatively profitable but unsustainable businesses can provide the resources to develop new, more sustainable strategies and technologies as replacements. For example, in 2006 Virgin Group announced that it would invest all profits over the following three years from its transport businesses directly into new alternative fuels businesses.[15]

It is worth noting that part of the process of strategic portfolio planning involves deciding which products and markets a company should withdraw from, as well as those that it should invest in. Conventionally, the case for market withdrawal has been made on grounds of economic viability, depending on the size, growth rate and prospects of a market and the strength of the company's position in it. Sustainability concerns could also encourage a company to withdraw from a market for ethical reasons or because it is strongly linked to a social or environmental challenge.

Competitive Advantage

The conventional marketing management mindset has traditionally considered responding to sustainability issues as a potential source of competitive disadvantage, especially where there were attempts to internalize social and environmental costs that were previously treated as externalities. This mainstream view was notably challenged in 1995 with the publication in the *Harvard Business Review* of the article 'Green and competitive' by Michael Porter and Claas van der Linde.[16] They argued against the assumption that responding to stricter environmental regulation or consumer demand for more sustainable products would incur costs and threaten competitiveness. They highlighted that sustainability concerns could generate market opportunities for new technologies, for example for pollution-control equipment required by regulation, or from customer demand for greener products. They also argued that the requirement to meet tougher environmental regulation provided a spur to rethink and reengineer products and production processes from first principles. This could lead to innovative approaches and more efficient production processes through 'whole system' design, which reduces inputs of energy, water and raw materials and seeks to convert by-products from costly waste to valued inputs for other businesses.

Competitive advantage for sustainability marketers can be generated in more than one way. The most common approach is to use superior social or environmental performance as a source of differentiation that sets a business and its products apart from its competitors in some way that is valued by customers. Although some products use the term 'sustainable' as a form of differentiation, competitive advantage is usually based on a more specific sustainability dimension such as being organic, fairly traded, local, energy efficient, low carbon or carbon neutral, or 'free from' particular ingredients or influences (such as phosphates, genetic modification, CFCs, child labour or endangered species like tropical hardwoods). A distinctive sustainability brand can also provide a source of differentiation, help customers to identify, recognize and understand products in a crowded retail environment, and be invaluable in generating customer loyalty (see p. 163–169).

Another form of sustainable competitive advantage is to follow a strategy based on low costs and prices. This approach is often neglected due to the conventional business wisdom that improving social and environmental performance incurs costs. Experience has shown that sustainability marketing strategies can also reduce costs. This could come from something as simple as saving money by reducing unnecessary packaging from a product, or from the sophisticated application of a radical, clean technology approach that reduces material and energy inputs, and cuts inefficient pollution and waste.[17]

Competitive advantage can also be generated by identifying, occupying and defending a particular market niche. This strategy is popular among small and specialist companies, and the early development of sustainability markets tended to involve identification of the market niches containing the most concerned consumers, and the development of new products to meet their needs. There is, however, a danger that successful niche strategies could effectively inhibit the development of mass markets for sustainable products. This occurs when niche players 'capture' those consumers who are most aware and concerned about sustainability issues. Satisfying their needs effectively removes a source of market opportunity and dilutes pressure on companies throughout the market to improve their sustainability performance even further. In many industries it will require sustainability issues to move beyond acting as the basis for a niche marketing strategy and to become the basis of mass market strategies (or better still, a prerequisite for being able to compete successfully in the market) to create substantive progress towards sustainability.[18]

Although discussions about competitive advantage and sustainability usually focus on the potential for sustainable strategies to generate competitive advantage, the corollary is that a failure to respond to societal and consumer concerns about social and environmental issues has the potential to generate strategic disadvantage.[19]

Targeting

Beyond evaluating the attractiveness of markets in order to decide which to compete within and how, it is important to understand which segments of the market to target and how to vary the company's market offering to appeal to different segments. In an era of increasingly diverse lifestyles and consumption, relatively few companies have the resources, or a broad enough product range, to attempt traditional mass marketing.

One profound impact of conventional approaches to targeting has been to exclude consideration of those who cannot afford a product. This has naturally focused the efforts of companies and marketers on the wants of relatively affluent consumers within industrialized countries, and away from the three billion people living on less than $2 (€1.44) per day, mostly in less industrialized countries. The priority within a sustainable development perspective to spread the costs and benefits of economic activity more equitably encourages marketers not to discount the relatively poor as a potential market, but to consider whether there are alternative strategies through which it might be commercially viable to meet their needs. From this perspective the concept of 'base of the pyramid' (BoP) marketing has developed (as introduced on p. 107), which seeks to include the numerous poor at the base of the economic pyramid.[20] Despite its ethical merits, this approach has created controversy. This is because the environmental consequences of improving the material living standards of the three billion poorest consumers, without constraining the consumption of the richest, risks exacerbating environmental crises in ways that are likely to affect the global poor and their quality of life directly and disproportionately. There are also concerns that BoP strategies may encourage the poor to abandon traditional, self-reliance strategies for meeting their needs in favour of joining the commercial market. If BoP strategies emerge from major companies as a form of conventional market development strategy, seeking growth from new markets for existing technologies, the contribution to sustainability is likely to be negative. BoP strategies have the potential to make a tremendous contribution to global sustainability, but only if they form one part of an overt reconception of the relationships between human development, the meeting of needs and the role of business.[21]

Positioning

Segmentation, differentiation and targeting combine in the concept of *positioning*, which can be considered as the competitive position that a product (or a company) occupies in the market, but is more accurately about the position it occupies in the minds of consumers in comparison to its competitors. Finding a new and distinctive position in a market can be challenging for a company, and in many markets there is an opportunity to establish a position as the most credibly sustainable, ethical or greenest product. In the UK the Co-operative Bank redeveloped its marketing strategy to establish itself as the bank that is responsible with its customers' money and will not use it to finance companies associated with arms trading, major environmental damage or the disadvantage of the global poor.

The ultimate aim of a positioning strategy is to create for a sustainability business, product or brand a 'unique sustainability selling proposition' (USSP), which encapsulates what makes it different to the competition, what makes it sustainable and what makes it attractive to consumers. Ringbeck and Gross, for example, use the context of sustainable tourism marketing to explore how countries as destinations, tourism operators or airlines have the opportunity to create a USSP to meet the needs of ecologically concerned consumers. They give the example of the opportunity for an airline to create a USSP based around welcoming and responding to ecologically concerned fliers using 'something like a "Green Pass" that allows customers to check in at green counters, collect and spend green points with a "Green Frequent Flyer Program," or even use a "Green Credit Card" to pay for a carbon-neutral flight and other environmentally superior products and services. Price differentiation between the regular and the "Green Booking Class" could be realized, and new sales channels could even be opened with customer groups that usually would turn away from air travel because of its negative environmental reputation.'[22]

In many consumer goods markets there is the phenomenon of polarization, in which market growth occurs around both the budget segment and the high-quality segment of the market, at the expense of mid-market segments. Sustainability strategies based around resource efficiencies and a low-cost strategy may be able to take advantage of the growth in low-cost market segments, or alternatively strong socio-environmental quality can allow a product to be positioned as high quality. For small companies, there is often little choice but to seek out a position based around a market niche (including geographic niches serving local markets). For larger companies, it may be possible to develop multisegment strategies with a multibrand concept. Migros, the largest food retailer in Switzerland, offers two different kinds of sustainability food brands. M-Bio is positioned in the premium segment and fulfils the high quality standards of controlled, certified organic farming. M-Budget is clearly positioned in the price conscious segment, but still fulfils the firm's social-ecological minimum standards, which go beyond the legal requirements.[23]

The process of developing a position as the most sustainable within a market is not restricted to individual products or companies. In some cases whole industries have sought to establish a position as particularly sustainable or responsible. In the packaging market, for example, the glass, plastic and paper industries have all sought to establish a position as the provider of the most sustainable packaging materials according to their recyclability or energy efficiency.

Sustainability Innovations

A key source of differentiation and competitive advantage for companies is through innovation. If marketing is to contribute to a transformation to a more sustainable society, it will require innovations in technologies, products, services and business models. The necessary innovations will not all be technological, since in many markets sustainability will require 'soft' innovations in social practices, financing and business relationships. Ironically, the conventional approach to marketing research and marketing strategy formulation has been accused of stifling innovation and limiting companies to relatively incremental changes to existing technologies, products and strategies[24]. The logic behind this accusation is based on a reliance on the marketing philosophy and on ensuring that all company activities are geared around meeting customer wants and aspirations as revealed by market research. A drawback to this approach is that consumers typically cannot envisage a technology that is not on the market, or a radically different way of meeting a particular need.[25] Most consumers will articulate their wants as being offered the same products and benefits that they currently enjoy, but with any outstanding annoyances removed or the price reduced.

This process yields continuous improvements, and in many cases improvements in the sustainability performance of products to achieve greater cost and resource efficiency or in response to growing customer concerns about sustainability issues. Therefore within consumer economies we have witnessed fuel efficiency improvements in cars, increased use of recycled materials in packaging and the growth in fairly traded commodities and organic foods. However, there are concerns that such product-improvement strategies are only capable of a certain level of eco-improvement, and that in many cases the potential gains have largely already been realized. Although environmental management systems (EMS) are viewed as integral to many companies' sustainability efforts, there is an argument that they have also prevented companies from making substantive progress towards sustainability. The quality management systems approaches that underpin EMS rely strongly on continuous and incremental improvement. As such they emphasize 'maintaining the status quo' approaches to sustainable development rather than the types of radical systems innovation that will be required to change the current trajectory of our economic and technical development towards something more sustainable. Critics of EMS argue that they need to be complemented by systems and approaches that foster the exploration of alternative approaches and discontinuous change in the search for more radical, 'step-change' solutions to sustainability challenges.[26]

The need to achieve more radical approaches to sustainability innovation has been envisaged, as shown in Figure 6.1, as a series of 'waves' or types of innovation that can deliver increasing levels of eco-efficiency until a sustainable global economy can be established.[27] Each wave follows the 'S-curve' that is typical of product life cycle models, and provides diminishing eco-efficiency improvements over time, therefore needing to be superseded by a newer and more radical approach. The first wave of innovation is classic incremental marketing product improvement, which has delivered more fuel-efficient homes, less-polluting cars, more ethical food choices and opportunities for ecologically oriented vacations. The second wave involves product redesign, in which reengineering creates new types of product and production processes.[28] These first two waves have reduced environmental impacts, but often restricted to a particular market niche or in a way that has been negated by other changes (for example the fuel efficiency of car engines has improved, but this has been negated by the growth in the number of cars and in the large-car segments of the market). They have in no way transformed either production or consumption. The third wave of 'function innovation' seeks to focus on finding alternative methods of delivering the same functional benefits, for example by switching from writing letters to sending e-mails or through a product to service switch such as by sharing cars instead of owning a car. The ultimate innovation involves the innovation of an entire system of consumption and production and the broader system within which they are embedded. The development of a sustainable

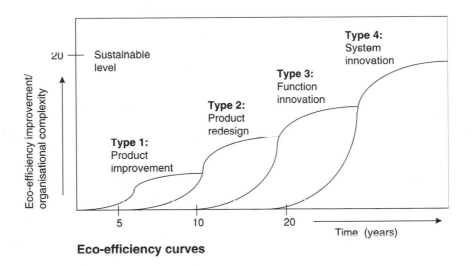

Eco-efficiency curves

Figure 6.1 Eco efficiency curve

Source: Brezet H., and van Hemel, C. (1997) Eco-Design: A Promising Approach to Sustainable Production and Consumption, United Nations Environment Programme (UNEP), Paris.

community within which sustainable transport solutions are developed would be an example of this.

The type of innovation that is required to contribute to sustainability will vary among markets and countries. Tukker's analysis of the need for, and opportunities for, more radical sustainable innovations suggested that there are significant differences between different types of economy.[29] The consumer economies of industrialized countries face political and social expectations that wealth and living standards will be at least maintained, combined with a need for a radical reduction in material resource use. Tackling this will require a targeted system innovation approach, but this is difficult because of the relatively high sunk costs (material, financial and emotional) invested in existing systems and infrastructure. There is an opportunity for the emerging and rapidly industrializing economies of the world to 'leapfrog' in their development path and move directly towards more sustainable systems of production and consumption without constructing the resource-inefficient 'dinosaur' infrastructures developed by the industrialized economies in the late twentieth century. Achieving this will require some proactive planning and investment. It will also only happen if consumer pressure to achieve an Americanized consumer lifestyle as soon as possible is resisted or redirected. For the 'base of the pyramid' economies of poorer countries, there should be more opportunity to experiment with radically different approaches to consumption and production through small-scale experiments.

Timing

Success in a market is not simply a question of making the right decisions about where and how to compete. The timing of entering and leaving a market or introducing new products or other forms of innovation is vital. In the development of new markets and market segments that reflect consumer concern about sustainability issues, there are benefits and challenges of being the first company to enter a market. Such pioneers risk entering a market in which demand will be unproven and may be based on consumers' expressed interest in more sustainable goods and services, which may differ from their actual willingness to purchase. Market pioneers also frequently face a challenge in both educating consumers and perfecting the technologies involved, and in gaining finance for an unproven technology or marketing concept. The reward for their efforts can be to establish a position in the marketplace that later market entrants may find difficult to challenge. Pioneers can build market-entry barriers by generating media coverage, consumer awareness and market share, and by having the opportunity to build relationships with consumers. Later entrants to the market may not have to worry about educating consumers or proving the case for the technologies involved, but they will face a different set of entry barriers and risks.[30]

In practice it can be difficult for successful pioneers within sustainability markets to maintain their first-mover advantage and sustain their businesses in the long term. Innovation often stems from small and nimble businesses that develop innovative products to target sustainability-oriented niches. As their technologies mature, and as market niches expand and move towards mass-market status, it can be difficult for entrepreneurial companies to maintain a leadership position. In many markets the innovative pioneers have ultimately been purchased by better-resourced major market players. The purchases of Ben & Jerry's by Unilever, The Body Shop by L'Oréal and Howies by Timberland demonstrate how hard it is for entrepreneurial brands that pioneer and grow the sustainability segment of a market to maintain that leadership position as the segment grows and moves towards the mainstream.

Sustainable Strategic Relationships

Conventional mainstream marketing strategy theory is dominated by a highly analytical approach based on the three metaphors of strategy. The emphasis on competitiveness and the dominance of the military analogy for strategy have framed strategic marketing as confrontations between individual companies, such as the battles between Coca-Cola and Pepsi, Microsoft and Apple or the 'Goliaths' of global corporations and the smaller 'Davids' among emerging greener companies. This view of strategy is not necessarily very helpful for several reasons. Some markets are composed of a myriad of small players, which makes direct confrontation relatively unusual. Many sustainability challenges confront entire industries rather than individual companies and require collective, cooperative responses rather than initiatives from individual companies pursuing competitive advantage. A single major chemical spillage will tend to create a backlash against all the companies within the industry, which encourages cooperative efforts to improve safety and sustainability.

An alternative approach to understanding sustainability marketing strategy is in terms of relationship management beyond just the relationship with consumers. Conventionally when market relationships were considered in marketing strategy it was from the perspective of power relationships and exchanges, with the actors in the market clearly distinct from one another and operating in a highly linear 'supply chain' (as exemplified by Porter's models of industry structure and the value chain[31]). Sustainability challenges often require suppliers, rivals, intermediaries and customers to work in partnership to improve social and environmental performance. The need to improve the material efficiency of our economies requires customers no longer to be the final destination of products (or the penultimate one prior to landfill), but to become the point within a supply loop from which reusable and recyclable products and materials are returned into the production system. In this way the customer also becomes a supplier of the business and a participant in the co-production of sustainable value.

Stakeholders

A central idea within management and marketing strategy is that of a 'stakeholder'. The stakeholder model (see p. 36) seeks to identify those parties in the marketing environment whose behaviour can potentially affect the interests of the company, or towards whom the company owes some form of social obligation. A stakeholder approach encourages companies to consider the relevance of parties beyond satisfying just the wants of the consumer and the financial expectations of investors (as shown by the Toyota example in Chapter 5, pp. 111–112), and it can be important in identifying strategic opportunities and threats that arise from elsewhere.[32] The drawback is that it complicates the strategy process considerably and introduces some difficult and subjective decisions about who should and should not be included as a stakeholder, and how to balance different types of stakeholders and their claims and interests in a way that is fair, ethical and sustainable.

The stakeholder concept has been important in helping marketing strategists to understand the implica tions of the sustainability agenda. Understanding the needs of consumers, meeting the expectations of investors and staying within the law were sufficient to develop strategies to ensure the short- to medium-term economic viability of a business. Developing strategies to ensure their long-term economic, social and environmental sustainability requires companies to consider the needs of a far broader range of stakeholders.[33] It also requires them to balance the needs of future generations of stakeholders against those with a current interest in the company. Internally and externally, organizations face growing interest in their eco-performance from an increasing range of interested parties.[34] Dealing effectively with these stakeholders involves understanding their perceived legitimacy and ability to affect the business, as well as how conflicting stakeholder interests can be managed and reconciled. Table 6.1 highlights a range of stakeholders and examples of socio-environmental issues that could be associated with the development, manufacture and marketing of a particular product.

One of the more radical and contentious ideas in the debate about stakeholders in relation to sustainability and marketing is whether the planet itself should be considered as a stakeholder. The argument that it should is based on the ultimate dependence of all business systems on the stability of environmental systems, and the power that environmental instability has to affect our systems of production and consumption. As Driscoll and Starik observed, 'business organizations exchange more with the natural environment than with any other stakeholder, interacting through myriad ecosystem service transactions that ultimately keep organizations alive'.[35] Others argue that because the environment does not consciously engage in any form of exchange with business, and does not intentionally try to influence businesses, it cannot be a valid stakeholder, even though there may be other stakeholders (such as environmental agencies or NGOs) that do represent its interests.

Table 6.1 Stakeholder Interest in Product Impacts

Stakeholder	Potential Issue	Indicator
Company shareholders and managers	Product safety and acceptability	Prosecutions; inclusion rate in ethical funds
Employees	Harmful processes and substances	Accident rate; time lost due to injury
Customers	Labelling	Customer satisfaction; breaches of government/industry guidelines
Business partners	Product-recall handling	Efficiency, speed and success of product recalls
Suppliers	Involvement in research and development	Results of supplier element of life cycle analysis and use of results in the design process
Competitors	Health and safety performance and effect on industry reputation	Performance against industry benchmarks and guidelines
Government and regulators	Product stewardship	Quantity of hazardous nonproduct output (NPO) returned to process or market by reuse/recycling
NGOs, pressure groups and other influencers	Product safety and socio-environmental impacts	Incidence of NGO/regulatory targeting
Communities	Harmful substances	Releases to air, land and water of NPO

Source: Adapted from WBCSD (2000) *Corporate Social Responsibility: Making Good Business Sense*, Geneva: World Business Council for Sustainable Development.

Identifying Critical Issues for Sustainability Strategies

For any company seeking to adopt a more sustainable strategy, particularly when it involves relatively radical changes in technologies, products, services and customer solutions, it is important to identify the strategically critical 'make or break' issues. In his *Journal of Marketing* paper 'Strategic marketing planning for radically new products',[36] Lee Cooper developed a useful 'critical issues grid' that takes the influences on a company's macro and micro environments and separates them between those that affect specific companies, those that affect the entire industry (viewed as a business ecosystem or value network) and those that are linked to the broader technical and social infrastructure on which the industry depends. By coincidence, one of the two products that he used to demonstrate the process of identifying critical strategic issues was the development of electric vehicles, a market sector that has become iconic in the debate about sustainability. The first analytical step involves identifying the relevant stakeholders, which for electric vehicles are set out in Table 6.2.

The second step uses the perspective and interests of each stakeholder to try to tease out potentially significant strategic influences from five macro-environmental forces (political, social, behavioural, economic and technical) as they can affect individual companies, entire industries (or business eco-systems) and the infrastructure on which they depend.

Table 6.2   Stakeholders in Electric Vehicles

Stakeholder groups	Parties	Interests
Consumers	Individual, rental, corporate fleet, public transportation	• Performance • Total cost of ownership • Convenience
Ecological	Environmental Protection Agency, Sierra Club, World Population	• Environmental protection
Petroleum	Petroleum companies, foreign governments of petroleum exporting countries	• Maintain demand for petroleum
Electric	Battery manufacturers, public utilities	• New sources of revenue • Technological gains • Efficient use of available capacity
Political	Local, national and foreign governments	• Decrease or maintain demand for petroleum (depending on perspective) • Serve constituents
Car manufacturers	World manufacturers, new ventures	• Profitable production • Servicing consumer demand

Source: Reprinted with permission from the *Journal of Marketing*, published by the American Marketing Association, Cooper, L. (2000) 'Strategic marketing planning for radically new products,' 64, 1–16.

Effective sustainability marketing strategy making involves developing a strategy that responds to consumer needs and marketplace opportunities, reflects company values and is well suited to the company's resources and capabilities. It also requires the company to consider the implications of the strategy from the perspective of its relevant stakeholders to identify the critical strategic issues that might threaten the success of its strategy and its survival. Once this process is complete, the marketer is ready to operationalize the strategy through the development of a sustainability marketing mix.

List of Key Terms

Competitive advantage
Competitors
Critical issues
Customers
Differentiation
Environmental management systems
Innovation
Low-cost strategies
Macro environment
Market niche
Marketing environment

Marketing research
Marketing strategy
Micro environment
Positioning
Publics
Relationships
Segmentation
Stakeholders
Supply chains
Targeting
Timing

REVIEW QUESTIONS

1. Which three metaphors form the basis of thinking about marketing strategy?
2. Which different types of actor make up a company's marketing environment?
3. How can marketers gather information about the internal marketing environment?
4. What are the three generic approaches to competitive advantage defined by Porter, and how can each be delivered through sustainability marketing strategies?
5. Name the four different 'waves' of innovation.

DISCUSSION QUESTIONS

1. If marketing is conventionally viewed as the satisfaction of customer needs at a profit, why does a sustainable marketing strategy require consideration of stakeholders other than customers and investors?
2. Experience suggests that competitive advantage based on superior sustainability performance is often difficult for companies to sustain in the long term. What reasons might explain this?
3. In what ways is a sustainable approach to marketing strategy requiring relationships with key stakeholders to be reconsidered?

SUSTAINABILITY MARKETING CHALLENGE: THE TESLA ROADSTER – A SHOCK TO THE CAR MARKET

If there is a 'Public Enemy Number One' in the sustainable consumption debate, the prime candidate would be the private car. It is a key contributor to greenhouse gas emissions and the depletion of oil reserves. It creates a trail of death and injury around the planet at a level that would cause daily global outrage if it was the result of the actions of a particular country. It brings benefits of safe, convenient and very personal mobility to the masses, and gets people where they want to go comfortably and quickly (provided that everyone else is not trying to go to the same place at the same time as well). However, the more our systems of retailing and urban planning are based around the assumption that most people have access to a private car, the more the proportion of the population without a car becomes disadvantaged.

The sustainability issues linked to cars concern their emissions and the contribution that CO_2 from cars makes to climate change, along with the damage done to human health by other pollutants such as carbon monoxide and low-level ozone. These concerns have led to an interest in electric cars, a concept first proposed in the late nineteenth century but swept aside by the low cost and high efficiency of cars driven by internal combustion engines. Towards the end of the twentieth century the idea resurfaced, but the failed launch of the British Sinclair C5 in 1985 suggested that the concept could never provide a serious competitor to conventional cars. With a top speed of only 15 mph (applied to avoid driving licence restrictions) and a range in cold weather of as little as 15 miles, the small, single-seater, open-to-the-elements C5 offered consumers more of an opportunity to dice with discomfort and death than to demonstrate their green credentials. Only 70 000 were sold, many to be used as buggies in closed environments such as holiday complexes or around the decks of supertankers. In the early 1990s, however, California's zero-emissions regulations kick-started efforts among the major industry players to develop an electric car, but once those regulations were watered down in the late 1990s, GM, Toyota, Honda and Ford all shut down their emerging electric vehicle programmes. The 2006 Sony movie *Who Killed the Electric Car?* seemed to signal yet another death of the electric car concept.

However, 2006 also saw the unveiling in America of a commercial electric car that was as different to the Sinclair C5 as could be imagined. The Tesla Roadster is an electric 'supercar', capable of 125 mph and doing 0–60 in under 4 seconds, offering a range of 220 miles, costing only 4 cents a mile and taking only 3.5 hours to recharge.[37] It is marketed at wealthy 'early adopters' as an environmentally conscious alternative to a Porsche or a Ferrari. Its combination of performance, aesthetics and environmental benefits gained it rapturous reviews in the media and has proved successful for the $100 000 (€73 400) price tag. By mid 2008 the company had accumulated back orders for 1200 cars without having spent any money on promotion. It certainly meets the consumer's interest identified in Cooper's analysis of performance, convenience and low cost of ownership (compared to the supercars it was competing against), and at a time when the conventional car industry is under increasing environmental, social and economic pressure, the Tesla Roadster appeared to be a sustainability innovation whose timing and market positioning were right, in just the way that the failed C5 got it all wrong.

Getting the car successfully to the market was not a simple matter, however. It was conceived by inventor and entrepreneur Martin Eberhard, but he found the financial community unwilling to back a new technology from someone without car-making experience, at a time when oil prices were still relatively low. It was PayPal founder Elon Musk who provided \$6.3 (€4.6) million in initial funding to develop the Tesla, becoming company chairman in the process. The car was unveiled as a concept in 2006 in front of celebrities like Arnold Schwarzenegger, but it was far from ready for the market. It was originally based on a Lotus Elise body, but changes from fibreglass to carbon fibre body panels and restyling of the seats and doorsills all added cost and delay to the project. A supplier able to manufacture the two-speed transmission the car needed to meet its performance potential couldn't be found, and the 2007 deadline for full production came and went. Eventually a one-speed transmission was used in initial production (with a promise to upgrade customers later once new transmissions were developed). Building the car to its list price of \$100 000 (€73 400) at a profit also proved to be a challenge, partly due to the unwieldy network of multiple suppliers that had evolved. The company moved away from using specialist suppliers for parts and instead bought from a smaller number of established vehicle parts makers, a simple step that reduced costs by \$1000 (€734) per car. During 2007 the original strategy of getting an electric supercar to the market quickly and at relatively low cost was clearly not going to happen, but such was the loyalty of the prospective customers that even a year's delay prompted only some 30 out of 1000 to ask for their deposit back.

The eventual launch timing for the Tesla in mid 2008 looked to be ideal, with the car hitting the market just when oil prices were steadily climbing and climate change fears had reached a new high. The Tesla came to market just as the major automakers were dusting off their own plans for electric cars to restart them. By that stage Tesla was already planning a second model, the \$60 000 (€44 160) Model S sedan, and thinking ahead to providing electric cars for the mass market.

By the second half of 2008 the company was gearing up to enjoy its first-mover advantage, but there were some storm clouds on the horizon. Musk and Eberhard had split acrimoniously, with the departing Eberhard writing a high-profile blog airing his grievances about the company. In the second half of 2008, as the credit crunch bit, the company, like many others, began to struggle to gain further financing. The plan for the Model S, which would require \$250–300 (€184–220) million in new capital, had to be put on hold, and the manufacturing operations were streamlined with some 80 job losses. The oil price, which had seemed to be a strategic factor so much in the company's favour in mid 2008, had plunged close to a five-year low in December, and the effects of the credit crunch were unlikely to help the long-term prospects in the supercar market. Potential competitors were also mobilizing. By 2010 the major automakers including General Motors, Toyota and Nissan all plan to launch their own electric cars. As James Hall, of automotive consulting firm 2953 Analytics, remarked, 'If the market wants [them] in the number Tesla is talking about, a larger auto company will bury them on cost.' The Tesla Roadster itself, and bringing it successfully to the market, were certainly both tremendous achievements. Whether the car could become commercially sustainable in the long term, and whether the company's vision of bringing electric cars to the mass market will prove achievable, are less certain.

Discussion Questions

1. Which actors and forces in Tesla's marketing environment have shaped the company's strategy, and what influence has each had?
2. How would you describe Tesla's positioning strategy, and what risks and benefits does its approach to positioning in the market bring?
3. What would you expect the future to hold for the company and its strategy?

Endnotes

1. Ries, A. & Trout, J. (1986) *Marketing Warfare*, London: McGraw-Hill.
2. Iansiti, M. & Levien, R. (2004) 'Strategy as ecology', *Harvard Business Review*, 82(3): 68–78.
3. See for example Smith, T.M. (1998) *The Myth of Green Marketing: Tending Our Goats on the Edge of Apocalypse*, Toronto: University of Toronto Press.
4. Fielder, A. (2006) *Choice Editing for Durability?*, London: National Consumer Council.
5. Jenkins, H. (2004) 'A critique of conventional CSR theory: An SME perspective', *Journal of General Management*, 29(4): 37–57.
6. Cartwright, R.I. (2001) *Mastering the Business Environment*, London: Palgrave Macmillan.
7. Peattie, K. (1995) *Environmental Marketing Management: Meeting the Green Challenge*, London: Pitman Publishing.
8. See Leiserowitz, A.A., Kates, R.W. & Parris, T.M. (2004) *Sustainability Values, Attitudes and Behaviours: A Review of Multi-national and Global Trends*, Center for International Development Working Paper 113, Boston, MA: Harvard University.
9. Driscoll, C. & Starik, M. (2004) 'The primordial stakeholder: Advancing the conceptual consideration of the natural environment's stakeholder status', *Journal of Business Ethics*, 49(11): 55–73.
10. Bonini, S.M.J., Hintz, G. & Mendonca, L.T. (2008) 'Confronting climate change', *McKinsey Quarterly*, 2: 52–61.
11. For details see http://www.iso.org/iso/home.htm (accessed 26 December 2008).
12. See http://www.sa-intl.org/index.cfm?fuscaction=Page.viewPage&pageID=473 (accessed 26 December 2008).
13. Wernick, I. (2003) 'Environmental knowledge management', *Journal of Industrial Ecology*, 6(20): 7–9.
14. The Boston Box model is described in detail at http://www.quickmba.com/strategy/matrix/bcg/ and http://www.themanager.org/Models/BostonBox.htm (accessed 26 December 2008).
15. Milmo, D. & Adam, D. (2006) 'Branson pledges $3 bn transport profits to fight global warming', *The Guardian*, 22 September, http://www.guardian.co.uk/environment/2006/sep/22/travelnews.frontpagenews (accessed 26 December 2008).
16. Porter, M.E. & van der Linde, C. (1995) 'Green and competitive: Ending the stalemate', *Harvard Business Review*, 73(5): 120–33.
17. Among the 181 waste-reduction projects within 29 chemical industry plants studied by Porter and van der Linde, *op. cit.*, only one led to a net cost increase and the average annual saving (on the projects where this could be meaningfully measured) was $3.49 per dollar spent.
18. Belz, F.M. (2006) 'Marketing in the 21st century', *Business Strategy and the Environment*, 15(2): 139–44.
19. Czinkota, M. & Ronkainen, I. (1992) 'Global marketing 2000: A marketing survival guide', *Marketing Management*, 1(1): 36–45.
20. Prahalad, C.K. & Hart S.L. (2002) 'The fortune at the bottom of the pyramid', *Strategy and Business*, 26: 54–67.

21. Boyer, N. (2003) *The Base of the Pyramid: Reperceiving Business from the Bottom Up*, San Francisco, CA: Global Business Network.
22. Ringbeck, J. & Gross, S. (2008) 'Environmental Sustainability as a Driver for Competitive Success', in *The Travel & Tourism Competitiveness Report 2008*, Geneva: World Economic Forum, pp. 27–40.
23. Belz, F.-M. (2008) 'Marketing in the Age of Sustainable Development', in Tukker, A., Charter, M., Vezzoli, C., Stø, E. & Andersen, M.M. (eds), *System Innovation for Sustainability: Perspectives on Radical Changes to Sustainable Consumption and Production*, Sheffield: Greenleaf Publishing.
24. Bower, J.L. & Christensen, C.M. (1995) 'Disruptive technologies: Catching the wave', *Harvard Business Review*, 73(1): 43–53.
25. Bennett, R.C. & Cooper, R.G. (1981) 'The misuse of marketing: An American tragedy', *Business Horizons*, 24(6): 51–61.
26. Könnölä, T. & Unruh, G.C. (2007) 'Really changing the course: The limitations of environmental management systems for innovation', *Business Strategy and the Environment*, 16: 525–37.
27. Brezet, H. (1997) 'Dynamics in ecodesign practice', *UNEP Industry and Environment*, 20(1/2): 21–4.
28. Porter, M.E. & van der Linde, C. (1995) 'Green and competitive: Ending the stalemate', *Harvard Business Review*, 73(5): 120–33.
29. Tukker, A. (2005) 'Leapfrogging into the future: Developing for sustainability', *International Journal of Innovation and Sustainable Development*, 1(1/2): 65–84.
30. Belz, F.-M. (2008) 'Marketing in the Age of Sustainable Development', in Tukker, A., Charter, M., Vezzoli, C., Stø, E. & Andersen, M.M. (eds), *System Innovation for Sustainability: Perspectives on Radical Changes to Sustainable Consumption and Production*, Sheffield: Greenleaf Publishing.
31. Porter, M.E. (1998) *Competitive Advantage: Creating and Sustaining Superior Performance*, New York: Free Press.
32. Polonsky, M.J. (1996) 'Stakeholder management and the stakeholder matrix: Potential strategic marketing tools', *Journal of Market Focused Management*, 1(3): 209–29.
33. Polonsky, M.J. & Ottman, J. (1998) 'Stakeholders in green product development process', *Journal of Marketing Management*, 14: 533–57.
34. Fineman, S. & Clarke, K. (2007) 'Green stakeholders: Industry interpretations and response', *Journal of Management Studies*, 33(6): 715–30.
35. Driscoll, C. & Starik, M. (2004) 'The primordial stakeholder: Advancing the conceptual consideration of the natural environment's stakeholder status', *Journal of Business Ethics*, 49(11): 55–73.
36. Cooper, L. (2000) 'Strategic marketing planning for radically new products', *Journal of Marketing*, 64: 1–16.
37. See http://www.teslamotors.com (accessed 26 December 2008); Welch, D. (2008) 'Electric carmaker Tesla downshifts', *BusinessWeek*, October 23; Copeland, M.V. (2008) 'Tesla's wild ride', *Fortune*, 9 July.

PART IV

DEVELOPING THE SUSTAINABILITY MARKETING MIX

CHAPTER 7

Customer Solutions

After Studying this Chapter You Should be Able to:

1. Define and characterize sustainable products and services.
2. Describe decisions that sustainability marketers make to provide customer solutions in purchase, use and post-use.
3. Understand the development of sustainability brands.

LOOKING AHEAD: PREVIEWING THE CONCEPTS

Now that you are familiar with the development of sustainability marketing strategies, we will take a closer look at the sustainability marketing mix: the tactical tools that marketers use to implement their strategies. In this chapter we will examine how companies provide customer solutions while taking social and ecological problems into account. To start off, we consider the automotive industry, which provides individual mobility by selling or leasing cars. The following example of Mobility CarSharing demonstrates that there are other ways of providing mobility and making money by doing so.

SUSTAINABILITY MARKETING STORY:
MOBILITY CARSHARING – SUSTAINABLE MOBILITY

Switzerland is famous for its watches, banks, chocolate and cheese. You may be surprised that this small country with its beautiful landscape and eight million inhabitants also has the largest, most successful car-sharing organization in the world. In 1997 two Swiss cooperatives, ATG Auto Teilet Schweiz and ShareCom, merged to become Mobility CarSharing. Its head office is in the city of Lucerne, employing more than 150 people.

Mobility CarSharing offers a unique mobility solution to private and business customers: car sharing and combined mobility. Customers have access to a fleet of 2000 cars at 1050 locations all over Switzerland. At locations in urban areas there is a wide range of car types and models available in ten different categories: Budget, Micro, Economy, Compact, Combi, Comfort, Convertible, Fashion, Minivan and Transport. Customers choose the most suitable car according to their needs: smaller cars for singles, mid-sized cars for families, premium cars for business people, fun and fashion cars for the weekend, and trucks for moving or transporting bulky goods. The cars can be booked by customers at any time from anywhere via phone or Internet. Registered customers hold an electronic 'Mobility card' providing easy access to the cars and their on-board computers, which are connected to the Mobility centre via a Global Positioning System (GPS) that transfers the data.

Mobility CarSharing is a well-known brand with a high recognition rate among the Swiss population. It stands for first-class quality service in car sharing and guarantees accessibility, transportation, safety, tidiness and ecological concern. In cooperation with the Swiss rail and regional public transport companies, Mobility CarSharing offers mobility cards, providing access to both car sharing and public transport. These are popular in urban areas and with commuters and are a unique solution to the mobility needs of some customer groups.

Customers pay per use; that is, per hour and kilometres driven. The prices depend on car categories. Take the Ford Fiesta in the Economy category: in this case the customer pays 2.70 Swiss Francs (€ 1.80) per hour and 0.60 Swiss Francs (€ 0.40) per kilometre. Prices seem to be high at first glance, but they reflect the total cost of driving: depreciation, tax, insurance, fuel, parking, maintenance, breakdown services and so on. Periodically, customers receive invoices with a detailed list of their trips as well as the *Mobility Journal*, which informs them about the latest news and developments in the world of Mobility. In communication the simplicity of car sharing is emphasized to reach out to new customers: 'Mobility CarSharing: Quite simple. 1. Make a reservation, 2. Get access, 3. Drive, 4. Pay.'

The growth of Mobility CarSharing has been impressive. Between 1997 and 2007 the number of car sharers almost quadrupled from 17 000 to 77 000. The potential for car sharing in Switzerland is estimated at half a million people, the equivalent of 20% of all Swiss car drivers. In 2007 Mobility CarSharing made revenues of 50 (€ 33.4) million Swiss Francs. Private customers are responsible for 80% of revenue, with commercial customers generating the remaining 20%. An increasing number of Swiss companies now outsource their fleet and fleet management to Mobility Business CarSharing in order to reduce overheads and mobility costs, save the environment and enhance their corporate image.

Almost half of the car sharers choose to become cooperative members of Mobility CarSharing. They own shares in the cooperative and reinvest most of the profits into improving and further developing car sharing. The ideas of ecology, intra- and intergenerational equity are essential for the founding members of the cooperative. As compared to private car ownership, Mobility CarSharing is more environmentally benign for a number of reasons. First, if a number of people share cars, fewer have to be produced, resulting in a smaller amount of material and energy flows. Secondly, Mobility CarSharing chooses cars with relatively low fuel consumption and CO_2 emissions. Eco-efficiency is an important criterion in supply management. Finally, empirical data shows that car sharing leads to changes in mobility behaviour. Paying per use (that is, per hour and kilometre) makes drivers aware of the total costs of driving a car. Thus, there is an economic incentive to think twice about taking a car. Often car sharers decide to walk, ride a bike or use public transport instead. By 2008 Mobility CarSharing had 80 000 customers and 2000 cars, which means that on average about 40 people share one car. This is a kind of mobility pattern that can be replicated on a global scale.[1]

Marketing Myopia

The nineteenth century was the great era of railroads. They connected cities, regions and countries. At that time no other form of transportation could compete with the railroads for speed, durability and economy. The advent of automobiles and airplanes led to a gradual decline of railroads in the twentieth century, however. Many railroad tycoons and companies went bankrupt. They suffered from 'marketing myopia', a preoccupation with products (or rather services) instead of customer solutions.[2] They defined their business in terms of railroads instead of transportation and providing mobility. They made the mistake of paying more attention to a specific technology than to the benefits it provided for the customer. The classic concept of the marketing mix consisting of the 'four Ps' enhances this kind of thinking. It takes the company's point of view and tends to focus on products and purchases.

In this chapter we change perspective: we take the customer's viewpoint and present solutions to problems that occur in the entire consumption process from the purchase of products or services to their use and post-use.[3] The challenge for sustainability marketers is to solve the direct problems of consumers' everyday living and their needs, while also improving social and environmental performance. We know from empirical research that most consumers want to be provided with more socially and environmentally responsible goods and services, but we also know that they are generally unwilling to compromise in terms of cost, performance and convenience of those goods and services. This is the conundrum that sustainability marketers have to solve to remain competitive.

Customer (Pre-)Purchase Solutions

When customers seek to satisfy a need, the solution might be provided by material products or immaterial services. Sustainable products and services offer solutions to customer problems as well as to socio-ecological problems. We define sustainable products and services as offerings that satisfy customer needs and significantly improve the social and environmental performance along the whole life cycle in comparison to conventional or competing offers.[4] This definition has the following six characteristics:

1. *Customer satisfaction*: if sustainable products and sustainable services do not satisfy customer needs, they will not survive in the market in the long run.
2. *Dual focus*: unlike purely environmental products, sustainable products have a dual focus on ecological and social aspects.
3. *Life-cycle orientation*: sustainable products have to consider the whole life cycle from cradle to grave: extraction of raw materials, transportation, manufacturing, distribution, use and post-use.
4. *Significant improvements*: Sustainable products and services have to make a worthwhile contribution to tackling socio-ecological problems on a global level (macro level); or provide measurable improvements in socio-ecological product performance as indicated by life cycle assessment; (see Chapter 3).[5]
5. *Continuous improvement*: Sustainable products and services are not absolute measures, but are dependent on the state of knowledge, the latest technologies and societal aspirations, which change over time. A product or service that meets customer needs and has an extraordinary social and environmental performance today may be considered standard tomorrow. Thus, sustainable products and services have to be continuously improved regarding customer, social and environmental performance.
6. *Competing offers*: a product or service that satisfies customer needs and provides environmental and social improvements may still lag behind competing offers. Thus, the offerings of competitors are yardsticks for improvements with regard to customer, social and environmental performance.

In addition to price, function, performance, aesthetics and design, an increasing number of customers want to know the 'world behind the product', how it was produced and processed. They care about the natural environment and the human beings involved in the production process. Consequently, they want to buy products that are produced and processed in a socially and environmentally benign way. Some examples of sustainable offerings include organic food products, MSC-labelled fish, FSC-labelled products and Fair Trade products:

- *Organic food products* have enjoyed high growth rates in many industrialized countries since the 1990s. They are produced according to the principles of organic farming, which seeks to work compatibly with natural cycles and processes in soil, plants and animals. Neither chemical fertilizers and pesticides nor genetically modified organisms (GMO) are allowed in organic farming. In times of food scandals and the advent of genetic engineering, organic food products offer security. Generally, consumers consider organic food products as natural and healthy. Furthermore, organic food products offer an authentic instead of artificial taste.

- *MSC-labelled fish*. The Marine Stewardship Council (MSC) is an international not-for-profit organization that was set up in 1997 to promote solutions to the problem of overfishing.[6] The MSC runs the widely recognized sustainable certification and labelling programme for wild capture fisheries, which is consistent with the guidelines of the Food and Agriculture Organization of the United Nations. MSC-labelled fish offers customers a good 'environmental conscience'. The purchase of MSC-labelled fish is a small contribution to fighting the problem of overfishing and the extinction of endangered species.
- *FSC-labelled products*. The Forest Stewardship Council (FSC) promotes forest management that is environmentally appropriate, socially beneficial and economically viable.[7] It ensures that the harvest of timber and nontimber products maintains the forest's biodiversity, productivity and ecological processes. The higher the demand for FSC-labelled products, the higher are the incentives for local people to sustain the forests (including rainforests), which absorb CO_2 and help fight the problem of climate change. The establishment of MSC and FSC shows that there is a growing interest in treating ecosystem goods and services not as free common goods, but as assets with a market value in order to provide incentives for their conservation.
- *Fair Trade products*. As defined above, sustainable products have a dual focus on ecological and social aspects. Products that are environmentally benign but neglect the social aspects of their production in developing countries cannot claim to be sustainable. Ethically traded products support internationally recognized standards and conventions, particularly those of the International Labour Organization (ILO), which seeks to eliminate all forms of forced or compulsory labour, abolish child labour and guarantee the right to form and join workers' associations. Moreover, Fair Trade products emphasize the idea of partnership between trade partners, by ensuring minimum prices for producers to allow them to make a living and providing an additional Fair Trade premium that can be invested in projects that enhance social, ecological and economic development. Both food and nonfood products like cotton textiles, cut flowers and sports balls are certified according to the international Fair Trade organization Transfair. These kinds of products offer customers a good 'social conscience'.

The world behind the product does not only involve the extraction of raw materials and the production of pre-products, but also the processing of the final product offered to customers. Processing companies whose operations are wasteful of resources, highly polluting or involve the exploitation of workers are ill advised to offer 'sustainable' products to the market, even if an aspect of the product's use or raw material sourcing is particularly sustainable. Sooner or later this strategy will backfire and the credibility of the company may be lost instantly and forever. Environmentally and socially responsible manufacturing is the foundation of credible sustainability marketing strategies for tangible products.

Cleaner production is an approach that minimizes emissions and waste. It involves analysing material and energy flows to pinpoint ways to improve the resource and energy efficiency of operational processes. The ultimate aim is to reach zero emissions and avoid negative impacts on the natural environment. The linear manufacturing systems of industrialized economies are highly inefficient in the amount of natural resource that is wasted compared to natural production systems, which make full utilization of resources and are more circular in nature. Elements of cleaner production include establishing cycles to reuse water, recover heat, reuse waste (internally or externally) and switch from nonrenewable to renewable energy. Solar Roast Coffee is a small company that switched totally to renewable energy. In

2004 the founders invented the first solar coffee roaster Helios 1, named after the Greek sun god Helios, which also appears in the company logo.[8] Solar Roast Coffee supplies Fair Trade coffee from organic farming and roasts it in a carbon-neutral way. The sustainable coffee with a 'sun in your cup' can be consumed in the company-owned café in Pueblo, Colorado, or ordered online. Thus, the company offers high quality by all means: taste, convenience, social and environmental aspects.

Cleaner production is a key element of ISO 14000, an international environmental management standard. ISO 14001 specifies the requirements for establishing an environmental policy, determining environmental aspects and impacts, planning environmental objectives and measurable targets, implementing programmes to meet these objectives and targets, checking and corrective action. The overall idea of ISO 14000 is to establish a systematic approach to reduce the environmental impact of an organization and its operations. In 2008 more than 14 000 companies were certified according to ISO 14000, most of them coming from Japan, Germany and the UK.

ISO 14000 focuses entirely on the environmental dimension of management. It does not cover the social dimensions, which are also quite important in the context of sustainability marketing. Chocolate from organic farming does not taste so sweet if consumers discover that child or forced labour is involved. Textiles without chemicals are not cool if the working conditions in developing countries are unacceptable. Thus, environmental and social dimensions go together in sustainability marketing. SA 8000 is an international social accountability standard for decent working conditions.[9] It covers the following areas of accountability: child labour, forced labour, workplace safety and health, freedom of association and right to collective bargaining, discrimination, working hours, remuneration and management systems for human resources. In 2008 there were about 1700 facilities certified according to SA 8000, most of them in apparel and textiles, agriculture and construction. The countries with the most certifications are Brazil, India and China.

Neither ISO 14000 nor SA 8000 is a product certification or product guarantee. Both refer to the activities on site. That is why the two standards may be suitable for corporate communications, but less so for product communications. Consumers are usually unaware whether a company is certified according to ISO 14000 and/or SA 8000. Nevertheless, there is an indirect effect that consumers profit from: some retailers request such standards from their suppliers. In these cases they become a pre-requisite for doing business.

Environmental and social management standards are not restricted to manufacturing companies. Both ISO 14000 and SA 8000 also apply to service providers. In a lot of service industries such as tourism, hospitality, cleaning or call centres, there are some important issues in terms of working hours and conditions and ensuring the physical health, safety and welfare of staff. The social well-being of the workforce and the integration of mentally and physically challenged people in the workplace are founding principles of the German retailer CAP.[10] In 2008 there were more than 60 CAP markets in villages in Germany, offering a full assortment of food and nonfood products. In addition, CAP offers delivery services for its customers. Obviously, CAP fills a gap in the market: large retailers tend to locate their stores in larger towns and cities, neglecting rural areas and elderly people who do not have a car.

Customer Use Solutions

When customers use products, they expect them to be safe. Despite safety regulations and health, safety and environmental testing by consumer organizations, there has been a series of scandals relating to product safety. Food with residuals of pesticides, plastic toys for children with traces of toxins and cellphone batteries catching fire are reported in the media and often alarm consumers. There are a number of reasons for these kinds of incidents, including international supply chains with a minimum of control, price competition and the necessity for cutting costs.

Offering *safe and healthy products* is a vital part of customer use solutions. For some, it is literally a question of life and death. More than 2.5 billion people around the world prepare food on open fires. The emissions of those fires contain hazardous concentrations of carcinogenic substances. The World Health Organization estimates that 1.6 million people die each year from that indoor air pollution. Philips co-created two wood-burning stoves in India, 'Saral' (basic) and 'Sampoorna' (complete), as low-cost, locally produced solutions that are able to reduce indoor pollution and are convenient (i.e. easy to distribute, access, install, use and maintain). The stoves were designed together with users and NGOs according to sustainable criteria (longevity, dematerialization, efficient and clean energy, cultural diversity and sharing).[11] Similarly, Bosch Siemens Home Appliances (BSH) explored ways to enter the market at the base of the pyramid (BoP). The company developed and tested a plant oil stove in developing countries to improve health and safety and fight deforestation.[12] The major challenge for the two multinationals is to turn the CSR design project into a business case; that is, to market the sustainable stoves successfully to make profits and elevate the quality of life of people in developing countries.

From an ecological point of view, the use stage is often the most critical for many durable products, as shown by life cycle analyses. This is the case for products that rely on energy or water in the usage stage, such as washing machines, refrigerators and cars. When petrol and energy prices are relatively low, energy efficiency becomes a low priority for most consumers when purchasing. Other criteria such as power, design, status and prestige are far more important then. A typical example of this kind of purchasing behaviour lies in sport utility vehicles (SUVs), which consume high quantities of fuel per kilometre as compared to conventional cars. At the turn of the twenty-first century about half of the cars sold in the United States were SUVs. Although not ecological at all, this segment was highly profitable at the time. However, times have changed and American car companies are not well prepared for the future. Between 2002 and 2008 the oil price rose from $20 (€ 14.44) per barrel to more than $100 (€ 72.18) per barrel, leading to a significant shift in consumer behaviour. Most consumers are more energy sensitive than ever before. As petrol prices rise, *energy efficiency* becomes more important. In 2008 there emerged a higher demand for smaller cars in the American and western European markets, which seems unlikely to diminish even though energy prices tumbled in the latter part of the year. The financial hardships caused by the global credit crunch ensured that fuel economy remained important to consumers. The sales of sport utility vehicles in 2008 almost dropped by half compared to the previous year. Thus, a key strategy to meet consumer expectations and environmental criteria during usage is to offer highly resource-efficient products.

The increase in oil and energy prices since 2002 has led to a growing interest in and demand for products such as hybrid cars, energy-efficient houses and energy-efficient appliances. Compared to other cars in its class, the Toyota Prius needs about half of the fuel per kilometre and emits much less CO_2.[13] The inherent consumer benefits are cost savings in the usage stage. Bundled consumer benefits are the design of the car, the power, the fun of driving and its status in society (see Chapter 2). In the market for new homes, energy efficiency is also becoming the name of the game. On average, around 70–80% of the energy used in households is for heating. The better the insulation of a dwelling, the lower the energy consumption will be, leading to greater comfort and significant cost savings. The rest of the energy used in households is for lighting and appliances such as washing machines, refrigerators, ovens and dishwashers.

Since 2000 Electrolux has offered refrigerators in China that only consume 0.38 kWh per day, matching the top European appliances listed by energy. That is about half the energy used by refrigerators ten years ago. The inherent consumer benefit of the energy-efficient refrigerator is saving money, which appeals to cost-conscious consumers. High energy efficiency is part of a bundle of benefits marketed as 'perfection in form and function'. The refrigerator has a very aesthetically pleasing design and keeps the food fresh for a long period due to an optimized cooling system.

Besides energy efficiency, the *durability* of products during the usage stage is important from an environmental viewpoint. Until the middle of the twentieth century consumer durables were regarded as investments and were designed to last as long as possible. Since then, however, planned obsolescence, which attempts to deliberately shorten a product's life span, has become commonplace.[14] There are three forms of planned obsolescence: built-in, psychological and technological. Some manufacturers build products with an intentionally limited life (built-in obsolescence). A number of appliances, particularly small items, do not last as long as in the past. Manufacturers also promote new products as fancy and fashionable, making previous products and models seemingly outdated (psychological obsolescence). This is common in the fashion industry and is also becoming more important in other consumer goods industries due to shorter development cycles. We once bought sofas, curtains and other furnishings and kept them until they wore out. They have now become items that consumers are encouraged to change regularly as interior design fashions change. Another form of obsolescence is the rapid and continuous upgrade of products like computers, home entertainment products and mobile phones (technological obsolescence). Planned obsolescence generates substitution purchases and revenues for companies. It is driven by a need for cost reductions in order to meet 'price points', fierce competition, the convenience of disposability and the appeal of fashion.[15] Planned obsolescence leads to a shorter lifetime for products and a high material throughput. It is part of the take-make-waste rationale commonplace in consumer societies at the beginning of the twenty-first century.

Extension of the product life is the antithesis of planned obsolescence.[16] The offer of long-lasting products and complementary product-related services for the right use, maintenance and repair is another approach to more sustainable customer use solutions. Some 'classic' high-quality products like hand-made shoes and furniture are still designed to last as long as possible. If products last ten years instead of five, resource productivity increases by a factor of two. Von Weizsäcker and his colleagues argue that 'durability is one of the most obvious strategies for reducing waste and increasing material productivity'.[17]

A good example of the strategy of durability is the modular furniture by USM Haller, which is manufactured in Switzerland and installed in offices as well as private homes around the world. Its durability is the result of three factors: the high quality of the materials, the versatility of the system and the timelessness of the design.[18] The supporting structure and outer elements of this modular furniture are made of steel, guaranteeing long-term sturdiness and stability. In the finish of the production process the elements are powder-coated in wear-resistant, nonfading colours. The modular furniture is constructed in such a way that it can easily be adapted to the changing needs of its users. The basic principles of USM Haller furniture are the open system and modular assembly. The design is inspired by the motto 'form follows function'. It represents simple solutions and refrains from following fashionable trends. Even USM furniture built more than a quarter of a century ago is still used today, because it is timeless and can easily be adapted. The classic design status was confirmed by its inclusion in the famous Museum of Modern Art (MoMA) in New York in 2001. USM Haller customers benefit from the functional design, the pleasing aesthetics and the long durability, which also saves money in the long run.

Product-related services are offered in addition to tangible products as part of a sustainable solution. This kind of service helps customers to optimize the application of the product sold. It includes training, consulting, maintenance and disposal services. Product-related services may add both customer value and ecological value. Take automobile companies offering courses on how to drive in a safe and ecological way. By driving responsibly, consumers can increase the eco-efficiency of cars during the usage stage and reduce their fuel consumption by more than 20%. Another example is repair services for washing machines, textiles or shoes. Such a product-service system is contrary to 'take-make-waste' thinking, which assumes indefinite supplies of resources and infinite sinks in which to dump waste.[19]

Another type of service is use-related. In this case, instead of selling the product itself the service provider sells the use of the product. The chapter-opening sustainability marketing story is a good example of such a service. The members of the Swiss car-sharing organization have the right to use available Mobility cars any time they want, but they do not own them. The ownership of the car pool stays with the cooperative, which takes care of it. The sharing of products and multiple product use have great environmental potential: if more cars are shared, fewer need to be produced and the environmental impact related to the extraction of resources and manufacturing is reduced. Additionally, we see that participation in car sharing influences mobility behaviour patterns, which become more flexible and less dependent on cars. This encourages consumers to make use of transport modes with a lower environmental impact such as public transport, riding a bike or going on foot.

Theoretically, *use-oriented services* can be applied to almost any kind of product category except for nondurable consumer goods such as food. Consumers do not really need to own cars, gardening tools, electric drills, hairdryers or coffee machines in order to make use of them. In practice, however, this business model has limitations. Often consumers do want to own and possess products. They take pride in the ownership of products to impress friends, neighbours and colleagues. Products are part of their self-identity and how they express themselves (see Chapter 4). Think about cars: in consumer societies this kind of product goes far beyond the basic function of taking us from A to B; it has a high degree of symbolic meaning. The same is true for 'cool' electronic devices like the iPod or the iPhone. In addition to the symbolic meaning of products and the pride of ownership, sharing of products implies higher transaction costs; that is, booking the product, picking it up and returning it after use.

A German study shows that the willingness to share is fairly high for washing machines, gardening equipment for special events, cars, electric drills and gardening tools (Figure 7.1). In contrast, the willingness to share is rather low for children's toys, children's furniture, toolboxes, dishes for special events, kitchens and grills. What do we learn from this study? Which kinds of products are suitable for sharing and which are obviously not? Generally, we can say that products that are expensive to buy and seldom used are most appropriate for sharing. Standardized products like books or DVDs are also suitable for sharing. If use-related services for these types of product are readily available, easy to access and use, then they are an alternative to conventional product sales.

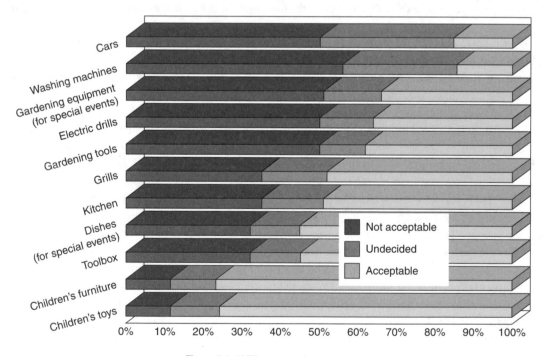

Figure 7.1 Willingness to share products

Source: Based on Schrader, U. (1998) *Empirische Einsichten in die Konsumentenakzeptanzöko-effizienter Dienstleistungen,* Research Paper No. 42, Hannover: University of Hannover, Chair for Marketing and Consumption.

Yet another type of service is result-related. Similar to the previous type, the provider does not sell the product any more. In the case of result-oriented services the buyer neither owns nor uses the product. They enjoy the 'fruits' of the product, the final result. Take a textile care centre, which cleans your clothes and irons them. You neither own nor use the washing and cleaning equipment, you simply get the result of the service. Another common example of *result-related services* is public transport, which represents a multibillion-dollar business. Passengers of trains, subways, trams and buses neither own nor operate the means of transportation. They are transported from one place to another in an environmentally efficient way.

The different types of service and the various combinations of products and services help marketers to focus on customer solutions instead of specific products. They open up the minds of marketers and enable creative, out-of-the-box thinking. Are washing machine producers bound to sell washing machines or can they provide the service of clean clothes in a profitable and environmental way? Are automotive companies limited to selling cars or should they also offer eco-efficient mobility services? What is the future business of computer and software companies in a connected world? Some visionaries already predict the end of conventional hardware and software as we inherited it from the 1990s. They wonder why we need bulky computers with software and data if we can get the same ability to process information via the Internet almost anywhere and at any time? Customers want solutions to their everyday needs: they want to write e-mails, communicate with friends, collect pictures, see a movie and so on. These kinds of services can be provided by small multimedia devices connected to the Internet using online software and storing data in the 'cloud'. Eventually, this kind of thinking may transform the computer hardware and software business. Difficult to imagine? Just think about answering machines from the end of the twentieth century, which were substituted by comboxes, a result-oriented service offered by telecommunication companies.

Customer Post-Use Solutions

When customers want to get rid of a product permanently, they have a number of options: they can give it away, trade it, sell it or dispose of it. The German telecommunication company T-Mobile asks its customers to give back their used mobile phones for charity. The collected mobile phones are tested and, if possible, repaired and reused. Thus, the product life of two thirds of those mobile phones is prolonged. The rest of them, which are no longer viable, are recycled and disposed of in an environmentally sound manner. For each mobile phone given back by customers, T-Mobile gives a donation to the Deutsche Umwelthilfe (German Environmental Fund), which endorses natural and environmental projects.[20]

In the past it was difficult to trade or sell used products due to high transaction costs. Now, online marketplaces like eBay create transparency in secondary consumer markets and lower transaction costs. They enable consumers to sell their used products easily. Thus, the original purchaser can recoup some of the money paid for the product. Furthermore, the lifetime of the product is extended.

Most products are disposed of after use. To make sure that used products are recycled in an environmentally friendly way, it is vital for companies and whole industries to establish retro-distribution schemes that are convenient for customers.[21] In consumer societies a lot of products are treated as disposables. They are used for a short period and then discarded. In the United States over 90% of products bought are thrown away after less than two months. Companies enhance this consumer behaviour by planned obsolescence and promotion of new products proclaiming that 'new' is 'better'. During the latter part of the twentieth century, 'disposable' was marketed as a consumer benefit on formerly durable products such as razors, nappies and cameras. The 'take-make-waste' rationale of the consumer society results in high material throughputs, which is a burden on both sources and sinks.

Holistic Systems Approaches to Providing Customer Solutions

As raw materials and landfills become scarcer due to the rising world population and higher demand, the take-make-waste rationale will slowly be substituted by a *cradle-to-cradle approach*, which is oriented towards a circular economy instead of a linear throughput economy (see Figure 7.2). There are both legal requirements and economic incentives for companies to adopt a closed-loop approach: landfill disposal bans for highly toxic products (e.g. batteries, electronics), rising disposal costs, increasing costs of raw materials and energy as well as extended product responsibility laws will encourage companies to think in cycles.[22] Product takeback programmes become an alternative to landfill.

The redistribution, remanufacturing and reuse of products begin with their design. One of the guiding principles of design for the environment (DFE) is to create products that are easy to disassemble at the end of their life cycle. Otherwise, the cradle-to-cradle approach becomes too costly and not worth the effort. The redistribution of products also requires new infrastructure. The consumer craves convenience and needs incentives to return used products.[23] A growing number of companies start by designing their products for recycling, repair, remanufacturing and reuse. Herman Miller, one of the world's largest office

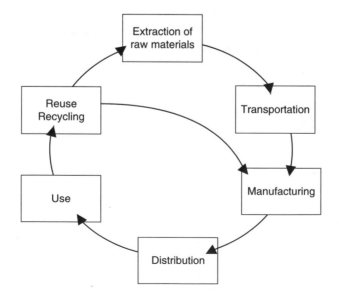

Figure 7.2 Cradle-to-cradle approach

furniture makers, created the Avian chair, which is designed for the lowest possible ecological impact and 100% recyclability.[24] This sustainability product won several awards for design and function, as well as environmental responsibility. Product takeback programmes help in building long-term relationships with customers, as the point of return provides an opportunity to offer new, sustainable solutions to customers.

Another complementary strategy of the cradle-to-cradle approach is to design products and use materials that are in harmony with natural cycles and systems. Houses, furniture and toys made of timber are in line with the natural environment. However, most products around us contain at least some plastic parts from nonrenewable resources: the chair you sit on, the basketball you play with, the plastic bottle you drink from, the cellphone you communicate with, the iPod you listen to and the laptop you use. All of these products are based on polymers made of fossil resources. As oil becomes scarcer and as climate change continues, there is a need for sustainability marketers to think of alternatives. Bioplastics that stem from renewable resources such as corn or potato crops are such an alternative. Bioplastic packaging for food and nonfood products has already entered some market niches. Take the plastic shopping bags from Natura Packaging, which are made of renewable resources and are fully biodegradable. To emphasize the strength and reliability of the bag, the company claims that the product 'can take a punch'.[25] To make consumers happy, the bags come in a refreshingly colourful design. The prices for most bioplastics are still higher than conventional ones. However, in contrast to plastic from fossil resources, prices of bio-based polymers tend to fall due to new technological developments, new production capacities and economies of scale. Eventually they will become competitive, even in highly price-sensitive markets.

Sustainability Branding

Sustainability brands are products and services that are branded to signify to the consumer a form of special added value in terms of environmental and social benefits. A brand is a name, term, sign, symbol or design that identifies the maker or seller of a product or service (although some argue that brands are something that real companies hide behind). However, a brand is also much more than that. It represents consumers' perceptions about a product and its performance.[26] It evokes positive or negative feelings, especially in the context of sensitive social and ecological issues. The more positive the perceptions and feelings are towards a brand, the higher will be the likelihood of identification and loyalty among consumers. It is therefore crucial in sustainability marketing to build up strong brands. To create and build sustainable brands that consumers associate with social and environmental added value, challenging decisions have to be made involving sustainability brand positioning, sustainability brand name selection and sustainability brand development.

Sustainability Brand Positioning

Sustainable products and services have to satisfy consumer needs and offer improved social-ecological performance. The first generation of sustainable products and services overemphasized the latter at the expense of the former. This kind of 'alternative' product served a cause, but not the customer. They were made to do good for people and save the planet. There are numerous examples of the first generation of sustainable products and services, including:

- Fair Trade coffee with a bitter taste
- natural detergents that did not wash the laundry properly
- textiles with fading colours
- energy-efficient light bulbs with clumsy shape and poor light
- electric cars that did not go fast or far
- car-sharing services that were unreliable

Obviously, these kinds of products and services were inferior to competing market offers. Some of them ended up in the 'green' graveyard. Others served a very small group of dedicated customers, living alternative lifestyles and emphasizing social and environmental issues. Certainly, these alternative products and services do not appeal to a broader market segment. If marketers overemphasize socio-ecological attributes at the expense of core benefits, sustainable products are likely to fail in the market or remain trapped in small alternative niches. The myopic focus on socio-ecological attributes over the broader expectations of consumers is termed *'sustainability marketing myopia'*.[27] For most customers, socio-ecological attributes are not core benefits. Usually, they are of secondary importance and play an auxiliary role.[28]

In general terms, there are two possible ways to avoid sustainability marketing myopia and broaden the appeal of sustainable products and services: identifying and emphasizing the inherent consumer value of socio-ecological attributes, including efficiency and cost effectiveness, health and safety, convenience, symbolism and status;[29] and aligning socio-ecological attributes with core benefits such as functionality, design and durability to create motive alliances.

Inherent Consumer Benefits

In times of rising fuel and energy prices, the resource efficiency of products in the usage phase becomes an important buying criterion for cost-conscious consumers. The inherent consumer benefit of resource efficiency is *cost effectiveness*. To put it simply, saving fuel and energy means saving money, even if energy-efficient products have a higher purchase price than conventional products. In the medium term the higher price for the purchase of energy-efficient products is overcompensated for by cost savings in the usage phase. As fuel and energy prices go up, consumers start considering life-cycle costs, which include purchasing prices, usage costs and post-usage costs. In the European Union this kind of life-cycle thinking is enhanced by means of obligatory labels, which categorize products like washing machines, dishwashers, refrigerators and light bulbs into five different classes. Products with the highest energy efficiency are awarded an 'A' label, whereas products with the lowest energy efficiency receive just an 'E' label. These labels make it easy for consumers to identify the products that are the best in their category in terms of energy efficiency and financial savings. Products performing well and also offering energy efficiency are destined for market growth. An example is Tide Coldwater, introduced to the North American laundry market by Procter & Gamble in 2006. The new product is designed to clean clothes effectively in cold water. Most of the energy used to wash clothes comes from heating water. Thus, using cold instead of warm water saves a lot of energy and some money. P&G calculates that on average an American household can save more than $60 (€ 43.30) annually using Tide Coldwater instead of competing offers.[30]

Concerns over exposure to toxic chemicals in everyday products make *health and safety* important choice considerations, especially among vulnerable consumers like pregnant women and children. For example, Hipp offers baby food from organic farming that is 100% residual free. The good quality of the baby food and the credible promise personally given by the owner of the company convince sensitized parents who want the best for their baby.[31] A number of empirical studies show that organic food products are not primarily bought for environmental reasons. Most consumers buy organic food products because they think they are healthier or because of their superior taste. In other words, inherent personal benefits make consumers buy organic food products, not so much environmental benefits, which are auxiliary. The same holds true for household cleaners. A joint study conducted by the Alliance for Environmental Innovation and SC Johnson comes to the conclusion that consumers are most likely to act on sustainability messages that are associated with their personal environments: household product benefits such as 'not toxic ingredients' and 'safe to use around children' are preferred to 'not tested on animals' or 'packaging can be recycled'.[32] Consequently, the main claim of the brand Seventh Generation, a nontoxic and environmentally safe household product, is 'Safer for You and the Environment'. In the claim the inherent personal benefit is placed first, whereas the environmental benefits come second.

In addition to efficiency and cost effectiveness, health and safety, *convenience* is another inherent consumer benefit that a number of sustainable products and services have to offer and that can be highlighted by marketers. Fuel-efficient cars require fewer refuelling stops, saving time and money. Energy-efficient light bulbs last much longer than conventional bulbs, saving the hassle of replacement. With society's increasing mobility and reliance on electronics, solar power is convenient on the go. The Juice Bag by Reware is a popular recharger for students, professionals and outdoor enthusiasts. It has a flexible, waterproof solar panel that has the capacity to recharge PDAs, cellphones, iPods and other gadgets in about two to four hours.[33] The increasing mobility of society is also one of the drivers for new packaging in the worldwide soft drink market. Refillable plastic bottles fulfil the need for convenience much better than glass bottles do. Plastic bottles are quite light and unbreakable, which is ideal for consumers on the move.[34]

The first generation of sustainable products and services attracted consumer groups who were generally perceived as outsiders by the rest of society. 'Alternative' consumers were not recognized as innovators by the mainstream. Product innovations like the Toyota Prius changed that image. Toyota managed to position the hybrid synergy drive system beyond the niche of 'techies' who are interested in the latest innovation. Through clever advertising, product placements in popular films and the endorsement of Hollywood celebrities, the Toyota Prius turned into a *status symbol* that is 'cool' and 'chic'.

The latest sustainability fashion is also far removed from combats and jute bags. Leading sustainability fashion brands include People Tree, Ciel, Edun, Ali Hewson and Noir. The target group is not the niche of consumers who are willing to make big sacrifices for environmental or social causes. Ciel's designer Sarah Ratty says, 'Our clothes are for cosmopolitan, busy, fashionable people who care about the planet, but don't want to sacrifice in style.'[35] The clothing label Noir represents the new face of sustainability fashion. Set up in 2005 by the Danish designer Peter Ingwersen, Noir wants to appeal to 25-plus women who combine a love of luxury with a social conscience. Noir is working in Uganda to provide trade rather than aid. The cotton industry in Uganda is on the brink of collapse. Ingwersen made a deal that has him paying above industry prices for the country's finest cotton, which will be woven into fabrics for Noir and also sold to other luxury fashion brands. The elegant and yet sexy style of Noir gives the chance for meaningful consumption.

Motive Alliances

Identifying and highlighting the inherent consumer benefits of socio-ecological attributes is one way of broadening the appeal of sustainable products and services. Another viable option is to align socio-ecological attributes with core benefits and main buying criteria such as functionality, performance, design, durability, taste, freshness and so on to create *motive alliances*.[36] The growth of organic food products in western European and North American markets has been based on transcending the relatively small segment of the market that would be attracted by the main inherent consumer benefit of healthier and safer food. One of the main reasons for the mainstreaming of organic – and partly Fair Trade – food products is the bundling of socio-ecological attributes with those core benefits. Leading organic groceries like Whole Foods Market as well as conventional retail chains present a wide range of organic food products that are fresh and delicious. Furthermore, they offer convenience goods of organic food quality such as readymade salads and meals.

In the case of low-energy houses, motive alliances are very important too. The inherent consumer benefits of energy-efficient houses are cost savings during the usage stage due to low consumption of heating fuel. However, even in times of soaring energy prices, that is not enough to appeal to a broader spectrum of customers if the comfort or design of the house is compromised. Pioneering planning and construction companies have learnt the hard way what counts most for private housebuilders. The main criteria for building and buying a house include location, layout, design and comfort. Since planning and construction companies began offering energy-efficient houses that fulfil these kinds of criterion, their market share has risen.

The chapter-opening sustainability marketing story shows that car-sharing and combined mobility services are successful if coupled with the convenience of easy access as well as the flexibility of booking any kind of car according to specific needs in different situations (e.g. a business trip with two people or a family outing with parents and three children). Furthermore, car sharing frees customers from the duties of owning a car: taking care of parking, insurance, tax, maintenance and so on.

Positioning sustainability brands is problematic because there is a temptation to overemphasize socio-ecological attributes at the expense of core benefits in an attempt to be distinctive. That is why the first generation of sustainable products and services from the 1980s and early 1990s failed or stayed in small niches. The later generation of sustainable products and services has been more successful in appealing to different, larger consumer groups. Learning from past experiences and mixed results, successful companies now emphasize the inherent consumer benefits of socio-ecological attributes and seek to create effective motive alliances. They connect the personal benefits of customers with the relevant sustainability issues at hand. Thus, they appeal to different consumer segments by enhancing sustainable products and services. There is also a particular positioning challenge for those companies that try to manage sustainable and conventional brands to appeal to different segments of a market. It can be very difficult to emphasize the social and environmental benefits of sustainable products without highlighting the social and environmental shortcomings of conventional brands.

Sustainability Brand Name Selection

The name of a sustainability brand can be an important factor in its success and choosing the right name is a difficult task. The name should suggest something about the brand's qualities and benefits. For example, Mobility CarSharing underlines that the Swiss company offers more than just car sharing; it provides unique solutions to the mobility needs of private and commercial customers. Prius means 'the way forward' or 'the next step', which refers to the new technology of the hybrid synergy system, which goes beyond the old technology of the petrol motor. It is not the ultimate but the next step towards sustainable mobility. Seventh Generation is a brand of nontoxic and environmentally safe household products. It derived its name from the Iroquois belief that in our deliberation, we must consider the impact of our decisions on the next seven generations. Furthermore, sustainability brand names should be easy to remember and pronounce, distinctive, extendable to other product categories, easy to translate into foreign languages and capable of registration and legal protection.[37]

One problem for sustainability marketers trying to break a new product into the market is that they may face a phalanx of well-established household brands backed by heavy promotional investment. It can be easier for a familiar and trusted brand to realign itself as social and ecological than for a new sustainability brand to gain consumer trust.[38] Starbucks embraced sustainability issues and added them to its brand. It is ideal for newcomers if they manage to establish a new playing field. Mobility CarSharing neither competes with automobile companies nor with public transportation providers; it set up a new service category with different prices and rules. If newcomers enter established markets, technological innovation is perhaps the best way to compete with known household brands.[39] Reware bridges the gap between what is and what should be by means of intelligent design. The newly founded company uses state-of-the-art solar conversion technology in everyday products to turn the sun's natural power into electricity. Juice Bags and Powerpockets are fitted with superflexible solar panels that can charge handheld devices in a couple of hours.

Sustainability Brand Development

Once a sustainability brand is launched and established in the market, there are different options for developing it further. In line with the sustainability brand name and the product category, we can differentiate between four different options: line extension, sustainability brand extension, multi-sustainability brands and new sustainability brands (Figure 7.3).

Line extension means that a company introduces additional items in a given product category under the same sustainability brand name. American Apparel was founded by Dov Charney in response to the outsourcing of the textile industry to sweatshops in developing countries. Its high-quality t-shirts are made in downtown Los Angeles, USA, where the company provides a number of social benefits to

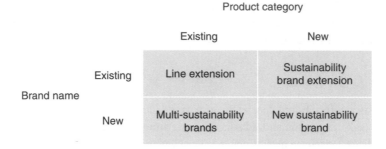

Figure 7.3   Sustainability brand development strategies
Source: Based on Kotler, P. & Armstrong, G. (2004) *1The Principles of Marketing*, 10th edn, Upper Saddle River, NJ: Prentice Hall, p 296.

its employees, including above-average wages, health insurance, subsidized lunches, English courses for Hispanic employees and financing of children's studies. Originally focused on basic cotton knitwear such as t-shirts and underwear, American Apparel has expanded to include tanktops, vintage clothing, dresses, trousers, denim and accessories for men, women, children and babies. It also sells a line of shirts under the 'Sustainable' label that are 100% organic cotton. The company plans to increase its use of organic cotton from over 20% in 2007 to 80% by 2011.[40]

Sustainability brand extension involves the use of a successful sustainability brand to launch new or modified products in a new category. Natura was founded in 1969 as a sustainability pioneer in cosmetics. It has become the leading South American cosmetic company, with a 19% market share and a brand valued at 113% of sales. The cosmetic products developed and branded by Natura are inspired by the diversity of Brazilian nature and culture. Their ingredients are environmentally and socially oriented (natural resources, sustainable forestry, Fair Trade).[41] Besides cosmetics Natura also sells skincare products, haircare products, perfume and solar filters under the same brand name.

Multi-sustainability brands imply that a company has two or more sustainability brands in the same product category. Multi-sustainability branding is a way to establish different features and appeal to different target groups. Since the 1970s the sustainability pioneer Rapunzel has offered organic and Fair Trade food products under the same brand name in small organic food stores around the world, aiming at sustainability actives. In 2007 the company launched a new sustainability brand called BioGourmet, offering tasty organic food products for gourmets. The brand is distributed via conventional food retail chains aiming at *sustainability approachables* (consumers who would could consider sustainability purchases). In 2000 Philips introduced a series of long-life light bulbs: Philips Marathon as the top-line product comes with a life guarantee of five to seven years. Due to high energy efficiency the brand promises substantial cost savings during the prolonged product life span. Philips Halogena is a middle-level product range with a guaranteed life of two years, while Philips DuraMax is the entry-line product range with a guaranteed life of one year. The full line concept allows consumers to choose the right light bulb for the right place.[42]

Some companies create a *new sustainability brand* name when entering a new product category. Sustainability is a key element in the brand development strategy of the Swiss retailer Coop, which created three sustainability brands in different product categories: Coop Naturaplan stands for organic and Fair Trade food products; Coop Naturaline represents textiles products that are produced and processed in an environmentally and socially benign way; and Coop Oecoplan indicates nonfood products with an ecological value added (e.g. recycling paper, FSC-certified furniture).

Well-known and highly reputed sustainability brands are valuable assets for companies that must be carefully managed and developed. Advertising helps to create name recognition, brand knowledge and maybe even some brand preference. However, what counts most is brand experience, which includes advertising but also personal experience with the brand, word of mouth, personal and virtual interactions with company representatives and other people. A crucial part of the communication of and about sustainability brands is trust and credibility, which is explained further in the next chapter.

List of Key Terms

Cleaner production
Cradle-to-cradle approach
Customer solutions
ISO 14000
Marketing myopia
Motive alliances
Planned obsolescence
Product durability
Product-related services
Recycling
Result-related services
SA 8000
Sustainability brand development
Sustainability brands
Sustainability marketing myopia
Sustainable products
Sustainable services
Use-related services
Zero emissions

REVIEW QUESTIONS

1. How do you define sustainable products and services? What are the main characteristics of sustainable products and services?
2. What are the different kinds of services? Explain using the example of washing.

3. What is a sustainability brand? Give specific examples from your everyday life.
4. What does sustainability marketing myopia mean? How can companies overcome sustainability marketing myopia?
5. There are four sustainability brand development strategies. Describe them briefly and give examples.

DISCUSSION QUESTIONS

1. What are the potential benefits and limitations of car sharing? Do you think it would work in your region? Why? Why not?
2. Sustainable products and services are defined as offerings that satisfy customer needs and significantly improve social and environmental performance along the life cycle in comparison to conventional or competing offers. Would you consider the development of an electric car like the Tesla a significant improvement?
3. Is product life extension really useful for the environment? Give pros and cons for this line of argument.
4. Do you think Toyota Prius is a good sustainability brand name?
5. Discuss the advantages and disadvantages of sustainability brand extensions.

SUSTAINABILITY MARKETING CHALLENGE: MOTOROLA – COMMUNICATION SOLUTIONS AT THE BASE OF THE PYRAMID

Motorola is one of the top mobile phone device manufacturers with net sales of \$36 (€ 26) billion in 2007, operating in 72 countries and employing 66 000 people worldwide. In the third quarter of 2008, the operating loss at Motorola's handset division grew to \$840 (€606) million from \$248 (€ 179) million the year before, unit sales dropped by 32% and the company's market share plummeted to 8.4% globally, down from 22% in 2006 when Motorola's Razr handset was a bestseller. Meanwhile, Motorola lost its No. 3 place among the world's largest handset makers to Sony Ericsson. Nokia is the uncontested market leader with almost 35% market share, followed by Samsung with 28%. As Motorola focuses on making its phones more profitable by cutting costs, analysts warn that it may sacrifice the scale that makes it able to compete with bigger rivals. The company currently sells about 100 million units a year; analysts estimate that once production drops below this landmark, per-unit costs could rise by 10–20%.

Do 'base of the pyramid' markets offer the solution to Motorola's problems? Can the company offer commercially viable communication solutions to BoP markets? The mobile phone sector in developing markets is booming, with new subscriber rates twice as high as in developed countries.

Averaging about 50% annual growth, Africa's market increased most rapidly during 2001–08, counting over 270 million subscribers in 2007 and expecting to reach 330 million by the end of 2008. Despite this high growth, penetration rates in 2007 remained low, averaging approximately 28 subscribers per 100 people in Africa, as compared to the global average of about 50 subscribers per 100 people. Though mobile device manufacturers have developed and introduced low-cost products specifically for the African market, priced at between $25 and $45 each (€ 18–32), this still represents a sizeable fraction of most households' disposable income and cannot be afforded by the masses. Another problem is the high illiteracy rate in African countries. Lack of infrastructure both enhances and hinders the use of mobile phones: on the one hand mobile phones offer people from remote, isolated areas the opportunity to connect to each other; on the other hand the phones cannot function without an adequate infrastructure, more precisely without electricity. Maintenance and end-of-life management also require innovative solutions.

To solve (some of) these problems, Motorola initiated several projects. In Namibia, the company is testing wind- and solar-powered base stations, which provide electricity and lower the cost of linking remote users to cellular networks. In Uganda, which has one of the lowest levels of electricity provision in Africa, Motorola launched the 'Motopower' project in 2007, under which 55 solar-powered kiosks were set up offering free mobile charging to local consumers. Each kiosk is charged by a 55 Watt inverted solar panel, capable of charging up to 20 phones at a time. While waiting for their phone to charge, customers can browse and purchase Motorola products. Additionally, the kiosks function as a local 'phone booth' for people who do not own a mobile phone. On-site repair services are also offered. Through these income-generating services, Motopower kiosks are designed as a viable business model for entrepreneurial local women.

Mobile phones themselves can be an efficient instrument of empowerment. Studies show that the use of mobile phones is boosting gross domestic product, enabling entrepreneurial opportunities and reducing costs. For example, mobile technology can help people avoid expensive journeys, strengthen businesses' contact with their customers, access market information and financial services. Mobile phones also ensure greater access to important social services such as education, healthcare and public safety, as well as entertainment.[43]

Questions for Discussion

1. What are the main sustainability issues regarding mobile phones? Consider health aspects, environmental impacts and social consequences in your discussion.
2. Which criteria should a 'sustainable mobile phone' fulfil?
3. What is the market potential for mobile phones at the BoP? Conduct some research on the Internet, quantify your results and discuss your assumptions.
4. Even at a low price, many BoP consumers cannot afford to buy a mobile phone. Are service sales instead of product sales a viable option for Motorola in BoP markets? Differentiate between product-, use- and result-oriented services and discuss which kinds of services could work in BoP markets.

5. Mobile phones require energy to operate. Providing electricity in remote areas remains a challenge in many BoP markets. What do the leading mobile devices manufacturers do to overcome this barrier? How do you evaluate their approaches from the perspective of sustainability marketing?

Endnotes

1. See Belz, F.-M. (1999) 'Mobility CarSharing. Successful Marketing of Eco-efficient Services', in Green, K. (ed.), *Ahead of the Curve, Cases of Innovation in Environmental Management*, Boston, MA: Kluwer Academic Publishers, pp. 133–41; Hockerts, K. (2007) 'Mobility CarSharing', in Hamschmidt, J. (ed.), *Cases Studies in Sustainability Management and Strategy: The Oikos Collection*, Sheffield: Greenleaf Publishing, pp. 252–76; www.mobility.ch (accessed 31 December 2008). Let us assume that the whole world shares cars collectively instead of owning cars individually. The calculation would be: 6.6 billion people divided by 40 people per car equals 165 million cars, which is less than the total number of cars in the USA (2002: 225 million cars) and far less than the total number of cars worldwide (2002: 808 million cars).
2. Levitt, T. (1960) 'Marketing myopia', *Harvard Business Review*, July–August: 45–56.
3. See Chapter 2 for the customer's viewpoint and the new marketing mix of the 'four Cs' (customer solutions, communication, customer cost, convenience) as contrasted to the company's viewpoint and the conventional marketing mix of the 'four Ps' (product, promotion, price, place). See Chapter 4 for the total consumption process.
4. See for a similar definition Peattie, K. (1995) *Environmental Marketing Management: Meeting the Green Challenge*, London: Pitman Publishing, p. 181.
5. See Chapter 3 for the impact matrix and life cycle assessment (LCA) as instruments to identify and analyse the main socio-ecological problems of products.
6. See the sustainability marketing story in Chapter 1.
7. www.fsc.org (accessed 31 December 2008). The basic idea and concept of sustainable development originates in forestry, where it was formulated at the beginning of the nineteenth century.
8. www.solarroast.com (accessed 31 December 2008).
9. www.sa8000.org (accessed 31 December 2008).
10. See www.cap-markt.de (accessed 31 December 2008). Actually, the name of the German retailer CAP derives from English ('handicapped people').
11. Rocchi, S. & Kusume, Y. (2008) 'Empowering Creativity. A Design-led Innovation Experience based on Value Co-creation and User Insights', in Kandachar, P. & Halme, M. (eds), *Sustainable Challenges and Solutions at the Base of the Pyramid. Business, Technology and the Poor*, Sheffield: Greenleaf Publishing, pp. 284–306.
12. www.bsh-group.com (accessed 31 December 2008).
13. See sustainability marketing story in Chapter 2.
14. Cooper, T. (2005) 'Slower consumption: Reflections on product life spans and the "throwaway society"', *Journal of Industrial Ecology*, 9(1–2): 57.
15. *Ibid*.
16. Fuller, D.A. (1999) *Sustainable Marketing: Managerial-Ecological Issues*, Thousands Oaks, CA: Sage, p. 148.
17. Von Weizsäcker, E.U., Lovins, A. & Lovins, L.H. (1997) *Factor Four: Doubling Wealth, Halving Resource Use*, London: Earthscan.
18. USM U. Schärer Söhne AG, 'USM and Sustainability 2005', www.usm.com (accessed 31 December 2008).
19. See Belz, F.-M. (1999) 'Eco-Marketing 2005. Performance Sales instead of Product Sales', in Charter, M. & Polonsky, M.J. (eds), *Greener Marketing: A Global Perspective on Greening Marketing Practice*, Sheffield: Greenleaf Publishing, pp. 84–94.

20. http://www.t-mobile.de/unternehmen/umwelt (accessed 31 December 2008) and www.duh.de (accessed 31 December 2008).
21. See Chapters 9 and 10 for the costs and convenience of retro distribution schemes from the customer perspective.
22. Ottman, J. (1998) *Green Marketing: Opportunity for Innovation*, 2nd edn, Lincolnwood, IL: NTC Business Books, p. 79.
23. See Chapter 10.
24. Kotler, P. & Armstrong, G. (2004) *The Principles of Marketing*, 10th edn, Upper Saddle River, NJ: Prentice Hall, pp. 651–2; and www.hermanmiller.com (accessed 31 December 2008).
25. www.naturapacking.com (accessed 31 December 2008).
26. Kotler, P. & Armstrong, G. (2004) *The Principles of Marketing*, 10th edn, Upper Saddle River, NJ: Prentice Hall, p. 291.
27. This term is derived from Ottman, J.A., Stafford, E.R. & Hartmann, C.L. (2006) 'Avoiding green marketing myopia', *Environment. Science and Policy for Sustainable Development*, 48(5): 22–36.
28. Fuller, D.A. (1999) *Sustainable Marketing: Managerial-Ecological Issues*, Thousands Oaks, CA: Sage, p. 131.
29. Ottman, J.A., Stafford, E.R. & Hartmann, C.L. (2006) 'Avoiding green marketing myopia', *Environment. Science and Policy for Sustainable Development*, 48(5): 22–36.
30. *Ibid.*
31. See the sustainability marketing story of Hipp at the beginning of Chapter 5.
32. Alston, K. & Roberts, J.P. (1999) 'Partner in new product development: SC Johnson and the Alliance for Environmental Innovation', *Corporate Environmental Strategy*, 6(2): 111–28.
33. www.reware.com (accessed 31 December 2008).
34. These issues of convenience are explored in more detail in Chapter 10.
35. Robson, J. (2006) 'Cred label', www.telegraph.co.uk (accessed 31 December 2008).
36. Belz, F.-M. (2001) *Integratives Öko-Marketing: Erfolgreiche Vermarktung von ökologischen Produkten und Leistungen*, Wiesbaden: Gabler.
37. Kotler, P. & Armstrong, G. (2004) *The Principles of Marketing*, 10th edn, Upper Saddle River, NJ: Prentice Hall, p. 293 for brand name selection in general.
38. Peattie, K. (1995) *Environmental Marketing Management: Meeting the Green Challenge*, London: Pitman Publishing, p. 166.
39. *Ibid.*
40. United Nations Environment Programme, UN Global Compact and Utopies (2005) *Talk the Walk: Advancing Sustainable Lifestyles through Marketing and Communications*, pp. 18–22, available at www.talkthewalk.net; www.americanapparel.net (accessed 31 December 2008).
41. United Nations Environment Programme, UN Global Compact and Utopies (2005) *Talk the Walk: Advancing Sustainable Lifestyles through Marketing and Communications*, pp. 18–21, available at www.talkthewalk.net; http://www.ethos.org.br/ Ethos/documents/natura_text.pdf (accessed 31 December 2008).
42. See the sustainability marketing story of Philips 'Marathon' at the beginning of Chapter 9.
43. International Telecommunication Union (n.d.) *Information and Communication Technology Statistics*, www.itu.int (accessed November 2008); Kharif, O. & Crockett, R. (2008) 'Motorola's turnaround plans meet with skepticism', *BusinessWeek*, 31 October, http://www.businessweek.com/technology/content/oct2008/tc20081030_659888.htm (accessed 31 December 2008); International Data Group (2008) 'Financial Crisis Hits Western European Mobile Phone Market–3Q Shipment Growth Drops Significantly', Press Release, 4 November, http://www.idc.com/getdoc.jsp?containerId=prUK21506708 (accessed 31 December 2008); Motorola (2008) *Corporate Responsibility Report 2007*, www.motorola.com (accessed 31 December 2008).

Communications

After Studying this Chapter You Should be Able to:

1. Understand the complexities and risks involved in developing marketing communications campaigns for sustainable products and services
2. Explain the approaches that companies can take to ensure that they develop open, credible and interactive marketing communications strategies.
3. Appreciate the difference between conventional marketing communications and sustainability marketing communications.

LOOKING AHEAD: PREVIEWING THE CONCEPTS

Communications, especially advertising, play a role in the marketing and sustainability debate that is contradictory. On the one hand, they help promote conspicuous consumption and create an unsustainable consumer society, but on the other they can be vital for enhancing the diffusion of sustainable products and services as well as sustainable lifestyles. In this chapter we will describe the decisions and difficulties involved in sustainability communications on both a product and a corporate level. The core elements of a communications campaign are described, including communications objectives, media and messages, along with the implications for each of these when communicating about a sustainability marketing strategy. To be credible a company requires an open, transparent, interactive and holistic approach to communications.

SUSTAINABILITY MARKETING STORY:
ONE WATER – A CAUSE-INSPIRED MARKETING VENTURE

ONE Water is a bottled water brand launched in 2005 that could most accurately be described as a 'cause-inspired marketing' venture. The social enterprise behind it, Global Ethics, was set up by former advertising executive Duncan Goose to fund clean water projects in Africa, after he had witnessed at first hand the extent to which the search for clean water dominated the health, development and quality-of-life agenda there. Having persuaded water producer Radnor Hills to work with him to bottle and label the water, Duncan had to find a way to break into a UK market worth £2.3 (€2.42) billion and dominated by four brands each of which was spending between £1 million and £4 million (€1.05–4.20 million) a year on advertising and, together with supermarket own brands, comprising 60–70% of the market. Additionally there were 200 other smaller brands fighting for a share of the remaining market, some of them already using ethical or environmental issues as their selling proposition. The challenge called for some remarkably creative approaches to communication.

The first step was to take advantage of the launch year's major event, the Live8 concert in Hyde Park. The expectation was that a major brand would become the official water for the event, and some companies offered significant sponsorship to secure it. Duncan's approach was a very direct one to the organizers of the event, Sir Bob Geldof, Harvey Goldsmith and Richard Curtis. He marched confidently into their offices to deliver a case of 'the water they'd want to use for Live8'. He left behind samples of the water and product literature explaining how money raised through sales of ONE was used to install 'PlayPump' water systems throughout Sub-Saharan Africa. These systems use an ordinary merry-go-round for children to play on, installed near the village school. This drives a screw pump that brings uncontaminated drinking water from deep below the ground and into a secure and clean 2500-litre water tank, providing the community with an uninterrupted and uncontaminated water supply for drinking and agriculture. For the children it means that instead of a long daily journey to collect water for their families, they can spend their time in school receiving an education, with something fun to play on as well.

The promoters of Live8 bought into the philosophy of ONE and adopted it as the official water, and the event yielded photos of celebrities such as Brad Pitt and Annie Lennox holding bottles. Duncan also had an unusual advantage in that his sister, Claire, was a well-known TV actress. She not only became a brand ambassador, she was able to persuade other actors such as David Tennant (well known to millions as Dr Who) to provide endorsements to be used on bottle labels and product literature. Despite these PR successes, gaining widespread market access was difficult for the new brand, largely because of the FMCG retailing practice of expecting new brands to pay a 'stocking fee' for access to shelf space and also to cover the marketing costs of in-store promotion. Duncan could afford neither of these. The breakthrough into the market came when the grocery retailing arm of petrol company Total agreed to adopt the fledgling brand, and to cover the costs of an in-store poster promotional campaign and a national PR campaign. Sales were slow at first, but a 'Buy Two for £1' sales promotion campaign boosted national sales up to 1000 half-litre bottles daily, settling at over 200 bottles daily once the promotion ended. With the relatively generous margin that Total allowed ONE, it took only a few months to sell the 25 000 bottles needed to fund the first ONE PlayPump. Both Duncan and Ian Mackie (the Total buyer he had worked with) flew out to Africa to help build and install that pump, which provided further communications opportunities for both companies. ONE's success via Total opened the doors to other retailers such as the Co-op, Tesco, Morrisons and Waitrose.

Despite early growth and success, the challenge for ONE was how to compete against some very long-standing, entrenched and well-resourced brands. In the absence of money to invest, Duncan and others invested time and creativity instead. Duncan's tireless efforts in speaking at events and to organizations to highlight the company's work, backed up by distributing leaflets, gradually built up awareness about the brand. His efforts were eventually rewarded when he was honoured at the Greatest Living Briton Awards in 2007, which generated considerable public relations benefits.

ONE also realized the benefits that online marketing offered to a young company with a limited communications budget. Its website (www.we-are-one.org.uk) featured information about the product, the retailers stocking it and the PlayPump projects. It also linked to a YouTube video showing Duncan's experiences in South Africa when the first pump was installed. The brand also utilized 'word-of-mouse' though the 'Message in a bottle' feature, which allowed visitors to send a message to a friend through the website in a way that also let them know about the product. Site visitors could also interact by nominating 'heroes' who had supported the brand, sign up a pledge of support for the brand and its ideals, post blog entries, photos or drawings relating to the brand and finally vote for other people's creative efforts, support pledges or hero nominations. The company also took interactive marketing communications to a new level by introducing 'smart codes' on bottles and posters that if snapped using a WAP-enabled camera phone could automatically link consumers through to the product's website. This would connect them to opportunities to donate money to water projects in Africa, stream video footage to their phone and access promotional benefits. This was the first time this technology had been used for marketing communications in Europe, which was a stunning achievement for a small company with little or no marketing budget.

Bottled water is a slightly controversial product from a sustainability point of view, due to the resources consumed to provide and package it compared to tap water. These issues are tackled on ONE's website, providing information on the company's efforts to be sustainable and some of the challenges it faces (particularly in relation to packaging). While a market exists for liquid refreshment on the move, and bottled water in particular, ONE represents a strongly sustainable choice given the contributions the company has made in bringing clean water to improve the everyday lives of communities in Africa. Within two years of being established, the company had raised £2 (€2.1) million and provided water for 18 communities, with many more almost literally in the pipeline.

The Ambivalence of Communication

Marketing communication has been a focus of social criticism for its role in promoting conspicuous consumption and creating an unsustainable consumer society.[1] This can make marketing communications for sustainability products a difficult area to manage. Advertising has frequently endured strong criticism for its social and environmental impacts, and in terms of whether it accurately reflects the experience that consumers can and will have.[2] The scale of marketing communications activity has also generated concern about the level of resources involved in delivering it to consumers. This is particularly the case for direct mail, sales promotion and print advertising.

The social consequences of advertising have been the subject of considerable debate among marketing scholars. Some argue that advertising is so pervasive and intrusive that it profoundly shapes the values and desires of society to make us more acquisitive, cynical, selfish and superficial, and it has led to a homogenous global culture that presents consumers with unrealistic stereotypes that can alienate or simply depress them.[3] There is also an argument that while marketing aims to create consumer satisfaction, marketing communication generates considerable dissatisfaction without intending to. Messages aimed at the target market to make them desire a particular product will also reach many consumers who can be made to desire it, but are not able to afford the product or to satisfy that desire. The effect of such dissatisfaction goes largely unnoticed because that portion of the audience is not normally included within the target market and therefore their response to the message is not considered or measured.[4] Those who defend advertising claim that it represents a mirror reflecting the existing values of society, rather than a tool that shapes them.[5] They argue that although advertising is capable of influencing consumers in choosing between brands and product categories, it is incapable of creating a demand that was not already present (or at least latent) within the consumer.

The debate about the social impacts of advertising and other forms of marketing communications is intensified when the target audience is children. Partly this relates to the growing childhood obesity crisis in industrialized (and an increasing number of less industrialized) countries. This has led to deep concern about the marketing of 'junk' foods high in fat, sugar and salt, such as soft drinks, sugared cereals, confectionery, savoury snacks and takeaway 'fast food'. These are both some of the most heavily advertised products and those most deeply implicated in contributing to childhood obesity.[6] Other concerns about the impact of marketing communications on children regard the advertising of toys, which have led countries like Sweden to ban television advertisements for toys (and food or beverages) that appeal to children under 12. There is also concern about the stereotypical gender roles in many adverts and the endemic use of sexual imagery to sell products.[7]

Although there is often concern about the social and environmental harm that commercial advertising can do, ultimately it is a tool that can be used in ways that work for or against the pursuit of sustainability. There is an increasing emphasis on social marketing for sustainability, and governments and NGOs frequently use advertising as part of their efforts to tackle sustainability issues such as climate change.[8] In Malaysia there are government-sponsored guidelines encouraging all commercial advertisers to include in their campaigns a secondary social message relating to issues such as racial harmony, energy saving, politeness, care for the elderly, litter avoidance or national pride. Although not necessarily adopted by all advertisers as intended, campaigns by major companies such as car manufacturer Perodua or oil company Petronas regularly feature these themes and are positively received by consumers.[9]

For the sustainability marketer, communication is as much a vital part of the marketing mix as it is for conventional marketers. Without effective communication it will be almost impossible to make consumers aware of sustainability solutions that have been developed, and how they will integrate with consumers' lifestyles and meet their needs. Effective communication to forge long-term relationships with consumers (which continue through use and post-use of the product) will also be crucial to ensure that a whole life cycle approach is taken to managing sustainable solutions. The challenge for sustainability marketers is to develop communications campaigns that suit the nature of their consumers and the solutions they develop for them, and that can take advantage of the power of marketing communications techniques, without being tainted by association with the social and ecological criticisms they attract.

Sustainability Marketing Communication in Context

Marketing communication is conventionally discussed as the fourth marketing mix 'P' of Promotion. This originally focused on promoting products to consumers through advertising, personal selling, sales promotions and public relations. Over time the notion of promotion evolved and grew to become communications, although in practice those original promotional techniques, particularly advertising, continue to dominate. The conventional view of communication that underpins conventional marketing thinking (and textbooks) reflects models of communication from the field of physics.[10] Communication is depicted as a process in which a 'sender' encodes a message and transmits it through a particular medium to a 'receiver', who decodes and interprets it. This is subject to more or less 'interference' depending on the circumstances under which the communication occurs. Communication is viewed as a 'magic bullet' travelling in one direction to achieve a desired and predetermined effect. This would equate to a marketing campaign in which adverts are devised to convey a certain message to a target audience. The adverts are broadcast on television during programmes that the target audience are likely to watch. Interference might occur if dramatic world events distract the audience from the programmes or the advert breaks, or if a competitor launches a critical comparative advertising campaign. Those who watch the adverts might take away from them the message that the advertiser intended, or they might interpret it or respond to it in their own unexpected way.

This conventional approach to marketing communications is very unidirectional and inflexible. It broadcasts a single predetermined message to an entire target audience, and provides no direct means of reply. It is an instrumental, mechanical and rather dehumanized view of communication, and is still rooted in the promotion of products to potential consumers. An alternative approach comes from sociology, which views communication as essentially about human interaction and understanding, and about the sharing of information, knowledge and meaning. This is more relevant for understanding and promoting sustainable development[11] and marketing that emphasizes the process of building and maintaining relationships with consumers. In recent years there has been a growth in interactivity in marketing communications through online communications, interactive sales promotion, experiential marketing (for example roadshows that take products out to consumers, often combined with entertainment) and relationship marketing approaches.

Sustainability marketing communications represents the next step in the evolution of marketing communications. Conventional promotional communications focused on the promotion of the product *to* the consumer. Relationship marketing focused more on communicating *with* the consumer, and particularly on learning more about consumers in order to market to them more effectively. Sustainability communications also opens up the company behind the product offering to allow the consumer to learn much more about the company, and to allow for dialogue between the consumer and company so that they can understand, and learn from, one another. This creates a dual focus for sustainability marketing communications strategies: to communicate with the consumer about the sustainability solutions the company provides through its products, and to communicate with the consumer and other stakeholders about the company as a whole.

Sustainability Product Communication

The communications efforts of a company to promote the sustainability solutions that its products provide need to be carefully planned, managed and controlled. The starting point for a communication strategy is the setting of objectives. Any communication activity has some form of objective, even if it is only to provide a response to a customer query or a story in the media. There are a number of common objectives of marketing communications efforts, including:

- *Generating awareness*, since any product, brand or technology, however excellent, will not succeed in crowded and fast-moving contemporary markets unless the consumer is made aware of them. One of the key factors that has held back the development of more sustainable products, and their extension from 'green' market niches to the mass market, is that they lack the broad awareness among consumers enjoyed by their longer-established conventional competitors.[12]
- *Informing* consumers about products and their availability, about the nature of the company and its activities or about special promotional offers. Sustainability marketing efforts may also require efforts to inform consumers about issues on the sustainability agenda and how they relate to lifestyles and choices. The Tom's of Maine toothpaste carton does not just list ingredients like a conventional toothpaste, it also lists the role each ingredient plays in the product and where each is sourced from. However, the provision of information alone is rarely sufficient to motivate consumers to adopt more sustainable consumption behaviours.[13]
- *Reminding* consumers about a product and its availability, or about the need to maintain or replace a product. Marketers can contribute to the sustainable use of durable products by reminding consumers of the need for regular maintenance, creating opportunities to market maintenance services at the same time.

- *Persuading* consumers to try a new product, switch their brand loyalty or change their behaviour in some other way. Korean car company Kia developed an unusual, award-winning campaign in the UK on the theme 'Think Before You Drive', which urged people to avoid using their cars for short journeys.
- *Reassuring* consumers in the face of direct or implied criticism of a product (perhaps from competitors' marketing communication) and reassure them that past purchases of the product were sensible choices. P&G's communication in support of its Tide Coldwater brand was based on strongly reassuring consumers that cold-water washing could work.
- *Motivating* consumers to respond, perhaps through a direct response by making a phone call or clicking through on a website to view a particular product or offer.
- *Rewarding* consumers through the provision of direct benefits for past custom and loyalty or for other behaviours. To promote product takeback, computer maker Lenovo rewards consumers returning a range of old electronic devices (regardless of brand) with pre-paid gift cards based on the residual value of the items.
- *Connecting* with consumers through relationship-building activities and interactive communications. The interactive website features highlighted in the ONE Water story are all aimed at encouraging consumers to develop a relationship with a brand for a core product (water) that is as basic and easy to take for granted as could be imagined.

There are a number of different media that marketers employ in their communications efforts. Conventionally this was often expressed in terms of the division of the communications effort and budget between 'above-the-line' advertising and 'below-the-line' promotional efforts that involved other media. In recent years this mythical 'line' (originally linked to the billing practices of marketing communications agencies) has become sufficiently blurred to be meaningless and most companies and marketing communications agencies tend to talk in terms of 'through-the-line' or integrated marketing communications efforts. The key media that sustainability marketers can employ include the same selection open to conventional marketers, but the implications of each media for the sustainability marketer are somewhat different.

Advertising

This is the medium people most readily associate with marketing. Advertising refers to mass media, including television, radio and print. It is a powerful medium capable of reaching a large or dispersed market repeatedly with persuasive and informative messages. It has the limitation that it communicates in a 'scattergun' way, providing a single, unidirectional message to the entire audience at once. Advertising has been widely used to support sustainability marketing strategies in markets including cars, white goods, coffee and cleaning products. Much of the early academic research into sustainability marketing focused on advertising, particularly on the credibility of the claims used and the types of messages and appeals.[14] The conclusions were that such ads tended to use vague, unsubstantiated or misleading claims and that they saw using 'moral' appeals to position sustainability consumption as the 'right' thing to do.

There are some challenges involved in using mass-media advertising to promote sustainability products effectively. Advertising is strongly associated with the conventional marketing paradigm that emphasizes the generation of demand and a presentational emphasis on the superficial style of products rather than their substance. Therefore it may feel 'wrong' to marketers (and to consumers) to use such a medium to communicate the sustainability credentials of a product. It can also be a challenge to communicate meaningfully about the complex interplay of social, environmental, economic, technical and consumer benefits of a product from a sustainability perspective using a 30-second radio or television slot or a single printed page.[15]

Personal Selling

Selling is a medium more closely associated with industrial and business-to-business marketing than consumer marketing. However, there are still some product categories and countries where traditional door-to-door sales techniques are employed. Natura, the leading Brazilian manufacturer and marketer of sustainable cosmetics with an annual revenue of $1.3 billion (€955 million), has successfully adopted a business model heavily dependent on direct sales. The company differentiates itself in the market by the quality of its relationships and its adherence to environmental and social principles. Natura's salesforce consists of consultants who carry out direct sales in the communities in which they live (in Brazil, Argentina, Chile, Bolivia and Peru). The retailing of complex consumer items such as cars or home electronics, or of upmarket brands of clothes or makeup, also still involves selling as an important communications technique.

The key issue in sustainability strategies is to ensure that sales staff understand the issues related to the sustainability performance of the product and are able to answer customers' questions. The sales staff of Toyota retailers undergo extensive training to learn about the complex technologies of hybrid cars, Toyota's sustainability aims and strategy, and the forces driving it (world population, climate change and sustainable mobility). It is not enough to brief salespeople about the sustainability benefits of a product. A customer who learns about a company whose production process is environmentally superior might then want to know whether it is also a socially responsible employer or ensure that it sources sustainably.

Direct Mail

The concept of 'junk mail' has made direct mail a target for environmental activist campaigns and also for grumbling by many householders. Ironically, however, it is also one of the major communications tools employed by environmental organizations in their efforts to raise funds for their campaigns. Part of the solution for companies that employ direct mail is to ensure that it is accurately targeted, since mailings that reach their intended targets who then respond to them are not junk.

There are a number of initiatives among direct mail companies, and the companies that use their services, to reduce their actual and perceived environmental footprint. These include the use of paper that has been recycled or produced from sustainably managed forests, moves from oil-based to vegetable-based printing inks, and the use of 'hybrid mail', in which mailings are distributed electronically to multiple distribution points for localized printing and delivery, significantly reducing the fuel used for distribution. In 2006 Charterhouse, an independent print management company, launched the Carbon Neutral Print Production programme in partnership with the Carbon Neutral Company. It measures the CO_2 emissions of any print job and neutralizes the effect through investing in positive carbon projects. This allows clients like Sony to produce high-profile carbon-neutral direct mail campaigns; financial firm ING Direct has gone further by pledging to link the printing of all the bank's consumer marketing and operational literature to carbon-offsetting programmes.[16]

Sales Promotion

Promotions include a range of techniques offering consumers additional benefits to generate a response, such as a purchase or product trial.[17] *Value-increasing promotions* offer a better deal to consumers through price reductions or by increasing the quantity (or quality) of the product. Money-off coupons, seasonal sales or buy-one-get-one-free (BOGOF) offers all improve the basic deal to consumers. *Value-adding promotions* provide additional but different benefits to consumers, such as the opportunity to join a club, enter a contest, access promotional merchandise or enjoy a free gift or complementary product. Since promotions are mostly geared around increasing material consumption, they may not appear to be an obvious choice for sustainability marketers. BOGOF offers in particular effectively double the material impact of a purchase's consumption without doubling consumer expenditure. However, promotions could potentially also encourage more sustainable consumption by offering additional benefits that encourage sustainable behaviours (e.g. 'cashback' offers to promote end-of-life product returns or free Tupperware products to help consumers avoid food wastage).

Labelling

This is an important means of communicating with consumers about sustainable consumption, and it plays a crucial role in shopping for food and for domestic appliances. As a promotional device, green or ethical labels provide customers with a simple and trustworthy signal of a product's social and environmental credentials. Labelling schemes include national schemes such as the German 'Blue Angel'; international labels like the European Union Eco-label; schemes that relate to particular industries or products (e.g. Rug-mark carpets made without child labour), to particular methods of production (e.g. organic farming), to the use of a particular method of transportation (e.g. air freight); or to business conduct (e.g. Fair Trade). It can also support consumer recycling behaviour, for example by labelling containers by type of plastic to simplify sorting and recycling. Some examples of sustainability labels for food and other products (e.g. child labour-free carpets or Fair Trade handicrafts) are shown in Figure 8.1.

Labelling programmes vary in terms of the following aspects:

- Whether or not they are mandatory or voluntary within a particular industry.
- Whether they involve single or multiple issues.
- The level of information they provide.

Figure 8.1 Examples of sustainability labels

- Whether they communicate properties that consumers might want to avoid (e.g. air freight) or properties that might attract consumers (e.g. organic or Fair Trade).
- The level and style of verification that underpins them.

Each of these dimensions has provided ample opportunity for controversies about labelling schemes within industries and between companies, regulators and NGOs. There are two main types of eco-label, those where a third, independent party verifies the achievement of certain environmental or social standards or criteria, and those created by individual producers to communicate or market (positive) sustainability attributes of products to consumers.[18] One challenge for consumers is being able to recognize, understand and cope with the sheer number of different labels that are emerging dealing with specific aspects of the sustainability agenda. In Germany a specific website (www.label-online.de) has been established providing consumer-oriented advice and evaluations of over 300 different environmental and social labelling schemes.

Sustainability labels have become one of the most widely employed communications techniques that aim to influence consumer behaviour. They have the advantage of being able to communicate on the packaging and in store, where many final purchase decisions are made, and there is evidence that consumers are increasingly willing to consider environmental and social aspects when buying food.[19] Sustainability labels can inform consumers about the environmental and social effects of the production, consumption and waste phases of a product or service, and can act as a potential source of competitive advantage.[20] Consumers vary in how they perceive sustainability labels, although generally they have been found to add value to a product.[21]

Point of Sale

As well as communicating at the point of sale through product labels, companies can employ displays, literature or posters to seek to inform and influence consumers. This is frequently done during

'Sustainable Weeks' in Austria in which the government, retailers and NGOs collaborate to develop in-store promotions for healthy, environmentally oriented, regional and Fair Trade produce.[22] The Grupo Eroski, one of Spain's largest retailers with more than 30 000 employees and €5.5 billion in revenues, has conducted a 'Comercio Jucio' campaign for two weeks each March since 2001. The campaign aims at raising consumer awareness of Fair Trade and promoting the purchase of Fair Trade products available at Eroski outlets. The retailer uses in-store promotions, awareness-raising sessions, customer loyalty mailings and adverts in its free *Idea Sana* magazine. As a result, Eroski has witnessed significant increases in sales of Fair Trade products.[23]

Online Communication

The Internet and other new information and communications technology has created a revolution in marketing communications technology that has evolved in parallel with the rise of the sustainability marketing agenda. The early days of online marketing communications mostly involved companies translating their print and advertising media campaigns onto their websites, and using them as a source for consumers to access advice and product information. This was still essentially the one-way provision of information to consumers, not a process of building relationships. As the Internet has evolved, it has spawned a range of new social media including blogs, social networks, podcasts, wikis, review sites, bulletin boards and newsgroups. These have the power to start, host or shape conversations about products, brands and companies and their relationship to a host of social and environmental issues. These are conversations that companies can join in with, but cannot control, and they have the power to enhance or destroy a brand and its reputation. Considerable attention has been given to companies being attacked, fairly or unfairly, online about aspects of their social and environmental performance. The risk is that an attack or rumour can escalate from the virtual world to affect the perceptions of consumers, investors and the media. Dealing with any online attacks on a company's sustainability performance and reputation requires it to respond in a proactive and open way to prevent the situation escalating into a crisis.[24]

There is also a trend towards companies establishing a separate website to inform and educate consumers about the sustainability issues related to a brand. Confectionery company Cadbury established a separate 'Dear Cadbury' website to communicate its sustainability report and engage with consumers by using actual customer feedback to illustrate areas of commitment, including the environment, supplier and employee relations and well-being.[25] Computer monitor maker ViewSonic has launched a dedicated microsite to educate customers about the environmental features of its products and how to recycle them, along with general tips on sustainable living.[26]

There are also sustainability-oriented 'communities of interest' developing in the online environment, which provide a direct communication channel to groups of consumers with the greatest commitment to sustainability issues. Examples include www.treehugger.com, www.utopia.de and www.lohas.de. These communities also bring far more than a potential audience to communicate to, they represent a source of expertise and insight about the sustainability agenda from which marketers can learn, and with which marketers can develop and test new ideas, strategies and campaigns. P&G used insights from online communities to assist in the introduction of Tide Coldwater.[27] It is also worth noting that although the Internet has the power to offer access to sustainability-oriented consumer information and consumption choices, 70% of the web's content is in English, a language that is the mother tongue of less than 10% of the global population, which may put limits on its reach and the equity of the benefits it brings.[28]

Like ONE Water, most companies will use a *communications mix* of different media according to their communications objectives, the particular audiences they are trying to reach and the nature of their product and industry. There is no one best media for a marketing campaign, and it is the integration and synergies developed between the different elements of a marketing communications campaign that are the key to its success.

Sustainability Marketing Messages

Every marketing communications message will have an appeal or 'hook' within its message with which it tries to engage with the audience and motivate them to respond. There are three generic types of appeal. *Rational appeals* target the consumer's self-interest, which could involve marketing organic foods as healthier or low-energy products as more economical. It is worth noting that the broader pursuit of the sustainability agenda is also deeply rational, since destroying the planet (at least as we know it) is hardly in the interests of any stakeholder. *Emotional appeals* seek to make an emotional connection with consumers, and this is often done by connecting the benefits of sustainability strategies to children's welfare or showing the plight of endangered animals or disadvantaged people from poorer countries. *Moral appeals* aim to engage with people's sense of right and wrong and, in the case of sustainability, stressing our duty to protect the quality of the environment for future generations or to try to put an end to poverty.

An early study of sustainability-oriented print advertising identified six types of appeal:[29]

1. *Financial appeals*: linked to price reductions from resource conservation or to donations to charitable causes.
2. *Management appeals*: in which companies seek to position the company itself as a part of the 'green movement' and part of the 'solution' rather than of the 'problem'.
3. *Euphoria appeals*: invoking a sense of well-being by highlighting the naturalness or health benefits of a product.
4. *Emotional appeals*: to evoke fear for the future or guilt about our impact on the planet, or to generate a sense of empowerment.
5. *Zeitgeist appeals*: an attempt to link into prevailing social concerns about environmental and social issues.
6. *Others*: such as comparative advertising or celebrity endorsement.

The first and second types are rather rational, while the third and fourth are emotional and moral appeals. Achieving the right style and tone of message, and selecting the appropriate appeal, can be a challenge for marketers. The seriousness of key sustainability issues such as climate change, global poverty or the erosion of biodiversity makes it tempting to employ fear appeals that seek to use fear and guilt to motivate consumers. The difficulty is that such emotions can be disempowering to consumers in a way that is demotivating; when faced with a message of guilt and fear, consumers will look for why the message might be exaggerated, why it might not apply to them, or reasons that would give them 'permission' not to attend to it.

In a study of consumers' response to marketing messages in relation to climate change, Rose *et al.*[30] concluded that for consumers who are 'outer directed' (that is, who seek the approval of others) in terms of their psychological nature, there was little hope of motivating them through appeals that used guilt, fear or the 'worthiness' of sustainability. Instead they suggest:

- Making the issue personally relevant (about your home and lifestyle) and personalized.
- Avoiding negative guilt-based messages and instead focusing on benefits relating to saving money, 'getting something' and convenience.
- Associating behaviours with positive self-images for the consumer ('shrewdness', 'flattery' and 'glamour') and with the here (local and familiar) and now (rather than something global and about the future).
- Being interactive, playful and entertaining as well as informative.

Getting the tone of sustainability product communication right is ultimately a careful balancing act. The sustainability agenda is made up of complex and serious issues. Communication that seeks to do them justice by providing a large amount of factual information and conveying the seriousness of the issues risks overwhelming consumers who are already suffering from information overload, or demotivating them with an overly gloomy message. Alternatively, messages delivered in a lively, upbeat, emotional and entertaining style risk being interpreted as trivializing serious issues or as superficial responses. Celebrity endorsement can be a very effective strategy, as ONE Water demonstrated, but again it involves risks in terms of how the chosen celebrity behaves and whether he or she is perceived as an appropriate spokesperson for the brand by consumers. Successfully communicating to make the connection between consumers' lives and the relevant sustainability issues via the product, delivered in a way that motivates them to attend and to respond by changing their consumption behaviour, is a unique and complex challenge faced by sustainability marketing managers.

Communication Throughout the Consumption Process

Sustainability communication is important at all stages of the consumption process, although at each stage the specific objectives, the most appropriate media and the nature of the message will vary.

Pre-Purchase

The emphasis will be on generating awareness, informing consumers about a product and persuading them to consider it. Free samples, product literature or product demonstrations are good means of persuading consumers to try a sustainable product or to reassure them about its benefits and suitability. Such communication techniques help to reduce the perceived risks associated with a purchase. This can be important for new sustainability-oriented brands, since they will often be perceived as 'risky' by consumers if they have an expectation of either impaired technical performance or increased cost linked to a brand's sustainability credentials.[31]

Purchase

Persuasive advertising campaigns that consumers recall or are influenced by when shopping, point-of-sale displays and promotional offers or the efforts of sales staff in store can all help to motivate consumers to buy a sustainability-oriented product. The nationwide PR campaign, in-store posters and promotional pricing offer that accompanied the launch of ONE Water at Total filling stations were all geared towards encouraging purchase.

Use

In conventional marketing the majority of communications activities are geared either to achieving sales relatively directly, or to building brand loyalty with the hope of increasing future sales. With the advent of relationship marketing, the emphasis on generating consumer loyalty evolved into efforts to build and maintain consumer relationships. In sustainability marketing communications, companies often seek to achieve a broader range of consumer responses across a wider range of consumption behaviours. Sustainability marketing may require changes to the way in which consumers use products, which requires communications efforts that are not sales-oriented (although if such campaigns improve consumer attitudes towards the company and its perceived social responsibility, increased sales may result). One example is the 'Ariel Turn to 30°C' campaign run by P&G, which persuaded consumers to reset their washing machines to take advantage of improvements in detergent technology, which allowed for effective cleaning at lower temperatures. It contributed to around one million UK households changing their behaviour, saving 60 000 tonnes of CO_2 annually (representing a 41% energy saving).

Post-Use

Another significant area for sustainability marketing communications is product disposal. Numerous government social marketing and producer-specific campaigns have aimed to encourage consumers to recycle used products and packaging, or engage in other forms of responsible disposal. The Marks & Spencer Oxfam Clothes Exchange project involved an advertising campaign, PR campaign, dedicated web pages, in-store posters, direct mail and a promotional offer to encourage consumers to recycle their old clothes via Oxfam (see pp. 124–26).

The Credibility of Sustainable Product Claims

One of the key determinants of success in sustainability marketing communications relates to credibility and trust. The perceived *value–action gap* between consumers' strongly expressed concerns about environmental and social issues[32] and their relatively unenthusiastic take-up of purchases of many more sustainable goods and services is typically explained in terms of consumers providing unrealistically positive responses to market research questions for reasons of social acceptability. An alternative explanation is that consumers are sceptical about businesses' sustainability claims.[33] A pervasive distrust of what consumers regard as marketing hype and little perceived association between the 'green' products they are offered and contributing to a better environment has regularly featured in research findings.[34] Credibility, like the meaning of communication, is something that is decided by the audience, not by the communicator. Consumers generally trust brands that they are familiar with, and therefore will also tend to trust marketing messages that feature those brands, including those that focus on positive aspects of their social and environmental performance.[35] Unfortunately, there is growing evidence that overuse of environmental advertising that involves weak or vague sustainability claims or associations is eroding that trust and increasing consumer scepticism about the sustainability efforts of business.[36]

Many socio-ecological qualities of sustainability solutions are credence qualities; that is, they cannot be directly verified by consumers before purchase through information gathering, nor after the purchase and during use through experience. Consumers rely on third parties to provide the information that will allow them to make confident decisions.[37] This is one of the reasons that sustainability labelling, particularly when endorsed by third parties, has been such an important communication medium for sustainability marketing. Other media may be able to attract consumers' attention, entertain them and create useful associations or emotional responses, but labelling has a crucial role in terms of generating credibility.

One of the most important factors in generating credibility is through consistency between a company's messages and its actions, and across different aspects of its product range and operations. A lack of consistency is likely to draw criticism from sustainability campaigners and the media. The Ford Motor Company, for example, produced television adverts featuring the company chairman, William Clay Ford Jr, pledging that the company is 'dramatically ramping up its commitment' to more sustainable cars like hybrid vehicles. This was viewed as an exaggeration, since if Ford was to meet the targets it had set, low-emission hybrids would still make up less than 4% of the company's fleet by 2010. Campaigners also objected to the advertising campaign on the basis that in 2003 the company had dropped its promise to increase average fuel efficiency on its sport utility fleet, and a year later it had joined forces with other car makers to block a California law that would limit emissions of gases linked to global warming.

The term *greenwashing* (which conflates 'greening' and 'whitewash') was first used by environmentalist Jay Westerveld when objecting to hoteliers' practice of placing notices in hotel rooms asking guests to reuse towels to 'save the environment'. Westerveld noted that there was little else to suggest that the hoteliers were interested in reducing their environmental impacts, and that their interest in washing fewer towels seemed to be motivated by a concern to save costs rather than the environment. Since then greenwashing has become a central feature of debates about marketing communications and sustainability, with 'awards' for greenwashing established and numerous campaigns, laws and advice developed in an attempt to reduce or curb it.

In 2007, US environmental marketing firm TerraChoice published a study called *The Six Sins of Greenwashing*, in which the marketing campaigns of more than 1000 common US consumer products were randomly surveyed and analysed. A total of 1753 environmental claims were made, with some products having more than one. Out of the campaigns studied, only 1% had avoided all forms of false or misleading claims; the other 99% had committed one of the following six 'sins' in the following order of commonality:

1. *Hidden trade-off*, e.g. 'energy-efficient' electronics that contain hazardous materials.
2. *No proof*, e.g. shampoos claiming to be 'certified organic' but with no verifiable certification.
3. *Vagueness*, e.g. products claiming to be 100% natural when many naturally occurring substances are hazardous, like arsenic and formaldehyde.
4. *Irrelevance*, e.g. products claiming to be CFC free, even though CFCs were banned 20 years ago.
5. *Fibbing*, e.g. products falsely claiming to be certified by an internationally recognized environmental standard like EcoLogo, Energy Star or Green Seal.
6. *Lesser of two evils*, e.g. organic cigarettes or 'environmentally friendly' pesticides.

Car companies, airlines and energy companies have often borne the brunt of environmentalists' concerns about greenwashing, since their products are essentially carbon intensive and although individual products may be more sustainable than their competitors, making absolute or overstretched claims is inviting trouble.

Audience Values

Consumers' values will influence their behaviour and responses when purchasing, and they will also influence how they perceive and respond to communication campaigns. For example, performance claims for environmentally oriented products are more likely to be believed by consumers with strongly pro-environmental values.[38] The challenge for the marketing communicator lies in being able to communicate with a target audience that may include segments with very different attitudes and values in relation to sustainability issues. This is crucial when seeking to expand the consumption of sustainability-oriented products beyond green market niches and into the mass market. In the case of attitudes towards sustainability, what would make a product attractive to different groups segmented by psychological type or attitudes towards sustainability issues can be diametrically opposed.

Ottman *et al.* propose that the secret to successful communications for sustainability products is to connect their attributes and the brand message effectively with the values that consumers desire (see also Chapter 7).[39] Some of the examples they highlight are summarized in Table 8.1.

Table 8.1   Marketing Messages Connecting Sustainability Products with Desired Consumer Value[40]

Desired Consumer Value	Message and Business/Product
Efficiency and cost effectiveness	'Did you know that between 80 and 85 percent of the energy used to wash clothes comes from heating the water? Tide Coldwater – The Coolest Way to Clean.' Tide Coldwater Laundry Detergent 'mpg:)' – Toyota Prius
Health and safety	'20 years of refusing to farm with toxic pesticides. Stubborn, perhaps. Healthy, most definitely ' – Earthbound Farm Organic
Performance	'Fueled by light so it runs forever. It's unstoppable. Just like the people who wear it.' – Citizen Eco-Drive Sport Watch
Symbolism	'Make up your mind, not just your face.' – The Body Shop
Convenience	'Long life for hard-to-reach places.' – General Electric's CFL floodlights
Bundling	'Performance and luxury fueled by innovative technology.' – Lexus RX400h Hybrid Sports Utility Vehicle

Source: Ottman, J.A., Stafford, E.R. & Hartman, C.L. (2006) 'Green marketing myopia', *Environment*, 48(5): 22–36

Sustainability Corporate Communications

Sustainability marketing is different to mainstream marketing in the extent to which all aspects of corporate social and environmental performance become relevant to consumers and liable to influence their behaviour. This requires companies to approach the management of sustainability performance, and communications about it, holistically. If a company makes claims about a specific environmental or social benefit of its products, this could become counterproductive if it is shown to use a highly polluting production process or one that exploits labour in poorer countries. From this perspective the means of production and the behaviour of the entire company become part of the 'product' that the consumer buys. This is very much in line with Peter Drucker's famous vision of marketing as the entire business seen from the customer's point of view.[41] Therefore communicating about the sustainability performance of the whole business is necessary for credible and effective sustainability marketing communications.

Such a holistic approach was proposed in McDonagh's model of *sustainable communications*,[42] which identifies four fundamental and interrelated principles relevant to sustainability marketing communications. Although the model focuses on ecological dimensions, it could equally apply to societal aspects:[43]

1. *Ecological trust*, which is built to reverse the trend towards a loss of confidence in businesses and business leadership and the resulting crisis of ecological legitimation.
2. *Ecological access*, allowing stakeholders access to organizations, their facilities and the information they hold, particularly about the ecological impacts of their strategies, decisions, products and production processes. Openness is important in building trust and creating innovations, although any company would need to be open within certain limits in order to protect commercially sensitive information.

3. *Ecological disclosure*, which when done voluntarily through corporate environmental reporting helps to build ecological trust, since consumers are more likely to trust organizations that routinely disclose information rather than those that are subject to revelations from third parties or forced disclosures.

4. *Ecological dialogue*, with stakeholders to build trust, to learn from stakeholders and their concerns, and to begin to draw them into the corporate decision-making process. McDonagh views this as the most radical difference to conventional marketing communications, in which the marketer seeks to control both the strategic agenda and the communication process.

The key to understanding marketing communication is that it is not what the marketer intends to communicate that counts, it is what the consumer interprets as the meaning of a message that is important. The implication of this is that marketing communication does not consist only of the deliberate efforts of marketers to send messages to consumers through conventional marketing communications channels. Anything can communicate. The product and its packaging will communicate to the consumer through their design and their performance. The fact that a product is low energy, designed to be easily repairable and recyclable, will communicate a great deal about the sustainability concerns of the manufacturer. The cost of a product may be interpreted by consumers as a proxy measure of quality by consumers, although in some markets low prices may be interpreted as meaning that a company cares about its consumers. Providing convenience for consumers and ensuring that products, information and support are accessible and available to consumers will also communicate a message about customer care. Similarly, the choice of channels through which a product is available can communicate about the nature of the product, including its environmental and social credentials.

In the case of retailers, or businesses where consumers visit the facilities of the business (as is the case with much leisure consumption), the nature of their facilities will also communicate much about the company's sustainability credentials. The sourcing of refreshments and the packaging they use, the availability of recycling facilities, the support for relatively sustainable transport methods, the efficient use of water and energy on site: all these factors will communicate something about the company's stance towards sustainability. They also provide opportunities to develop improvements in the sustainability performance of the business as a whole and to become the subject of positive communications efforts in the future. The Body Shop, for example, opened its Littlehampton headquarters for use as a primary communication tool, with visitors able to see the company's values put into practice. The name of a product will communicate, and in the case of many sustainability-oriented offerings the use of 'eco' as a prefix is often used to denote environmental quality, often combined with economy. The actions of a company will also communicate a great deal about its social and environmental credentials and the depth of commitment to the sustainability agenda. As Jon Bernstein neatly expressed it:

> Everything communicates. But does everything communicate coherently? A buyer takes a supplier to task for operating environmentally unsatisfactory manufacturing processes and then gives him a lift in the company 3-litre car. The chief executive sends out an environmental statement on non-recycled paper... The local environmental group is called in for a community meeting around the boardroom table of tropical hardwood veneer. Conversely a favourable message will be conveyed by converting part of the reserved car park to a bike rack.[44]

Sustainability marketing communications require a holistic perspective that integrates the deliberate promotional communication techniques of conventional marketing management, the interactive two-way communications approaches of relationship marketing, and the open approach to disclosure about social and environmental performance that is associated with corporate social responsibility (CSR). Sustainability corporate communications mostly tend to be discussed in the context of public relations (PR). PR traditionally combines marketing communication for products (often in terms of brands) alongside communication for corporate branding, identity and reputation. Sustainability marketing requires a close integration between the two. It also requires a communications focus on internal as well as external audiences.

Kanatschnig suggests that the internal audience is the most important one for corporate sustainability communications, and the one that the communications process should start with.[45] This will allow employees to become attuned to the company's sustainability performance and efforts to improve it, allowing them to act as ambassadors and generate positive 'word-of-mouth' communication, still the most trusted and effective marketing communication medium, but one that the marketer cannot control. To reach external audiences, a variety of public relations approaches can be employed, including sponsorship, speeches, literature, educational materials, audiovisual materials and information services. Lobbying is an externally focused communications approach that tends to have a bad reputation from a sustainability perspective, and is associated with companies lobbying governments defensively to prevent, delay or dilute regulations that may have a negative impact on their competitiveness. However, there are examples of companies that have proactively lobbied government for stricter legislation and higher social and environmental standards within their industries. This is usually an attempt to force less sustainable competitors to implement better social and environmental standards and to remove any cost advantages they may enjoy as a result of 'free riding' (see Chapter 11).

The Consumer as Communicator

The early phases of sustainability marketing communications featured predominantly one-way communication efforts in which the consumer took the passive role of audience. Examples include the publication of sustainability statements, declarations and commitments, providing information about environmental performance, or publishing sustainability-oriented advertising campaigns or web pages. A more interactive approach to communication requires a shift towards more two-way dialogue with stakeholders.

If a dialogue is to be meaningful, it involves more than simply a two-way flow of information. True dialogue is based on a willingness to listen to (as opposed to simply 'hearing') and learn from the other party; it should be an interactive and 'symmetrical' exchange of information in pursuit of mutual understanding.[46] Dialogue also needs a 'bias for action' so that it can shape strategies and decisions rather than simply debating or endorsing them. This means that dialogue needs to occur early while there is scope for making changes, and before reactions and positions become entrenched. Dialogue needs to be open and inclusive to ensure that all relevant stakeholders, issues and information are included.

Finally, any dialogue process needs to be properly resourced in terms of time and financial resources to meet the costs involved (e.g. travel costs of participants), including the provision of a neutral facilitator.

There are a number of ways in which companies can engage in dialogue with customers and other stakeholders in order to build trust and benefit from listening to, as well as talking to, them. These include:

- *Roundtables*, which involve facilitated discussions with interested stakeholders about particular issues and problems to seek to find equitable, constructive and workable solutions. For example, in the wake of several serious accidents, Hoechst Chemicals set up a Neighbourhood Circle near its Frankfurt site to allow for dialogue about issues such as air pollution and emissions, the transportation of hazardous materials and environmental auditing.
- *Citizens' panels*, which involve groups of typically 20–25 randomly selected people who are invited to participate in facilitated discussions about the sustainability performance of the business. They usually result in the publication of a 'Citizens' Report', that is fed back to the organization and made publicly available. This technique helps to understand ordinary citizens and consumers rather then the most interested and articulate who become involved in roundtables. Citizens' panels are similar to consumer focus groups used in market research, but have a broader focus on all aspects of an organization's sustainability, and are more geared towards problem solving than providing responses about particular company offerings.
- *Consensus conferences*, which are similar to citizens' panels but are organized as a specific event and involve presentations by, and questions to, expert witnesses as well as facilitated discussion. This is an approach that has mostly been used in political circles in countries such as Denmark, the Netherlands and the UK, but it has potential for companies seeking to adopt sustainability communication.

As well as specific events, dialogue can also be incorporated into the daily operation of an organization by establishing procedures and an organizational culture that encourages staff to listen to, and enter into dialogue with, consumers and other stakeholders. The Austrian Federal Forest Corporation (Österreichische Bundesforsten) realized the potential value of its 180 forestry staff as a communication channel with its key publics. Research revealed that those 180 staff had about 520 000 direct contacts (personal communications) with members of the general public annually. These staff were then trained to communicate the company's sustainability vision to the public, and also to become a conduit for ideas and opinions from the public about how to improve its sustainability performance further and adapt to the public's evolving expectations.[47]

A more radical shift in the nature of marketing communication, which has been facilitated by new digital media, is the trend towards consumers generating, rather than just consuming, campaigns. The distributive power of the Internet and the creative power of inexpensive media software are combining to allow consumers to create their own messages and 'adverts', which can be affectionate pastiches, subversive manipulation of brand identities and messages, laudatory salutes or critical assaults. In these cases the liberation of the consumer to become involved in the marketing communications process and to evolve from a passive audience to an engaged and creative message producer can create significant challenges for marketers.[48] This new world of marketing communications is a long way from the carefully constructed, orchestrated and controlled broadcasting of promotional campaigns from the producer to the consumer that is enshrined in yesterday's marketing textbooks.

The shift from conventional marketing communications to a sustainable approach to marketing communications requires a change in thinking, mindset and practices among marketing communicators. The emphasis on openness, dialogue, credibility and authenticity, and the need to consider the (often unintended) social and environmental consequences of marketing communications activity, will dominate the sustainability marketing communications agenda.

List of Key Terms

Advertising
Cause-related marketing
Communications
Credibility
Dialogue
Direct mail
Disclosure
Interactive marketing
Greenwash
Media
Messages
Promotion
Public relations
Openness
Sales promotion
Sustainability corporate communication
Sustainability product communication
Word of mouse
Word of mouth

REVIEW QUESTIONS

1. What specific communications objectives might a campaign for a sustainable product or service have?
2. How can direct mail companies reduce their environmental impacts and the negative connotations of 'junk mail'?
3. What are the three basic types of appeal that a sustainability marketing message aimed at consumers can apply?

4. What are the four components of McDonagh's concept of sustainable communication?
5. What is greenwashing, and which six sins can lead to it?
6. How can a company establish greater dialogue with its stakeholders?

DISCUSSION QUESTIONS

1. Why might marketing managers at a firm that has not previously embraced a sustainable approach to marketing strategy feel uncomfortable with the concept of sustainable marketing communications outlined in this chapter?
2. Is advertising an appropriate medium for sustainable marketing campaigns, or do the limits of the medium doom almost all ad campaigns to be perceived as 'greenwash'?
3. What steps could a company take to transform its approach to marketing communications from conventional promotion to the open and interactive dialogue at the heart of sustainable marketing communications?

SUSTAINABILITY MARKETING CHALLENGE: IS SHELL COMING OUT OF ITS SHELL?

The public relations battle over Shell UK's decision in 1995 to dump its *Brent Spar* oil installation at sea is used as an iconic example of many things, including the ability of NGOs like Greenpeace to harness the media, the way that the balance of credibility has shifted from big companies to campaigning groups, and how not to succeed in risk communications.[49] At the time the company thought that it was entirely in the right in implementing a disposal solution that had been approved by the UK government and for which it felt it held convincing evidence that it was technically and economically the best solution. However, once Greenpeace landed 12 people on the rig, media coverage of their 'occupation' went into overdrive, and the public perception was rapidly shaped into a simple story of Shell as the enemy of the oceans and Greenpeace as their defender. The resulting protest campaign escalated into a massive boycott by consumers of Shell petrol stations in Europe, particularly in Germany, where there were even acts of violence against the facilities. Other European governments, other signatories of the Business Charter for Sustainable Development like Novo Nordisk, dissident shareholders and even other parts of the Shell Group turned against Shell UK, forcing the company to abandon its original strategy and instead search for a new disposal strategy, this time in consultation with all the relevant stakeholders.

The most interesting lesson is perhaps the effect that the experience had on Shell's culture and communications style. It perceived itself as a highly respected company that had the law and the scientific evidence on its side. It failed to recognize the contested nature of the scientific evidence and the emotional nature of the issues involved. It also demonstrated a complete lack of understanding of the symbolic dimensions of communication by originally announcing the decision to dump the *Brent Spar* in the North Sea in the same week that a major conference on environmental protection for the North Sea was taking place. Shell's communication during the crisis remained a one-way process with an emphasis on rational, legal and scientific arguments and it accused critics of being overemotional and irrational, even suggesting that the campaign had made people 'emotionally disturbed'.

The failure to understand or engage with its stakeholders is a mistake that Shell decided not to repeat. The company launched a dialogue with stakeholders over the fate of the *Brent Spar* and began an international competition to generate alternative solutions. The company explicitly sought to change its corporate culture to become more outward looking and developed the Shell.com website to promote debate about the company's wider responsibilities. Shell's first annual social accountability report said, 'we are now trying hard to be more accessible and open in the way we deal with requests for information and in the style with which we communicate ... We are also determined to listen more and get involved in debate and dialogue.' Readers of the report were encouraged to send Shell their views, or post them on the website, on a range of policy dilemmas facing the group.

Whether this new spirit of openness can repair the damage the *Brent Spar* did to Shell's credibility remains to be seen. In an era of growing societal concern about the contribution of fossil fuels to the threat of climate change, the communications agenda for oil companies remains challenging. Keeping a low profile at a time of record oil company profits invites criticism for profiting at the expense of the planet. Emphasizing investments in alternatives to oil, as BP has done with its 'Beyond Petroleum' campaign, risks accusations of greenwashing while the alternative fuels part of the business remains small. Either way, as the *Brent Spar* case illustrates, despite the extent to which our economies depend on oil companies, sustainability-related communication remains a risky and complicated business for them.

Discussion Questions

1. Why do you think Shell found the communications aspects of its *Brent Spar* strategy so difficult to get right?
2. What other steps do you think Shell could take to become more open and credible in its communications?
3. Do you believe that the *Brent Spar* experience has fundamentally changed Shell's approach to communication, or do you believe that its response is based around 'damage limitation'? Use Internet coverage of Shell's communication efforts since to find evidence to support each viewpoint.

Endnotes

1. Southerton, D., Warde, A. & Hand, M. (2004) 'The Limited Autonomy of the Consumer: Implications for Sustainable Consumption', in Southerton, D., Chappells, H. & van Vliet, B. (eds), *Sustainable Consumption*, London: Edward Elgar, pp. 32–48.
2. See for example Lantos, G.P. (1987) 'Advertising: Looking glass or molder of the masses?', *Journal of Public Policy and Marketing*, 6: 104–28; Richins, M.L. (1991) 'Social comparison and the idealized images of advertising', *Journal of Consumer Research*, 18(1): 71–83.
3. Pollay, R.W. (1986) 'The distorted mirrors: Reflections on the unintended consequences of advertising', *Journal of Marketing*, 50(2): 18–36.
4. Peattie, K. (1995) *Environmental Marketing Management: Meeting the Green Challenge*, London: Pitman Publishing.
5. Holbrook, M.B. (1987) 'Mirror, mirror, on the wall, what's unfair in the reflections on advertising?', *Journal of Marketing*, 51 (July): 95–103.
6. Hastings, G., Stead, M., McDermott, L., Alasdair, F., MacKintosh, A.M. & Rayner, M. (2003) *Review of the Research on the Effects of Food Promotion to Children* (Final report), London: Food Standards Agency.
7. Kilbourne, J. (2005) 'What else does sex sell?', *International Journal of Advertising*, 24(1): 119–22.
8. NESTA (2008) *Selling Sustainability: Seven Lessons from Advertising and Marketing to Sell Low-carbon Living*, London: National Endowment for Science Technology and the Arts.
9. Woo, C. & Peattie, K. (2008) *The Era of Corporate Citizenship: Perodua's Advertising with a Social Dimension*, Hong Kong: Hong Kong University.
10. As an example of classic communications models see Schramm, W. (1954) 'How Communication Works', in Schramm, W. (ed.), *The Process and Effects of Communication*, Chicago, IL: University of Illinois Press, pp. 3–26.
11. Leydesdorff, L. (2001) 'A Sociological Theory of Communication: The Self-Organization of the Knowledge-Based Society', unpublished paper, Boca Raton, FL.
12. Pickett-Baker, J. & Ozaki, R. (2008) 'Pro-environmental products: Marketing influence', *Journal of Consumer Marketing*, 25(5): 281–93.
13. Rose, C., Dade, P. & Scott, J. (2007) *Research into Motivating Prospectors, Settlers and Pioneers to Change Behaviours that Affect Climate Emissions*, London: Campaign Strategy.
14. See for example Iyer, E. & Bannerjee, B. (1993) 'Anatomy of green advertising', *Advertising Age*, 20: 494–501; Carlson, L., Grove, S.J. & Kangun, N. (1993) 'A content analysis of environmental advertising claims: A matrix method approach', *Journal of Advertising*, 22(3): 28–39.
15. Prothero, A., Peattie, K. & McDonagh, P. (1997) 'Communicating greener strategies: A study of on-pack communication', *Business Strategy and the Environment*, 6(2): 74–82.
16. Weissberg, T. (2008) 'Print media: Footprints with a lighter touch', *Marketing Week*, March 27, p. 23.
17. Peattie, S. & Peattie, K. (2003) 'Sales Promotion', in Baker, M.J. (ed.), *The Marketing Book*, 5th edn, London: Butterworth-Heinemman, pp. 458–84.
18. Tews, K., Busch, P.O & Jörgens, H. (2003) 'The diffusion of new environmental policy instruments', *European Journal of Political Research*, 42: 569–600.
19. Judge, K. (2008). 'Energy matters: Carbon labeling', *Geography Review*, 22(1): 36–7.
20. Nancarrow, C., Wright, L.T. & Brace, I. (1998) 'Gaining competitive advantage from packaging and labelling in marketing communications', *British Food Journal*, 100(2): 110–18.
21. D'Souza, C., Taghian, M. & Lamb, P. (2006) 'An empirical study on influence of environmental labels on consumers', *Corporate Communications*, 11(2): 162–73.
22. Schmidt-Pleschka, R. & Dickhut, H. (2005) *Guiding Systems for Sustainable Products in the Retail Industry: Sales-enhancing Consumer Communication at the Point of Sale*, Berlin: Die Verbraucherinitiative e.V. (Bundesverband).
23. United Nations Environment Programme, The Global Compact and Utopies (2005) *Talk the Walk. Advancing Sustainable Lifestyles through Marketing and Communications*, www.talkthewalk.net (accesssed 1 January 2009), p. 28.
24. Adapted from Goodman, R. (2008) 'Managing crises through social media', *PR News*, 64(1): 2.
25. http://www.dearcadbury.com (accessed 26 December 2008).

26. http://www.viewsonic.com/company/green (accessed 26 December 2008).
27. Kotler, P. & Armstrong, G. (2004) *The Principles of Marketing*, 10th edn, Upper Saddle River, NJ: Prentice Hall.
28. Dragon, A.G. (2006) 'The World is Not Enough: Sustainable Communication for a Sustainable Planet', *Proceedings of the World Congress on Communication for Sustainable Development*, 24–27 October, Rome: FAO.
29. Iyer, E. & Bannerjee, B. (1993) 'Anatomy of green advertising', *Advertising Age*, 20: 494–501.
30. Rose, C., Dade, P. & Scott, J. (2007) *Research into Motivating Prospectors, Settlers and Pioneers to Change Behaviours that Affect Climate Emissions*, London: Campaign Strategy.
31. Pickett-Baker, J. & Ozaki, R. (2008) 'Pro environmental products: Marketing influence on consumer purchase decision', *Journal of Consumer Marketing*, 25(5): 281–93.
32. Kollmuss, A. & Agyeman, J. (2002) 'Mind the gap: Why do people act environmentally and what are the barriers to proenvironmental behaviour?', *Environmental Educational Research*, 8(3): 239–60.
33. Gray-Lee, J., Scammon, D.L. & Mayer, R.N. (1994) 'Review of legal standards for environmental marketing claims', *Journal of Public Policy and Marketing*, 13(1): 155–9.
34. See for example Moore, K.J. (1993) 'Emerging Themes in Environmental Consumer Behavior', in Sheffet, M.J. (ed.), *Proceedings of the 1993 Marketing and Public Policy Conference*, East Lansing, MI: Michigan State University, pp. 109–22; and Mohr, L.A., Ellen, P.S. & Dogan Eroau, D. (1998) 'The development and testing of a measure of skepticism toward environmental claims in marketers' communications', *Journal of Consumer Affairs*, 32(1): 30–55.
35. Pickett-Baker, J. & Ozaki, R. (2008) 'Pro-environmental products: Marketing influence', *Journal of Consumer Marketing*, 25(5): 281–93.
36. Pfanner, E. (2008) '"Green" marketing loses buzz and credibility', *International Herald Tribune*, 6 July.
37. Karstens, B. & Belz, F. (2006) 'Information asymmetries, labels and trust in the German food market: A critical analysis based on the economics of information', *International Journal of Advertising*, 25(2): 189–211.
38. Pickett-Baker, J. & Ozaki, R. (2008) 'Pro environmental products: Marketing influence', *Journal of Consumer Marketing*, 25(5): 281–93.
39. Ottman, J.A., Stafford, E.R. & Hartman, C.L. (2006) 'Green marketing myopia', *Environment*, 48(5): 22–36.
40. Drucker, P. (1974) *Management: Tasks, Responsibilities, Practices*, New York: Harper & Row.
41. McDonagh, P. (1998) 'Towards a theory of sustainable communications in risk society', *Journal of Marketing Management*, 14(6): 591–622.
42. *Ibid.*
43. Bernstein, D. (1992) *In The Company of Green: Corporate Communication for the New Environment*, London: ISBA.
44. Kanatschnig, D. (2005) 'Corporate Social Responsibility, Corporate Sustainability and Communications', Seminar for the Austrian Business Academy for Sustainable Development, Bad Blumau, Austria, quoted in Signitzer, B. & Prexl, A. (2008) 'Corporate sustainability communications: Aspects of theory and professionalization', *Journal of Public Relations Research*, 20(1): 1–18.
45. See Zoller, K. (1999) 'Growing Credibility through Dialogue', in Charter, M. & Polonsky, M.J. (eds), *Greener Marketing: A Global Perspective on Greening Marketing Practice*, 2nd edn, Sheffield: Greenleaf Publishing.
46. Kanatschnig, D. (2005) 'Corporate Social Responsibility, Corporate Sustainability and Communications', Seminar for the Austrian Business Academy for Sustainable Development, Bad Blumau, Austria, quoted in Signitzer, B. & Prexl, A. (2008) 'Corporate sustainability communications: Aspects of theory and professionalization', *Journal of Public Relations Research*, 20(1): 1–18.
47. Berthon, P., Pitt, L. & Campbell, C. (2008) 'Ad lib: When customers create the ad', *California Management Review*, 50(4): 6–30.
48. *Ibid.*
49. See Neale, A. (1999) 'Coming out of their Shell', in Charter, M. & Polonsky, M.J. (eds), *Greener Marketing: A Global Perspective on Greening Marketing Practice*, 2nd edn, Sheffield: Greenleaf Publishing; and Löfstedt, R.E. & Renn, O. (2006) 'The Brent Spar controversy: An example of risk communication gone wrong', *Risk Analysis*, 17(2): 131–6.

CHAPTER 9

Customer Cost

1. Identify total customer cost, including prices, purchase costs, use costs and post-use costs.
2. Understand how to reduce the costs to customers of sustainable products and services.
3. Discuss the nature of prices.

LOOKING AHEAD: PREVIEWING THE CONCEPTS

In this chapter, we will shift the focus from prices to total customer cost, which goes further to include purchase costs, use costs and post-use costs. In the first part of the chapter we will look at the individual components of total customer cost from the consumer's perspective. In the second part we will take the marketer's perspective and identify two goals of sustainability marketing management: reduce total customer cost and make customers aware of total costs. Several options for attaining these two goals are presented. In the last part, we will switch to the external perspective and discuss how the (lack of) internalization of socio-ecological costs will alter competition mechanisms in the future.

SUSTAINABILITY MARKETING STORY: PHILIPS 'MARATHON' – SAVING CUSTOMER COST THROUGH LONG LIFE AND ENERGY EFFICIENCY

Philips Lighting, the lighting division of Netherlands-based Royal Philips Electronics, invented compact fluorescent bulb technology in 1980 and has led the way in product refinement and market development ever since. Despite the obvious advantages of the new lighting technology, such as extended lifetime, energy efficiency, and absence of heat emissions, consumers still preferred the traditional incandescent lamps for their brightness, instantaneousness and low price. Early generations of compact fluorescent light (CFL) bulbs were big and bulky, forcing consumers to replace lampshades or get modification kits to make the bulbs fit some of their fixtures. Additionally, consumer dissatisfaction was caused by the humming, buzzing and flickering associated with the early bulbs' magnetic ballasts, together with the delayed start, lack of dimmability, poor outdoor performance, poor light levels and colour rendition. In the 1990s, the penetration rates of CFL bulbs in the residential light market were generally disappointing, with ownership levels ranging from just 0.1 CFL per household in North America to approximately 1.5 CFL per household on average in Europe.

After years of languishing sales of CFLs in the US market, in 1994 Philips made its first attempt to market a standalone CFL bulb. The product was branded EarthLight and was sold at a unit price of $15 (€10.80) versus $0.75 (€0.55) for incandescent bulbs. What followed were numerous awards, such as 'Best of What's New' in the environmental technology category of *Popular Science* magazine in 1997 or the award for technological innovation from *Discover* magazine. However, neither the awards nor the environmental benefits of the product persuaded consumers to buy the EarthLight. On the contrary, the bulb had a clumsy shape and was incompatible with many existing lighting fixtures, which kept acceptance low.

This situation made Philips determined in 1998 to reconsider its marketing approach. The first step was to find out through market research what was really important to consumers of light bulbs. As Steve Goldmacher, director of corporate communications for Philips Lighting in the US, explained, 'It turned out the environment wasn't their primary need. Environmental responsibility was the number-four or -five purchase criterion. Number-one is that they wanted the bulb to last longer. Being green is wonderful, but no one wants to pay the extra nickel.' Another major problem uncovered was a high level of consumer confusion concerning CFL bulbs, especially regarding their expected lifetime.

The market research prompted Philips to react to the misunderstood consumer benefit and the consumer confusion by offering a whole series of new long-life light bulbs. Thus, it reintroduced the EarthLight under the Marathon brand in 2000, underscoring its new 'super long life' and promising savings of over $20 (€14.40) in energy costs over its lifetime. The lifetime of the product was guaranteed, meaning that if a light bulb failed to last as long as Philips promised, the customer would be able to mail it back to the company for a refund. The market research had revealed that consumers wanted their light bulbs to have a traditional shape, so the new design of

Marathon bulbs offered the look and versatility of incandescent light bulbs. To add credibility, the products were labelled with the US Environmental Protection Agency's Energy Star label. Within the new series, Marathon would be the top-line product family with a guaranteed life of five to seven years. Additionally, in 2000 Philips introduced Halogena as a middle-level product range with a guaranteed life of two years, and in 2002 DuraMax, as the entry-level product range with a guaranteed life of one year. This full line concept would allow consumers to choose the ideal light bulb for different locations and needs. These measures, backed up by increasing sensitivity to rising utility costs and electricity shortages, led to an increase in sales of 12% in 2001 in an otherwise flat market. Due to the initial success, the full line concept has been adopted by Philips on a worldwide basis.[1]

Total Customer Cost: The Consumer Perspective

Reduced costs through longer life, the fact that the light bulb doesn't have to be changed so often and significant energy savings were key factors in Philips' successful repositioning of its bulb range. By introducing a product series that addressed different needs through different value propositions, Philips improved the acceptance and diffusion of its CFL bulbs, despite their higher prices. Price is an important element in consumers' product-evaluation process, yet it is not the only one, as we will see in this chapter. In a narrow sense, price represents the amount of money charged for a product or service.[2] As suggested by this definition, price is a relatively producer-oriented and exchange-based concept, since it refers to the amount of money that the producer receives and the consumer pays at the point of exchange. In a wider sense, price can take on various facets and functions, being considered a reflection of the cost of production, a signal of quality to consumers, a basis for market segmentation, a reflection of the demand that exists for a product and the available supply, an important basis for competition and, last but not least, a key marketing variable that can be influenced to achieve a wide variety of marketing objectives.[3]

From the producer's perspective, price is the only element of the marketing mix that generates revenue and (at least in the long term) must therefore cover all the costs incurred by the company for producing, distributing and selling the product.[4] From the consumer's perspective, price represents only one element of the costs that the consumer incurs by acquiring, recycling or disposing of a product, referred to as *total customer cost* (TCC). Some use the concept of *total cost of ownership* as the total cost of a purchase from a particular supplier. We will, however, refer to total customer cost, as this goes beyond the 'ownership' of goods as a response to consumer needs. Consequently, price is a concept that fails to reflect the total costs arising from buying decisions. An approach that is oriented to the total consumption process, including the acquisition, use and post-use phases, is to switch from the price perspective to the total customer cost perspective; in other words, a switch from the producer's to the consumer's perspective (see Figure 9.1).

The consumer's purchase decision is based on an analysis of expected and perceived benefits and costs. Conventional marketing theories and microeconomic theories assume that consumers try, either

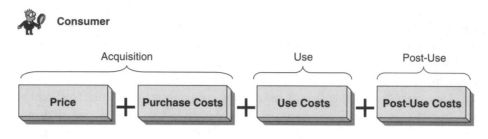

Figure 9.1 Total customer cost – the consumer perspective

consciously or unconsciously, to maximize benefits and minimize costs. In other words, the decision to buy is made in favour of the product that delivers the highest net benefit or highest perceived value; that is, the highest difference between total benefits and total costs (see Chapter 4).[5] Consequently, sustainable products will be bought only if they perform better in terms of perceived value than other competing offers. This implies that sustainable products must provide a higher net benefit than conventional products in order to be bought.

In this chapter we will focus on the costs side of the benefit–cost balance. In the following, we will take a closer look at the individual components of consumer costs.[6] These costs go beyond the retail price of a product insofar as they also include purchase costs, use costs and post-use costs.

Consumer costs for sustainable products are individually perceived, evaluated and weighted based on a number of personal and situational factors such as socio-ecological awareness, socio-ecological knowledge, disposable income, peer groups and purchasing situation. If the other cost components are more or less visible or predictable to the individual consumer, *price* has a special status in the cost assessment process for the following reasons: it is known prior to the purchase; it is expressed in monetary units; and it (generally) belongs to the up-front costs. Since consumers tend to minimize present and *not* future costs, price takes the lion's share in the cost evaluation process.[7]

Purchase costs include the costs of searching for a product (search costs), gathering information on prices, specific features and comparing the product to alternative marketing offers (information costs), and finally obtaining the product (transportation costs), also known collectively as transaction costs.[8] Often, the purchase costs of sustainable products are higher as compared to conventional products. One of the reasons is that specific features of sustainable products are 'experience qualities' or 'credence qualities'. Generally, the theory of information economics[9] distinguishes between three types of product qualities: search, experience and credence qualities. Search qualities can be fully evaluated prior to purchase (e.g. the colour of a shirt). Experience qualities can be evaluated only after the purchase, during the use or consumption phase (e.g. the shirt's colour fastness during washing). Credence qualities can never be fully evaluated by the consumer, neither prior to nor after the purchase (e.g. the shirt's fabric being made from organic cotton). In the case of the latter, the customer has to rely on the information given by the company itself or by a third-party organization. Each type of product quality is associated with different consumer search and information costs. The highest search and information costs occur when experience and credence qualities dominate. In the case of sustainable products, social and ecological qualities are very often experience (e.g. energy consumption of electric appliances) and/or credence qualities (e.g. organic production). Credence qualities stem from the production process prior to the purchase or from the post-use process, which is emphasized by sustainability marketing and is distinctive compared to conventional marketing (with its focus on purchase and use).

Making an initial purchase of a product also involves higher search and information costs than subsequent purchases. When confronted with the decision to buy a new product, consumers perceive a certain level of risk arising out of the purchase decision. The literature distinguishes several dimensions of perceived risk:

- Financial risk captures outcomes for consumers after they adopt products that are anticipated to be financially negative.
- Performance risk relates to concerns that products will not perform as anticipated.
- Physical risk is the perception that products could be harmful to adopters.
- Time risk relates to the perception that the adoption and use of the product will take too much time.
- Social risk involves negative reactions from a consumer's social network.
- Psychological risk concerns the nervousness arising from the anticipated post-purchase emotions such as frustration, disappointment, worry and regret.

Associated with psychological risk is the loss aversion that people have when it comes to giving up current benefits, for promised yet not experienced higher benefits. People irrationally overvalue the benefits of the products they currently possess relative to those of products they do not own.[10] This is one of main reasons consumers are hesitant about buying new sustainable products when they are first introduced to the market. On the other hand, it may encourage relatively sustainable consumption behaviour if consumers are slow to replace existing products that are performing satisfactorily for the sake of new technologies or fashions.

Transportation costs are directly related to the distribution intensity of the product. The less available the products, the higher the probable distance a customer has to travel to get the product, and consequently the higher the incurred transportation costs.

Use costs are often underestimated and even ignored at the moment of purchase. In the case of long-lasting products such as houses, cars, washing machines and refrigerators, a considerable amount of money is paid for energy or maintenance during the usage stage. Also included within use costs are switching costs, which customers face when switching from one product or supplier to another. Especially when customers have to learn new behaviour and unlearn old in connection with the use of a new product or service, switching costs can be extremely high.[11] Sustainable products or solutions can involve a different usage pattern. For example, living in a passively heated house makes opening windows for airing superfluous; using car sharing involves a totally different approach to mobility. But even if the necessary adjustments in product usage are not that radical, and even if no behaviour adjustments at all are required, customers can become 'captive' to a product through sheer habit. Therefore switching from conventional to sustainable products requires customers' willingness to give up old habits and eventually learn new ones.

Post-use costs comprise costs related to the collection, storage and disposal of products. Key variables affecting post-use costs are the amount of packaging involved, the product's design, the product's durability, the amount and type of materials used and available resale or recycling opportunities. Generally, consumers have a low awareness of post-use costs. In developed countries with an advanced waste collection infrastructure, the waste service fees, set by municipal authorities, are included in property taxes or are attached to the billing for another public service such as water supply and are thus paid 'automatically'. Collection services for bulky items like furniture or appliances, household hazardous waste or garden and construction waste are charged separately. Local authorities increasingly seek to implement variable-rate systems based on the actual costs of solid waste management and related, as far as possible, to the volume of collection service actually provided. 'Pay-as-you-throw' systems offer households a direct incentive to reduce their waste.[12]

In developed countries the collection, disposal and recycling of materials are provided by the formal sector, driven by law and the general public's concern for the environment, and often at considerable expense. In many less developed countries resource recovery is partly conducted by the informal sector.[13] An example is household waste management in Dhaka, Bangladesh, a city with more than 6 million inhabitants who produce over 3000 tons of household waste each day. The Dhaka City Corporation collects less than half of it, while the rest of the waste remains nearby in open sites, along main roads or railroad tracks, in drains or waterways. This poses serious threats to human health and the environment through water and soil pollution. In 1995 the nongovernmental organization Waste Concern started a community-based project in Dhaka to reduce, reuse, recycle and recover waste (the '4 Rs'). It is based on the idea that the organic content of Dhaka's household waste, which accounts for more than 70% of the total, can be converted into valuable compost. Activities include house-to-house waste collection, composting of the collected waste and marketing of the compost to fertilizer companies and plant nurseries. Since there is a market for the compost, the waste collection is financially viable. The initial project was so successful that it was expanded to other communities in Dhaka, helping to clean up areas, create new jobs for poor people, reduce the Dhaka City Corporation's waste-management costs and create business opportunities.[14]

In developed countries households are encouraged (or even compelled by law) to recycle waste streams for items such as paper, glass, metals, plastic and textiles. The recycling infrastructure can take two forms:

1. A 'bring' or 'drop-off' system, which means that the materials have to be taken by the consumer to a collection point.
2. A 'collect-type' or 'kerbside' scheme, which requires households to separate recyclables from the waste stream and place them in specially provided boxes or bags at the kerb for collection.

From the consumers' perspective, recycling involves transportation costs in the case of drop-off systems or nonmonetary costs from separating waste, such as storage costs, time and learning costs. Deposit-refund systems, for example for beverage containers, as well as product charges on batteries, cars, tyres and home appliances, are further instruments used in many OECD countries to promote the collection and recovery of post-use consumer waste.[15] Although some of the costs presented above are monetary costs or can be easily monetized, a significant amount of the perceived consumer costs are nonmonetary in nature. The transportation costs, for example, consist of monetary fuel costs or public transportation costs and of nonmonetary costs related to the time expenditure, the associated stress or the missed opportunity to do other things.

Resale is a way for consumers to reduce post-use costs. In the past, secondhand markets were limited in space and time. The digital age has changed that. Online market places like eBay enable trade on a local, national and international basis. Since 1995 secondhand markets provided by the Internet have become a multibillion business worldwide. Online trade allows the original purchaser to recoup some of the costs associated with purchasing, owning and using a product. Furthermore, by selling the product, the lifetime is extended and the material value of the product is enhanced.

Total Customer Cost: The Marketer Perspective

So far we have looked at total customer cost from a consumer perspective. In this section, we will analyse TCC from a marketer's perspective (see Figure 9.2). Marketers of sustainable products must move beyond pricing decisions to consider the total cost to the customer for purchasing, using and disposing of the product, and integrate this perspective into their marketing strategy. As a consequence, sustainability marketing management should seek both to reduce the total customer cost and to make customers aware of total customer cost.

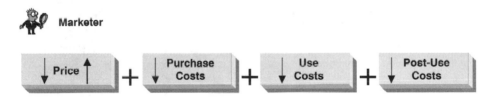

Figure 9.2 Total customer cost – the marketer perspective

Reduce Total Customer Cost

One way of managing the cost balance in favour of sustainable products is to reduce the total customer cost; that is, the sum of all costs related to a product, comprising price, purchase costs, use costs and post-use costs. In this section we will look at possibilities of lowering the total customer cost.

Price

Price is a marketing tool that can influence demand. Conventional economics tells us that in general, as prices decrease consumer demand increases and vice versa. There are exceptions to this relationship, however, for example when consumers interpret price levels as an indicator of quality or exclusivity. The sensitivity of consumers to price changes also varies between types of purchase and among consumer segments. By setting prices companies can increase demand or even reduce it.[16] Power companies, for instance, sometimes have trouble meeting demand during peak usage periods. By lowering the prices for water and energy during the night, power companies try to shift the demand of customers temporarily. Similarly, public transportation companies offer special rates during the day, when trains, buses and subways are not used by commuters. Consequently, active price management helps in fully utilizing existing capacity and improving the resource efficiency of these types of service.

In general, companies can choose between two general price-setting approaches: value-based pricing or cost-based pricing (see Figure 9.3). Value-based pricing is based on a differentiation strategy and uses buyers' perceptions of value, not the seller's cost, as the key to pricing. It is often expressed in terms of charging whatever price the market will bear. Highly fashionable or unique items exemplify value-based pricing. While value-based pricing is customer driven, cost-based pricing is product and production driven. The latter means that a price will be set that covers all the costs of production and includes a target profit margin.[17] The predominant focus on costs is typical for low-cost strategies, which aim at cost reductions in purchasing and production processes to offer low prices for mass markets. Discount retailers like Wal-Mart follow such a strategy. In times of rising prices for basic necessities such as food, water and energy, people with low incomes can have difficulties covering their everyday costs. Low prices make (basic) products affordable for them. In this way it can be argued that low prices contribute to sustainability because they meet certain social criteria. A key question, however, is whether low prices are offered to customers at the expense of ecological and social costs somewhere else.

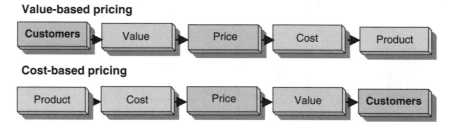

Figure 9.3   Value-based pricing vs cost-based pricing[18]
Source: Kotler, P. & Armstrong, G. (2004) *The Principles of Marketing*, 10th edn, Upper Saddle River, NJ: Prentice Hall, p. 360.

Value-Based Pricing

Consumers generally expect sustainable products to be more expensive than conventional ones, though this may be a perception based on experience rather than a market necessity. In this context, marketing managers face two basic questions: Should the company go for a price premium for sustainable products? How much of a price premium will the customer be willing to pay for a sustainable product? In answering these questions several factors must be taken into account:

- *The nature of the product and the level of differentiation in the market:*Differentiating a company's marketing offer is about gaining competitive advantage by offering the customer more value than competitors' offers. A product's differentiation potential depends on the product's nature. In general, the differentiation potential of convenience products (e.g. toothpaste or laundry detergents) is lower than that of shopping goods (e.g. furniture, clothing) and speciality goods (e.g. cars, watches).[19] Products can be differentiated on features, performance, style, design, durability, reliability, image and, last but not least, sustainability aspects. The more unique the product appears in the eyes of the customer, the higher the marketer's leeway to demand a price premium relative to competition.

- *The profile of the sustainability issues to which the product is linked*: Some social and environmental issues have a high public concern profile and 'emotional load', which allow them to command a premium price. Sustainability issues related to food usually receive a lot of public attention. The use of antibiotics and hormones in industrial livestock farming to help animals grow faster and put on weight more efficiently, the threat to human health of food additives or the depletion of fish stocks are examples of issues that received intense public coverage through the media, NGOs and ultimately through companies that took up these concerns. It is a challenge to communicate parts of the ecosystem that are not glamorous but vital. Promoting products because they help protect the marvellous rainforest or photogenic mammals is relatively easy; promoting products that protect something more mundane like bees is much harder (although the fate of bee populations in the wake of the outbreak of 'colony collapse disorder' threatens agricultural systems globally. In the USA bees account for the pollination of one third of food output, but during 2007 the American bee population slumped by 30%).[20]

- *The credibility level that the company and the product enjoy in the market*: The higher the ability of the company to transform credence qualities into quasi-search qualities, the easier it is for the customer to accept premium prices. Basically, the company has to transfer information to the customer that signals credibility. This type of information forwarding is referred to as signalling.[21] Credence qualities can be transferred into quasi-search qualities through various communication instruments such as labels, self-declarations, product brand, corporate brand, personality and Internet presence (e.g. Hipp and The Body Shop).[22]

- *The perceived value of sustainable products vs conventional products*: A premium price is enforceable only if it matches its perceived value in the eyes of the customer. This implies that sustainable products should be perceived as having a higher value than conventional products. One way of making the product's added value more transparent to the customer is to break down its sustainability premium into sustainability-related cost components (i.e. x% of this premium is to cover the costs of responsible disposal or carbon offsetting). Empirical studies in the UK show that most consumers believe that higher prices of sustainable products are a ploy to part consumers from more of their money, rather than a genuine attempt to benefit the natural and/or social environments. Transparency regarding premium prices could help counteract that consumer impression.

- *The price sensitivity of customers, and their awareness of and interest in sustainability issues related to the product*: Before setting a premium price, the company should carefully consider which customer groups it will target with its sustainable product. Will it address *socio-ecological actives*, sustainability enthusiasts who most certainly draw a higher value from sustainable products than conventional ones, thus being willing to pay a premium/higher price? Will it go for the *socio-ecological approachables* (e.g. LOHAS or Lifestyles of Health and Sustainability), who are often willing to pay a higher price for the perceived value added, but who are reluctant to make any compromise when it comes to the quality and service of the product? Or will it approach the mass market, the *socio-ecological passives*, where price sensitivity is higher and socio-ecological value does not always translate into individual value? Hessnatur, a German clothing company, aims at the socio-ecological actives in a niche market. The socio-ecological value of organic cotton textiles is communicated as one of the primary customer benefits. Patagonia, a manufacturer of sportswear and outdoor clothing, targets the customer group of socio-ecological approachables, especially young, wealthy singles, mostly men, for whom price is of secondary importance. They value superior durability, functionality and performance, while the product's environmental performance completes the positioning strategy. Patagonia can thus demand prices up to 50% above those charged by competitors by targeting a LOHAS segment. For its Coop Naturaline clothing collection, the Swiss retailer Coop emphasizes both price and environmental superiority, derived from the use of organic cotton. The Coop Naturaline collection is priced the same as conventional collections, renouncing sustainability-based price premiums in favour of appealing to the mass market.[23]

- *The existence and use of reference pricing in the product category*: Reference prices are prices that buyers carry in their mind and refer to when they look at a given product.[24] For sustainable products with a price premium, this may entail difficulties in moving consumers beyond habitual pricing brackets. The record industry in the UK, for example, spent years trying and failing to move consumers past the £5 (€5.25) price bracket for a vinyl LP, before CDs allowed them to charge £15 (€15.75) for something that rapidly cost less to produce. The best solution for sustainable products might be to avoid competing through a market offering that looks like the existing products and instead provide something that stands out through innovative technology (e.g. a hybrid car) or alternative service solutions and new pricing systems (e.g. car sharing).

Cost-Based Pricing

The assumption that sustainable products will necessarily cost more has underpinned the sustainability marketing debate for the last two decades. This assumption may be misleading, however. On the one hand, the green premium may relate more to company pricing strategy than to economic necessity. If a company feels it is adding value by adding sustainability benefits, it may feel justified in increasing the price, regardless of the underlying cost structure. On the other hand, cost-based pricing means that products that have sought to internalize the social and ecological costs associated with consumption and production (i.e. more sustainable products) will be at a cost/price disadvantage to those that do not.[25]

For many companies, developing and implementing a sustainability marketing strategy may indeed involve increased costs, which are reflected in higher prices. This additional cost burden will often come from production technologies that are implemented end-of-pipe (e.g. an air filter) and as something added to the existing production system they inevitably add to costs. Cleaner production or integrated production technologies may require a higher initial capital cost, but the changes in operations usually result in lower long-term costs by minimizing waste and reducing water and energy consumption.[26]

The problem of higher costs associated with sustainable products may also stem from (initial) low production volumes. Higher production volumes generate economies of scale, thus reducing costs and prices. Manufacturers that can negotiate large volume discounts from suppliers cause cost/price distortions in the market by producing artificial economies of scale. As a consequence, suppliers push up prices for smaller competitors, confining sustainable products to a niche strategy. To avoid this trap marketing and operations should work hand in hand, with marketing seeking to increase sales volume (e.g. by reaching other market segments or approaching the mass market), while operations try to achieve savings in packaging, production and logistics, which can be passed on to the consumers.

81[Fünf] High-Tech and Holzbau AG is a good example of how to reduce costs and trim prices. This German company has been one of the pioneers in offering wooden, low-energy houses since the 1990s. The purchase price of its energy-efficient houses is usually up to 10% higher than conventional houses due to the increased cost of insulation. To compensate for the premium price, 81[Fünf] High-Tech and Holzbau AG reengineered both products and processes. By simplifying and standardizing the designs to utilize industrially produced high-quality wooden elements, and through close cooperation with production craftspeople to identify where time and money could be saved in the construction process, it cut costs, a saving that could then be passed onto the customer.

Rent/Lease Pricing

Renting or leasing is an alternative pricing approach to value-based or cost-based pricing. Under rent or lease pricing, the right to use the product is transferred for a specified period from the seller to the buyer, but no title transfer occurs.[27] At the end of the specified period the product is taken back by the vendor for reuse or recycling. The basic principle of renting and leasing is the same. The main difference between the two lies in the length of the time period: renting transfers the right to use the product for a couple of hours or days (e.g. videos), while leasing transfers it for a couple of years (e.g. automobiles). An advantage of renting and leasing is that the customer does not have to bear the capital costs.[28] Disadvantages are less (self-)esteem as attached to product ownership, no possibilities of modifying or customizing the product, as well as higher transaction costs. Usually, renting requires time and effort getting access to the product. Thus, there is a trade-off between capital costs, (self-)esteem, rental and transaction costs.

The importance of the product to the consumer and the frequency of usage will influence decisions to buy or rent/lease products. Heavy users, who identify themselves with the product and who use it frequently, will probably buy; light users, who do not express themselves through the product in question, are more likely to rent. That was the original business idea behind Rentaski, a Swiss service company that rents winter sports equipment such as skis, snowblades, Nordic skis, snowboards and sledges. Since 1987 Rentaski has become the dominant market leader in renting winter sports equipment represented in 29 Swiss ski resorts (e.g. Arosa, Davos, Klosters, Laax and St Moritz).[29] By renting the winter sports equipment dozens of times per season, the resource efficiency of the material is increased.

Purchase Costs

Purchase costs play an essential role in the consumer's evaluation process of product alternatives. The challenge for sustainable products is to reduce purchase costs (search costs, information costs, transportation costs, perceived risks) and overcome the initial buying barriers to achieve a first purchase. In recent years, suppliers of organic food, for instance, have done a good job of minimizing purchase costs and bringing them to the same level as for conventional products. From a niche sector, sold only via health-food and specialized organic food stores or directly from the farms, organic food has become mainstream, entering conventional retail chains from the early 1990s and giving rise to a new form of retail outlet, the specialized organic supermarket (e.g. Whole Foods Markets in the USA, Planet Organic in the UK, Alnatura and Basic in Germany). These supermarkets have mushroomed in the last decade, with demand and growth rates rising steadily. Information and advertising campaigns increased both the level of awareness and knowledge of organic food products. Increased awareness among consumers was backed up by the fact that the organic food sector has become increasingly moulded by marketing professionals. The product appearance of organic food has become as attractive as conventional alternatives. Branded organic product ranges are highly visible in supermarkets and marketing campaigns in the mass media are no longer a rarity.[30] As a result of the high visibility and availability of organic food, the purchase costs in the form of information, search and transportation risks as well as perceived risks have been reduced.

Use Costs

Sustainable products like hybrid cars, low-energy houses, eco-efficient refrigerators and washing machines may cost more upfront, but they involve lower running costs due to energy and water savings during usage. Philips Marathon energy-saving bulbs represent a typical example of such a product, by reducing energy costs and eliminating the inconvenience of changing bulbs frequently. The competitive advantage of higher eco-efficiency and lower usage costs should be highlighted and can be enhanced further by sustainability marketers. The amount of cost savings realized is a function of the (sustainable) product's performance and the consumer's patterns of use. A number of empirical studies show that the energy consumption of (sustainable) products varies by 10–20% depending on usage patterns. To leverage the full cost savings potential of sustainable products, marketers have to inform consumers.

The Washright campaign initiated by the International Association for Soaps, Detergents and Maintenance Products aims to educate customers throughout Europe about more efficient washing habits, by featuring the Washright panel on detergent products. The key messages are:

• Washing more clothes in one wash reduces the water and energy used.
• The amount of detergent used should relate to the hardness of the water in your area and the soil level of the laundry.
• Most of today's washing detergents work well at low temperatures, so high-temperature washes are not usually necessary and use more energy than required.
• Keep permanent or refillable packaging and buy refill packs where available.[31]

These messages make consumers aware that they can reduce their use costs on two levels: by buying sustainable products (buying behaviour) and by using those products in an efficient way (use behaviour).

Switching from one product to another may also incur costs. The so-called switching costs associated with sustainable products are mostly underemphasized, despite being of utmost importance to the market success of a product. Take hybrid or electric cars. Many people are hesitant to buy this new kind of car, because they are concerned that they might have to change their driving habits (which is a switching cost). To achieve market breakthrough, the product must either offer exceptionally compelling features or be demonstrably easy to learn and use. Several options are available to minimize switching costs: use trained sales personnel to demonstrate the use of the product at key points of contact with the customer (e.g. trade fairs, point of sale); provide easy-to-understand, accessible instructions for use; develop entertaining multimedia learning applications to visualize the functioning of the product for the customer; leverage early adopters and communities to support those who may need more help to use the new product or service. These kinds of measure help to reduce the perceived risks and switching costs of buying sustainable products for the first time.

Post-Use Costs

Post-use costs involve both direct and indirect costs. Direct costs refer to those that the consumer experiences at the end of the product's life (or period of use), through, for example, transportation and disposal costs. One of the most efficient ways to reduce *direct post-use costs* is to extend the product's life cycle through repair, reuse and upgrading, thus slowing down the throughput of resources.[32] Extended guarantee programmes and attractive maintenance and support services can be implemented to promote a 'repair instead of replace' mentality. Another alternative, especially for technology-intensive products with high innovation rates, is to design upgradeable products. Miele, for example, offers PC Update, a service that allows customers to have washing machines, tumble dryers and dishwashers reprogrammed according to the latest software. Hewlett-Packard offers asset recovery services to its customers. The programme focuses on three primary methods to address product end of life: extending the life of systems when possible through a refurbishing process; responsibly disposing of units that cannot be refurbished; extracting useful components and materials from recyclable systems to make use of them elsewhere. From the customer's point of view, the options available are trade-in, return for cash, leasing return and donation (see Figure 9.4).[33]

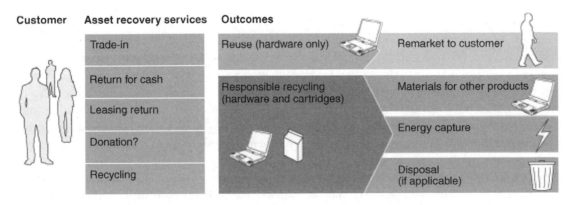

Figure 9.4 Hewlett-Packard asset-recovery services to reduce customer post-use costs
Source: HP (www.hp.com)

Particularly relevant, especially to *indirect customer post-use costs*, is the 'extended producer responsibility' (EPR) concept, which has become very important in the public policy arena in recent years. EPR is a policy approach in which producers of consumer products are required to accept responsibility for the management or disposal of the products they have placed on the market at the end of their life cycle. The idea behind EPR is that if manufacturers are made to pay more directly for the waste created by their products, they will improve their design processes to reduce that waste (and thus reduce costs). A wide range of programmes (both mandatory and voluntary) fall under the EPR umbrella, including 'take-back' programmes and deposit and refund systems. EPR programmes are now well established internationally and many initiatives exist in a number of OECD countries (e.g. for packaging, electrical and electronic equipment, automobiles, tyres and small consumer batteries).[34] The EU Directive on End-of-Life Vehicles, for example, stipulates that member states should ensure that the last holder and/or owner can deliver the end-of-life vehicle to an authorized treatment facility without any extra cost. Member states should ensure that producers meet all, or a significant part of, the costs of the implementation of these measures and/or take back end-of-life vehicles.[35]

The extent to which EPR programmes ultimately result in waste prevention (e.g. through changes in product design) has not yet been conclusively researched and documented. Most existing EPR programmes do, however, show a clear improvement in recycling rates. In South Korea, for example, Samsung and LG Electronics have reportedly reduced the weight of televisions. Manufacturers of computer disk drives are apparently using fewer circuit parts, and vacuum cleaner manufacturers have made product design changes. In Japan, the new vehicle recycling law has prompted Honda to increase the proportion of recycled material in vehicles, increase the recyclability of certain automobile components, and create markets for other secondary materials from vehicles.[36] All these changes prompted by voluntary or mandatory participation in EPR programmes involve new costs structures for producers, which will consequently translate into higher or lower market prices, depending on the achieved trade-off between compliance costs and realized cost savings through eco-design and material savings.

Making Customers Aware of Total Cost

Often customers are not aware of the total costs of various product alternatives. They make decisions based on incomplete information and suffer from a phenomenon called *bounded rationality*.[37] Take decision-making behaviour in the case of refrigerator purchases. A representative survey in Finland reports that consumers are likely to use biased information sources, such as sales personnel or brand-specific brochures, instead of more impartial ones. According to the study, price is the most frequent criterion used to evaluate and compare brands. Because consumers seem more concerned with immediate losses than future gains, energy-efficient refrigerators are at a disadvantage. These may cost more upfront, but they will yield downstream benefits over their life in the form of reduced energy costs.[38]

Why is price often the main purchase decision criterion, prevailing over quality, sustainability value, performance or lifetime costs considerations? The answer may lie in the individual situation of the customer, but also in the marketing and competitive practices that many companies endorse. Price-focused promotions resulting in 'price wars' inculcate price-dominated buying behaviour in the consumer. Matching this fact with the usually higher (perceived) prices of sustainable products as compared to conventional products leads to a challenge to sustainability marketers to make total costs more salient to the customer. How can marketers enhance customers' awareness of the costs of sustainable products versus conventional products? A broad range of instruments can be used for this purpose: online tools such as savings calculators, life cycle costs information sheets or labelling instruments. These instruments can be implemented either by producers or by third-party organizations.

Producer Instruments

Companies can provide product-specific information on the costs associated with their sustainable product(s), mostly in comparison with conventional products. An example of such an approach is the Savings Calculator provided by Philips, where a current lighting solution is compared with a Philips energy-saving solution, highlighting the monetary and CO_2-saving effects both in the short and long term.[39] Continental, one of the world's leading suppliers to the automotive industry, communicates the fuel-saving potential of its tyres as compared to those of its main competitors by means of an online calculator on its website.[40] Phoenix Motorcars, a manufacturer of zero-emission, freeway-speed, all-electric vehicles, offers a tool to calculate the return on investment from buying a Phoenix car versus a comparison vehicle of the consumer's choice.[41] Another example of a company-based instrument is the EcoSavings Calculator developed by Electrolux, where the best products available in the Electrolux Group today are compared with 1997 standard appliances (see Figure 9.5). The difference in consumption between the 1997 standard and the most efficient appliances currently is used to calculate the annual savings potential for a household, for major cities, for any of the 22 countries analysed and for all countries aggregated. The savings are illustrated as annual economic savings expressed in local currency and euros, and as ecological savings, expressed in metric tons of water, kWh electricity and related CO_2 emissions.[42]

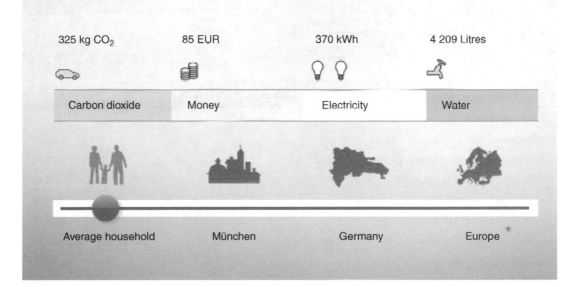

Figure 9.5 The Electrolux EcoSavings Calculator – switching from 1997 standard appliances to best available technologies
Source: Electrolux, www.electrolux.com/ecosavings.

Table 9.1   Savings Calculator Tool: Energy Star Qualified vs Standard Clothes Washer

Annual and Life Cycle Costs and Savings for 1 Residential Clothes Washer(s)

	1 ENERGY STAR Qualified Unit(s)	1 Conventional Unit(s)	Saving with ENERGY STAR
Annual Operating Costs*			
Electricity costs	36.18	52.79	16.61
Water costs	17.39	38.35	20.96
Gas costs	0.00	0.00	0.00
Maintenance costs	0.00	0.00	0.00
Total	**$54**	**$91**	**$38**
Life Cycle Costs*			
Operating costs (electricity, water, and maintenance)	469.32	798.46	329.14
Electricity costs	316.95	462.45	145.50
Water costs	152.37	336.00	183.63
Gas costs	0.00	0.00	0.00
Maintenance costs	0.00	0.00	0.00
Purchase price for 1 unit(s)	500.00	300.00	−200.00
Total	**969.32**	**1098.46**	**129.14**
Simple payback of initial additional cost (years)[†]			**5.3**

* Annual costs exclude the initial purchase price. All costs, except initial cost, are discounted over the products' lifetime using a real discount rate of 4%. See "Assumptions" to change factors including the discount rate.
† A simple payback period of zero years means that the payback is immediate.

Summary of Benefits for 1 Residential Clothes Washer(s)

Initial cost difference	−$200.00
Life cycle savings	**$329.14**
Net life cycle savings (life cycle savings - additional cost)	**$129.14**
Simple payback of additional cost (years)	**5.32**
Life cycle electricity saved (kWh)	**1882.35**
Life cycle air pollution reduction (lbs of CO_2)	**2889.40**
Air pollution reduction equivalence (number of cars removed from the road for a year)	**0.25**
Air pollution reduction equivalence (acres of forest)	**0.36**
Savings as a percent of retail price	**26%**

Source: US Environmental Protection Agency, www.energystar.gov. (31 December 2008)

Third-Party Organization Instruments

An increasing number of companies provide ecological information about their products and models. In addition to this, governmental and nongovernmental organizations make systematic product comparisons on the basis of economic *and* ecological criteria to provide information and create transparency. A good example is EcoTopTen from the Ökoinstitut in Germany, which 'offers consumers credible recommendations on a range of attractive products and helps them make environmentally sensible and cost-effective choices'.[43] The information is presented mainly in the form of charts, where available product offers are compared according to factors such as purchase price, performance criteria, yearly costs of use, CO_2 emissions and expected lifetime. The US Environmental Protection Agency offers a customized savings calculator tool for a broad range of appliances, where an Energy Star qualified product is compared with a standard model based on input data from the user (e.g. initial cost per unit, type of water heating, average number of loads per weeks, gas rate, water rate, electricity rate); see Table 9.1.

Comparative energy labels, such as the EU Energy Label, the US Energy Star, the Japanese National Standard Energy-Saving Label, the Australian Energy Rating Label, the Korean Energy Efficiency Label or the China Energy Label, are widespread means of signalling the expected operating costs of electrical appliances (see Figure 9.6). Such national labelling schemes have evolved from voluntary to mandatory forms, for an ever-growing range of product categories and countries.[44]

Figure 9.6 Comparative energy labels from around the world

In comparison to company tools, the information provided by third-party organizations, especially governmental bodies or government-sponsored initiatives, tends to be less biased. A systematic comparison of a number of products within a category provides neutral information. By doing so, the EcoTopTen initiative in Germany seeks to create market transparency in economic and ecological terms and, ultimately, to change consumer behaviour. Online tools such as the saving calculator from the US Environmental Protection Agency provide useful individualized information regarding the total cost of various household appliances. A limitation of this type of tool is that it is typically used by consumers who are already sensitized and active. Other consumers, who do not actively seek information on the Internet or elsewhere, cannot be reached in this way. That is why easy-to-read energy labels stuck to the product are probably one of the most efficient tools for making customers aware of the total cost of ownership and reducing search and information costs.

The Nature of Price Systems

A key barrier in marketing sustainable products is the emphasis on price as opposed to cost. By highlighting total customer cost, sustainability marketers may overcome this barrier. Yet another key barrier is the externalization of social and ecological costs. Did you ever ask yourself why a radio is available for less than €10? Does that price really cover all the costs? Does it include the full cost of the extraction of natural resources at the beginning of the product life cycle, such as petroleum for the plastic parts, and copper and silicon for the circuit board and transistors? What about shipping and transportation costs? Do they include the contribution to global warming and climate change? What about production cost? Where, and under what working conditions, are radios for the price of less than €10 assembled? And what about the cost for the disposal of the product at the end of its life cycle? Who pays for that? It becomes apparent that the price of the radio does not cover all the social and ecological costs. In many cases the price paid by consumers in the shop is just a fraction of the real, total cost incurred by others in the present (e.g. underpaid workers) or in the future (e.g. coming generations, which suffer from the consequences of global warming and climate change). The current price system fails to cover the external costs of the social and natural environments.[45] Thus, many products available on the market are unreasonably cheap. They are effectively subsidized by other individuals, nature and by the general public, who (willingly or not) bear the external cost. This leads to a biased competition mechanism in favour of unsustainable products. As long as prices do not reflect their true social and ecological costs, conventional products often have a decisive cost advantage over the more sustainable competitors they face.

However, as socio-ecological problems become increasingly pressing, and as more people become aware of them, local, national and supranational governments will have to use a mix of different policy instruments to internalize those external costs (see Figure 9.7).[46]

Sustainability marketers are well advised to anticipate these changes, which are ultimately unavoidable and will eventually alter consumer behaviour. Again, a thorough analysis of the social and ecological problems along the whole product life cycle is a good starting point.[46] It gives a basic understanding of the major social and ecological issues and some insight into the hidden costs that have been

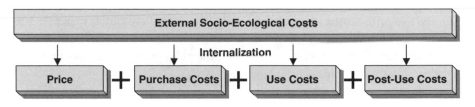

Figure 9.7   Total customer cost – the external perspective

externalized so far. Based on the analysis of socio-ecological problems, it is useful to consider different scenarios. What does happen, if the external costs of a particular problem are partially internalized? What will happen in the case of full internalization of external costs regarding a particular problem? To what extent does it affect the cost structure and the value proposition of a product? In which way does it change the rules of competition? To give profound answers to these questions, a full cost/environmental accounting is required.[48] Take cars and climate change. If CO_2 emissions are given a price, as planned by the European Union, the market will favour cars that emit less or no CO_2. Since the development of hybrid cars or electric vehicles takes years or even decades, it becomes apparent how important it is to be aware of the key socio-ecological problems and to anticipate the internalization of external costs well in advance. In Chapter 11 we will come back to the internalization of external costs. Before that we will discuss the fourth 'C' of the SM mix, the convenience of SP and customer solutions.

List of Key Terms

Cost-based pricing
Information costs
Information economics
Internalization of external costs
Post-use costs
Price
Purchase costs
Search costs
Switching costs
Total customer cost
Transaction costs
Use costs
Value-based pricing

REVIEW QUESTIONS

1. Identify and describe the components of the total customer cost for a) a refrigerator; b) a car; c) a frozen pizza.
2. Explain various types of purchase costs. Outline their importance in the context of sustainable products and show how they can be reduced.

3. Explain the two price-setting approaches, value-based vs cost-based pricing, and their implications for sustainable products.
4. What does the term 'switching costs' mean? Give examples of switching costs for two sustainable products that you would consider buying.
5. List possible ways to reduce use costs.

DISCUSSION QUESTIONS

1. Compare the total customer cost of compact fluorescent light bulbs versus incandescent bulbs. How did Philips manage to reduce the (perceived) costs of CFL bulbs? What other factors do you think may have played an important role in the success of CFL bulbs?
2. What is the total customer cost of energy-efficient or low-energy houses as compared to conventional houses? Select a construction company of your choice and discuss how it could market energy-efficient houses effectively.
3. Making customers aware of total costs is crucial for sustainability marketers. Discuss the pros and cons of the environmental information and tools provided by companies as compared to third-party organizations.
4. Use costs are a function of the product's performance and the consumer's patterns of use. Empirical studies show that energy consumption varies significantly depending on user behaviour. Search the Internet for studies that show the variance of energy consumption in the case of a) houses; b) cars; and c) washing machines. Discuss behaviour patterns as influencing factors of energy consumption in the case of the three different kinds of products.
5. The European Union plans to increase the fuel-efficiency standards of cars so that emissions are no more than 130 g CO_2/km, down from 162 g/km in 2005. For every extra gram automobile companies would have to pay a fine up to €95 from 2012 onwards. To which extent would that change the costs of a new a) Volkswagen Golf; b) Toyota Yaris; c) Mercedes; and d) Porsche? Moreover, discuss how the plans of the European Union would change the rules of competition in the automobile business.

SUSTAINABILITY MARKETING CHALLENGE: EVERGREEN LEASE BY INTERFACE

Interface specializes in the design, manufacture and supply of carpet tiles for commercial and residential use. The company was founded in 1973 and is based in Atlanta, USA. It has manufacturing capacity in the United States, the UK, the Netherlands, Australia and Thailand. The distribution network is global, with sales and marketing offices in most countries. More than 5000 employees work for Interface. Its products are sold under the Interface and Heuga brand names. The company has always been at the forefront of design innovation and technological expertise, and together the two brands have combined to become the world leader in modular flooring (market share over 35%).

Since 1994 Interface has been dedicated to sustainability. The company mission is to become truly sustainable by 2020, balancing people, process, product, place and profits. A major part of the journey towards sustainability is 'Mission Zero', a promise to eliminate any negative impact by the company on the natural environment. Since 1996 waste sent to landfill has been reduced by 75% and greenhouse gas emissions (GHG) by 82%. In 2008, 27% of the company's total energy use was either renewably purchased via Renewable Energy Credits or received directly from renewable sources. As part of its commitment to sustainability, Interface developed a ReEntry scheme to reclaim as much end-of-life product as possible. Under the ReEntry scheme any Interface carpet will be reused for noncommercial organizations, recycled into new products or 'downcycled' into other products. In 2007, 25% of the total raw materials used in manufacturing consisted of recycled and bio-based raw materials.

To make sure that the modular carpet tiles are reclaimed at the end of their life cycle, Interface promotes leasing instead of selling its products. Under the Evergreen Lease system it provides carpet installation, maintenance, selective tile replacement and reclamation at the end of the carpet's life or usage. In exchange, the customer pays a monthly fee for these services. In 1995 Interface signed the first Evergreen Lease agreement with the Southern California Gas Company. A number of commercial customers expressed interest in the carpet-leasing idea, including British Petroleum, the Environmental Protection Agency, Ernst & Young, the Federal Reserve Bank, General Motors, Procter & Gamble, Tennessee Valley Authority and the University of Texas. Despite the sales effort led by the former CEO Ray Andersson and other senior officers of the company, the majority of negotiations ended up going nowhere. Since 1995 only six lease agreements have been signed. The current CEO Dan Hendrix questions the viability of Evergreen Lease considering that the record of sales has been slow. To develop it to a successful marketing and environmental tool, a number of internal and external obstacles have to be overcome.[49]

Questions for Discussion

1. What are the advantages and disadvantages of (eco-)leasing from the customer point of view?
2. An obstacle for the market adoption of Evergreen Lease is the seemingly high monthly payment of leasing the carpet. Interface needs more innovation to close the loop and lower the cost of the carpet service. Search the Internet and find out what Interface does to close the loop. How could the company lower the cost of the carpet service?
3. Most customers do not perceive the full cost of purchasing and maintaining carpets. Analyse what the total cost of owning a carpet is and compare it to the alternative of leasing a carpet. What can Interface do to make customers aware of the total cost of carpet ownership?
4. Basically, there are two different types of leases: operating leases and capital leases. Find out what the differences between the two are and the consequences for a company's balance sheet. Why is an operating lease instead of a capital lease more favourable for companies from accounting and tax points of view?
5. According to the Generally Accepted Accounting Principles (GAAP) a lease agreement is considered a capital lease if it meets at least one of the following four criteria: a) the lease

transfers title of the lease asset at the end of the term; b) the lease contains a 'bargain purchase option'; c) the lease term is 75% or more of the estimated useful time of the asset; and d) the present value of the future lease payments is 90% or more of the market value of the leased asset. Does Evergreen Lease qualify for the (unfavourable) capital lease? If so, why?

Endnotes

1. Kofod, C. (1999) *A Strategy Study Concerning Promotion of Energy Efficient Lighting in IEA Member Countries: Energy Savings by Use of CFLs (Compact Fluorescent Lamps) in the residential sector. The potential for an Effort Coordinated by the IEA*, Paris: Energy Piano for the IEA; Ottman, J.A., Stafford, E.R. & Hartman, C.L. (2006) 'Avoiding green marketing myopia', *Environment*, 48(5): 22–36; Johnson, W.B. (2004) *Powerhouse Marketing Plans: 14 Outstanding Real-Life Plans and What You Can Learn from Them to Supercharge Your Own Campaigns*, Boston, MA: AMACOM, pp. 58–80; Sandahl, L.J. (2006) *Compact Fluorescent Lighting in America: Lessons Learned on the Way to Market*, prepared by Pacific Northwest National Laboratory for US Department of Energy Office of Energy Efficiency and Renewable Energy Building Technologies Program, http://www.netl.doe.gov/ssl/PDFs/CFL%20Lessons%20Learned%20-%20web.pdf (accessed 31 December 2008). Company information available at www.philips.com (accessed 31 December 2008).
2. Kotler, P. & Armstrong, G. (2004) *The Principles of Marketing*, 10th edn, Upper Saddle River, NJ: Prentice Hall, p. 345.
3. Peattie, K. (1995) *Environmental Marketing Management: Meeting the Green Challenge*, London: Pitman Publishing, p. 280.
4. Kotler, P. & Armstrong, G. (2004) *The Principles of Marketing*, 10th edn, Upper Saddle River, NJ: Prentice Hall, p. 345.
5. *Ibid.*; Varian, H.R. (1992) *Microeconomic Analysis*, New York: Norton.
6. The discussion of customer costs is based on Belz, F.-M. (2001) *Integratives Öko-Marketing. Erfolgreiche Vermarktung ökologischer Produkte und Leistungen*, Wiesbaden: Deutscher Universitäts-Verlag, pp. 75–8; and Bänsch, A. (1993), Marketing für umweltfreundliche Güter', *UmweltWirtschaftsforum*, 1(2): 13–18.
7. Kuusela, H. & Spence, M. (1999) 'Factors Affecting the Acquisition of Energy Efficient Durable Goods', in Charter, M. & Polonsky, M.J. (eds), *Greener Marketing. A Global Perspective on Greening Marketing Practice*, Sheffield: Greenleaf Publishing, pp. 224–32.
8. Transaction theory focuses on the individual transaction, defined as the transfer of property rights, as the unit of analysis. The costs occurring in this process are referred to as transaction costs. Picot (1982) has defined and systematized transaction costs, as including initiation, agreement, execution, control and adaptation costs. For a more detailed discussion of transaction costs and transaction cost theory, see e.g. Coase, R.H. (1937) 'The nature of the firm', *Economica*, 4(16): 386–405; Picot, A. (1982) 'Transaktionskostenansatz in der Organisationstheorie: Stand der Diskussion und Aussagewert', *Die Betriebswirtschaft*, 42(2): 267–84; Williamson, O. (1985) *The Economic Institutions of Capitalism: Firms, Markets, Relational Contracting*, New York: Free Press.
9. For the following discussion on information economics see Nelson, P. (1970) 'Information and consumer behaviour', *Journal of Political Economy*, 78(2): 311–29; Nelson, P. (1974) 'Advertising as information', *Journal of Political Economy*, 83(4): 729–54; Darby, M.R. & Karni, E. (1973) 'Free competition and the optimal amount of fraud', *Journal of Law and Economics*, 16(1): 67–88.
10. Hirunyawipada, T. & Paswan A.K. (2006) 'Consumer innovativeness and perceived risk: Implications for high technology product adoption', *Journal of Consumer Marketing*, 23(4): 182–98.
11. Meyer, A. (2001) 'What's in it for the Customers? Successfully marketing green clothes', *Business Strategy and the Environment*, 10(5): 320.

12. Research indicates that 'pay-as-you-throw' systems save the average household money. Nevertheless, they are often portrayed in the media as an 'extra' household charge. Therefore such schemes are quite unpopular in countries like the UK. They have been poorly explained by the government and the media has gone into protest overdrive.

13. Zurbrügg, C. (2002) 'Urban Solid Waste Management in Low-Income Countries of Asia. How to Cope with the Garbage Crisis', paper presented for Scientific Committee on Problems of the Environment (SCOPE), Urban Solid Waste Management Review Session, Durban (South Africa), December, http://www.eawag.ch/organisation/organisation/abteilungen/sandec/publikationen/publikationen_swm/downloads_swm/USWM-Asia.pdf (accessed 31 December 2008).

14. Enayetullah, I. (2005) 'Household Waste Management in Dhaka, Bangladesh', http://tilz.tearfund.org and www.wasteconcern.org (accessed 31 December 2008).

15. OECD (2006) *Improving Recycling Markets*, Paris: OECD Publishing.

16. Kotler, P. & Armstrong, G. (2004) *The Principles of Marketing*, 10th edn, Upper Saddle River, NJ: Prentice Hall, p. 11.

17. *Ibid.*, pp. 359–60.

18. *Ibid.*, p. 360.

19. *Ibid.*, pp. 259–60.

20. Alexander, H. (2008) 'US fears over honey bee collapse', BBC News Online, 25 March, http://news.bbc.co.uk/1/hi/sci/tech/7312358.stm (accessed 26 December 2008).

21. Spence, M. (1976) 'Informational aspects of market structure: An introduction', *Quarterly Journal of Economics*, 90(4): 591–7.

22. Karstens, B. & Belz, F.-M. (2006) 'Information asymmetries, labels and trust in the German food market: A critical analysis based on the economics of information', *International Journal of Advertising*, 25(2): 189–211.

23. Meyer, A. (2001) 'What's in it for the customers? Successfully marketing green clothes', *Business Strategy and the Environment*, 10(5): 323–7; Hessnatur, company information available at www.hess-natur.info (accessed 31 December 2008).

24. Kotler, P. & Armstrong, G. (2004) *The Principles of Marketing*, 10th edn, Upper Saddle River, NJ: Prentice Hall, p. 377.

25. Peattie, K. (1999) 'Rethinking Marketing', in Charter, M. & Polonsky, M.J. (eds), *Greener Marketing. A Global Perspective on Greening Marketing Practice*, Sheffield: Greenleaf Publishing, p. 62.

26. Porter, M.E. & van der Linde, C. (1995) 'Toward a new conception of the environment–competitiveness relationship', *Journal of Economic Perspectives*, 9(4): 97–118; Porter, M.E. & van der Linde, C. (1995) 'Green and competitive: Ending the stalemate', *Harvard Business Review*, 73(5): 120–33.

27. Fuller, D.A. (1999) *Sustainable Marketing: Managerial-Ecological Issues*, Thousand Oaks, CA: Sage, p. 311.

28. Tukker, A. (2004) 'Eight types of product-service system: Eight ways to sustainability? Experiences from Suspronet', *Business Strategy and the Environment*, 13(4): 253.

29. www.swissrent.com (accessed 22 April 2009).

30. Sahota, A. (2007) 'The International Market for Organic and Fair Trade Food and Drink', in Wright, S. & McCrea, D. (eds), *The Handbook of Organic and Fair Trade Food Marketing*, Oxford: Blackwell, pp. 4–13.

31. Washright Initiative by AISE, http://www.washright.com/uk/index.html (accessed 31 December 2008).

32. See Chapter 7.

33. Fuller, D.A. (1999) *Sustainable Marketing: Managerial-Ecological Issues*, Thousand Oaks, CA: Sage, pp. 303–10; Miele Sustainability Report 2006, p. 23, http://www.miele-presse.de/media/presse/media/Sustainability_Report_2006.pdf, (accessed 4 January 2009); HP Asset Recovery Services, information available at www.hp.com (accessed 4 January 2009).

34. OECD (2006) *EPR Policies and Product Design: Economic Theory and Selected Case Studies*, http://www.olis.oecd.org/olis/2005doc.nsf/LinkTo/NT00005AA6/$FILE/JT03204660.PDF (accessed 31 December 2008).

35. Directive 2000/53/EC of the European Parliament and of the Council of 18 September 2000 on end-of-life vehicles, amended by Directive 2008/33/EC of the European Parliament and of the Council of 11 March 2008, available at http://eur-lex.europa.eu (accessed December 2008).

36. OECD (2006) *EPR Policies and Product Design: Economic Theory and Selected Case Studies*, http://www.olis.oecd.org/olis/2005doc.nsf/LinkTo/NT00005AA6/$FILE/JT03204660.PDF (accessed 31 December 2008).

37. The concept of bounded rationality was coined by Herbert Simon (Simon, H.A. (1957) *Models of man: Social and rational*. New York: John Wiley & Sons) and embraced by the newer literature streams of new institutional economics and new economic sociology. See Chapter 4 for further details.

38. Kuusela, H. & Spence, M. (1999) 'Factors Affecting the Acquisition of Energy Efficient Durable Goods', in Charter, M. & Polonsky, M.J. (eds), *Greener Marketing. A Global Perspective on Greening Marketing Practice*, Sheffield: Greenleaf Publishing, pp. 224–32.

39. Philips Savings Calculator, http://www.start-saving.com/?site=3-1&universe=3&lang=global (accessed 31 December 2008).

40. Continental Fuel Savings Calculator, http://www.conti-online.com/generator/www/de/en/continental/transport/themes/goods/fuel_saving/fuel_saving_calculator_en.html (accessed 31 December 2008).

41. Phoenix Motorcars, ROI Calculator, http://www.phoenixmotorcars.com/why-choose-phoenix/calculation.php (accessed 31 December 2008).

42. Electrolux, Ecosavings, http://www.electrolux.com/ecosavings (accessed 31 December 2008).

43. Öko-Institut e.V., EcoTopTen, The Initiative, http://www.ecotopten.de/download/EcoTopTen_Broschuere0502e.pdf (accessed 31 December 2008).

44. Sammer, K. & Wüstenhagen, R. (2006) 'The influence of eco-labelling on consumer behaviour – Results of a discrete choice analysis for washing machines', *Business Strategy and the Environment*, 15(3): 185–99; CLASP (Collaborative Labeling and Appliance Standards Program), Energy Efficiency Standards & Labeling Information Clearinghouse, www.clasponline.org (accessed 31December 2008).

45. Peattie, K. (1995) *Environmental Marketing Management: Meeting the Green Challenge*, London: Pitman Publishing, pp. 288–90.

46. See Chapter 11 for the internalization of external costs and the role of companies in sustainability marketing transformations.

47. See Chapter 3 for qualitative and quantitative instruments to analyse the socio-ecological problems of products along the entire life cycle 'from cradle to grave'.

48. Schaltegger, S. & Burrit, R. (2000) *Contemporary Environmental Accounting. Issues, Concepts and Practice*, Sheffield: Greenleaf Publishing.

49. Feld, A., Fowler, A., Haq, A. & Schrader, C. (2003) Transition to a Functional Service Economy, NTRES 318, Ithaca, NY: Cornell University; Oliva, R. & Quinn, J. (2003) 'Interface's Evergreen Services Agreement', Harvard Business School N9-603-112, Boston, MA: Harvard Business School; www.interfaceflor.eu (accessed 31 December 2008); www.interfaceinc.com (accessed 31 December 2008).

CHAPTER 10

Convenience

After Studying this Chapter You Should be Able to:

1. View the process of delivering customer solutions to consumers from the unconventional perspective of convenience.
2. Appreciate the different aspects of marketing that influence consumer convenience.
3. Discuss strategies that could be developed to deliver more sustainable solutions that are also convenient for consumers, and the challenges this may involve.

LOOKING AHEAD: PREVIEWING THE CONCEPTS

There are many aspects to convenience. Some reflect distribution issues and the process of making products accessible and available to purchase at a place and time that suit consumers. Convenience can also be delivered during other stages of the consumption process, including pre-purchase choice through the provision of information, product usage through the incorporation of convenient features or supporting services, through to making responsible disposal of a product easy. Delivering successful sustainability solutions to consumers will depend on them being convenient for those consumers, as well as technically effective and affordable.

SUSTAINABILITY MARKETING STORY: FAMILYMART CONVENIENCE STORES

In a contemporary marketing context, the epitome of convenience in marketing is represented, perhaps not surprisingly, by 'convenience stores'. This retail format of relatively small stores in urban locations providing quick and easy access to goods and services for busy and time-pressed city dwellers is a global phenomenon. In Japan, nearly 50 000 *conbini* stores have been established after the first 7-Eleven store opened in Tokyo in 1974. Since then they have grown into a major component of Japanese life, acting as a convenient focal point for picking up groceries, paying bills, eating and drinking, and dropping off laundry, and they generate annual sales of over ¥7 trillion (€5.5 billion).

FamilyMart Co. is the third largest convenience store chain in Japan with over 7000 stores (and a further 5300 in other countries). Like most *conbini* it is a franchise business, with stores mostly owned and run by a family assisted by 15 to 20 employees working in rotation. A typical store has a floor space of some 120 square metres, carries 2800 products, such as food and drink, magazines and daily-use items, and is open 24 hours a day. FamilyMart is moving away from competing on just the basis of convenience and accessibility and has developed a new strategy of 'co-growing', which means growth by building mutually beneficial relationships with its customers. It has rebranded itself as 'an important place' in its customers' lives, and sought to compete by becoming an integral as well as a convenient part of household and community life and by demonstrating social and environmental responsibility. Providing consumers with convenient access to almost everything they need, near their homes, in one place, at any hour of the day, inevitably has significant environmental consequences such as packaging waste, unsold food waste and the energy needed for 24/7 operations. The company's sustainability report states, 'FamilyMart believes that realizing a society that can permanently coexist with the global environment is the vision for an environmentally conscious convenience store of the 21st century.'

Offering sustainable convenience is a considerable challenge. The average FamilyMart store consumes 180 000 kWh of electricity, 360 cubic metres of water and 662 litres of cooking oil each year. It also produces 4.5 tonnes of food waste, 8 tonnes of burnable waste and 1.5 tonnes of plastic waste. The lighting needed to offer 24/7 convenience is the largest driver of the stores' energy bills and associated emissions. To reduce this stores have been redesigned to adjust the lighting levels needed for each of the five 'zones' within them (e.g. magazine zones were placed to take advantage of daylight) and FamilyMart took an industry lead by introducing energy-efficient white light-emitting diodes (LEDs) for its sign boards. Integrated heat-utilization systems were also installed to combine the functions of air conditioning, cooling and refrigeration, to reduce electricity consumption.

In dealing with waste, the chain has set up Japan's largest network collection points for recycling waste cooking oil at 5500 of its stores, and introduced a system to collect food items that have passed their freshness date, which are recycled into fertilizer and feed. To handle logistics and deliveries, the company replaced its entire fleet with hybrid vehicles.

The company has also sought to combine convenience with social responsibility, including an emphasis on health with a move away from its traditional pre-packaged convenience food range and towards providing fresh foods on a convenient basis. Fresh and freshly prepared foods now account for 70% of a typical store's sales. With the ageing population in Japan, the stores have become important for elderly consumers, allowing them easy access to the products they need within walking distance of their homes. Convenience stores already fulfil a community role as government-appointed communication networks in the case of national disasters such as earthquakes. FamilyMart is seeking to take this role further through schemes such as offering stores as recognized safe refuge points for children. The company is explicitly aiming ultimately to fulfil a role within local communities to promote a sustainable society, and to serve as a disseminator for initiatives with a social dimension and for sustainable lifestyles.

As well as extending its social and environmental contributions, FamilyMart has continued to bring convenience to other aspects of Japanese consumers' lives. The ATMs that exist in the majority of stores can be used to borrow as well as access money, and the company has formed partnerships with DVD distributors to cater for consumer entertainment needs. It entered into a joint venture with Bears Co., a household services provider, to offer cleaning, washing and even childminding for ¥9800 (€77) per 150 minutes. Tickets for such services can be purchased in advance and then arranged by phone when needed, and have proved extremely popular.

FamilyMart is leading the industry in many of its sustainability schemes, and is already working on future challenges to reduce store CO_2 emissions and switch to biodegradable packaging. Like other convenience stores, FamilyMart has been reluctant to charge consumers ¥5 (€0.04) for shopping bags, as some regional governments have been suggesting, but it has instituted its own reusable 'Eco-bag' scheme. For the convenience it offers, and its role in tackling sustainability issues and seeking to contribute to progress towards sustainability within its communities, FamilyMart has succeeded in making itself 'an important place' in its customers' lives.[1]

Consumption and Convenience

One of the traditional four P variables of the conventional marketing mix is 'place', which is usually focused on issues of distribution and, in the case of consumer goods, of retailing. There are three key weaknesses in the conventional place mix variable from a sustainability perspective. First, with its emphasis on the distribution of products, place suffers from being envisaged largely from the producer's perspective. Conventional marketing books focus on how distribution channels are organized and managed, and on the relationships between producers and the intermediaries within those channels. Provided that these channels work effectively, how they work is not particularly interesting to consumers.

If the benefits provided by the product or service are as expected, and if the cost of the product is afford-able, then the remaining issues that can be influenced by the distribution process are largely related to convenience, which is the core benefit that consumers seek from retailing and distribution. Secondly, thinking about place creates a focus on the point of exchange (or the service encounter), when in practice consumers increasingly demand convenience through all phases of the consumption process, including the acquisition of products, their use and their disposal. Finally, the conventional concept of place in many markets is becoming less relevant as consumption, or elements of the consumption process such as information search, move into a virtual environment through the rise of electronic commerce.

The concept of 'convenience' is defined in several different ways, all of which are significant to marketers. Something is convenient if it is appropriate in time and place; if it removes discomfort or trouble and promotes ease; and if it is well suited to one's wants. The pursuit of convenience is therefore central to the whole evolution of marketing, and much of the environmental damage resulting from the rise of the consumer society and the growth in consumption can be linked back to attempts to make goods and services increasingly convenient for consumers. Elizabeth Shove's book about the nature of everyday consumption, *Comfort, Cleanliness and Convenience*, proposed convenience as one of the three defining elements of lifestyles and consumption habits within the consumer society.[2] She proposes that a move towards more environmentally sustainable lifestyles and patterns of consumption will require us to rethink our ideas about what constitutes comfort, cleanliness and convenience and how these are achieved. A fourth 'C' factor not covered by Shove is the idea of *'cosmetic perfection'*, in which we consume everything from fruit and vegetables, from consumer electronics to celebrities and politicians, on the basis of their superficial external appearance. In the case of fruit and vegetables, until 2008 this concept was enshrined in European regulations that prevented the sale by retailers of cauliflowers less than 11 cm in diameter, 'forked' carrots (with more than one root) or onions not at least two thirds covered with skin. This rejection of nature's variety resulted in 20% of such products grown in the UK being disposed of instead of sold, resulting in price premiums to customers of up to 40%.[3]

Convenience is highly valued by consumers, and for those who are relatively cash rich and time poor it is the convenience offered by marketers, rather than the financial cost of the product, that will ultimately determine their behaviour and satisfaction. A simple example is the use of batteries, a ubiquitous product in industrialized economies awash with iPods, mobile phones, remote controls, electronic toys and games, and all manner of household items from smoke detectors to electronic weighing scales. The use of rechargeable batteries in such products would save the consumer money and reduce the environmental impact. However, the additional effort involved in managing the recharging process, and in having to replace batteries slightly more often, has ensured that disposable batteries continue to dominate the market.[4] It is also worth noting that convenience is a relative concept, and it is achieved by offering products and services that are quicker and easier to find out about, access, purchase, consume and dispose of than those currently being offered to consumers.

Within conventional marketing, convenience has usually been discussed in two ways, both originating in how consumers purchase things. The first is in relation to *convenience goods*, one of the three types of consumer goods originally proposed in 1923 by Melvin T. Copeland, following his observations of shoppers.[5] These were items purchased frequently, immediately and with a minimum of thought and effort. The other categories were *shopping goods*, which consumers would only purchase after comparing products, and possibly stores, for quality, price and style; and *speciality goods*, for which consumers would make a special dedicated purchasing effort. Convenience is also considered in relation to 'convenience stores' (like FamilyMart in Japan), also sometimes referred to as 'corner stores' or 'corner shops' and a variety of other regional variations. These small retailers in suburban areas, city centres or on major traffic routes offer consumers quick and easy access to a variety of products. They typically stock a limited selection of leading brands, offered at premium prices when compared to discount stores or supermarkets. There are some iconic convenience store chains such as 7-Eleven and Spar, and there is an increasing trend towards major supermarket chains expanding their businesses by opening convenience-format stores. In the following we will cover convenience aspects along the whole consumption process, that is, convenience in purchase, convenience in use, and convenience in post-use.

Convenience in Purchase

Accessibility in Distribution

It is by making goods and services physically accessible that a company's distribution channels contribute most to convenience. The very root of 'marketing' is in the establishment of physical markets where buyers and sellers are conveniently and efficiently brought together in place and time. Those same principles underpin all forms of retailing from the local corner store, the giants of online retail like Dell and Amazon, through to the creation of new hypermarkets and giant retail malls, such as the South China Mall in Dongguan, which houses over 1500 different stores within 892 000 square metres of retail space.

For consumers, the convenience of having products together in one location allows for a wide range of goods to be bought, and services to be accessed, within a single shopping trip. Understanding the environmental impacts of the co-location of goods in supermarkets, hypermarkets and shopping malls is not straightforward. Single-trip/location shopping is certainly time efficient, and could be considered resource efficient compared to making numerous trips by car to different locations. However, in practice retail development trends have been towards 'out-of-town' retail centres that are distant from most customers' homes, making shopping trips resource inefficient compared to more traditional local shopping on foot, by bicycle or using public transport. Taking the UK as an example, if all grocery shopping by car was replaced by bus, bicycle or walking, the associated environmental and congestion costs would fall from an estimated £1.3 (€1.37) billion to just over £100 (€105) million.[6] The 2005 UK Food Miles report from Defra[7] calculated that one eighth of total food transport CO_2 is generated by the final car journeys of food (mostly relating to the movement of foodstuffs from shop to home), which equates to some 2.4 million tonnes of CO_2 annually.

For sustainability marketers, there are a number of channels through which consumers can gain access to solutions. The tendency of mainstream retailers to act as 'gatekeepers' and only cautiously to add sustainability-oriented products to their shelves led to an emergence in the 1980s and 1990s of speciality eco-retailers. In many cases these were cause-driven marketers or social entrepreneurs with an explicit goal of building markets for sustainability-oriented products.[8] Such retailers emerged during the early 1990s with product ranges featuring recycled paper products, t-shirts, cleaning and personal care products and organic/natural food and clothing products. They were largely small, independent businesses whose financial sustainability was often not very secure.[9] In the USA there has been an emergence of sustainability-oriented convenience stores on the campuses of universities, and some successful recent launches based around organic foods such as the Full Moon Foodies chain in Oregon in 2007. There has also been a growth in sustainability catalogue retailers such as Gaiam and Real Goods, and an increase in cause-related catalogue campaigns from a growing number of NGOs (e.g. WWF).

Distribution Chain Impacts

The process of operating supply chains to make them accessible to, and convenient for, customers accounts for a considerable amount of the environmental and social impacts of individual products. The key environmental issues linked to distribution are packaging and waste creation, the disposal of waste, noise and emission levels and the consumption of fossil fuels.[10] The environmental impacts associated with the distribution of physical products will partly reflect the geography of supply and demand. The fuel required to transport products to customers will depend on:

- the distance between producers and consumers,
- the transport infrastructure that connects the two, and
- the pattern of depots involved in supplying goods to intermediaries or direct to customers.

There are pre-existing economic pressures on manufacturers to reduce their distribution fuel costs to create more economically and also environmentally efficient structures for their distribution channels. However, from a sustainability perspective, while the full social and economic costs of using fossil fuels (including their contribution to climate change) are not internalized, the costs of fuel and of operating centralized distribution systems remain artificially low. More sustainable distribution systems in future are therefore likely to see a return to more localized systems of production, consumption and distribution (although quite possibly within a framework of international or global ownership).

How product distribution channels are structured can have social as well as environmental impacts. Trends towards 'out-of-town' retail complexes on major roadways, and away from residential areas, dominate in both the USA and western Europe as part of 'the great car economy'. As a form of retailing this disadvantages those without a car, particularly those who are on low incomes, are elderly or suffer from health problems (or some combination of those factors). This trend can lead towards the creation of urban 'food deserts' and promote social exclusion among those without access to a car, who may become very restricted in terms of the range of outlets and products that are available to them and may be forced to pay higher prices for the products they consume.[11]

Availability in Distribution

For consumers, convenience is dependent on goods and services being accessible and available where and when they want them. Availability is crucial to marketing success, and one argument is that it is the availability of leading brands that plays a large part in maintaining their success. The retailers will stock the most successful brands, which will then be chosen because they are available, which will ensure that they continue to be successful. Within fast-moving consumer goods markets, the major retailers play a crucial role in determining the accessibility and availability of products through a role as 'gatekeepers' between consumers and producers. A product may be appealing to consumers, but unless retail buyers allow it shelf space it is unlikely to attract customer attention or to succeed. Major retailers routinely require 'stocking fees' from manufacturers as an upfront payment to gain access to retailer shelf space, which can make it extremely difficult for new alternative offerings from smaller and more sustainability-oriented suppliers to compete.[12] This was one of the reasons many embryonic sustainable products and brands have used alternative methods of distribution. Ecover, one of the pioneering green brands, built its early success on distribution through outlets such as health food stores, rather than through conventional grocery retail chains. Even established manufacturers introducing new sustainability-oriented brands, or more sustainability-oriented versions of existing products as a form of brand extension, will face the same struggle for a share of the available shelf space. Ensuring availability for more sustainability-oriented goods and services is crucial for their success, since even motivated consumers who want to purchase them are often unwilling to compromise on convenience-oriented attributes such as availability.[13]

One aspect of promoting convenient product availability in mainstream marketing is the emergence of the 24/7 service economy in which goods and services become permanently available as retailers move towards opening 24 hours a day, seven days a week. The development of 24/7 retailing (and in some manufacturing sectors, round-the-clock manufacturing based on three 8-hour shifts) has had significant social impacts. Studies in America reveal that millions of workers are involved in 'nonstandard' work patterns including weekend and evening work. These work patterns can have a substantial impact on their health and well-being, and those regularly working late or on shift patterns are prone to problems including a higher risk of cardiovascular disease, breast cancer, miscarriage, fatigue from sleep deprivation and a higher rate of accidents and injuries at work.[14] There is also an environmental cost in the 24/7 operation of the retail economy, as it requires stores to remain permanently heated and lit for the convenience of those customers who wish to shop at nonstandard times. Whether the emerging global 24/7 retail and service economy is compatible with the drive to achieve a more socially and ecologically sustainable economy is an interesting question for the future.

One area where availability management has a considerable environmental impact is in the provision of fresh, seasonal food produce. Global purchasing and distribution systems allow retailers to import products between hemispheres to ensure that seasonal products like fresh strawberries are available throughout the year. This typically involves having them air-freighted in, with a considerable impact in terms of embedded CO_2 emissions. Similarly, using heated greenhouses or chilled storage facilities to extend the seasonal availability of more locally grown produce can effectively increase the level of energy embedded in a product.

Convenience through Packaging

Packaging is an aspect of marketing whose profile has risen as sustainability concerns about current patterns of consumption and production have emerged. Packaging represents a large proportion of municipal solid waste (20–36% by weight in EU countries)[15] and reductions in the amount of packaging reaching landfill has been a primary objective of many policymakers and marketers. Reducing or changing the packaging of a product in response to environmental concerns is typically attractive to marketers, because it can create opportunities to reduce costs or even add consumer benefit, and avoid any need to make changes to the core product. When HP was seeking to respond to Wal-Mart's Eco-Challenge and develop product ideas with reduced packaging, HP in France came up with a simple solution: sell notebook computers in a readymade carrying case instead of disposable packaging. This cut packaging material by 97%, leaving only the cardboard box used to group five notebooks for stacking on a pallet. The consumer gets a useful case (made from recycled material) and the company has one less packaging waste issue to deal with.

The packaging of a product fulfils several roles that may have value for either the producer or the consumer:

- Protecting the product and helping to ensure its quality. Food and drink accounts for almost half of all the packaging used for goods. By keeping food fresh and protected it can help to reduce or avoid product wastage.
- Facilitating the transport and storage of goods by allowing physical products to be efficiently stored and stacked in ways that would be impossible if they were loose.
- Helping to 'sell' products within stores by attracting the consumer's attention and ensuring that a product has 'shelf presence', which can be extremely important within the typical supermarket containing more than 40 000 different products.
- Providing information to consumers to inform them about issues such as ingredients, quantity, country of origin and product use. This may also be important in ensuring that the product complies with all relevant regulations governing labelling, hygiene and the display of pricing information.
- Portioning products so that they can be sold in different portion sizes to suit different customer needs, and to help maintain the freshness of perishables. This has also led to environmental concerns about the packaging required to deliver foodstuffs in individual portions.

Another key role that packing plays is in delivering convenience to the customer. Research has shown that a package's ability to communicate convenience and ease of use to the consumer is the most important marketing communication role it fulfils.[16] The whole concept of convenience food, for example, is based around food products that are pre-prepared and packaged to allow for ease of consumption (e.g. frozen food and readymade meals).

Convenience through Augmented Benefits

There are ways in which the consumption process can be made easier and more convenient for consumers that are not linked to distribution issues and do not require significant changes to the core benefits of the customer solution. Instead, they augment the customer offering with additional convenience benefits, including:

- *Convenience from information*: Marketers can deliver convenience to their customers through the provision of information that helps them choose, use and appropriately dispose of products. Valued information for consumers will include information on foodstuff ingredients (particularly about potential allergens) and suggestions and recipes about how to use them; safety information, including safe disposal advice for hazardous products; usage advice for durable products; and even interestingly abstract and symbolic artwork wordlessly explaining how self-assembly furniture is meant to be assembled. Some information will be embedded within the packaging of a product (such as labelling), while in other cases it will be delivered via a publication, website or advice service. From a sustainability perspective, green consumer guides and online information resources such as sust-it.net make the process of identifying more sustainable purchase options easier and more convenient.
- *Convenience from credit*: Extending credit to customers and the use of credit cards for payment contribute to consumer convenience as well as to making products affordable. Overextending credit can lead to social problems of excessive debt, however. The provision of credit also has implications for environmental sustainability because the availability of consumer credit has acted as one driver of economic growth. To an extent consumer credit 'writes forward' the consumption of physical resources by allowing the consumption of products today in exchange for a promise of payment from the financial wealth that will be generated in the future.
- *Convenience from choice editing*: There is a common perception that the ability to select from a wide range of available choices is highly valued by consumers. However, there is evidence to suggest that in practice consumers find it increasingly stressful to handle the information-processing and decision-making activities that are a side effect of a growing range of consumption choices. The integration of social and environmental considerations, alongside more conventional issues relating to the functionality and desirability of products, has made the consumer's decision-making process even more complex. There is growing evidence that many consumers who are concerned about environmental and social issues would like this to be dealt with by manufacturers and retailers by removing through 'choice editing' those products that are most socially and environmentally damaging. This reduction in choice makes the purchasing process easier and provides a convenient way for consumers to integrate social and environmental criteria.

Delivering Sustainability and Convenience in Purchase

Sustainability-Oriented Retailing

The impact of sustainability in retailing has not been limited to the emergence of speciality retailers; mainstream retailers have increasingly sought to respond to consumer concerns about environmental and social issues to integrate sustainability into their operations and policies. These efforts have been a combination of changes to product ranges (particularly the expansion of organic and ethical foodstuffs), reuse of store-generated packaging materials, and energy and refrigerant conservation programmes.[17] This will involve both the provision of new, more sustainable goods and services and changes to existing product ranges and practices to improve sustainability performance. In grocery retailing, for example, there is often considerable wastage in products that become damaged, go beyond their sell-by dates, are part of a discontinued line or are residual stock from failed product launches. These 'unsaleable' products represent an avoidable cost incurred by the entire supply chain that represents between 1 and 2% of gross sales[18] and delivers little or no benefit to consumers (although some does accrue through charitable food distribution programmes).

Tackling the energy requirements for store lighting, heating and refrigeration has been a major priority for retailers, and one with significant economic benefit in times of more expensive energy. New England supermarket Star Market is building a sustainability prototype store opening in 2009 in Newton, Massachusetts. It will use fuel-cell energy for refrigeration, heating and ventilation, elevators, cash registers and lighting along with low-impact glycol/carbon dioxide refrigeration systems. Light-emitting diode-based lighting will be used for the store, both inside and out, which will also lower energy usage by 50% to 65%.[19]

The world's largest retailer, Wal-Mart, is a controversial company that has sometimes attracted criticism relating to its employment and competitive practices. However, it is an organization whose roots lie in a socially oriented community business and it has been explicitly addressing its environmental performance since the mid 1990s. In 2005 CEO H. Lee Scott made a commitment to reduce the company's environmental impact by embedding sustainability in the business model and pursuing goals to sell products that sustain natural resources and the environment, to use only renewable energy and to create zero waste. Targets were set to reduce greenhouse gases at existing facilities by 20% by 2012, and to design and open a commercially viable store prototype that is up to 30% more energy efficient and will produce up to 30% fewer greenhouse gas emissions by 2009. The resulting pilot store in practice is up to 45% more energy efficient than the 2005 baseline store.

Convenience stores might appear to be the retail format that is least likely to make a substantive contribution to sustainability due to their emphasis on convenience, their stress on a small number of mainstream leading brands and their close associations with major traffic routes and fuel retailing. However, as the FamilyMart story illustrates, there is an argument that convenience stores could offer a route back towards more localized and less energy-intensive patterns of retailing and consumption and that they could help to regenerate a sense of community. This could be particularly valuable in improving social cohesion and access to goods and services to the elderly and those with health problems and without access to cars. Such stores could also represent a communal hub through which tangible products could be made available through rental services in ways that could aid in the dematerialization of the economy.[20] This model in some ways takes retailing back towards the model of the locally based 'general store' that preceded the supermarket.

Sustainability-Oriented Logistics

A key part of the environmental impacts of the products we consume is accounted for by transporting them from their place of origin to a place where we can conveniently and cost effectively purchase. One way to create more sustainable systems of consumption and production will be to reduce the distance that products travel by creating more localized supply chains. If all food were sourced from within 20 km of where it was consumed, then in the case of the UK, the associated environmental and congestion costs would fall from more than £ 2.3 (€ 2.41) billion to under £ 230 (€ 241) million.[21] Such a change would, however, limit all food consumption patterns to an extent that would impoverish consumers in terms of their quality of life, and literally impoverish countries whose economies are based around food exports. Sensible use of more localized supply chains therefore needs to be complemented by reductions in the environmental impacts of distribution and logistics processes.

One way to achieve this is through shifts from road to rail for domestic freight and from air to sea for international freight. If it were possible to shift from road to rail 50% of all food journeys over 300 km, this could reduce environmental impacts by as much as 4.5%, but it would be highly dependent on the development of infrastructure.[22] In Japan modal shifts for freight distribution have been made a national priority and have generated considerable success. Through a partnership with Japan Freight Railway and Nippon Express, Shihoro Agricultural Cooperative Association in Hokkaido managed to shift the transportation of *tokachi* potatoes from road to rail, which reduced carbon dioxide emissions by 53%. Other ways to achieve a reduction in distribution impacts are summarized in Table 10.1, which provides numbers for the environmental changes that could be achieved for current patterns of UK domestic food deliveries.[23]

Table 10.1 Opportunities to Reduce Environmental Impacts in Distribution

Logistics and Distribution System Change	Total Eco-Saving	CO_2 Reduction
Larger-capacity vehicles (using double-decker or double-length articulated trailers)	5.3%	6.5%
Vehicle engine changes (upgrading vehicles to most efficient and lowest-emissions engines available)	3.5%	0.4%
Vehicle telematics (vehicle-tracking and route-planning systems to optimize fleet use and delivery times)	3.0%	2.3%
Transport collaboration (between manufacturers, retailers, wholesalers and food service operators to share vehicles and combine loads)	3.2%	3.8%
Logistics systems redesign (to optimize distances between distribution centres and retail outlets)	2.3%	2.8%
Total	**15.3%**	**14.2%**

As well as environmental savings from shifting transport modes, programmes to promote 'eco-driving' have been adopted in distribution companies in many countries. Anshin Distribution in Okinawa,

Japan, adopted an eco-drive management system that gathered and analysed vehicle driving data (including on speed, engine revolutions and braking patterns), which is then used to educate drivers and improve their driving safety and fuel economy. Since introducing the system in 2007, the company has saved an average of 11 000 litres of petrol per month, equivalent to a 10% reduction in CO_2 emissions.

Convenience in Use

Convenience is not simply a function of the time and effort involved in purchasing, it is relevant to all stages of the consumption process. Automatic cars, the Apple iPod, ready-pasted wallpaper and instant coffee are all products that revolutionized a market by offering consumers something that was more convenient to use than the conventional products on the market.

Convenience as a Product Feature

Convenience is a key influence on consumer behaviour in all of the key domestic consumption markets for sustainability of food, homes and transportation (particularly cars). A product's level of convenience (along with its sustainability impacts) is determined by the attributes of the product and the ways in which consumers find them to be convenient. In food, the rise of 'convenience foods' was one of the most remarkable transformations in both a market and a central aspect of society during the twentieth century. These allowed the preparation of meals from basic ingredients to be replaced by pre-prepared and packaged meals and ingredients that could be rapidly heated and served. The rise of convenience foods drove, and was driven by, significant social changes in working patterns, equality between the sexes and household lifestyles. It has also had social consequences in a loss of food-preparation skills in some countries, and health consequences linked to overconsumption of processed foods. Food processing and packaging that deliver consumers convenience in food preparation and storage also contribute significant environmental impacts.

In transportation, the convenience of private car ownership has led to the dominance of the private car within industrialized economies. Generally, public transport is far more efficient in terms of environmental impacts and, depending on journey patterns, can be far more economical, but for most people this is outweighed by the 'go anywhere, any time' convenience of the private car. In car technologies, in some countries (such as the USA, the world's largest market for cars) the convenience of automatic gearboxes has outweighed the losses in fuel efficiency compared to manual gearboxes in making them popular among consumers.

Within homes, energy use has grown in part through central heating and the increasing ownership of labour-saving devices that deliver convenience, but require electric power to wash and dry our clothes, open our cans or slice and mix our foods. Convenience can be integral to a particular product as a primary product feature, and it is quite common for convenience to be emphasized at the expense of environmental performance. A simple example would be the emergence of disposable products including disposable pens, razors and cameras. Such products are engineered to be relatively inexpensive to purchase and to deliver single or limited use before disposal and replacement.

One of the most obvious examples of convenience being designed into products at the expense of sustainability performance is in the widespread use of 'standby' buttons on electrical equipment. The 2002 OECD Working Party Report on Decision-Making and Environmental Policy Design for Consumer Durables[24] estimated that the standby power alone of appliances and other domestic equipment is responsible for 1.5% of total electricity consumption, and also contributes 0.6% (68 million tonnes) of CO_2 emissions. The energy consumption of equipment left on standby (and delivering no consumer benefits while they are idle) can account for as much as 85% of their total energy consumption (depending on frequency of use). The standby power consumption of a typical Japanese household is approximately 400 kWh per annum; considering that a household consumes 4227 kWh per annum on average, the standby power accounts for almost 10% of household electricity use.[25]

There are also potential social impacts from the development of products that seek to deliver convenience to consumers. Convenience tends to be expressed as a function of appropriately meeting the needs of the individual consumer in time and place and reducing the level of effort and compromise involved in the individual's consumption. The technologies that deliver this convenience include freezers and microwave ovens that allow consumers to eat when convenient; DVD recorders or on-demand cable television that allows consumers to be entertained when convenient; and cars that allow individuals to travel when convenient. Such technologies tend to promote an increasing level of individualism and, in allowing household members to eat at different times or watch the same television show at different times, can increase levels of household fragmentation and social isolation.[26]

Convenience in Post-Use

Conventional marketing supply chains are envisaged as very linear structures through which products flow, ending when the product reaches the end of its life (or the end of the consumer's use for it), at which point it is disposed of. The aim of the distribution or 'place' variable within the conventional marketing mix was to ensure that products were made accessible and available to consumers to allow for them to be purchased. Product disposal was rarely considered by marketers during most of the twentieth century, or even by consumers, for whom the most convenient method of disposal was simply to throw away used products and packaging as waste to be collected by municipal authorities and disposed of as landfill. Environmental concerns and the growing shortage of landfill space in many countries have led to increasing efforts to reuse, remanufacture and recycle used products and packaging. This has reoriented municipal waste collections around recycling rather than disposal, but recycling systems typically require some form of waste segregation in the home. This allows different types of materials such as glass, paper, metal cans and biodegradable waste to be collected separately and then recycled (or in the case of biodegradable food and garden waste, composted). Although this does introduce an element of inconvenience for consumers, since it is less easy than simply dumping all waste into a single receptacle, municipal recycling schemes have generally involved a growing number of consumers. This is partly because there is a high level of support for recycling as a consumption behaviour: even those consumers who are sceptical about climate change and other elements of the green agenda can usually relate to the benefits and common sense of recycling in terms of frugality and resource conservation.[27] Also, changing product disposal behaviour requires no compromise from the consumer in terms of their level of consumption or the nature of the products they purchase. It is therefore a behaviour that consumers who are concerned about sustainability, but unwilling to make substantive changes to their lifestyles, are happy to embrace.

The success of schemes to involve consumers in recycling is also strongly influenced by their convenience from a consumer perspective. The most important contribution to increased recycling rates comes from offering consumers kerbside collection of waste from their homes, rather than expecting them to take materials for recycling to a municipal 'bring' site. Similarly, in many countries reverse distribution operations are being established among retailers to reclaim post-use products such as batteries or bottles, often under the auspices of extended producer responsibility regulations (see Chapter 9).

Another packaging issue that has become symbolic of the potential collision between convenience as a consumer benefit and sustainability as a benefit for both consumers and society concerns the humble plastic shopping bag. Different countries and retailers have tackled the challenge of ending consumer addiction to the convenient plastic bag. The government of Ireland introduced a €0.15 tax on plastic shopping bags, which cut demand by more than 90%. Marks & Spencer has levied a 5p (€0.05) charge on plastic bags as part of its Plan A initiative, and has invested the money raised in environmental projects. Other retailers like Stop & Shop in the USA or Sainsburys in the UK have given a small discount to consumers for bringing bags back to reuse. Texan grocery retailer HEB trained staff to increase the number of grocery items going into each bag on average at the checkout, a simple step that has reduced the number of bags it uses by an estimated 136.4 million. Many retailers are now offering durable and reusable bags, often on a free replacement 'bag for life' basis.

From Chains to Loops: Towards Sustainable Distribution

In some key markets such as cars and electronics, reducing consumer waste has been tackled through extended producer responsibility regulations and a requirement for companies to reclaim end-of-life products for consumers to be reused or recycled. This requires distribution and logistics channels, which were set up to make new products available to consumers, to be reengineered to provide reverse logistics channels that will reclaim used products from consumers and make them available for remanufacturing or recycling. This might sound like a relatively straightforward challenge that involves ensuring that vehicles leaving a manufacturer with finished goods return with a load of end-of-life goods. The practicalities make it a complex challenge, however. Forward logistics are based around economies of scale and moving large quantities of standardized products to central points from which consumers can access them. Reverse logistics require manufacturers to access used products that will have become dispersed among households, which will return into the supply chain in varying conditions and at a time convenient to the consumer. Doing so makes sound strategic sense from an economic as well as an ecological perspective, since end-of-life products represent a store of potential value.

Some of the best-known examples of reverse logistics systems come from business-to-business markets and feature equipment manufacturers such as IBM, Xerox and Dell. Consumer goods companies are also becoming increasingly proficient at reclaiming, managing and extracting value from unsold, returned or end-of-life products. Cosmetics firm Estée Lauder, for example, has created a reverse logistics system using its own software in which boxes of returned products are scanned when they re-enter the warehouse. The scanned data provides information about expiration dates, and the system selects which products can be resold into other markets profitably and which will be given away to charities to prevent it needing to be landfilled.[28] For the principle of 'extended producer responsibility' to work, and for markets to be transformed into sustainable supply loops, such innovative systems and thinking will need to become the norm across a range of industries.

Online Convenience

The emergence of the Internet and the growth of online commerce have created profound changes in the world of marketing and to the way in which products are made available to consumers, purchased and consumed. Online commerce can give consumers access to an astonishingly wide range of products, available for purchase 24/7; in the case of Amazon.com, it offers consumers millions of products in different categories. One of the great hopes for online marketing is that it allows for the combination of both increased convenience for the consumer and the reduction of the environmental impacts associated with their consumption. Consumers express satisfaction with the convenience of online purchasing for product categories such as electronic hardware, computer software, books and music, and the booking of tickets for concerts or plays. Product categories that require a more experiential aspect for purchasing of 'touch', 'feel' or 'fit', such as for sunglasses or clothing, are not viewed as so convenient to purchase online.[29] Being able to peruse and purchase products from home at the click of a mouse allows the consumer to save the time, energy and fuel that are typically associated with shopping trips. Ultimately this could reduce the number of shopping centres that society requires and their relatively inefficient use of land.[30]

However, the reality is unlikely to be as predictable and as significantly benevolent as these arguments suggest. Although the purchase and distribution process may become more materially efficient in many markets, this will not change the level of environmental impacts in production, use or disposal, where the most significant impacts will occur. There can also be unforeseen displacements of environmental impacts when particular types of consumption or distribution move into a virtual environment. One of the sectors predicted to benefit from this and become more sustainable was photography, where digital photos were forecast to replace hard-copy photographs and the chemicals, paper and water they consumed. What was not predicted was the extent to which the convenience (and low cost per picture) of digital photography would lead to an explosion in the number of photographs taken. Many of these pictures are now left perpetually posted on the web pages of individuals or placed in digital photo frames, both of which will consume electricity for as long as the pictures are stored or displayed.

There is also a social aspect to the convenience of online marketing purchasing that is significant but often overlooked. Leaving the house in order to access goods and services, particularly at local outlets, is an activity that is often important in maintaining individuals' social contacts and links with communities. The ability to use the Internet to consume (and sometimes also to work) from home creates the danger of growing social isolation and reduced quality of life. The most extreme example of this is the Japanese phenomenon of *hikikomori*, a form of acute social withdrawal prevalent among young men. This is the emergence of a lifestyle of convenient home-based consumption that leads to a withdrawal from almost all other aspects of society. An exact definition of *hikikomori* and accurate data on its prevalence have yet to emerge, but it has been recognized as an illness and described in medical journal *The Lancet* as follows:

> there is broad agreement that this illness is a product of the affluence, technology, and convenience of modern Japanese life. Many hikikomori spend most of their waking hours on the internet or playing video games, while snacking on food and drink delivered to their homes.[31]

So, although convenience is widely recognized as a consumer benefit, it is important to realize that it also often comes at a social and environmental cost. For sustainability marketers, the challenge is to make the solutions they offer convenient in a way that minimizes those costs. Offering customer solutions that are as convenient as their conventional competitors is one of the key challenges for sustainability marketing, and the need to do so has been a recurrent theme among many commentators, particularly the leading green marketing expert Jacqueline Ottman.[32] The relationship between convenience and environmental and social performance is currently imbalanced. More sustainable products and services are expected to match conventional marketing offerings in convenience, but products and services primarily designed to be convenient are not currently expected to match the environmental and social performance of more sustainable products. While only 'win–win' solutions that do not involve any compromises on the part of the consumer are acceptable as a marketing strategy, the opportunities to make any transformational changes to markets will be limited.

List of Key Terms

Accessibility
Availability
Channels
Choice editing
Convenience goods
Convenience stores
Disposal
Distribution
Electronic commerce
Logistics
Out-of-town retailing
Packaging
Retailing
Reverse logistics
Shopping bags
Supply chains
Supply loops

REVIEW QUESTIONS

1. How can 'convenience' be defined?
2. What are the potential social disadvantages of trends towards out-of-town retailing?
3. How could convenience stores play a key role in a more sustainable future economy?
4. What methods could allow existing retailing logistics operations to become more environmentally sustainable?

DISCUSSION QUESTIONS

1. Can substantive progress towards sustainability marketing be made unless consumers are willing to trade off some elements of convenience against other sustainability-oriented benefits?
2. What are the social and environmental implications of the growth of online consumption, and can increasing levels of e-commerce make a substantial contribution to sustainability marketing?
3. How might increasing trends towards product takeback and supply loops affect the management of relationships with key marketing stakeholders?

SUSTAINABILITY MARKETING CHALLENGE: FAIRMONT HOTELS – CONVENIENT, LUXURIOUS AND SUSTAINABLE?

In the hotel market, two of the principal benefits consumers seek are luxury and convenience, and often it is the provision of convenience that contributes to the sense of a luxurious experience. If convenience is the removal of discomfort and the provision of ease, and providing something well suited to the consumer's needs, then it is the essence of hotel marketing. In a hotel, we expect all the things we do for ourselves at home to be done for us. Our living space is cleaned and tidied, our bedding is changed daily, our food is prepared for us and there are staff on hand 24/7 to bring us food and drink (or whatever else we desire), wake us up and otherwise arrange for our needs to be met. The typical hotel room itself provides a convenient combination of entertainment technology, telecommunications, fridge and other facilities.

All this convenience comes at a significant environmental cost. The average hotel guest creates between 1 and 2 kg of solid waste and 6 litres of liquid waste per overnight stay. It is not difficult to see why so much waste is created. Individual bars of soap unwrapped and used once; coffee-making facilities featuring individually packaged coffee, sugar, milk and biscuit portions; breakfast buffets composed of individual-serving cereal packets and pots of conserves; towels used once and sent for laundering. Interestingly, in energy use more luxurious hotels (4 and 5 stars) use an average of around 33 Kwh per overnight stay, compared to nearly 59 Kwh for 2-star hotels. Although counterintuitive, this reflects the attempts by the more upmarket hotel chains to manage their energy consumption actively. In water the situation is reversed, with the average 5-star hotel guest using 594 litres in an overnight stay compared to 454 litres for a 2-star hotel.[33]

The hotel industry is one of many seeking to address their sustainability impacts and to seek competitive advantage and build good relationships with consumers by demonstrating their social and environmental concern. The question remains, however, whether a hotel can really deliver convenience, luxury and home comforts to guests in a sustainable way.

The Fairmont Hotel chain has sought to establish a leadership position as an environmentally responsible hotel.[34] The chain has 50 hotels with 23 000 rooms around the world. In 1990, its Canadian operations pioneered a 'Green Partnership' programme, a comprehensive commitment to minimizing environmental impacts, accompanied by a guide to sustainable best practices for the whole industry. The Green Partnership programme and its underlying values has now become a core part of the global group's strategy and philosophy, and 26 000 Fairmont employees have become 'environmental ambassadors', helping to protect the habitats, resources and cultures of the countries in which they operate. Fairmont is also part of the World Heritage Alliance, an industry-leading initiative established by Expedia and the United Nations Foundation to promote sustainable tourism and awareness of World Heritage sites and communities.

Fairmont's Canadian operations have implemented a range of sustainability initiatives. In 2007 the Fairmont Winnipeg switched to all energy-efficient lighting and donated more than 1000 replaced bulbs to the charitable sector to keep them from landfill. Energy savings are anticipated of more than 882 000 kWh per (equivalent to the power used by 327 typical homes), saving around $44 000 (€ 31 760) annually. In 2005 the Fairmont Royal York, Toronto, installed a commercial water softener to reduce laundry water use, which saved nearly half a million litres of water daily. The Fairmont in Vancouver organized the donation of leftover food to the Vancouver Food Runners Program, feeding people in need. This avoided food waste of around one tonne every three months.

The group has also developed a range of products based around ecologically oriented holidays and partnerships to deliver joint hotel and community projects locally (called Eco-Innovation signature projects); globally it is the first hotel brand to partner with WWF to tackle climate change. The efforts Fairmont has made in trying to lead in sustainable tourism have led to numerous awards, including Top Eco-Hospitality Program in *Strategy Magazine*'s Cause and Action Awards, Best Corporate Social Responsibility Platform in the Worldwide Hospitality Awards, and recognition as the best global example of responsible tourism and sustainable operations in the World Tourism and Travel Council Awards. The company's strategy is based on developing a range of partnerships to strive towards sustainable tourism and responsible travel practices. The improvements it has delivered are impressive, but the journey to reach a genuinely sustainable hospitality sector looks set to be a very long one.

> **Discussion Questions**
>
> 1. Can the concept of sustainability marketing be compatible with the process of trying to compete within the luxury hotel market?
> 2. Why do you think Fairmont produced a guide to sustainability practices for the whole industry?
> 3. How could Fairmont try to build relationships with its guests in order to encourage them to play a part in more sustainable use of Fairmont's services, while still delivering luxury and convenience?

Endnotes

1. See Kobayashi, K. (2005) 'From "Convenience to Co-Growing"', *Japan for Sustainability, Towards a Sustainable Japan. Corporations at Work Series*, September: Article 30; Betros, C. (2007) 'Convenience Stores Changing with the Times', *Japan Today*, December 17, http://archive.japantoday.com/jp/feature/1315 (accessed 26 December 2008).
2. Shove, E. (2003) *Comfort, Cleanliness and Convenience: The Social Organization of Normality*, Oxford: Berg.
3. Press release from the UK retailer Sainsburys on 4 November 2008.
4. The total global battery market is estimated at $50 billion, with rechargeables accounting for around $5.5 billion, according to battery market research group Freedonia
5. Copeland, M.T. (1923) 'Relation of consumers' buying habits to marketing methods', *Harvard Business Review*, 1 (April): 282–9.
6. Pretty, J.N., Ball, A.S., Lang, T. & Morison, J.I.L. (2005) 'Farm costs and food miles: An assessment of the full cost of the UK weekly food basket', *Food Policy*, 30(1): 1–20.
7. Watkiss, P. (2005) *The Validity of Food Miles as an Indicator of Sustainable Development*, Report produced for DEFRA, Didcot: AEA Technology.
8. Gupta, U. (1994) 'Cause-driven companies' new cause: Profits', *Wall Street Journal*, November 8, p. B1.
9. Fuller, D. (1999) *Sustainable Marketing*, Thousand Oaks, CA: Sage.
10. Szymankiewicz, J. (1993) 'Going green: The logistics dilemma', *Logistics Information Management*, 6(3): 36–43.
11. Oppenheim, C. (1998) 'Poverty and Social Exclusion: An Overview', in Oppenheim, C. (ed.), *An Inclusive Society: Strategies for Tackling Poverty*, London: Institute for Public Policy Research.
12. See the chapter opening story on ONE Water in Chapter 8.
13. Ginsberg, J.M. & Bloom, P.N. (2004) 'Choosing the right green marketing strategy', *MIT Sloan Management Review*, 46(1): 79–84.
14. Presser, H.B. (2003) *Working in a 24/7 Economy: Challenges for American Families*, New York: Russell Sage Foundation.
15. Fonteyne, J. (2000) 'Packaging Recovery and Recycling Policy in Practice', in Levy, G. (ed.), *Packaging, Policy and the Environment*, Guildford: Springer.
16. Silayoi, P. & Speece, M. (2007) 'The importance of packaging attributes: A conjoint analysis approach', *European Journal of Marketing*, 41(11/12): 1495–1517.
17. *Ibid.*
18. GMA/Food Marketing Institute/Deloitte (2008) *Joint Industry Unsaleables Report: The Real Causes and Actionable Solutions*, Washington DC: Grocery Manufacturers Association.
19. Business Wire (2008) 'New Star Market at Chestnut Hill to be Pilot for Comprehensive Use of Innovative Technology that's Sustainable', *Business Wire*, 10 September.

20. Ueda, E.S. (2003) 'Exploring possibilities for sustainable services in convenience stores: An introduction', *Proceedings of EcoDesign 2003: Third International Symposium on Environmentally Conscious Design and Inverse Manufacturing*, 8–11 December, Tokyo, pp. 441–44.

21. Pretty, J.N., Ball, A.S., Lang, T. & Morison, J.I.L. (2005) 'Farm costs and food miles: An assessment of the full cost of the UK weekly food basket', *Food Policy*, 30(1): 1–20.

22. *Ibid*.

23. Faber Maunsell (2007) *Reducing the External Costs of the Domestic Transportation of Food by the Food Industry: Scoping Report*, St Albans: Faber Maunsell.

24. OECD (2002) *Working Party Report on Decision-Making and Environmental Policy Design for Consumer Durables*, Paris: OECD.

25. Sasako, M. (2001) 'Standby power consumption of household electrical appliances in Japan', *Third International Workshop on Standby Power*, Tokyo, 7–8 February.

26. Shove, E. (2003) *Comfort, Cleanliness and Convenience: The Social Organization of Normality*, Oxford: Berg.

27. Future Foundation (2007) *Climate Change and the Future of Brands*, London: Future Foundation.

28. Caldwell, B. (1999) 'Reverse logistics', *Information Week*, 729: 48.

29. Bhatnagar, A., Misra, S. & Rao, H.R. (2000) 'On risk, convenience and Internet shopping behaviour', *Communications of the ACM*, 43(11): 98–105.

30. Cohen, N. (1999) 'Greening the Internet: Ten ways e-commerce could affect the environment and what we can do', *Information Impact Magazine*, October, http://www.cisp.org/imp/october_99/10_99 cohen.htm (accessed 26 December 2008).

31. Watts, J. (2002) 'Tokyo: Public health experts concerned about "hikikomori"', *The Lancet*, 359: 1131.

32. Ottman, J. (1992) 'The four Es make going green your competitive edge', *Marketing News*, 26(3): 7; and Ottman, J.A., Stafford, E.R. & Hartman, C.L. (2006) 'Green marketing myopia', *Environment*, 48(5): 22–36.

33. See Hamele, H. & Eckardt, S. (2006) *Environmental Initiatives by European Tourism Businesses. Instruments, Indicators and Practical Examples*, ECOTRANS/IER, http://sutour.ier.uni-stuttgart.de/englisch/downloads/sutour_lores_en.pdf (accessed 26 December 2008).

34. See http://www.fairmont.com/EN_FA/AboutFairmont/environment/GreenPartnershipProgram/ (accessed 26 December 2008).

PART V

DEVELOPING THE FUTURE OF SUSTAINABILITY MARKETING

CHAPTER 11

Sustainability Marketing Transformations

After Studying this Chapter You Should be Able to:

1. Explain how socio-ecological problems evolve into market and marketing issues.
2. Understand internal sustainability marketing transformations *of* companies.
3. Describe the starting points of external sustainability marketing transformations *by* companies.

LOOKING AHEAD: PREVIEWING THE CONCEPTS

Transformation means change, conversion or alteration, especially radical change in the sense of a revolution. In this chapter we will look at three different sustainability marketing transformations. We will learn how socio-ecological problems turn into forces of competition and issues of sustainability marketing (*outside-in perspective*). We will examine the types of transformations that companies pursuing sustainability marketing go through (*inside perspective*). Finally, we will see why and how some leading companies play a part in promoting the great transformations required within societies seeking to make progress towards sustainable development (*inside-out perspective*).

SUSTAINABILITY MARKETING STORY: GASSER CONSTRUCTION MATERIALS – BUILDING HAPPINESS

Josias Gasser is a visionary corporate leader. He bears a striking similarity to Doc Brown, the eccentric and yet sympathetic scientist who invented the first time travel machine in the *Back to the Future* movie trilogy. Although Josias Gasser did not invent time travel, he looked back in time when he took over the family business in 1984. He also thought about the future and came to the conclusion that to face the ecological and societal challenges of the twenty-first century, his construction material company could not go on with 'business as usual'. In the 1990s he developed a vision based on sustainable development and transformed the family-owned and family-run company. Ever since, Josias Gasser Construction Materials has focused on offering ecological construction materials, as well as systems and solutions for energy-efficient buildings.

In order to 'walk the talk', Josias Gasser rebuilt the company's headquarters at Chur (Switzerland) in 1999. The new wooden office building and warehouse are characterized by the reuse of materials from the old building, the careful selection of ecological construction materials, the use of rainwater and a high degree of energy efficiency. The bright and well-insulated offices are mainly heated by the sun. If the room temperature falls below the comfort level of 20°C, two small wood stoves provide heat and warmth. As a result, the annual energy consumption for room heating is less than 0.5 kWh (equivalent of half a litre of oil) per square metre. The construction cost of the new headquarters was 450 Swiss Francs (€300) per cubic metre, which is 3% higher than a comparable conventional office building with warehouses. However, its energy efficiency means that around 15 000 litres of oil are saved each year. The initial extra investment will pay off in 10–15 years (depending on future oil prices). The new headquarters provide a visible symbol of the sustainability strategy pursued by the company, and form part of its corporate culture and design. Employees feel comfortable in the offices. They identify with the company and its mission to 'Build Happiness'. Professional and private customers are welcome to inspect the headquarters, become acquainted with the new technologies for energy-efficient buildings and experience at first hand their quality and comfort.

In 1999 Gasser construction materials received an award for sustainable planning and construction by the Swiss Association of Engineers and Architects, generating national publicity. Encouraged by the positive results and responses, Gasser decided to enter the do-it-yourself market with energy-efficient offices and warehouse at Samedan in 2004. Samedan is 1728 metres above sea level, close to the famous winter skiing area of St Moritz. Despite the long and cold winters, the new building works well with the kind of technology for energy-efficient houses sold in the do-it-yourself market. Sustainability marketing has become a source of innovation and differentiation in construction materials: Since 1984 Gasser has established eight new sites in the south-eastern region of Switzerland, employing more than 90 people and increasing revenues as well as profits.

Besides transforming his company towards sustainability during the last 25 years or so, Josias Gasser also seeks change in the broader environment. He is active in a number of public and political organizations pursuing sustainable development. In 2004 he was one of the founding members of the interest group Passive House Switzerland. Between 2004 and 2008 he was president of the network, which establishes and enhances future standards of houses offering the best comfort and the highest energy efficiency. The interest group informs and educates its members, develops new quality standards, and promotes passive houses to the general public. In politics Josias Gasser is president of Ö+, an association for economy, ecology and society that aims to achieve sustainable production and consumption patterns in the Swiss canton of Graubünden, where Gasser is located. The association promotes regional products and services that contribute to the quality of life and value of the region. One of the main activities of Ö+ is the certification of hotels according to sustainability criteria, including quality, environmental and social standards. The certified hotels receive the 'Capricorn', the first holistic sustainability label for hotels worldwide. Furthermore, Josias Gasser is a founding member of the Green Liberals in the canton of Graubünden, a new Swiss political party that combines liberalism with the idea of sustainable development. The Green Liberals favour market-based instruments of environmental policy over command-and-control policies to internalize external costs. In addition, Josias Gasser is engaged in education and science. For years, he has been a supporting member of the Oikos Foundation for Economy and Ecology at the University of St Gallen (Switzerland), which seeks to integrate sustainability issues into the agenda of business schools.[1]

Sustainability Marketing Transformations: The Outside-In Perspective

In this chapter we will take a close look at transformations for sustainability marketing. There are three different, complementary perspectives of sustainability marketing transformations. The *outside-in perspective* gives us a better understanding of how ecological and social problems evolve into market and marketing issues. The *inside perspective* shows what kind of transformations companies go through internally through the pursuit of sustainability marketing. The *inside-out perspective* emphasizes objectives and options for companies to contribute to external change and the transformation of societies on their way towards sustainability.

So how do ecological and social problems such as local waste, toxic contamination, global warming, working conditions in sweatshops and child labour evolve into market and marketing issues, and how do they lead to sustainability marketing transformations from the outside in? Downs suggests that public attention rarely remains focused on any one ecological or social issue for very long – even if it is crucial to society.[2] Based on his observations of environmental concern in North America (and in other industrialized countries) in the late 1960s and early 1970s, he came to the conclusion that public attention on any issue goes through a cycle of five stages (see Figure 11.1):

1. *Pre-problem stage*: At the beginning the problem exists in society or the environment, but has not yet attracted much public attention. Scientists, other experts and concerned citizens may be aware

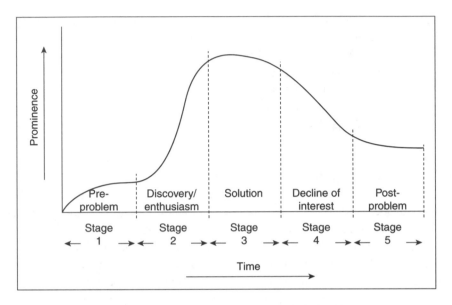

Figure 11.1   Issue–attention cycle of socio-ecological problems

Source: Based on Downs, A. (1972) 'Up and down with ecology: The "issue attention cycle"', *The Public Interest*, 28 (Summer): 38–50; and Dyllick, T. (1990) *Management der Umweltbeziehungen*, Wiesbaden: Gabler.

of the problem, investigate and discuss it, but their debates remain widely unheard. There is no coverage in the mass media or resonance with the general public yet.

2. *Discovery stage*: In the second stage some critical and newsworthy incidents or developments occur. They receive widespread coverage in the mass media and attract public attention. As a result, the public becomes aware of, and alarmed about, the particular problem.

3. *Solution stage*: Public attention creates pressure on politicians to 'do something' and 'solve the problem'. In some cases there are short-term remedies with a high symbolic meaning (e.g. an expert committee established to analyse the matter). In most cases there are no easy solutions. Often new institutions have to be established, new programmes initiated and new policies formulated, which take time and money.

4. *Decline stage*: As the difficulties and costs of tackling the problem become evident, the general public's attention to the issue wanes. There are fewer reports in the media, which turns to some new event or problem as more 'newsworthy'.

5. *Post-problem stage*: In the final stage the issue, having slipped down the agenda, receives reduced attention or only spasmodic recurrences of interest. Nevertheless, due to the newly established institutions, programmes and policies, issues that are placed on the back burner may become newly 'hot' as new events occur or discoveries are made. Problems that have already gone through the whole cycle are more likely to receive a higher than average level of attention, public effort and general concern than those still in the pre-discovery stage.[3]

The length of the issue–attention cycle and the timing of its different stages may vary depending on the nature of the problem involved and particularly on the media's reaction to it. In some cases it is a matter of weeks or months, in others it can take years or even decades. In the case of environmental concern, a series of sporadic but separate incidents and crises related to different aspects of the environment kept forcing the issue up the agenda over a period of decades. Critical incidents like the chemical disaster at Bhopal (1984), the nuclear disaster at Chernobyl (1985), the Sandoz chemical spill into the Rhine river (1986), the Exxon oil spill (1989) and the destruction of forests received worldwide news coverage and a lot of public attention, leading to unprecedented heights of concern for the environment in the late 1980s and early 1990s.[4] Initially, environmental concern was kept in the public consciousness through the endless variety of new problems. Then more recently the focus has shifted from concern about specific issues and incidents to concern about enduring global problems such as climate change and global poverty, the scale of which ensures that they command attention.

It is when looking at a specific problem such as global warming and climate change that the issue–attention cycle model has the greatest explanatory power. A content analysis of US media (print, broadcast television and radio) shows that in the late 1980s and the first half of the 1990s the issue of global warming went through the first three stages of the cycle.[5] The conference in Kyoto (Japan) in 1997 and the environmental treaty to limit the emissions of greenhouse gases, particularly carbon dioxide, represented the preliminary peak of the cycle. With critical incidents like Hurricane Katrina in 2005 (one of the most costly and deadly hurricanes in the history of the United States) the issue of global warming regained public attention. It was further fuelled by the documentary *An Inconvenient Truth*, which was released in 2006 and presented by former US Vice President Al Gore. When the Intergovernmental Panel on Climate Change (IPCC) collated and published mounting empirical evidence of global warming and the influence of human beings on climate change in its Fourth Assessment Report, the issue became omnipresent in public and political discourse. It reached an all-time high when *An Inconvenient Truth* won the Oscar for the Best Documentary Feature, and when IPCC and Al Gore received the Nobel Peace Prize in 2007. However, as the financial crisis and fear of recession set in during 2008, the issue of global warming waned again.

We can see that the issue–attention cycle is useful for sustainability marketers in understanding when and how ecological and social problems can interest the public and influence their behaviour as consumers. It does, however, have shortcomings. One is that it considers issues one at a time, but in practice several issues may be vying for public attention at the same time and the focus may switch between them as circumstances and media priorities change. Another shortcoming is that the cycle focuses on public attention, without showing how that attention can turn socio-ecological problems into competitive forces and issues for marketers.

To understand sustainability marketing transformations from the outside in, Dyllick *et al.* conducted empirical studies in six different industries (chemicals, computers, construction, food, transportation and machinery). They analysed the main ecological problems from 'cradle to grave' of the product as well as the main stakes by public, political and market stakeholders in the selected industries.[6] They identified two basic ways in which a particular ecological or social problem is transformed into a market and marketing issue: indirect and direct sustainability transformation processes (Figure 11.2).

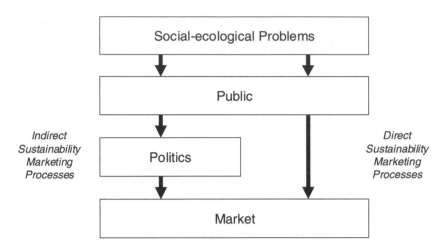

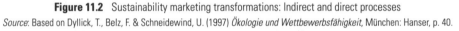

Figure 11.2 Sustainability marketing transformations: Indirect and direct processes
Source: Based on Dyllick, T., Belz, F. & Schneidewind, U. (1997) *Ökologie und Wettbewerbsfähigkeit*, München: Hanser, p. 40.

Indirect Sustainability Marketing Transformation Processes

Following Downs'[7] logic, scientific issues of interest initially only to experts and enthusiasts evolve into media issues, which turn into public issues and then into political issues. Some socio-ecological problems are solved by setting standards, which are enforced by law or other political regulations. Other socio-ecological problems are addressed through market-based approaches and by 'setting the prices right'; that is, giving economic incentives for producers and consumers to behave in a more socially and ecologically benign way.

The automobile industry presents a clear example of an indirect transformation process. As described above, the issue of global warming first received widespread public attention in the late 1980s and early 1990s. In 1995 the European Union adopted a strategy to reduce CO_2 emissions from cars resting on three pillars: promotion of fuel-efficient cars by means of fiscal measures (e.g. tax reductions for low-emission cars); consumer information by means of a label attached to the vehicle showing the fuel consumption and CO_2 emissions; and a voluntary agreement with the European Automobile Manufacturers Association (EAMA).[8] In 1999 European automobile manufacturers committed themselves to reduce CO_2 emissions from passenger cars and improve fuel economy. The agreement negotiated with the European Union was that the average emissions of new passenger cars sold in Europe should be 140 g CO_2/km. This means that the fleet of new passenger cars put onto the market in 2008/09 was supposed to consume on average about 5.8 litres of petrol per 100 km or 5.25 litres of diesel per 100 km. As it became evident that this commitment had failed, the European Union increased the political pressure on automobile manufacturers. In 2007 the EU Commission proposed a renewed strategy to increase fuel-efficiency standards so that emissions from new cars sold in Europe would be no more than 130 g CO_2/km in 2012, down from 162 g/km in 2005. For every extra gram automobile companies would have to pay a fine, starting in 2012 and gradually rising each year. Thus, fuel efficiency and CO_2 emissions will become inescapably important for purchasers and marketers within the automobile industry. By the end of 2008 there were already some signs of a significant shift. After a long period of 'business as usual' and upsizing cars with more power, a new era of downsizing and low-emission cars like hybrids and electric cars had begun.

Direct Sustainability Marketing Transformation Processes

As illustrated by the case of global warming and the automobile industry, a particular ecological or social problem usually goes through the issue–attention cycle and the political process before it begins to influence markets and marketers. This indirect transmission of concern from the general public via policy and politics to the market may take years to occur. However, in some cases pressure for sustainability marketing transformation processes goes directly from the general public to the market.

Take the activist protests against sportswear company Nike in the 1990s.[9] The first reports on low pay and bad working conditions in so-called sweatshops were published between 1988 and 1991 and attracted hardly any public attention. In 1990 David Taylor, vice president of Nike, said to the press: 'We don't pay anybody at the factories, and we don't set policy within the factories. It's their business to run.' At that time Nike took no responsibility for the working conditions of its suppliers throughout Asia. This attitude changed, however, when the company became the centre of activist protests that provoked public interest. Between 1996 and 1998 more than 1500 critical newspaper articles were published dealing with the unacceptable working conditions of young women and children in Asian sweatshops supplying Nike. Consumer protests, demonstrations at Niketown stores and worldwide boycotts hurt Nike's image and sales. They culminated in the outburst of a 13-year-old Afro-American on the occasion of a protest in September 1997: 'Nike, we made you. We can break you!'[10]

The protest in front of Niketown on Fifth Avenue in New York City and the youngster's outburst were broadcast across all the major American television networks during prime time. The example shows how activists attracted public attention and support by attacking Nike and its brand, the most valuable asset of the company. The activists deliberately chose Nike as their target, not because its supply chain had the worst labour practices, but because it was the leader in the global market for sports apparel with one of the highest-profile brands. If the market leader is made to deal with the problem of its suppliers' unacceptable working conditions, reasoned the activists, the rest of the companies in the market will follow suit. In this kind of sustainability marketing transformation process, politicians were not directly involved.

As we enter the digital information age, it becomes clear that technologies such as the Internet and mobile communications are powerful tools in the hands of activists, concerned citizens and critical consumers. New information and communication technologies help them to disseminate information on a particular social and ecological problem, exchange their ideas and views with like-minded people in virtual communities, learn from each other and coordinate protest and consumer boycotts in an efficient manner. They are increasingly well connected and more powerful than ever at pushing companies to confront socio-ecological issues and problems.

In both indirect and direct transformation processes, there are *key actors* who drive a particular ecological or social issue forward.[11] Key actors are those powerful stakeholders who exert an influence on others and keep the sustainability marketing transformation going. In general, there are three different kinds of key actors: public, political and market actors. The power of each stems from different sources: morality, political legitimacy and economic influence respectively.

Well-known and credible *public* stakeholders have power through moral legitimacy (e.g. Greenpeace). They highlight a particular ecological or social problem and appeal to the moral conscience of the general public. They often reduce complex issues to relatively simplistic ideas of right and wrong, good and bad, and if possible present them in a dramatic, exciting and newsworthy way. They will often use direct action and symbolic images to get their message across via the mass media despite their limited human and financial resources. Consider the dramatic occupation by Greenpeace activists of the *Brent Spar* North Sea oil platform in 1995.[12] Greenpeace successfully played with the image of David fighting against Goliath; that is, the multinational corporation Shell, which planned to dump the ageing oil facility in the sea. The pictures went around the world and mobilized intense protest across Europe, most notably in Germany (see Chapter 8).

Political key actors include national governments and supranational organizations like the European Union that play an important role in defining and dealing with ecological and social problems. As shown by the example of global warming and the automobile industry, integrated product policy within the European Union is backed by a variety of tools to establish a new institutional framework for competition with the aim of internalizing external costs, including economic instruments, command-and-control bans on substances, consumer information such as product labelling, as well as voluntary agreements. In the UK part of the government's response to sustainable development has been to establish the Market Transformation Programme, which supports sustainable product policy through the provision of information and evidence, and through working with industries and other stakeholders to agree action plans and measures aimed at transforming markets.[13]

Market key actors influence the whole value chain and competition within the market. They play a crucial role in the diffusion of socio-ecological solutions in the market. If global retailers like Wal-Mart announce their commitment to the purchase of sustainable fish, for example, it sends a strong signal to suppliers and competitors. By means of its purchasing power and dominant market position, Wal-Mart can change the rules of competition. In many consumer goods markets such as food, electronics, textiles and furniture, retailers have sufficient purchasing power to act as socio-ecological gatekeepers or diffusion agents for the entire value chain.

We can conclude that sustainability marketing transformations follow two typical patterns: ecological and social problems either make their way indirectly from the general public via politics to the marketplace, or go directly from the public to markets influencing the behaviour of consumers, companies and competitors. This is a useful way for marketers to understand how sustainability issues can and may affect their businesses, but in practice the model of indirect and direct transformation processes depicted in Figure 11.2 is a simplification of complex realities. Sustainability marketing transformation processes are often complex, nonlinear and discontinuous. That makes it difficult, if not impossible, to describe and predict the progression of a particular ecological or social problem in advance. Some critical incidents that influence the public and political agenda simply happen. The response to any issue will not simply be rationally economic and technical, it will also be a socio-political process constructed and shaped by various stakeholders and their often competing agendas. Some will try to promote the process of transformation while others defend the status quo.

In the past there were clear distinctions and opposition between environmental and social groups on the one side and companies on the other. At the beginning of the twenty-first century the boundaries between former antagonists have become blurred. Some forward-thinking companies are taking a lead in tackling ecological and social problems instead of simply following consumer demand or the requirements of regulation. Some companies, such as Gasser construction material, build partnerships with nongovernmental organizations. They also cooperate with other like-minded companies (including competitors) to create sustainable business models and to establish new business associations that support and enhance the ideas of sustainable development. These new associations frequently position themselves as an alternative to the established, rather conservative business and industry associations. Sometimes surprising alliances emerge. Usually, environmental organizations like Greenpeace and energy corporations with nuclear power plants are deadly enemies. Regarding electric vehicles as means of transportation, however, there is an extraordinary consensus. Environmental organizations see this as a great opportunity to revolutionize the automobile industry and to approach the problem of global warming, while energy corporations see it as a new business opportunity

Sustainability Marketing Transformations: The Inside Perspective

Faced with outside-in pressure to transform, companies have a number of options for how to respond. They can ignore or deny the pressure. They can try to hinder and delay the process. They can accommodate to it, accept responsibility and do what is demanded by different relevant groups. Or they can go beyond industry norms and anticipate future expectations by doing more than is expected.

One company that is doing far more than is expected by its stakeholders is Interface, one of the world's largest interior furnishing companies (see Chapter 9).[14] In 1994 Ray Andersson, the founder and CEO, established the goal of converting Interface into a sustainable enterprise. That represented nothing less than a total transformation of the company – culturally, strategically and structurally. To describe the long and intertwined journey for Interface towards sustainability Ray Andersson uses a powerful metaphor: for him, the journey is like 'conquering a mountain higher than Everest'. To motivate employees to start climbing 'Mount Sustainability', Interface started setting up informational and educational programmes such as:

- 'Play to win' exercises and training to view sustainability as a challenge, not a threat.
- EcoSense, which helped them to discover what sustainability means for Interface.

- QUEST (Quality Utilizing Employee Suggestions and Teamwork) invited employees to make things happen and be part of the change.

Evidence of the lasting cultural change at Interface can be found in a number of innovative solutions conceived and implemented by employees. An example is the Entropy carpet, a new product that emulates the forest floor and where no two pieces are alike. Therefore it is practically waste free in production and installation. The appeal of the Entropy carpet is that it brings part of the outdoors indoors. After its introduction it became one of the company's top-selling products. In the future a major step for Interface will be the use of bio-based materials that allow completely safe post-use degradation. This is vital to achieve 'Mission Zero', the company's commitment to eliminate any negative impact on the environment by 2020.

What can we learn from the example of Interface and its founder? Addressing the needs and limits of nature while exceeding customer expectations usually requires fundamental change. For Interface, the journey towards sustainability has been a 'momentous shift' in the way it perceives and operates its business, and in the way it develops and markets new products and services. There are a number of barriers to such radical transformations, which basically fall into three categories:[15]

- *Individual barriers*: lack of awareness, unwillingness to change, fear about necessary changes and how to deal with them, and extra work added to daily business.
- *Organizational internal barriers*: short-term perspectives focusing on economic aspects, faith in technology and market solutions, and lack of a clear business case, especially for marketing management.
- *Organizational external barriers*: lack of consumer interest, lack of investor interest, lack of coherence in public policies and regulations, especially regarding products.

To overcome the barriers and make changes towards sustainability marketing management, the following *six essentials* are required: a committed CEO; sustainability change agents; empowered employees; sustainability marketing information systems; a clear corporate sustainability mission; and sustainability incentive structures.

Committed CEO

The examples of Josias Gasser and Ray Andersson show that it takes a visible and committed CEO to make lasting changes.[16] Their role in the sustainability marketing transformation process can hardly be overestimated. Their personal commitment and communication empower employees and help to forge an emotional link between the company and its customers. A CEO who owns the company and has a personal stake in the outcome of the sustainability endeavour will be particularly credible in the leadership role.[17]

Sustainability Change Agents

A single CEO, however, will not bring about fundamental change towards sustainability. He or she needs sustainability change agents at all levels of management, particularly in research and development and marketing. There are three different types of change agents: some have power and resources to enable internal change (e.g. senior management); others have knowledge of the natural environment to inspire internal change (e.g. creative inventor); and others have knowledge about transitional processes regardless of the content or direction of change (e.g. organizational developer). Ideally, all three types of change agents will be employed and will complement each other.

Empowered Employees

Committed CEOs supported by change agents do not guarantee the success of sustainability change strategies. To complete the transformation of the company, its products and services, informed and empowered employees are also essential. In many companies environmental and social issues are delegated to an environmental department, or one handling CSR, corporate affairs or public relations. Sustainability marketing transformations from the inside require the integration of environmental and social issues throughout a company's core business and daily activities,[18] particularly in innovation and marketing management.

Conventionally trained marketing decision-makers are often poorly equipped to deal with environmental and social realities. Like Neo, the hero in *The Matrix*, they seem to live in a virtual world. They are imprisoned in an artificial world constructed of advertising imagery, without any reference to the real world of bio-mass, energy flows, endangered species and social problems, which follow their products through the whole life cycle from cradle to grave.[19] As long as these environmental and social problems do not change regulations or consumer behaviour, they do not exist in the world of conventional marketing. This kind of ignorance can be dangerous, if not fatal, for brand image and product sales. That is why marketing decision-makers need the capacity to see, feel, understand and respond to sustainability issues that go beyond the immediate needs and wants of customers.

Sustainability Marketing Information Systems

To develop these kinds of capacities, marketing decision-makers need information and education. They require sound information about the sustainability issues relevant to the products and services offered, provided by qualitative and quantitative life cycle assessments (see Chapter 3). Furthermore, marketing decision-makers have to be informed about stakeholder attitudes to sustainability issues that are relevant to sourcing, production, use or post-use of products. That gives them an understanding of how socio-ecological problems turn into market issues. Finally, marketing decision-makers have to research customer needs, preferences and expectations regarding sustainability issues, which involve questions such as: Are customers aware of sustainability issues regarding certain types of products and services? To what extent do different customer groups value social and environmental benefits? If social and environmental performance plays an auxiliary role in consumer decision-making processes, how can it be aligned to the overall quality and performance of products and services? In which way and to which extent should environmental and social performance be communicated to different kinds of customer groups? Without such information, marketing managers will have difficulties in identifying markets that are likely to grow as a result of sustainability concerns, and position products and services on the basis of social and environmental performance within sensitive markets.[20] Thus, a comprehensive sustainability marketing information system or an overall sustainability management information system is required to provide a basis for these key strategic decisions.

Toyota developed Eco-VAS, an ecological vehicle assessment system, which provides environmental information for R&D and production management. On the basis of the system, the chief engineer sets quantitative targets for reducing the environmental impact of future Toyota cars. Electrolux conducts regular consumer research on the importance of energy efficiency regarding household appliances. It also sets targets for its product managers to increase the number and profitability of 'green range' products. In 2007, Electrolux products with the best environmental performance accounted for 17% of total units sold within household appliances in Europe and 22% of gross profit. In 2008, the green range appliances will be expanded to all business sectors in the Electrolux Group.[21]

Corporate Sustainability Mission

Promoting a positive vision of a sustainable future for society as a whole, and a company mission to contribute to a better and more sustainable world, can help to motivate a company and set free the positive energies of its members.[22] Creating a sustainability mission that works is not easy. Something too general risks sounding clichéd and empty; too specific, and it becomes too unwieldy to be motivating. It has to be challenging and far-sighted enough to be inspiring, but not so difficult or distant to achieve that it becomes demotivating. The conversion of all products sold to bio-based materials by the year 2050 might be a fine aim for a company, but if it is beyond the time frame that most employees would expect to be with the company it will not mean very much to them. Conversely, expecting too much change too quickly allows insufficient time for research and development and to bring new technology or organizational processes onstream or bring new sustainable products and services to the market. This leads to a sense of frustration and failure that can also be demotivating. An example of a premature announcement was Mercedes' plan to introduce fuel-cell cars in serial production by 2007, which by the end of 2008 remained unfulfilled. The solution may be for companies to move away from the 'soundbite' mission to create something more layered. Marks & Spencer's Plan A contains both five broad areas for open-ended progress towards sustainability and 100 specific pledges (see Chapter 6).[23]

A powerful metaphor can also energize and motivate employees. Ray Andersson's comparison of the sustainability journey to conquering a mountain summit greater than Everest is one such metaphor. Although few people are climbers, this is a familiar image from television programmes, movies or dramatic stories like *Into Thin Air* by Jon Krakauer. It frames sustainability as a long, difficult and even dangerous journey requiring extraordinary will, dedication, effort and teamwork. To prevent such a journey from being too daunting, it needs to be broken into stages, with intermediate goals that are achievable in the medium term. This can provide a sense of progress and positive feedback as milestones are reached. This is perhaps the paradox of sustainability marketing transformations from the inside: even though the ultimate aim of truly sustainable products and services requires radical change, its institutionalization needs to be done incrementally, step by step.

Sustainability Incentive Structure

The achievement of intermediate goals towards sustainability should be coupled with a balanced incentive structure, in which both immaterial and material rewards play a role. Empirical studies show that there are four different types of employees regarding sustainability attitudes and activities:[24]

1. *Defeatists*: disinterested in sustainability issues, but may adapt (even easily) to new circumstances as they emerge.
2. *Conventionalists*: show a low level of interest and activity regarding sustainability issues, but potentially hard working in pursuit of sustainability goals if they are linked to material rewards.
3. *Active realists*: show a high level of interest and activity that is not dependent on monetary incentives. Potentially proactive and assertive contributors, but less adaptive.
4. *Nonconformist idealists*: highly interested in and active on sustainability issues, engaged and idealistic, but potentially uncompromising and prone to dissatisfaction with corporate efforts towards sustainability.

Different types of employee will require different approaches and incentives. The majority of employees belonging to the groups of conventionalists or defeatists may primarily respond to material rewards related to sustainability metrics and objectives. The nonconformist activist might interpret the same incentives as a subversive form of the company to 'buy' them and keep them quiet. In this case, immaterial rewards such as praise, a commendation or sustainability-related promotion prospects will be more promising.

A committed CEO, sustainability change agents, empowered employees, sustainability information and incentives are key ingredients to make sustainability marketing transformations from the inside possible. Sustainability challenges, however, cannot be solved by corporations alone: they need collaborative efforts with a number of external actors involving customers, suppliers, competitors, consultants, scientists, universities, governmental bodies and nongovernmental organizations on the way towards a sustainable society. The internal change has to be accompanied by an external change to guarantee a 'strategic sustainability fit' between the company and its environments. In the following section we will describe the sustainability marketing transformation from the inside out.

Sustainability Marketing Transformations: The Inside-Out Perspective

The outside-in perspective described at the beginning of the chapter provides insight into the transformation of ecological and social problems into market issues. What can companies do regarding sustainability marketing transformations from the outside in? Generally there are two approaches. The first is reactive and seeks to prevent, retard, diffuse or divert the changes taking place. The main aim of this approach is to defend existing markets and business models. The second is proactive and tries to enhance and enlarge the ongoing processes towards sustainability.[25] We refer to it as sustainability marketing transformations from the inside out, because companies and their representatives can act as sustainability change agents themselves and engage in collaborative efforts towards sustainable development.[26] This broad understanding of sustainability marketing takes the relationship building approach one step further: from the level of the micro environment with a special focus on the customer to the macro environment including public and political stakeholders.

Sustainability marketing transformations from the inside out are not straightforward. From a business perspective they are risky, could be misinterpreted and, as well as creating new value for the company, can destroy existing value.[27] This is why the majority of companies are unwilling to move into this territory. Why do some companies and CEOs take a lead and act as 'trailblazers'[28] by actively participating in public and political processes to change institutions in favour of sustainability? For some the rationale is an ethical one. Many owners of family businesses and some managers feel a social obligation and want to be good citizens. For others there is a strategic rationale: as illustrated by, and discussed in, a number of cases throughout this book, the successful marketing of sustainable products and services is possible within the present institutional framework, but it is limited in width and depth. Extending opportunities for the business means changing that framework.

Sustainability pioneers and leaders can participate in enlightened self-interest by changing public and political institutions to enhance sustainable development.[29] They can help to develop the free-market system towards a socio-ecological market system. The more social and political institutions favour sustainable consumption, the easier it is for companies to introduce sustainable products and services into mass markets. The more external effects are internalized, the easier it is for marketing decision-makers to balance the triple bottom line in a responsible way. The ultimate objectives of sustainability marketing transformations from the inside out are to initiate institutional changes that

- either set positive incentives for the purchase, use and post-use of sustainable products and services;
- or set negative incentives for the purchase of conventional/unsustainable products and services.

If we consider the issue–attention cycle and the transformation of socio-ecological problems into market issues via public and political engagement, there are three possibilities for sustainability pioneers and leaders to enhance these processes: problem exploration, public development and political development.[30]

Problem Exploration

The point of departure for sustainability marketing is ecological and social problems, both in general and in relation to products and services.[31] The research that reveals these problems is usually associated with university scientists, concerned citizens or NGOs investigating ecological and social problems at local, national and international levels. Instead of simply responding to such research activity, companies can also play a proactive role in investigating problems and searching for solutions. Doing so can add credibility to later sustainability marketing efforts and also serve as an early warning function. Companies that actively participate in research studies can be among the first to get results and develop appropriate solutions.

Since 1994, the German air carrier Lufthansa has been involved in basic atmospheric research: its A340-300 long-range aircraft has been equipped with sensitive sensors that continually take inflight measurements of the ozone, water vapour, carbon monoxide and nitrogen oxide content of the atmosphere to form a database for more precise global climate models.[32] In 2003 the Swiss retailer Coop established the Naturaplan Fund, which supports sustainable (research) projects to the tune of 10 million Swiss francs per year (€6.7 million). Major initiatives so far include large-scale projects at the Research Institute for Organic Agriculture (FIBL), the financing of training centres for Naturaline organic cotton growers in Maikaal (India) and Meatu (Tanzania) and a project in conjunction with WWF to promote sustainably produced soy.[33] In 2006 BP announced funding for radical research aimed at probing the emerging secrets of bioscience and applying them to the production of new and cleaner energy, principally fuels for road transport. From 2007 onwards the company will spend $500 (€361) million over ten years to establish a biosciences energy research laboratory attached to the University of California at Berkeley (USA).[34] Holcim, one of the world's leading suppliers of cement, endowed the Chair of Sustainable Enterprise at the University of Michigan (USA) and the Holcim Foundation is the donor of the Chair in Sustainable Construction at the Swiss Federal Institute of Technology (ETH) in Zurich (Switzerland).[35]

Such research is not always proactive in its intentions. In some cases research becomes an alternative to action, and a strategy aimed at delaying or preventing a problem being tackled rather than at solving it.[36] Examples from the asbestos and cigarette industries show companies using their own research to prevent the clarification of health risks associated with their products. Similarly, some oil companies still challenge the latest scientific results of climate change, despite an increasing amount of empirical evidence from leading researchers. In 2006 the Royal Society, one of Britain's top scientific institutions, accused US oil giant Exxon Mobile of deliberately undermining the scientific consensus on climate in its own communications and by funding organizations that mislead the public.[37]

Public Development

Socio-ecological problems that have been identified will remain unaddressed if they fail to capture the public's attention. Sometimes critical incidents occur that temporarily draw public attention to a particular problem. To keep the issue 'live' and sensitize the general public towards socio-ecological issues, further information and education are needed, which are usually provided by schools, universities and nongovernmental organizations (e.g. Amnesty International, Food Watch, Greenpeace, Peta and WWF). Companies may find it difficult to educate their stakeholders about socio-ecological problems if the public perceive them as having high professional competence but low credibility due to their selfish interests, a tendency to present one-sided information and biased communication.

Some companies have been able to build credibility by pursuing a sustainability marketing approach and providing information on social and ecological issues in a more balanced way, including achievements and objectives, advances and drawbacks. Many now report on their economic, environmental and social performance according to the Sustainability Reporting Guidelines developed by the Global Reporting

Initiative (GRI).[38] Such standardized sustainability reports allow for comparisons over time and among companies within the same sector. They are of special interest for scientists, nongovernmental organizations and also to the investment community, as they indicate how well social and environmental risks have been addressed. Although the average consumer may be unlikely to read corporate sustainability reports, they can still affect consumer perceptions and behaviour indirectly. Such reports can influence media coverage of a company and will act as a source of information for consumer guides such as *Shopping for a Better World*, which evaluates the social and ecological performance of companies to promote sustainable consumer buying behaviour.

Providing information on the economic, ecological and social performance of companies with a special focus on their operations and products is a key part of public development towards sustainability. Engaging in dialogue with public stakeholders and cooperating with NGOs to pursue mutually beneficial socio-ecological goals are further steps. Traditionally, companies have viewed social and environmental organizations, especially activists, as important stakeholders, but ones to be kept at arm's length.[39] While many companies still see this kind of group as a potential strategic threat, others are adopting a cooperative approach. They engage in dialogue and seek to involve public stakeholders in the development of solutions for social and ecological problems linked to the products and services offered by the company.

Consider Migros, the largest retailer for food and nonfood products in Switzerland. In 1999 its managers learnt that a number of food and cosmetic products in the company's range contained palm oil from timber corporations that were claimed to be setting fires in Indonesia and Malaysia in the pristine rainforests.[40] Once the land is burnt, the timber companies may apply for crop cultivation licences. In 2000 Migros started collaborating with WWF to develop compulsory standards and labelling criteria for sustainable palm oil. The initial project resulted in an international Roundtable on Sustainable Palm Oil (RSPO), which has become a global industry standard.[41] The example of Gasser construction materials shows that public development is not restricted to global problems and multinational companies (MNCs), but is also applicable to local problems and small- and medium-sized companies (SMEs). The traditional family-owned Bavarian brewery Neumarkter Lammsbrau is a well-known sustainability pioneer in the niche of organic beer.[42] In 2001 its owner, Dr Franz Ehrnsperger, won the prestigious German Environmental Award. The prize money was invested in a new energy- and water-efficient production plant. The annual costs savings due to energy and water reductions were used to set up the Neumarkter Lammsbrau Sustainability Award, which intends to enhance public involvement in sustainability. Each year the total prize money of €10 000 goes to individuals and organizations that are engaged in a culture of sustainability. In addition, the brewery is an initiator and active member of Local Agenda 21 in Nuremberg, which strives towards sustainable development on a regional level.

These examples show how sustainability marketing managers can create a long-term advantage through the development of new standards and labels that create change within the industry or markets.[43] Sustainability alliances with public stakeholders allow firms to become more involved in solving environmental and social problems, particularly those problems that transcend geopolitical boundaries or are poorly suited to command-and-control approaches.

Political Development

The illustrative case examples of Migros, Unilever, Gasser and Neumarkter Lammsbrau may be quite different, but they have one common trait. Collaboration between these companies and nongovernmental organizations sought to enhance the process of direct sustainability marketing transformation from the public to the market. New labels such as MSC from the Marine Stewardship Council, for instance, promote sustainable buying behaviour. However, as long as sustainable products and services are more expensive than conventional ones, they are unlikely to move beyond niches and into the mass market. Policy and politics have to advance the institutional framework in such a way that it either encourages the purchase, use and post-use of more sustainable products or discourages the purchase of conventional ones. Some companies that pursue sustainability marketing management actively seek to shape the legal and political framework to support improved social and environmental performance among companies, their products and services.[44] They break ranks and advocate government intervention on a range of sustainability issues.

Electrolux, for example, urges policymakers to introduce tax credits for the purchase of energy-efficient appliances. In 2007 it said on the title page of its sustainability report: 'Appliances can help tackle climate change. With the right market framework we can do more. That is why we urge governments to offer consumers incentives to go energy-smart.'[45] The same year, Vestas embarked on an international information campaign to present the benefits of wind power over other sources of energy and to put it at the top of the global energy agenda. Vestas' government relations department is responsible for the group's dialogue with politicians and NGOs all over the world. It assists in providing information about wind power and its potential in specific markets, including not least the required regulatory framework.[46] BP was the first major oil company acknowledging the link between rising CO_2 emissions and climate change in 1997, making a plea to ratify and implement the Kyoto protocol. Similarly, e5, the European Business Council for Sustainable Energy, urges the EU to adopt progressive energy and climate policies.[47] It considers the Kyoto protocol as an important first step to give a clear market perspective and provide a more level playing field for companies offering products and services requiring lower greenhouse gas emissions (e.g. renewable energies, hybrid cars, electric cars, low-energy houses). The World Business Council for Sustainable Development provides a platform for exploring sustainable development, sharing knowledge, experiences and best practices, and advocating business positions on these issues in a variety of forums, working with governmental and nongovernmental organizations.[48] Such business associations embracing sustainability is a relatively new phenomenon. As they enter the political arena there is the potential danger of them hijacking the agenda.[49] By defining the breadth and the depth of sustainable development from the business point of view, the strong opinions of businesses may drown out other voices in the debate. Sustainability approaches such as voluntary simplicity, sufficiency, happiness or aesthetics may be overshadowed by corporate calls for more investment, the adoption of new technologies and different products for consumers.

Another critical aspect is the lack of transparency regarding business–government relations. There are concerns that companies whose corporate image is very pro-sustainability may also lobby against progress towards it by employing lobbyists or through collective trade bodies. The main accountancy body in the UK recommends that sustainability reports should disclose the lobbying positions an organization takes on key public policy issues.[50] Accordingly, some companies have begun adopting more transparent practices on their relations with government.[51]

Despite some genuine corporate involvement in policy and politics towards sustainability, many companies remain focused on short-term returns.[52] It would be too short-sighted to view sustainability marketing transformation from the inside out as merely another from of lobbying to reinforce corporate and business interests. Instead, it reflects the commitment of many companies to sustainable development and their active participation in public and political processes. It is a discourse with stakeholders to realize institutional frameworks for a market system that is stable, fair and just, serving the vital purposes of human beings and a good life.[53]

List of Key Terms

Committed CEO
Corporate sustainability mission
Direct sustainability marketing transformation process
Empowered employees
Indirect sustainability marketing transformation process
Inside-out perspective
Issue–attention cycle
Outside-in perspective
Political development
Problem exploration
Public development
Sustainability change agents
Sustainability incentive structure

REVIEW QUESTIONS

1. Describe the five stages of the issue–attention cycle according to Downs (1972).
2. Explain the two kinds of sustainability marketing transformations from the outside in by means of examples.
3. List and describe the different kinds of key actors who play a vital role in sustainability marketing transformations from the outside in.
4. Empirical studies show that there are four types of employees regarding sustainability attitudes and activities. Describe them and show what kind of incentives might work for each of them to engage in sustainability marketing.
5. What are the rationale and the aims of sustainability marketing transformations from the inside out?

DISCUSSION QUESTIONS

1. Select a social or ecological problem of your choice (e.g. household waste) and describe its issue–attention cycle. Which indicators would you use to define and differentiate the five stages of the issue–attention cycle?
2. What role does the energy efficiency of household appliances play as a purchasing criterion for consumers in your country? Analyse how the energy consumption of household appliances was transformed from an ecological problem into an issue of markets and marketing.
3. 'Mission Zero' is part of Interface's corporate vision. It represents the company's commitment to eliminate any negative impact on the natural environment by the year 2020. What do you think are the positive and negative implications of such a corporate mission?
4. BP announced that it would fund radical research aimed at applying bioscience to the production of new and cleaner energy, principally fuels for road transport. From 2007 onwards the company will spend $500 (€361) million over ten years to establish a biosciences energy research laboratory attached to the University of California at Berkeley (USA). What are the positive and negative aspects of this corporate-funded sustainability research?
5. Discuss the pros and cons of corporate involvement in public and political processes towards sustainability.

Endnotes

1. www.gasser.ch; www.gr.grunliberale.ch; www.igpassivhaus.ch; www.oe-plus.ch; Dubacher, J. (2006) 'Schwarze Zahlen mit grünen Ideen', *Swiss Economic Forum*, 1: 15–18; Gasser, J. (n.d.) *Bürohaus Gasser: Nachhaltigkeits-Vision mit Praxis*, Chur: Gasser.
2. Downs, A. (1972) 'Up and down with ecology: The "issue attention cycle"', *The Public Interest*, 28 (Summer): 38–50.
3. *Ibid*.
4. Dunlap, R.E. & Scarce, R. (1991) 'The polls-poll trends: Environmental problems and protection', *Public Opinion Quarterly*, 55(4): 651–72.
5. Trumbo, C. (1995) 'Longitudinal modelling of public issues: An application of the agenda-setting process to the issue of global warming', *Journalism and Communications Monographs*, 152; Trumbo, C. (1996) 'Constructing climate change: Claims and frames in US news coverage of an environmental issue', *Public Understanding of Science*, 5: 269–83; Ungar, S. (1992) 'The rise and (relative) decline of global warming as a social problem', *Sociological Quarterly*, 33(4): 483–501.
6. Compare Chapter 2 for stakeholder theory and Chapter 6 for the different types and roles of stakeholders. See for sustainability marketing transformation from the outside in Belz, F.-M. (1994) 'Ökologische Wettbewerbsfelder in der Lebensmittelbranche', *Der Markt. Zeitschrift für Absatzwirtschaft und Markt*, 33(129): 51–61; Belz, F.-M. & Hugenschmidt, H. (1995), Ecology and competitiveness in Swiss industries', *Business Strategy and the Environment*, 4(4): 229–36; Dyllick, T., Belz, F. & Hugenschmidt, H. (1994) *Ökologischer Wandel in Schweizer Branchen*, Bern: Paul Haupt; Dyllick, T., Belz, F.-M. & Schneidewind, U. (1997) *Ökologie und Wettbewerbsfähigkeit*, München: Hanser, pp. 39–45.
7. Downs, A. (1972) 'Up and down with ecology: The "issue attention cycle"', *The Public Interest*, 28 (Summer): 38–50.
8. http://ec.europa.eu/environment/air/transport/co2/co2_home.htm (accessed 31 December 2008).
9. Klein, N. (2000) *No Logo*, München: B&T.

266 SUSTAINABILITY MARKETING

10. *Ibid.*
11. See for different key actors in sustainability marketing transformation processes Dyllick, T., Belz, F. & Schneidewind, U. (1997) *Ökologie und Wettbewerbsfähigkeit*, München: Hanser, pp. 43–5.
12. Crane, A. & Matten, D. (2004) *Business Ethics. A European Perspective*, Oxford: Oxford University Press, pp. 176–80.
13. See www.mtprog.com (accessed 26 December 2008)
14. See for the following account of Interface Andersson, R.C. (1998) *Mid-Course Correction: Towards a Sustainable Enterprise: The Interface Model*, White River Junction, VT: Chelsea Green; www.interfaceinc.com (accessed 31 December 2008).
15. See DeSimone, L.D. & Popoff, F. (2000) *Eco-Efficiency: The Business Link to Sustainable Development*, Boston, MA: MIT Press; Doppelt, B. (2003) *Leading Change Toward Sustainabilty. A Change-Management Guide for Business, Government and Civil Society*, Sheffield: Greenleaf Publishing.
16. See also Chapter 5 for the crucial role and different types of corporate leaders.
17. Ottman, J. (1998) *Green Marketing: Opportunity for Innovation*, 2nd edn, Lincolnwood, IL: NTC Business Books, p. 186.
18. See Hoffmann, A.J. (2000) *From Heresy to Dogma: An Institutional History of Corporate Environmentalism*, Stanford, CA: Stanford University Press, pp. 1826.
19. See Chapter 3.
20. Charter, M., Peattie, K, Ottman, J. & Polonsky, M.J. (2003) 'Marketing and Sustainability', Cardiff: BRASS Research Centre and Centre for Sustainable Design, http://www.cfsd.org.uk/smart-know-net, pp. 19–20.
21. Electrolux (2008) *Sustainability Report 2007*, http://www.electrolux.com/Files/Sustainability/PDFs/2008_PDF/Electroux_Sustainability_07_low.pdf (accessed 31 December 2008).
22. See Chapter 5 for sustainability mission statements from companies like SC Johnson, Electrolux and Toyota.
23. See for further details the sustainability marketing story Marks & Spencer's Plan A at the beginning of Chapter 6.
24. Franz, G. & Herbert, W. (1987), Wertewandel und Mitarbeitermotivation', *Harvard Manager*, 9(9): 96–102.
25. Dyllick, T., Belz, F. & Schneidewind, U. (1997) *Ökologie und Wettbewerbsfähigkeit*, München: Hanser, pp. 759.
26. See Belz, F.-M. (2001) *Integratives Öko-Marketing: Erfolgreiche Vermarktung von ökologischen Produkten und Leistungen*, Wiesbaden: Gabler, pp. 91–9.
27. British Telecommunications (2003) *Just Values. Beyond the Business Case of Sustainable Development*, http://www.btplc.com/Societyandenvironment/OurApproach/CSRresources/Reports/Archichedreports/Onlinedebates/JustValuesdebate/index.htm (accessed 31 December 2008), p. 17.
28. *Ibid.*
29. Bendell, J.& Kearins, K. (2005) 'The political bottom line: The emerging dimension to corporate responsibility for sustainable development', *Business Strategy and the Environment*, 14(6): 372–83.
30. See for that and the following Dyllick, T., Belz, F. & Schneidewind, U. (1997) *Ökologie und Wettbewerbsfähigkeit*, München: Hanser, pp. 155–74.
31. See Chapter 3 for the socio-ecological problems at macro and micro levels as a point of departure for sustainability marketing management.
32. See http://konzern.lufthansa.com/en/html/verantwortung/engagement/forschung/ (accessed 31 December 2008). The research projects CARIBIC (Civil Aircraft for the Regular Investigation of the atmosphere on an Instrument Container) and MOZAIC (Measurement of ozone, water vapour, carbon monoxide and nitrogen oxides about Airbus in-service aircraft) are financed by the European Union.
33. www.coop.ch (accessed 31 December 2008).
34. www.bp.com (accessed 31 December 2008).
35. www.holcim.com and www.holcimfoundation.org (accessed 31 December 2008).
36. Dyllick, T. (1990) *Management der Umweltbeziehungen*, Wiesbaden: Gabler, p. 261.
37. http://www.guardinan.co.uk/environment/2006/sept/20/oilandpetrol.business (accessed 31 December 2008).

38. The Global Reporting Initiative is a large multistakeholder network of thousands of experts, in dozens of countries worldwide. See www.globalreporting.org (accessed 31 December 2008).
39. Hartman, C.L., Staffard, E.R. & Polonsky, M.J. (1999) 'Green Alliances: Environmental Groups as Strategic Bridges to Other Stakeholders', in Charter, M. & Polonsky, M.J. (eds), *Greener Marketing. A Global Perspective on Greening Marketing Practice*, Sheffield: Greenleaf Publishing, pp. 164–80; Murphy, D.F. & Bendell, J. (1997) *In the Company of Partners: Business, Environmental Groups, and Sustainable Development Post-Rio*, Bristol: Policy Press.
40. Hamprecht, J. & Corsten, D. (2007) 'Purchasing Strategies and Sustainability. The Migros Palm Oil Case', in Hamschmidt, J. (ed.), *Case Studies in Sustainability Management and Strategy: The Oikos Collection*, Sheffield: Greenleaf Publishing, pp. 123–42.
41. www.rspo.org (accessed 31 December 2008).
42. www.lammsbraeu.de (accessed 31 December 2008). All ingredients of the 'eco-beer' are sourced from local farmers who produce grain and hops in accordance with organic standards. The eco-beer is brewed in a natural and eco-efficient way considering the principles of cleaner production.
43. Menon, A. & Menon, A. (1997) 'Enviropreneurial marketing strategy: The emergence of corporate environmentalism as market strategy', *Journal of Marketing*, 61(1): 51–67.
44. Bendell, J. & Kearins, K. (2005) 'The political bottom line: The emerging dimension to corporate responsibility for sustainable development', *Business Strategy and the Environment*, 14(6): 372–83.
45. Electrolux (2008) *Sustainability Report 2007*, http://www.electrolux.com/Files/Sustainability/PDFs/2008_PDF/Electroux_Sustainability_07_low.pdf (accessed 31 December 2008).
46. Vestas (2008) *Vestas Annual Report 2007*, Randers: Vestas, pp. 15–16, www.vestas.com (accessed 31 December 2008).
47. e5 stands for Energy, Environment, Economy, Employment and Efficiency. See www.e5.org (accessed 31 December 2008).
48. www.wbscd.org (accessed 31 December 2008).
49. Welford, R. (1997) *Hijacking Environmentalism: Corporate Responses to Sustainable Development*, London: Earthscan.
50. ACCA (2003) *ACCA UK Awards for Sustainability Reporting 2002, Report of the Judges*, London: Certified Accountants Educational Trust, p. 18.
51. Bendell, J. & Kearins, K. (2005) 'The political bottom line: The emerging dimension to corporate responsibility for sustainable development', *Business Strategy and the Environment*, 14(6): 372–83.
52. *Ibid.*, p. 381.
53. Ulrich, P. & Maak, T. (1997) 'Integrative business ethics: A critical approach', *CEMS Business Review*, 2(1): 27–36.

CHAPTER 12

Reframing Sustainability Marketing

After Studying this Chapter You Should be Able to:

1. Review the key elements of sustainability marketing.
2. Understand the role that social marketing and social enterprise can play in contributing to a more sustainable economy.
3. Discuss sustainability marketing in its broader social and economic context.

LOOKING AHEAD: PREVIEWING THE CONCEPTS

This chapter summarizes the key points of sustainability marketing. Furthermore, it describes the use of social marketing in achieving behavioural change to meet social goals, and how alternative forms of business such as social enterprises may be able to contribute to a more sustainable economy in the future. To conclude, the chapter considers some of the 'big picture' issues of sustainability marketing such as macromarketing, which considers the relationship between marketing and society as a whole.

SUSTAINABILITY MARKETING STORY: THE FATE OF THE NORTHERN COD

The social, environmental and economic consequences of an approach to business that is not sustainable are most vividly and poignantly illustrated by the fate of the Canadian fisheries off Newfoundland in the 1990s.[1] Traditional, local, small-craft fishing had yielded around a quarter of a million tonnes of northern cod there annually for almost a century prior to 1950. The advent of foreign fleets of new-style 'factory trawlers' then pushed catches of cod up to a peak of 810 000 tonnes by 1968. Concern about overfishing prompted the Canadian government to legislate to keep foreign boats beyond a 200-mile (322-kilometre) exclusion zone. Canadian-only fishing continued to yield around 250 000 tonnes annually throughout most of the 1980s, but in 1990 the *Independent Review of the State of the Northern Cod Stock* examined the existing scientific evidence and concluded that the remaining population of cod totalled only 400 000 tonnes and was declining rapidly. In 1992 the Canadian Minister of Fisheries and Oceans declared a ban on fishing northern cod, and for the first time in 400 years cod fishing ceased in Newfoundland. It was too little, too late for the cod. Overfishing had already pushed the cod population beyond its threshold of sustainability. By 1994 new research demonstrated that a cod population that had once yielded a sustainable annual catch of 250 000 tonnes had been reduced to a total of only 1700 tonnes.

Each of the boats in the Newfoundland fleet represented all or part of a business, and onshore there were many communities based around fish-processing businesses. The total job losses attributed to the fishing moratorium was over 40 000 and the social impacts arising from the devastation of several hundred communities and the businesses that served them can only be guessed at. The economic costs amounted to a billion Canadian dollars (€ 594 million) of government expenditure in social welfare and the costs of retraining workers and developing alternative opportunities in Newfoundland during 1993 and 1994 alone.

The story of Newfoundland cod demonstrates how rising consumer demand for fish products, combined with new technologies that allowed them to be extracted from the sea with ever-greater economic efficiency, virtually destroyed the natural resource on which so many businesses and livelihoods depended. It is a sobering thought that it occurred in a fisheries region in which there was a government fisheries management programme that was considered to be advanced and based on comprehensive scientific research. The fate of the northern cod led to a number of initiatives such as the formation of the Marine Stewardship Council, which seeks to promote sustainable seafood consumption and production through setting and promoting standards for sustainable fishing, and labelling and education initiatives to engage consumers (see Chapter 1).

Despite such positive developments, there is still a real danger that the fate of the Newfoundland fisheries is soon to be replayed on a global basis. An authoritative international study published in 2006 in *Science* demonstrated that one third of existing global fisheries had 'collapsed' and that the impact of current fishing practices on marine ecosystems would destroy the others by 2050.[2] If fish is to remain a product that future generations can consume, then a fresh and more sustainable process of delivering fish products to our table will be needed on a global basis in the near future.

Thinking Again about Sustainability Marketing

At the start of the book we explored how our understanding of the relationship between sustainability and marketing has continued to evolve over time. It began with the ecological marketing of the 1970s in which the importance of a small number of environmental issues (such as oil use or pollution) for a narrow range of industries (such as cars and chemicals) was framed as something that was relevant to engineers, lawyers and marketers within companies. During the 1980s, with a growing understanding of social and environmental problems, the idea of the 'green consumer' emerged. Green consumers represented a potential market for any businesses that could identify those consumers who were particularly concerned about environmental issues, and who could be convinced to purchase products and brands that successfully differentiated themselves on social and environmental performance. This concept of 'green marketing' delivered many products to consumers that were more resource efficient, less polluting or produced with greater care taken over the welfare of workers or of other species. It also delivered many marketing campaigns that were dismissed as 'greenwash' and damaged the credibility of the green marketing movement.[3] The emphasis of these early days was entirely on accommodating social and environmental concerns in existing marketing principles and practices. Social and environmental concerns represented a set of issues within the marketing environment that companies could respond to and take advantage of (or that could generate strategic threats if ignored). Improving social and environmental performance was viewed as one optional strategy that companies could adopt and use as a source of differentiation to generate competitive advantage. At its heart it was simply a continuation of conventional marketing and it did not represent a significant change to the discipline, nor did it significantly change markets or the world within which marketing activity occurs. It certainly did not make our economies or our societies measurably more sustainable.

Closing the gap between conventional marketing thinking and sustainability thinking will additionally require the reframing and rethinking of many specific aspects of marketing that have been explored throughout this book, including:

- An appreciation of social and ecological problems on a macro level.
- A basic understanding of the socio-ecological impacts of products on a micro level.
- A shift from a focus on purchasing to considering consumption as a holistic process.
- A change of emphasis from economic exchange to building and maintaining relationships with consumers.
- A critical reflection on the basic assumptions of marketing, its norms and values.

- Moving beyond the consideration of products and services to see the delivery of benefits to consumers in terms of providing them with solutions.
- An emphasis on the total economic and noneconomic cost of consumption instead of simply price.
- Communication as a two-way dialogue that builds relationships with consumers rather than an emphasis on the unidirectional promotion of products to them.
- The necessity of sustainability marketing transformations within and by companies.

In the first 20 years following the publication of the Brundtland Report (which roughly coincided with the first 20 years during which humankind's average ecological footprint exploited the Earth's resources at a level beyond that which the planet can sustain), we have not yet seen a transformation towards a more sustainable economy or more sustainable marketing. Achieving that transformation before it becomes too late to avoid significant environmental, social and economic upheaval will require marketing thinking to break out of the habits of mind and constraining assumptions of conventional, unsustainable marketing.

In Chapter 1 we referred to Christian Grönroos' analysis of marketing as 'a discipline in crisis'.[4] He is not the only scholar to draw such conclusions: others have described the discipline as suffering a 'mid-life crisis'[5] or as 'stereotyped on a derelict foundation in commodity-like textbooks'.[6] Interestingly, although his critique is not rooted in the sustainability agenda, the foundation of Grönroos' 'new logic of marketing' is on principles that are remarkably close to those that have emerged within this book as the key foundations of sustainability marketing management:

- A greater orientation to the creation of value for consumers.
- An emphasis on interactions, dialogue and relationships with consumers instead of on the process of economic exchange.
- An extended and more holistic concept of consumption.
- A move away from conventional product marketing being the 'norm' and a greater emphasis on the provision of services and on services marketing wisdom.
- An emphasis on expectations management to deliver satisfaction.[7]

As the new millennium approached, the academic debate about marketing and sustainability began to change. Growing concerns about the wider social and environmental impacts of business activity and its sustainability led to a renewed interest in corporate social responsibility. This moved sustainability issues beyond the relatively amoral territory of responding to consumer needs, in which marketers were conventionally used to operating, and into the realm of corporate values and the company's moral responsibilities to stakeholders beyond the consumer.[8] Instead of simply seeking to fit sustainability issues into existing ideas about markets and marketing, new ideas began to emerge that challenged the basic assumptions of the marketing academy.[9] One of these assumptions is that marketing is a relatively passive and reactive discipline, whose function is to respond effectively to threats and opportunities in the marketing environment, and to understand, respond to and meet consumer needs. This assumption underestimates the power of marketing, and the role that it could play in shaping the marketing environment and in influencing the behaviour of companies and consumers.

Chapter 11 examined the 'inside-out' efforts in which sustainability marketing managers can engage to influence individuals and institutions proactively within their environment through research, raising public awareness and political engagement. Although such efforts may be value driven, they typically focus on the generation of future opportunities for customer solutions that the company offers. The discipline of marketing has the potential to contribute to more widespread social change and to making progress towards more sustainable societies. In order to do this, however, we need to look afresh at marketing in the context of sustainability and in terms of the role that it can play. As William Kilbourne put it, to shift away from the traditional growth-oriented path of development to sustainable development is a 'transformation [that] entails a fundamentally different way of looking at the world and marketing's place in it'.[10] If we are going to complete the transformation of marketing to become significantly more sustainable, it will also be important to reframe how we think about marketing in relation to sustainable development.

Social Marketing and Sustainability

The focus of this book has been on commercial marketing. However, another branch of marketing that has a longstanding tradition of influencing behaviour in pursuit of social and environmental goals is *social marketing*. This can be defined as 'the use of marketing principles and techniques to influence a target audience to voluntarily accept, reject, modify, or abandon a behavior for the benefit of individuals, groups, or society as a whole'.[11] The development of social marketing emerged from a realization that attempts to pursue social goals through education, social communication and awareness raising often failed, because raised awareness alone rarely leads to changed behaviour.[12] Social marketing is based on achieving behavioural change by basing social campaigns on commercially derived marketing concepts such as market research, segmentation, product development and the provision of incentives.[13] Social marketing's origins are mainly in the field of public health, and the majority of social marketing campaigns have tackled health issues such as smoking cessation, preventing obesity by promoting exercise and healthy diets, promoting safe sex or responsible drinking or encouraging the uptake of vaccinations or screening programmes. Since the beginning of the twenty-first century social marketing has been increasingly applied to other social and environmental issues.[14]

Social marketing campaigns can involve the *de-marketing* of particular products or behaviours (e.g. wasting energy or buying tourist souvenirs made from endangered species) or the promotion of particular products or behaviours (e.g. engaging in recycling or insulating your home). Like commercial marketing, social marketing is founded on research that seeks to understand the target market, the marketing context and the competition (from other behaviours or from other interests, e.g. the anti-smoking social marketer must compete with the smoker's addiction, possible peer pressure and the marketing efforts of tobacco companies). As with commercial marketing, social marketing uses market research information to develop a marketing 'mix' of variables that can be adjusted in pursuit of behaviour change.[15] This makes social marketing a potentially powerful tool in the pursuit of sustainability because, as Tim Jackson concluded in his comprehensive research review on the challenge of motivating more sustainable consumption, 'Behavioural change is fast becoming the "holy grail" of sustainable development policy'.[16]

The social marketing mix shares considerable synergy with the sustainability marketing mix, the 'four Cs' of customer solutions, communication, costs and convenience. Instead of offering the customer a solution, social marketers develop a 'social proposition' (based around the benefits that will accrue from a particular behaviour) that they encourage their target audience to 'buy into'. A simple example of a sustainability-related social proposition (that has been the focus of campaigns in countries including Australia, Denmark and Canada) is that 'cycling (or walking) instead of driving is good for you and good for the planet'. Such campaigns seek to move people away from an unsustainable and energy-intensive form of consumption to a healthier, lower-carbon behaviour to meet the same need.

Social marketing is generally not based around physical products (although they may be involved), it is not particularly appropriate to talk about 'distribution' or 'place' issues and, like sustainability marketing, the emphasis is on 'convenience' and 'accessibility'. To continue the example of promoting cycling as an alternative to driving, access to appropriate cycling routes and route information, the availability of bikes, secure bike parking and bike maintenance services are all important to motivate and maintain cycling behaviours. In the Australian states of Victoria and Western Australia, the TravelSmart campaign to reduce car journeys used survey data to target households that were potentially interested in cycling as a means of transport. These households were then provided with cycling route maps and other information to make cycling travel solutions more accessible and practicable. Within the pilot city of Perth, this led to a 90% increase in cycling levels during the first year.[17] Such campaigns have encouraged a move away from car commuting and towards cycling in Australia that saw bike purchases outstrip new car sales during 2006.

In most social marketing campaigns there is no 'price', since the costs of changing behaviour are generally social rather than financial (although a financial cost can sometimes be involved). Costs may be in terms of time and effort, or in terms of overcoming psychological barriers to change. It is a much more holistic concept than that of economic prices, and has more in common with the transaction cost theory derived from economics. For the example of encouraging people to cycle instead of drive, this could be achieved by raising the costs of driving through congestion charging or parking restrictions. It can also be achieved by providing incentives that reduce the financial costs or by lowering any psychological costs involved in cycling. The Bike Bus'ters campaign run in the Danish city of Århus provided participants with a free bike (worth 4000 Danish crowns = €540) for one year, with the option to buy it for only 1000 Danish crowns (€135) at the end of the year. The Bike Smarts programme aimed at encouraging children to cycle in British Columbia identified that parental fears about cycling risks were a key barrier to children's involvement, as was the continued use of cars for short journeys to school and to transport children locally. The programme successfully tackled this by communicating its safety orientation and by encouraging parents to become involved and witness their children's cycling skills, thus reducing the perceived risks and psychological 'costs' of allowing their children to cycle.

Social communication is a crucial part of the social marketing mix, just as communication is in conventional or sustainability marketing. To continue the cycling theme, the Århus Bike Bus'ters initiative used many conventional marketing communication tools including flyers, a launch event and a regular magazine for participants. Less conventionally, but more interactively, participants were also asked to sign a contract that committed them to reducing their car use by cycling or using public transport when possible instead.

The use of social marketing to promote more sustainable behaviours is well established. The health campaigns that have been the mainstay of social marketing development all aim to deliver quality-of-life and well-being benefits that are central to sustainability. Since the early days of social marketing, there have also been explicitly environmentally oriented campaigns to promote behaviours such as recycling.[18] Beyond a focus on environmental issues within industrialized economies, social marketing is also already playing an important role in tackling a range of development issues in the context of less-industrialized nations. In a review of social marketing's application in a development context, Dholakia and Dholakia highlight its successful use on issues such as family planning, the provision of micro-credit, disease prevention and literacy. Despite some concerns that social marketing has weaknesses that can hinder its contribution to sustainability (e.g. a tendency to consider current generations of stakeholders only rather than taking a multigenerational view), they conclude that it is a potentially valuable tool for tackling the social, economic and ecological crises in many poorer countries that are at the heart of the sustainable development agenda.[19]

Overall, social marketing approaches have the potential to contribute to sustainability, both through specific campaigns focusing on social, health or environmental issues, and by promoting the broader concept of sustainability itself as a social goal. Its contribution can go beyond a role in influencing the behaviour of individual citizens. One of the architects of the discipline, Alan Andreasen, has articulated the concept of 'upstream' social marketing to complement 'downstream' social marketing campaigns aimed at citizens.[20] Upstream efforts involve also changing the behaviour of those organizations and individuals that influence the target audience's behaviour. One example Andreasen gives is tackling childhood obesity. To support downstream campaigns to influence children's eating and exercise behaviours, you also need effective upstream campaigns to target parents, school administrators, the media, regulators, urban planners and food businesses. With each of these stakeholders, social marketing efforts can seek to influence their behaviour by understanding their interests and then developing an appropriate social marketing mix to motivate them. Such an approach demonstrates how marketing does more than merely respond to the world around it, it can help to reshape the world in the pursuit of sustainability.

Such holistic social marketing campaigns also produce considerable opportunities for partnerships and alliances between social marketers and commercial marketers. Many social marketing interventions rely on the provision of commercial products such as bicycles as alternatives to cars, or healthy snack alternatives for children. The efforts of social marketers to influence the behaviour of citizens as consumers, often by structuring the choices available to them, will create new market opportunities for those commercial marketers who can provide more sustainable solutions.

This book has been written from a commercial sector perspective and focuses on marketing managers seeking to develop more sustainable solutions to meet the needs of consumers that will allow them to lead more sustainable lives. With the adoption of social marketing techniques to promote and pursue sustainability within the public sector, there is also a new group of social marketers trying to establish ways to encourage citizens to adopt more sustainable behaviours and lead more sustainable lives. The opportunities for synergies between the two, and for the development of future strategic partnerships in which public social marketing campaigns are integrated with commercial sustainability marketing campaigns, are considerable. There are also opportunities for mutual learning. Conventionally, social marketing has learnt from commercial marketing how to apply marketing techniques to social and environmental issues. Commercial marketers have a great depth of expertise when it comes to persuading us to adopt one very specific type of behaviour: making a particular purchase and choosing one brand over another. Changing purchasing behaviours will be important for sustainability, but many different forms of behaviour and behavioural change will also be needed. The emphasis on behavioural change within social marketing means that in future, sustainability marketers seeking to influence consumer behaviour over and above purchasing behaviour will be able to learn from the experience of social marketing.

Towards a More Sustainable Economy

This book has mostly focused on the challenge of developing more sustainable solutions for customers from the perspective of individual companies. The reality is that an individual product or company cannot, of itself, become sustainable. The sustainability of a product or an enterprise will depend on a wide range of stakeholders and factors beyond the control of an individual business. The actions of customers, suppliers, investors and infrastructure providers will all affect a company's ultimate sustainability performance. The pursuit of sustainability by an individual business will be relatively meaningless unless the economy and society within which that business exists is also making progress towards sustainability. Similarly, this book has considered the pursuit of sustainability from the perspective of the marketing discipline, but for a company to progress towards sustainability it will also need support from the other business functions such as accounting, operations management and human resources management.

To understand what a more sustainable economy might look like, and the role that sustainability marketing can play within it, it is useful to consider the different sectors of the economy. Pearce created a useful model of an economy that illustrates the three key systems within it (see Figure 12.1).[21] The first system is the private or commercial sector, comprising businesses large and small, from the local to the global, marketing services and products to consumers, to other businesses or to the public sector. The second system consists of public service providers including those involved in healthcare, law enforcement, education and waste management and who also provide tangible products from infrastructure projects to medicines. The third system is known as the Third Sector and comprises voluntary organizations such as charities together with social enterprises, and the self-help and family-based economy in which needs are met on a noncommercial basis. One reason that this model is helpful to consider is that it demonstrates that there are a range of different ways in which needs within society are addressed, and how a more sustainable economy may partly emerge by shifts among the sectors of the model from which needs are met. This could involve a shift within the private commercial sector from global companies to more local companies. It could also involve a shift in the provision of

Three Systems of the Economy

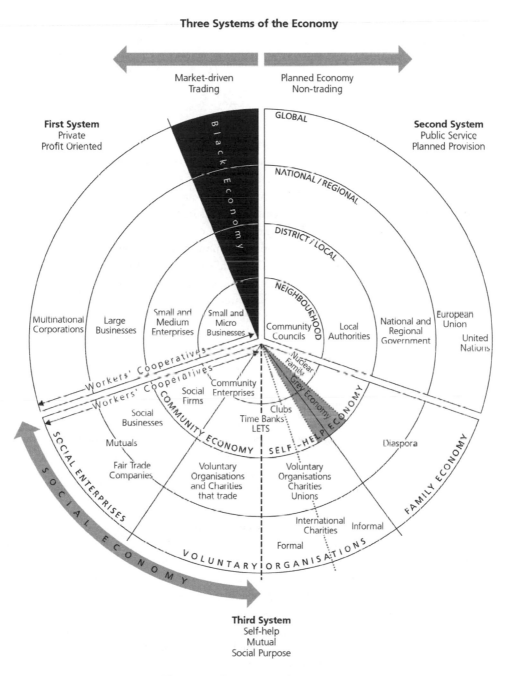

Market-driven
Trading

Planned Economy
Non-trading

First System
Private
Profit Oriented

Second System
Public Service
Planned Provision

GLOBAL

NATIONAL / REGIONAL

DISTRICT / LOCAL

NEIGHBOURHOOD

Black Economy

Multinational
Corporations

Large
Businesses

Small and
Medium
Enterprises

Small and
Micro
Businesses

Community
Councils

Local
Authorities

National and
Regional
Government

European
Union

United
Nations

Workers' Cooperatives

Workers' Cooperatives

COMMUNITY ECONOMY

SELF-HELP ECONOMY

FAMILY ECONOMY

Community
Enterprises

Social
Firms

Nuclear
Family

Grey economy

Social
Businesses

Clubs
Time Banks
LETS

Mutuals

Diaspora

Fair Trade
Companies

Voluntary
Organisations
and Charities
that trade

Voluntary
Organisations
Charities
Unions

International
Charities

Informal

Formal

SOCIAL ENTERPRISES

SOCIAL ECONOMY

VOLUNTARY ORGANISATIONS

Third System
Self-help
Mutual
Social Purpose

Figure 12.1   Three systems of the economy

Source: Pearce, J. (2003) *Social Enterprise in Anytown*, London: Calouste Gulkenkian Foundation.

services from the public sector to the private (or vice versa), or households or communities becoming more self-reliant and able to meet their own needs rather than relying on commercial solutions. This could allow the formal economy to contract, while not directly reducing the level of goods and services consumed.

Social Enterprises

Within Pearce's model, social enterprises are businesses whose primary activity is business (i.e. they trade in goods and services) but whose primary aims are social (such as the generation of employment, the improvement of the environment or the generation of funds for investment in the community).[22] The majority of social enterprises are relatively small, entrepreneurial community businesses and are typified (but not defined) by being relatively democratic and inclusive in the way they are run, and by investing the majority of the profits they generate into community or social causes rather than returning them to shareholders. Some of the most common forms of social enterprise include Fair Trade companies, cooperatives, community banks, mutual societies and the trading arms of charities. Both Mobility CarSharing and ONE Water, which were featured in Chapters 7 and 8 respectively, are examples of social enterprises. In recent years social enterprise has become an increasingly significant element of many economies throughout the world. Their exact scale and scope are contentious because of some difficult issues in consistently delineating them from commercial companies or voluntary-sector organizations. However, commonly quoted figures suggest that there could be as many as 55 000 social enterprises in the UK (equating to 5% of all businesses) turning over £27 (€ 28.4) billion.[23] Their growth worldwide is being characterized as explosive, and some commentators are portraying them as the potential engine of future economic growth.[24]

Social enterprises are an interesting type of business from the perspective of sustainability marketing for several reasons. They represent an alternative form of business that can address consumer needs when conventional markets fail and where government cannot provide a solution. Since they are largely free from the profit motive, many of them fulfil a role as work-integration organizations, seeking to provide meaningful employment opportunities, including salaried training, for the long-term unemployed, people with learning difficulties, ex-offenders, those lacking in qualifications or other groups with relatively low employment rates.[25] They also often operate within marginalized communities and provide goods and services for consumers who are otherwise neglected by mainstream businesses.[26] In this way, social enterprises have proven very effective in contributing to social equity and the provision of opportunity and the social side of the sustainability agenda. Social enterprises have also frequently evolved to tackle environmental needs within communities, including the provision of recycling and product-reclamation services or the management of community land. A survey of Scottish social enterprises reported that nearly half had environmental sustainability as a core business purpose. In addition, 51% reported that they undertake environmentally oriented procurement practices compared to only 28% of the conventional business population in Scotland, suggesting that they have a greater potential to become sustainability marketing-oriented than more mainstream businesses.[27] Future opportunities for the development of more social enterprise activity in sustainability-oriented business may come from the 'downshifting' phenomenon. People who leave conventional high-earning careers to find a more personally rewarding lifestyle may be attracted to use their business skills and experience to establish or contribute to social enterprises.[28]

A key weakness that has been observed among social enterprises is in relation to marketing. Their marketing efforts tend to involve intense personal promotion by the founding entrepreneurs, who often lack the time, skills and marketing orientation to develop more formal marketing strategies, plans and activities. The problems that social enterprises tend to encounter when competing against commercial enterprises are often linked to marketing and include a poor understanding of pricing dynamics, a tendency to underprice products and a lack of emphasis on packaging and labelling quality and providing information for customers.[29] In terms of culture and values, social enterprises represent a type of business that is well suited to playing an increasing role in the development of more sustainable solutions in the future. To succeed in doing so, however, they will need to develop their capacity for effective marketing.

Progress towards sustainability will require changes in all sectors of the economy, and there will be a role for marketing within the private sector, social enterprises and charities, and for social marketers within the public sector to contribute to the change process. The more their efforts involve partnerships, synergies and mutual learning, the better the prospects for success are likely to be. An example from this book would be the cooperation of Mobility CarSharing as a social enterprise with public transport companies (railway, subway, tram) and private companies (car rental) to provide sustainable mobility (see pp 152–153).

From Sustainability Micromarketing to Sustainability Macromarketing

Kilbourne argues that the prospects for progress towards sustainability are currently limited by the existing 'dominant social paradigm' (DSP). A society's DSP represents the values, beliefs, institutions and habits that combine to create the 'lens' through which its people view, interpret and understand the world around them.[30] The current DSP in most industrialized countries is based on a belief in the value of economic growth, faith in scientific evidence and technological solutions, and trust in the effectiveness of commercial markets and marketing to meet individual consumer needs (and also many societal needs) and to manage the use and distribution of resources. The existing DSP is also one that has placed the individual needs, rights and freedoms of current consumers above the welfare of other species, future generations and those who live outside the consumer economy. The fate of the northern cod illustrates many of the key aspects of the existing DSP and why it leads to the unsustainable exploitation of nature. Cod is a natural resource that had been harvested for many years in a traditional and sustainable way. The application of technology in the search for greater efficiency allowed the resource to be exploited almost four times as fast, and trust was placed in scientific research and government regulation to monitor and protect the fish stocks. The anecdotal evidence from the local fisherman about the declining numbers of fish, and the pleas from conservationists to reduce the fish catch on a precautionary basis, were both ignored. By the time the scientific research had proven that overfishing had been taking place, the level of the cod population had crashed and the businesses that were based around it soon followed suit.

Creating an economy within which we can make substantive progress towards more sustainable production and consumption will require our old worldview to be challenged and a new one to emerge. In a much quoted article, Dunlap and van Liere argued for the need for a 'new environmental paradigm' for society and for business as long ago as 1978,[31] although their vision was purely environmentally focused and its implications were not fully developed.[32] The concept of sustainable development both requires and offers an alternative worldview that seeks harmony between economic development, social justice and environmental quality. Making the transition from the existing DSP to a new, sustainability-based social paradigm will require significant changes to our social values, beliefs, institutions and habits. The process of challenging the conventional worldview and the assumptions behind it is something to which marketing and marketers can also contribute, along with policymakers, educators, the media and opinion leaders. Some commentators argue that escaping from the unsustainable nature of contemporary capitalism and its commodity culture will require exactly the same type of persuasive communications and marketing efforts that have been used to promote consumption to be employed instead to promote alternative, less consumption-oriented lifestyles and behaviours.[33]

Micromarketing approaches to sustainability led by a myriad of companies making individual efforts to deliver customer solutions more sustainably, however well intentioned, may struggle to make substantive progress towards more sustainable consumption and production, because companies are operating within the DSP and are ultimately limited by it.[34] The current DSP in western industrialized countries is one in which the quality of life and well-being are viewed in terms of increasing levels of consumption. Faced with a growing global population and a finite world, seeking to achieve increased well-being through ever-increasing material consumption is clearly not sustainable.[35] Making progress towards sustainability marketing transformations will therefore depend on changes to the broader political, technological and economic systems within which marketing exists. Marketing as a discipline and a field of study can also promote the social changes needed through sustainability-oriented macromarketing efforts. In this way sustainability marketing can also contribute to the emergence of a new, alternative, sustainability-oriented social paradigm.

Macromarketing as a field is concerned with the total marketing system rather than with the actions of individual companies, and considers the collective implications of society's consumption, rather than the consumption of individual consumers. If the field of marketing is to become more oriented towards sustainability, it will require a much greater emphasis on macromarketing. However, as Stanley Shapiro, former editor of the *Journal of Macromarketing*, remarked:

> It seems likely that macromarketing ... will remain the primary intellectual pursuit of a relatively limited number of academics. But while the number of such scholars may not increase all that much, the work they do will continue to be of very great importance. This follows from the fact that their research will focus on marketing matters that really matter.[36]

He goes on to lament the fact that despite the importance of many macromarketing issues such as sustainability, both macromarketing and 'marketing and society' courses remain a relative rarity in the teaching of marketing at all levels.[37] Similarly, Wilkie and Moore point out that marketing as an academic field over time has become increasingly focused on individual consumer behaviour, on managerial issues within companies and on statistically rigorous research, all of which has acted to obscure the 'big picture' view of marketing within the economy and within society.[38] It is yet another way in which the discipline of marketing has become 'myopic'.

One fundamental aspect of the macromarketing discipline is the consideration of markets as systems, and the application of systems theory and systems thinking. This is something that macromarketing shares with the concept of sustainable development. The concept of 'sustainability' is perhaps most easily and clearly understood in terms of systems thinking and system stability. If, over time, the inputs and outputs of a system do not achieve some form of balance and stability, the system will become unstable and crash, as happened to the northern cod's marine ecosystem (or at least be forced to change dramatically until some state that can be maintained is found). Whether you are discussing levels of predators and prey within an ecosystem or the 'balancing of the books' within a company viewed as a financial system, if the inputs and outputs of a system become unbalanced, the ability of that system to cope will become compromised.

Understanding the responses of individual consumers to the solutions offered by individual companies is vital in sustainability marketing. The consumer is at the very centre of any contemporary industrial economy. If you accept the argument that even government spending and infrastructure are ultimately there to serve the needs of the population, you could view all the environmental resource consumption linked to a national economy (minus trade balances) as being driven by the needs and wants of private citizens.[39] However, understanding sustainability marketing as a whole also requires an appreciation of the nature and implications of the total systems of consumption and production that exist to meet our needs. It also requires an understanding of the world itself, not from the conventional marketing perspective of geopolitical boundaries, sales territories and the distances between producers and consumers, but as a complex and dynamic set of interlocking physical systems which our lifestyles and economics depend on.

Towards a 'One Planet' Economy

Ultimately, for marketing activity to become sustainable it must occur within a sustainable economy. This obviously poses the question of what a sustainable economy might look like. One vision comes from WWF's 'One Planet Economy' project, which seeks to encourage progress among governments, companies and consumers to move the global economy towards an ecological footprint that can be sustained by the planet without eroding environmental quality. Within industrialized economies this means moving away from a lifestyle that would require several planet Earths to meet our needs (if that lifestyle was adopted globally) to one that requires only one planet's worth of resources. Some of the dimensions that are envisaged in moving towards such a One Planet Economy include:

- The development of more localized, small-scale, low-impact solutions to meet needs in sectors such as food and construction by taking advantage of local produce and materials.
- The use of environmental management practices, intelligent logistics, packaging and waste minimization to reduce the impacts of production and distribution systems.
- The development of clusters on industrial ecology principles, bringing groups of suppliers, processors, distributors and utilities together to achieve major progress in energy/water/waste minimization and creating cost savings.
- Major investments in sustainable energy technologies to reduce our dependence on oil and reduce CO_2 emissions.
- The use of financial and other business services to promote more sustainable business practices and principles, such as carbon trading or accounting based on triple bottom line principles.
- Harnessing ethical trading and the power of public-sector purchasing to develop markets for more sustainable products.
- The use of social marketing campaigns to promote more sustainable behaviours among citizens and consumers.
- The use of IT to enable 'distributed intelligence' and provide digital solutions for the development of reuse and recycling services, as well as community networks.
- Encouraging the development of social enterprises and community-based businesses and greater partnerships between businesses, communities and governments.

The model of a One Planet Economy that is emerging from this project is one that emphasizes new types of business, and new types of relationships between businesses and the stakeholders in their marketing environment.

Conclusions: A Final Rethink

Issues are already emerging that are challenging the existing DSP and providing opportunities for a new worldview to emerge in which sustainability marketing may be allowed to move from the margins of the marketing field to become more mainstream. The analysis within the Stern Review and its 2008 follow-up demonstrated that unless societies collectively invest around 2% of GDP to prevent or prepare for the destructive consequences of climate change, those consequences could shrink the value of the global economy by 20%. This challenged the dominant view that environmental measures are something that come at the expense of economic growth, rather than something that helps to ensure it is not compromised. The global 'credit crunch' that began during 2008 provided many painful lessons for many people. One of the things it most vividly demonstrated was that the existing financial market, with its pursuit of ever-increasing profits through increasingly arcane financial products and irresponsible lending, was fundamentally unsustainable. The lesson that if something is not sustainable for economic, financial or social reasons it will eventually fail is clearly demonstrated by the examples of the Canadian fishing industry and the American subprime mortgage debacle.

Ironically, it may be evidence of financial unsustainability, rather than social or environmental issues, that finally forces a rethink of our existing economic, political and social systems. By the end of 2008, the collective debt of the USA, the country at the vanguard of the capitalist consumer-driven economic model, stood at over $67 (€ 48.4) trillion (including unfunded social security and Medicare liabilities).[40] This debt has reached a level at which further economic growth is simply servicing the interest payments on the debt, not reducing it, and the search to maintain economic growth is being financed by further borrowing. Ecological economist Herman Daly likens this debt-based system to a cancer, in which the cancer (the debt) continues to grow until it destroys its host.[41] So on a simple test of economic viability, it is clear that our current approach to business, economics and living is not sustainable.

The social and environmental crises that were explored in Chapter 3 are also, unfortunately, getting worse rather than better. The forecast trends in population growth, population movements and the decline in the health of ecosystems and their ability to provide ecosystem services all point to a challenging future for governments, businesses and societies. The old idea that the social and environmental challenges facing the world can be solved, if only we can generate enough economic growth to fund the development of solutions, has been discredited. The economies and lifestyles that the global consumer class enjoys at the beginning of the twenty-first century are achieved at the expense of others and are not sustainable. It is a simple, if often overlooked truism that if something is not sustainable then it cannot be sustained. A new approach to economics, business and marketing for the future is required, and that approach needs to be more sustainable. This requires us to reframe marketing principles, practice and education from the perspective of sustainability, however uncomfortable that feels to marketers and consumers who have grown up with an absolute belief in the power and legitimacy of the consumer economy.

There are many ways in which making the transformation to sustainability marketing will require us to reframe different elements of marketing theory and practice and how we think about it, learn about it and teach it. The authors hope that this book will represent a valuable tool in the toolkit of future marketing educators and practitioners as they seek to understand how marketing can be brought together with sustainable development in a way that makes economic, social and environmental sense.

This suggests that those who are willing to think deeply about marketing will recognize the need for change, and that whether or not they begin from the perspective of sustainable development, the need to transform the discipline to be more sustainable will become apparent. The authors hope that this very un-commodity-like textbook will allow readers to take a fresh and critical look at the world of marketing, and inspire them to play a part in transforming it into something that will sustain, instead of consume, our world.

List of Key Terms

De-marketing
Dominant social paradigm (DSP)

Downshifting
Macromarketing
One planet economy
Social enterprise
Social marketing
Sustainable lifestyles
Systems thinking
Three systems of the economy model

REVIEW QUESTIONS

1. What are the key differences between the conventional and the sustainability marketing mindsets?
2. Why are social enterprises potentially well suited as vehicles for sustainability-oriented businesses?
3. What is social marketing?
4. How is macromarketing different from micromarketing?
5. What is the 'dominant social paradigm' and what is its significance for marketers seeking to become more sustainable?

DISCUSSION QUESTIONS

1. The Brundtland Report said that sustainable development required us to 'break out' of old patterns of development. Why do you think this has proved so difficult, and what role can marketing play in the process of breaking out from our old ways of doing things?
2. The response of governments around the world to the 'credit crunch' during 2008/09 was to borrow money to support ailing businesses in industries including financial services, car manufacture and steel making in order to restore growth. Discuss whether you believe these were responsible and sustainable measures.
3. How can a new sustainability-oriented marketing mindset challenge and displace entrenched ways of thinking within the marketing discipline?

Endnotes

1. Pilkey, O.H. & Pilkey-Jarvis, L. (2007) *Useless Arithmetic: Why Environmental Scientists Can't Predict the Future*, New York: Columbia University Press.
2. Worm, B., Barbier, E.B., Beaumont, N. *et al*. (2006) 'Impacts of biodiversity loss on ocean ecosystems', *Science*, 314(5800): 787–90.

3. Crane, A. (2000) *Marketing, Morality and the Natural Environment*, London: Routledge.
4. Grönroos, C. (2007) *In Search of a New Logic for Marketing*, Chichester: John Wiley & Sons.
5. Wilson, R. & Gilligan, C. (1997) *Strategic Marketing Management*, London: Butterworth-Heinemann.
6. Gummesson, E. (2002) 'Practical value of adequate marketing management theory', *European Journal of Marketing*, 36(3): 325–49.
7. Grönroos, C. (2007) *In Search of a New Logic for Marketing*, Chichester: John Wiley & Sons Ltd.
8. Crane, A. (1997) 'The dynamics of marketing ethical products: A cultural perspective', *Journal of Marketing Management*, 13(6): 561–77.
9. Kilbourne, W.E. & Beckmann, S.C. (1998) 'Review and critical assessment of research on marketing and the environment', *Journal of Marketing Management*, 14(6): 513–32.
10. Kilbourne, W.E. (1998) 'Green marketing: A theoretical perspective', *Journal of Marketing Management*, 14(6): 641–56.
11. Kotler, P., Roberto, N. & Lee, N. (2002) *Social Marketing: Improving the Quality of Life*, 2nd edn, Thousand Oaks, CA: Sage.
12. Andreasen, A.R. (2005) *Social Marketing in the 21st Century*, Thousand Oaks, CA: Sage.
13. Fox, K. & Kotler, P. (1980) 'The marketing of social causes: The first ten years', *Journal of Marketing*, 44(4): 24–33.
14. See Barr, A., Gilg, A. & Shaw, G. (2006) *Promoting Sustainable Lifestyles: A Social Marketing Approach*, Final Summary Report to Defra, London; and NESTA (2008) *Selling Sustainability: Seven Lessons from Advertising and Marketing to Sell Low-carbon Living*, London: National Endowment for Science Technology and the Arts Research Report
15. Peattie, K. & Peattie, S. (2003) 'Ready to fly solo? Reducing social marketing's dependence on commercial marketing theory', *Marketing Theory*, 3(3): 365–86.
16. Jackson, T. (2004) *Motivating Sustainable Consumption: A Review of Evidence on Consumer Behaviour and Behavioural Change*, Guildford: Centre for Environmental Strategy, University of Surrey.
17. James, B. (2002) 'TravelSmart, large-scale cost-effective mobility management: Experiences from Perth, WA, Proceedings of the Institution of Civil Engineers', *Municipal Engineer*, 1: 39–48
18. Zikmund, W.G. & Stanton, W.J. (1971) 'Recycling solid wastes: A channels of distribution problem', *Journal of Marketing*, 35(3): 34–9.
19. Dholakia, R.R. & Dholakia, N. (2000) 'Social Marketing and Development', in Bloom, P.N. & Gundlach, G. (eds), *Handbook of Marketing and Society*, Thousand Oaks, CA: Sage.
20. Andreasen, A.R. (2005) *Social Marketing in the 21st Century*, Thousand Oaks, CA: Sage.
21. Pearce, J. (2003) *Social Enterprise in Anytown*, London: Calouste Gulbenkian Foundation.
22. Peattie, K. & Morley, A. (2008) *Social Enterprises: Diversity and Dynamics, Contexts and Contribution*, Swindon: ESRC.
23. UK Government (2005) *Annual Small Business Survey* 2005, London: HMSO.
24. Harding, R. (2004) 'Social enterprise: The new economic engine?', *Business Strategy Review*, Winter: 40–43.
25. Defourney, J. & Nyssens, M. (2006) 'Defining Social Enterprise', in Nyssens, M. (ed.), *Social Enterprise: At the Crossroads of Market, Public Policies and Civil Society*, London: Routledge.
26. Evers, A., Laville, J.L., Borgaza, C., Defourny, J., Lewis, J., Nyssens, M. & Pestoff, V. (2004) 'Defining the Third Sector in Europe', in Evers, A. & Laveille, J.L. (eds), *The Third Sector in Europe*, London: Edward Elgar.
27. Triodos (2007) *Saving Money, Saving the Planet: Triodos Bank Report into the Environmental Practices of Social Enterprise across Scotland*, Bristol: Triodos Bank.
28. Peattie, K. & Morley, A. (2008) *Social Enterprises: Diversity and Dynamics, Contexts and Contribution*, Swindon: ESRC.
29. See Bird, A. & Aplin, J. (2007) *Marketing Analysis for Social Inclusion Enterprise Organisations*, Powys: SIREN & Powys Equal Partnership; and Shaw, E. (2004) 'Marketing in the social enterprise context: Is it entrepreneurial?', *Qualitative Market Research*, 7(3): 194–205.
30. Milbrath, L. (1984) *Environmentalists: Vanguards for a New Society*, Albany, NY: University of New York Press.
31. Dunlap R. & van Liere, K.D. (1978) 'The "new environmental paradigm"', *Journal of Environmental Education*, 9(4): 10–19.

32. Kilbourne, W.E. (1998) 'Green marketing: A theoretical perspective', *Journal of Marketing Management*, 14(6): 641–56.

33. Prothero, A. & Fitchett, J. (2000) 'Greening capitalism: Opportunities for a green commodity', *Journal of Macromarketing*, 20(1): 46–55.

34. Kilbourne, W., McDonagh, P. & Prothero, A. (1997) 'Sustainable consumption and the quality of life: A macromarketing challenge to the dominant social paradigm', *Journal of Macromarketing*, 17(1): 4–24.

35. Kilbourne, W.E. (1998) 'Green marketing: A theoretical perspective', *Journal of Marketing Management*, 14(6): 641–56.

36. Shapiro, S.J. (2006) 'Macromarketing: Origins, development, current status and possible future direction', *European Business Review*, 18(4): 307–21.

37. See also Wilkie, W.L. & Moore, S.E. (2003) 'Scholarly research in marketing: Exploring the "4 eras" of thought development', *Journal of Public Policy and Marketing*, 22: 116–46.

38. *Ibid.*

39. Spangenberg, J.H. & Lorek, S. (2002) 'Environmentally sustainable household consumption: From aggregate environmental pressures to priority fields of action', *Ecological Economics*, 43(2/3): 127–40.

40. Anielski, M. (2008) 'The Economics of What Matters', *CitiesGoGreen.Com*, December: 27–30.

41. *Ibid.*

Index